OUR SEPARATE WAYS

*Black and White Women
and the Struggle for
Professional Identity*

ELLA L. J. EDMONDSON BELL
STELLA M. NKOMO

HARVARD BUSINESS SCHOOL PRESS
BOSTON, MASSACHUSETTS

Cherríe Moraga's "The Welder," from *This Bridge Called My Back: Writings by Radical Women of Color*, 3d ed., edited by Cherríe Moraga and Gloria Anzaldúa (Berkeley, CA: Third Woman Press, 2001), is reprinted by the kind permission of Cherríe Moraga and Third Woman Press. The excerpt from Kate Rushin's "Word Problems" is reprinted by the kind permission of Kate Rushin.

Library of Congress Cataloging-in-Publication Data

Bell, Ella L. J. Edmondson, 1949–
Our separate ways : Black and white women and the struggle for
professional identity / Ella L. J. Edmondson Bell and Stella M. Nkomo.
p. cm.
Includes bibliographical references and index.
ISBN 1-57851-277-8 (alk. paper)
1. African American women executives. 2. African American women in the
professions. I. Nkomo, Stella M., 1947– II. Title.
HD6054.4.U6 B45 2001
331.4'089'96073--dc21
2001016791

ISBN 1-59139-189-X (pbk)

The paper used in this publication meets the requirements of the
American National Standard for Permanence of Paper for Publications
and Documents in Libraries and Archives Z39.48-1992.

Our book is dedicated to those
who will one day stand tall
on our shoulders

April, Chanel, Christina, Delilah, Eric, Evelyn, Isaac, Jeremy, Kai,
Keenan, Keli, Marc, Maricho, Morgan, Nomthandazo, Nqobile,
Sebenza, Sergio, Shari, Sherita, Sicelo,
Sparkle, Sybil, Sylvia, Tara,
Venus, Zamile

And to our beloved Dubie,
whose spirit remains deep in our hearts

CONTENTS

ACKNOWLEDGMENTS

OUR SEPARATE WAYS has been a joint project since its inception, and we want to jointly acknowledge all the people who have supported our work over the years. During times when we felt overwhelmed or even discouraged, we found encouragement from many different people. But the greatest source of inspiration came from the women who shared their life stories. They believed in this project at its very start. We are forever grateful for their generosity and willingness to share very personal stories of triumph and challenge. Our hope is that we have done justice to their lives and that our readers will be touched, as we were, by their remarkable stories.

No project of this magnitude could have been undertaken without resources. The Rockefeller Foundation funded the first stage of the study. This was followed by additional funds from the Ford Foundation. We especially want to thank June Zeitlin at the Ford Foundation for her personal interest in our project. During the years after the initial data collection, Yale University, MIT, and the University of North Carolina at Charlotte provided both funding and graduate assistants. A yearlong stay as visiting scholars at the Bunting Institute at Radcliffe and Harvard Universities allowed us much-needed time together to focus on data analysis and writing. We owe an immeasurable debt to Florence Ladd, former director of the Bunting Institute, for her special encouragement, friendship, and support of our work. Most currently, we would like to thank our present institutions, The Amos Tuck School at Dartmouth and the Graduate School of Business Leadership at the University of South Africa, for their support. To all these institutions and their staffs we owe a debt of gratitude.

One of the challenges of carrying out our work was finding women to participate in the study. We are thankful for the help of Jewel Jackson McCabe, founder of the National Coalition of 100 Black Women; Elaine Carter; George Tunick, former president of the National Coalition of Female Executives; and Susan Taylor, publication director for *Essence Magazine*, for their assistance in gaining access to many of the participants in the study. Special thanks to advisory board members Lotte Bailyn, Ann Morrison, Johnnetta Cole, and Paula Giddings for so graciously and wisely contributing to our thinking.

We were blessed to have a talented, hard-working, and caring research team. Lisa Horvath, Jennifer Ire, and Susan Corriher gave countless hours of work, energy, and emotion to this project even as they pursued their own graduate education. Their willingness to do the work on both a professional and personal level was truly amazing. Without their hard work and insights, this project could not have been completed.

Another blessing was the constellation of support we received from our women colleagues in the managerial sciences. Our dream team of Marta Calas, Deborah Meyerson, Linda Smircich, Colleen Jones, Joann Martin, and Judi Marshall kept the passion of our vision for this project alive even when we were on the verge of giving up. Their continual belief in our work and its contribution to management scholarship was a deep source of inspiration for us. To Deborah King, longtime friend and thoughtful colleague, thank you for sharing your wisdom, for pointing us in the right direction toward locating new scholarly insights, and for all those late-night chats. As always, we are deeply fortunate to have Maureen Scully as a sister-mate. Who else would have read the many versions of this manuscript? Who else would have helped with line edits? Thank you for your unrelenting faith in our project.

Throughout the course of this project we were lucky to have colleagues who were interested in our work and read earlier drafts of this manuscript. We are appreciative of Philomena Essed, Taylor Cox, Jr., Rosalyn Mickelson, Jim Walsh, Martin Davidson, and Bill Hicks. We hope they will see that their contributions did not fall on deaf ears. For their statistical savvy we are very thankful to Brenda Allen and Lynn Foster-Johnson.

No project of this scope could survive without the strong assistance of a support team. We are grateful to Debra Joyce for her speed and her accuracy in typing the manuscript under impossible deadlines and wide geographical distances. But even more, we value her wonderful spirit and warm personality. Rosemary Kirby worked long hours into the night transcribing the life history interviews. Her careful attention in capturing every detail in print was truly amazing. Patricia Hunt, with her wonderful sense of humor and caring nature, came to us just in the nick of time, as we were trying to finish the manuscript under difficult circumstances. She kept everything under control, including the logistics of communicating between South Africa, Charlotte, North Carolina, and San Francisco, California. Karen Lacey's keen sociological perspective brought greater insights to the analysis of the women's narratives. Karen Sluzenski, the reference librarian at Feldberg Business and Engineering Library at Dartmouth College, saved us more than once in locating critical references. In addition to our support team, a number of graduate assistants contributed to this project: Ellen Simpson, David Kraus, Lyndall Hare, Tara Perry, and Jen Liu.

We want to thank Nikki Sabin, our first editor at Harvard, for her quick grasp of the story we wanted to tell and her belief that this was indeed a book for Harvard Business School Press. We are indebted to David Thomas for leading us to her. To Melinda Merino, Sylvia Weedman, and Barbara Roth we say thanks for your professionalism in bringing this book to press in Nikki's absence. Words cannot express how much we love the portraits of the two women that cover our book. To Hyun Kounne, thank you for capturing the true essence of our book in such a beautiful way.

After several attempts, we were totally frustrated and overwhelmed with trying to figure out how to tell the women's stories so readers could really hear and appreciate the fullness of their voices. Enter Connie Hale, our development editor. Her way of thinking about this project propelled us to a new and better vision of the manuscript. Writer extraordinaire, she taught us the craft of writing, and we were humbled by her lessons.

Ella Acknowledges

Early on in this project several colleagues at Yale's School of Organization and Management provided me with an intellectual community where I developed as a young scholar. To David Berg, Ivan Lansberg, and my students at SOM, I will always think of all of you with great respect.

My heartfelt thanks goes especially to Clayton P. Alderfer, whose invaluable conversations, constructive criticism, and acceptance of me as a researcher enabled me to grow and to engage in scholarly work with integrity. I also was fortunate to have Charlene Alderfer as a friend and colleague. Thank you for encouraging me to think more deeply about relationships between black and white women. Joe Feagin was a guardian angel, picking me up, dusting me off, and sending me back into the world when I was most discouraged about doing race work.

I am deeply saddened that my cousin Harley Jones passed away before we were able to complete this book. His creative talent, intellect, and courage will always be sources of inspiration. His spirit is always with me. Dr. William Edmondson, my father, thank you from the bottom of my heart for helping me to reconstruct my own life while I was in the process of writing about the lives of other women. Dad, I am very proud to be your daughter. To Morgan Washington, my delightful seven-year-old goddaughter, I am grateful for your teaching me how to play again and helping me to discover what a wonderful remedy it is for writer's block. To Morgan's parents, Joe and Donna Washington, I am grateful for all those wonderful home-cooked dinners that gave me the energy to work late into the night. To Sebenza Nkomo, my godson, I think your mother has said it all. Please know how blessed I am to have you in my life. Finally to Kevin Jones, I appreciate all the encouraging words you offered and the space you gave me for writing this book. Our friendship sweetened the long, tiring process necessary for doing the work and continues to enrich my life.

Stella Acknowledges

I have many people to thank for giving me their unrelenting support over the years. I want to thank my parents, Fred and Eva Brown, for setting me on the right path and for the sacrifices they made to ensure that I got an education. I only wish my father were alive today to read this book and share my joy in its publication. Mom, I thank you for your commonsense questions about the book and your inimitable style for getting to the heart of things. You have no idea how much your simple question, "How's the book coming?" near the end of almost every long-distance conversation meant to me. I also want to thank my sisters and brothers, Mamie, Ollie,

Clara, Betty, Yvonne, Freddie, Isaac, Rosemarie, and Eddie, for their stead-fast encouragement and belief in me.

I want to thank my son, Sebenza. He was just old enough to get roped into helping when time was of the essence. His computer skills helped with the insertion of codes into the data. There were many times when he helped retrieve articles from the library. But what I valued most was his loving support and understanding—especially during the times when the research and writing limited my time with him. The words "Thank you, Sebenza" can never convey how I feel about your love and support.

Finally, I want to thank my husband, Mokubung. Words could never adequately express my heartfelt appreciation for your unquestioning sup-port of my career, my intellectual interests, and this book. Your love and gentle pushing kept me energized even when I felt overwhelmed. Thank you also for your unwavering patience when this project kept us apart and for never doubting its importance.

PROLOGUE

Your train is traveling
South at 73 miles per hour.
Mine is headed north doing 68.
How long will it take us to arrive at
Our separate definitions?
What time shall we begin, for real?
What time can we call it home?

—KATE RUSHIN, WORD PROBLEMS

WHETHER YOU COME to this book traveling south at seventy-three miles per hour or heading north at sixty-eight, whether you see yourself staring out from its front cover or from its back, you are probably familiar with the struggle for professional identity.

You are hardly alone.

Our Separate Ways represents an eight-year research effort spotlighting the life and career struggles of successful black and white women in corporate America. We found, as we conducted our studies, that women come to the workplace not just from separate directions but from what

Kate Rushin calls "separate definitions": they have followed their own distinct paths—created out of an individual juncture of family background, educational experience, and community values. Racial differences amplify this separation.

When these women enter the workforce, however, they all begin with a common assumption: I have a *chance*. They believe their business degrees, their raw talent, their ingenuity, and their industry will be the keys to their success. Then, somewhere along the way, the women—especially the black women—begin to see that people still question their authority, challenge their intelligence, and discount what they think. They are told to wait for opportunities, to prove themselves. So they wait. They continue to prove themselves. They contribute to the company's bottom line, they take on leadership positions, and they put in excessive time, often to the detriment of their personal lives. Yet even the most successful women reach a point where they realize that their own expectations haven't been met. That the rewards are not always commensurate with the costs. Many keep searching—and aching—for an answer. Others find this too toxic and, regrettably, bow out.

To the extent that our book may chronicle this all-too-familiar pattern, it may prove painful reading. Simply decrying sexism may not assuage the pain, for anger is not always redemptive. Recognizing the burden of gender is a demoralizing exercise. Recognizing the burden of race is even more demoralizing.

This book may be especially painful for black women, who face special hurdles in the journey to the top and who, when they get there, may find corporate America a lonely, hollow, haunted place. But it may also be painful for white women, who may learn that their black "sisters" are more like stepsisters, and that in the workplace they may have—perhaps unwittingly—shown more camaraderie with white men than with black women. Anyone who realizes that she may have been so consumed by her own plight that she abandoned the struggle to enhance the workplace for all may find a certain loneliness settling around her as well.

We have opened with Kate Rushin's poem because she eloquently raises the dilemma of "our separate definitions" while at the same time suggesting the promise of a resolution. When Rushin asks, "What time shall we begin, for real?" our reaction is to think about the relationships we can build with each other once we have learned more about each other's separate experiences. These need to be real relationships, not nonstarters. By shedding light on the images working women have of each other—whether a once-poor woman's resentment of a colleague's life of privilege, a white woman's belief that a black woman carries a racial chip on her shoulder, or a black woman's assumption that white women are allies of white men—we believe we will be able to shed stereotypes and to bind together in new, dynamic relationships, to experience each other fully, and to revel in each other's vibrancy, vulnerability, and vision.

When Rushin implores, "What time can we call it home?" she posits the notion of a new, common direction. In our view, "home" refers, paradoxically, not to our separate private worlds, but to a new kind of common space—a workplace that becomes a living, breathing space where women unite to create companies free of racism, sexism, and other forms of oppression. It is up to us to create that space, to roll up our sleeves and start building safety zones for each other and for our relationships. In that "home" rests the power of our combined forces, the wellspring of change—at work, in our communities, and in the greater world.

But, first, let us sketch the dimensions of the challenge.

In 1986, the National Coalition of 100 Black Women commissioned Louis Harris and Associates to conduct a survey of black women and leadership.[1] The polling firm interviewed sixty chief executive officers of Fortune 500 companies, asking them, among other things, whom they considered the top two or three black female leaders in the United States. Thirty-two percent of the CEOs identified Barbara Jordan, the powerful orator, brilliant lawyer, and groundbreaking Congresswoman from Texas. Twenty-five percent named Coretta Scott King, the widow of the slain Martin Luther King, Jr., who continued her husband's fight for social justice in the name of antipoverty causes and human rights.

Strikingly, though, 32 percent of the CEOs could not name one black woman in a leadership position in the United States—at a time when Shirley Chisholm had already been a Congresswoman, Eleanor Holmes Norton had served as chair of the Equal Employment Opportunity Commission, and Patricia Harris had been U.S. Ambassador to Luxembourg, as well as Secretary of Housing and Urban Development and Secretary of Health, Education, and Welfare.

In another twist, 22 percent of the executives who could not name a "leader" mentioned black women from outside the public service arena.[2] The sultry-voiced and sensual entertainer Lena Horne was a favorite among this group. Lena Horne was certainly a fighter in the civil rights movement, a breakthrough black actress in film and television, and a talented singer. But one of the top black female leaders in the United States in 1986?

Ten years later, Ella Edmondson Bell gave a talk on diversity to a group of senior executives at an East Coast bank. It was a small group, so she sat with them around a large conference table, drinking coffee and talking frankly about the bank's low success in recruiting, hiring, and retaining black women managers. At a loss to pinpoint what they were doing wrong, the senior executives honestly wanted to know what they should do to change this situation. At one point, the CEO confessed he really did not understand the black women in his bank. "Who are they?" he asked. "Are their experiences, expectations, and behaviors more akin to those of white women? Do their experiences more resemble those of black men? Where do they fit?" His quizzical look revealed how puzzled and confused he was when race intersected with gender.

Both anecdotes make important points about the status of black women managers. When Fortune 500 CEOs cannot name one black woman leader from the corporate world, resorting instead to identifying political celebrities from the public sector or, failing that, a Hollywood star, they cannot be facilely accused of middle-aged white-male myopia. For in 1986 it would have been difficult for anyone to list black women in the executive offices of corporate America. They were not present. Black women leaders were more prominent in government, public service, and education. Not one black woman even figured in the top twenty-five black managers in U.S. companies in a survey conducted in 1988.[3] In the larger culture, images of black female executives and managers were almost nonexistent.

Today, however, black women are making inroads into corporate America, entering higher paying career-track managerial and professional jobs. According to the U.S. Department of Labor, the number of black women holding such jobs increased by 79 percent between 1986 and 1996.[4] We can even point to black women sitting in executive suites—from Anne Fudge, executive vice president of Kraft Foods, to Brenda J. Gains, North American president of the Diners Club International, and Sylvia Rhone, president of Electra Records.[5]

Yet, despite their growing presence, black women executives remain a mystery to others in their organizations. Colleagues know little about who they are, where they come from, or how their life and career experiences set them apart. Some assume black women and white women share similar personal and professional histories because they share the same gender. Others see race as the key variable and assume the experiences of black women executives mirror those of their black male colleagues.

When the bank CEO confesses he knows little about his black women managers, he is candidly revealing a dearth of understanding that is universally shared. Should black women be likened to black men, who have had a presence in corporate America—albeit limited—longer than black women? Or should they be positioned with white women, whose status and numbers in management have grown significantly over the past two decades? What indeed do race and gender explain about how black women fit in organizations? Unfortunately, even in the year 2001, black women remain in the shadows. Whether subsumed by the category of "women" or the category of "blacks," they are invisible. Their colleagues seem unaware of the day-to-day realities they face in the workplace.

CEOs are not the only ones ambivalent and confused about how to interact with the black women in their companies. Colleagues wonder whether gender connects women across racial lines, or whether race determines commonality. Others wonder whether black women executives have their own leadership style and whether it helps them navigate the hierarchy. Still others wonder if black women are squarely on the company team.

We suspect many reading this book will assume it is intended for black women. But this book contains important information for everyone, regardless of race or gender. Our reader might be:

- A white male supervisor who thinks a black woman in the department overly attributes conflicts with white colleagues to racism.

- A black male middle manager who worries that the company has room for only one black executive.

- A white woman who has noticed that a black female rarely joins her coworkers on Friday afternoons for happy hour.

- A white female manager curious about why the black women in the company have developed a strong supportive network among themselves.

- A white male director of human resources who has wondered why the company cannot retain black women.

- A black male manager who keeps a cool distance from a black female colleague so people in the office won't suspect a sexual liaison.

- A black woman manager who believes white women use their sexuality to form alliances with powerful men in the company.

To make sense of the complex dynamics of heterogeneous workplaces, everyone from CEOs to secretaries would do well to fully understand the effects of race and gender on black women's life and career experiences. Previous efforts to discuss the advancement of women in management are based on a too-narrow slice of women workers, overemphasizing the career needs of white women in management positions. Statistics indicate black women currently represent the largest number of minority women in management. If the present trend continues, they may soon make up the largest pool of minority women managers. In addition, black women are surpassing black men in executive and managerial positions.[6]

What are the career needs of black women managers? How do these women understand and work with their racial and gender identity? How can corporate leaders advance the careers of black women and rid their companies of debilitating cross-race and cross-gender dynamics?

This book starts the process by bringing black women managers and corporate executives out of the shadow of their white counterparts. It also illuminates the different paths traveled by black and white women as they navigate the corporate world. It places black women in the foreground— not just to shed light on their experiences but also to learn from the juxtaposition of their experiences with those of white women.

We recognize that what happens to black and white women in organizations is irrevocably entwined. In the hierarchy of most organizations, white men are at the top; below them, white women exceed black women both in number and placement in executive positions.[7] Consequently, black women and white women in managerial roles do not have the same access to power and privilege because of their different positions relative to white men. These different positions influence the way black and white women experience organizational life. They also have profound implications for each group's roles and attitudes in the workplace and for their career paths. By juxtaposing the career and life experiences of black and white women, we demonstrate how the combined effects of race and gender create not only very different organizational identities and career experiences, but also very separate paths to the doors of corporate America. *Our Separate Ways* is the first book to offer a comprehensive, holistic, in-depth analysis of the ways black and white women executives' lives diverge and converge, both before and after they enter the corporate world.

We believe our findings and interpretations are relevant to several audiences. Practicing managers, HR executives, and organization leaders concerned with grooming women managers and enhancing cross-race and cross-gender relationships; academics studying race and gender in organizations, career development, and the sociology of work; and black and white women executives seeking to become more effective in their careers and to resolve the conflicts in their relationships.

How This Book Is Structured

The Introduction lays the groundwork for our study. We discuss the scholarly works supporting our research and share the conceptual framework that was our road map for conducting this study. The research methods and procedures used in our work are also provided, along with the demographics of all the women who so generously agreed to participate in our project. If the research underpinnings of this work are not of interest to you, then you may want to skip directly to Part I, "Flashbacks." Here we acquaint you with the fourteen women who appear as principal characters throughout the book. We let them tell the stories of their childhood and families as well as the psychological and educational training that set them on their various life paths. These women have been highlighted because their lives are representative of other women interviewed and because their stories most clearly articulate the themes that surfaced continually in our research.

We present them as completely as possible up front to enable the reader to get to know all of them as full-fledged persons, so that the pieces of their stories revealed later in the book will be coherent parts of a whole character rather than disembodied quotes. To protect their privacy, however, we have changed their names and certain identifying details.

In the interstices of their stories, we highlight the most relevant themes that surface in their early life narratives, amplifying elements that contribute to the separateness of the paths of black and white women. For example, when Julia Smith, an African-American woman in our study, recounts how as a young girl she learned how to survive and endure racism without taking it in, we explain how this is an example of "armoring," a theme that crops up again and again in black women's lives.

In Part II, "Flashpoints," we organize the women's professional experiences thematically. Flashpoints are the common denominators among corporate women—the difficult patches and necessary passages that seem inherent to the experience of being a female manager or executive, but which may nevertheless be experienced in distinctly dissimilar ways by black and white women. We found that six significant flashpoints surfaced in the women's narratives: breaking into a management career, adjusting to the corporate environment, encountering barriers to advancement, climbing over the barriers, making change in the work environment, and coming to terms with personal life choices.

We return here to our principal characters and their stories—allowing their individual experiences to illustrate the patterns our research revealed. In addition, we add the voices of fourteen other interview subjects to reinforce, shade, and supplement the presentation of our findings. These ten women act as a chorus, completing the drama. (For a full list of all the principal and supplemental participants whose narratives we used, see Appendix A.)

In addition to reporting, interpreting, and analyzing our findings, we will discuss the predominance of each of the three lenses—race, gender, and social class—through which we are viewing the women's careers and lives. All data were considered simultaneously through these lenses, but we found that the lenses were not always equally helpful. For example, when our subjects struggle with obstacles to career advancement, the gender lens proved especially relevant: elements of the experience are most attributable to the fact that these subjects are women trying to advance in a male-dominated profession. However, the race lens was also relevant—elements of the experiences of black women managers and white women managers are also shaped and defined by their respective races. We found, however, that a woman's social class of origin had less impact on the way she experienced barriers to advancement, making the social-class lens less helpful to our understanding of this set of her experiences.

In Part III, "The Self and The Other," we examine the way white and black women managers view themselves and their female colleagues. Chapter 11 focuses on the role of racial identity in the professional woman's overall sense of self. Chapter 12 examines the stereotypes that often unwittingly delimit the relationships among female corporate leaders.

Finally, in the Epilogue, we initiate a badly needed dialogue. First, we offer suggestions for how black and white women executives can begin the sometimes difficult conversation needed to bridge the gulfs between them. Second, we lay out a set of suggestions and prescriptions to provide a map for corporate leaders and national policy makers. We hope that our ideas will help corporate America maximize the talents of black and white women and encourage their advancement.

For that is the ultimate benefit of studies such as ours: to posit a new, broader range of role models for young women, to promote understanding of our hardworking colleagues, and to unleash unrealized talent and energy.

$$\clubsuit$$

INTRODUCTION

Foundations on Which This Study Was Built

As black women academics going through twists and turns in our own careers, we became curious about the career experiences of black women executives. Like us, they were few in number, often the sole black woman in their companies, and were also in highly visible positions of authority. Did they, too, experience discrimination in their organizations? How did they perceive their roles? What were the obstacles they experienced? What were some of the joys of being in those positions? And how did their experiences differ from white women?

When we looked to the managerial literature, we were dismayed to find little information. The stories of black women were just not there. Take, for example, the groundbreaking books on women managers. *Managerial Woman*, written by Marilyn Hennig and Ann Jardim and published in 1977, did not include one black woman manager in its sample.[1] *Breaking the Glass Ceiling* by Anne Morrison and her colleagues at the Center for Creative Leadership, a frequently cited 1987 book, contained only three black women in its sample, effectively precluding any meaningful study of both race and gender.[2] Its authors never acknowledge the

11

significance of race in understanding women's experiences with the glass ceiling. Subsequent books on women managers such as the 1993 *Members of the Club: The Coming of Age of Executive Women* by Dawn-Marie Driscoll and Carol Goldberg repeat the same omission.[3]

Rosabeth Moss Kanter's 1977 work, *Men and Women of the Corporation*, is still viewed as the seminal study of gender in organizations.[4] It gives us insight as to the barriers white women experience, particularly in their roles as tokens—the one and only female in a work group. Tokens are stereotyped, viewed as the representative of their gender rather than perceived as individuals. A woman in solo status has her job performance scrutinized more, is highly visible for all the wrong reasons, and encounters hostility from male colleagues. While it is not clear that the consequences of tokenism for African-American women is the same as for white women, Kanter's framework remains useful because she also introduces the idea that as the number of minorities—tokens—increased, there would be less hostility toward them and they would be stereotyped less. Her emphasis on the significance of relative numbers and the symbolic consequences of being a minority encouraged many companies to increase the numbers of African-Americans they employed. However, recent studies have found that a greater presence of African-Americans does not necessarily translate into a greater acceptance of them by white peers. On the contrary, white colleagues tend to show greater psychological discomfort as the number of African-Americans increases in work settings.[5] Both academics and practitioners are even questioning the effectiveness of the current diversity initiatives in companies.[6]

Some researchers conclude that managerial theories based on the experiences of white men and women are inadequate for understanding the experiences of black women.[7] Career literature reflects the same assumption: What we know about executive career entry, as well as career advancement and career paths, largely reflects the realities of white men, with some attention given to white women.[8] According to Harvard Business School professors David Thomas and John Gabarro, "In the absence of research on the effects of race on executive development, we do not know if systematic differences exist between the career paths taken by whites and minorities to reach the executive suite, or in the way they experience that climb."[9] Thomas and Gabarro's conclusion may seem surprising, but in-depth managerial studies dealing centrally and thoroughly with the career experiences of groups other than white men and white women are rare. Thomas and Gabarro's book, *Breaking Through: The*

Making of Minority Executives in Corporate America, is one of the first-in-depth studies focusing on minorities and career development. However, the authors do not treat gender specifically in their study.

There are a few recent studies examining race in combination with gender that point to the unique situation of African-American women. Ella Edmondson Bell examined the bicultural life experiences of seventy-one African-American career-oriented women.[10] For African-American women, biculturality, or moving from one cultural context to another, requires that they shape their careers in the white world, while shaping other dimensions of their life in the black community. Bicultural stress is a concomitant psychological barrier black professional women feel when they are compelled to suppress or diminish one part of their identity in order to exist in either of the cultural contexts where they work or live. Bell reports that because of bicultural stress, professional black women have unusually complex life structures with inordinate amounts of responsibilities and obligations in all dimensions of their lives. Consequently, these women must manage dual roles and social responsibilities within both cultural contexts, often without adequate social support in either. The women simply become worn out from juggling the multiple and conflicting roles in their lives.

David Thomas investigated the impact of race and gender on managers' mentoring relationships.[11] He found an interesting dynamic that he believes is grounded in the legacy of slavery: black women in his study were reluctant to establish a mentoring relationship with white men because of the lingering images of African-American women as concubines of white slave owners. Likewise, senior white men were ambivalent for the same reasons. Thomas referred to such discomfort as a "racial taboo." For black women, the racial taboo reflects a fear of being sexually linked to a senior white male in the company. The senior white men also fear others would interpret their relationships as a sexual liaison. These unspoken and unsanctioned racial taboos complicated or blocked the forming of mentor-protégé relationships.

Catalyst, a nonprofit research and advisory organization for the advancement of professional women, recently undertook a survey to examine the factors in the corporate culture and work environment that contribute to or impede the retention, development, and advancement of women of color. Catalyst compared what it learned from the women to earlier survey results from white women professionals, finding striking differences between white women and minority women in their perceptions of progress made. Sixty percent of white women thought there had been improvements in their opportunities the last five years, while only 47 percent of minority women agreed. Additionally, African-American women in the study believed:

- They need to adjust their styles to fit into the corporate environment.

- Many stereotypes exist about women of their racial group.

- Other employees feel uncomfortable around members of their racial group.

- Affirmative action had an impact on their recruitment to their companies.[12]

Unlike scholars in the managerial sciences, social scientists, particularly sociologists, have a long tradition of investigating race in combination with gender and class. We turned to these scholars to find relevant, in-depth theoretical treatments of race and gender. Their work laid the theoretical groundwork for our study. Patricia Hill Collins, a noted sociologist, articulates a theory of the relationship between race, gender, and class.[13] She argues that the relationship between black and white women across race, gender, and class is embedded in systems of oppression versus systems of privilege within the social structure and broader social systems. For Collins, race, class, and gender are historically constructed systems of power that support one another. Collins's concept calls into question how the interlocking elements of race, gender, and class translate in the executive careers of black and white women. She examines the characteristic themes that emerge for these groups of women in the workplace, as each one occupies a particular place in the race, gender, and class nexus.

Similarly, Aida Hurtado, in her pioneering construction of the effect of race on how women are positioned in society, argues that the critical distinction between women of color and white women has been their differential positions to white men in the context of a larger social system privileging those with white skin.[14] In Hurtado's view, the processes by which women of color and white women are subordinated and treated differ in any system favoring white men. White women as a group are kept in a subordinate position by seduction. They are accepted and treated well as long as they are submissive and responsive to the authority of white men. Women of color, on the other hand, are subordinated through rejection and exclusion. Her work strongly suggests that African-American and white women in organizations may not experience sexism the same way. Thus, sexism takes on a racial overtone.

This possibility is reinforced by the work of another sociologist, Philomena Essed.[15] In her work comparing the organizational experiences of black women in the United States and the Netherlands, Essed uncovered what she labeled "everyday racism," a subtle form of modern racism. The women in her research experienced this modern racism in their everyday, ongoing, routine encounters with whites both at work and outside the workplace. She defined everyday racism as "the integration of racism into everyday situations through practices that activate underlying power relations."[16] Essed's work lays out the particular racist encounters and prejudicial actions black women experience in professional settings that keep them in marginal positions.

Joe Feagin, a Pulitzer Prize–nominated sociologist with more than thirty years of extensive research on racial and gender discrimination issues, along with his colleague Yanick St. Jean, recently examined the experiences of middle-class African-American women in both the workplace and in their communities.[17] Their work describes gendered discrimination—negative white reactions, individual and institutionalized, to black female characteristics. St. Jean and Feagin show that in the everyday lives of black women there are distinctive combinations of race- and gender-related factors. These women face not only the double burden of having to deal with both racism and sexism separately but also the problems that come from having to deal with the combination of the two.

The Conceptual Framework Underlying Our Research Approach

In conducting our research study, we constructed a framework that responded to the omissions we saw in the managerial literature and the insights we gained from sociologists studying race, gender, and class. Even though black women executives were to take center stage in our research, we believed that placing them in context would yield a deeper and richer understanding of their career and organizational experiences. We settled on a comparative investigation: both black and white women executives and managers participated in this study. We wanted to learn from these women how their identities informed both their life course—especially their work experiences—and their ability to pursue career paths not traditional for women.

Our framework captures the complex factors shaping the life and career experiences of black and white women. It consists of the three interlocking core elements of identity: gender, race, and social class (presented in Figure 1-1). Sexual orientation could well be another interlocking circle in the framework, but given that all the women who participated in this study identified themselves as heterosexual, we intentionally omitted this element. Our decision does not devalue the importance of sexual identity and orientation in organizational life; we simply did not have the data to make any contributions in this area.

Gender is much more than a biological categorization. At its most elemental level, gender is a system of classification distinguishing men from women. It is also a set of assumptions and beliefs on both individual and societal levels that affect the thoughts, feelings, behaviors, resources, and treatment of women and men.[18] In Western society an infant is "gendered" to be male or female. To be gendered, in this context, is to incorporate societal orientations about roles for men and women and the relationships between them. As professor Elizabeth Fox-Genovese points out, gender is "a system of relations—specific relations—between women and men."[19] Throughout history and in every society, gender has been one of major structures of domination perpetuated by patriarchy.

In the past decade, scholarship has substantially increased our knowledge of gender differences. Feminist researchers espouse differences in the psychological makeup of women and men.[20] Harvard professor of education Carol Gilligan, for example, discovered that the way women connect

FIGURE 1-1 *Theoretical Framework*

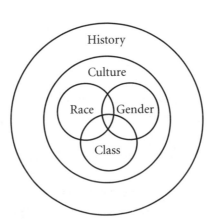

to others stresses emotional relatedness, while men seem to function by separation and autonomy. Gilligan's notion is supported by the research of Judy Rosener, who has reported that women managers used more relational styles of leadership than did male managers.[21] Gender significantly affects what happens to women in management.[22] Research has also indicated that women's lives develop in more complex patterns than men's lives,[23] especially as women structure their lives to accommodate motherhood and the world of work.[24]

Race is the second interlocking element in the framework. Even in the new millennium, race remains one of the most hotly controversial and highly complex issues in our society. In the social sciences, definitions of race have long been fraught with multiple meanings, causing Gordon Allport to proclaim, "The concept of race is badly abused and exaggerated."[25] Race is no longer a concept used to classify groups of people based on physical traits such as skin color, but rather denotes the meanings given or attached to phenotypical differences among people. In American society, race is politically and socially defined. Race has been used to reinforce already powerful groups, while weakening those groups with less power; prior to and even into the twentieth century, race determined a woman's political rights and social status.

Today race still determines a woman's position within the labor market and her economic well-being. Race prevents minority women from fully participating in organizational life, with minority women managers reporting greater scrutiny and extra challenges because of their race.[26] Race also shapes a woman's identity, influencing how she defines herself and how others define her. Of course, white women have a racial identity as well.[27] This book sheds light on how both groups shape their racial identities and how women define themselves racially.

The third interlocking circle is social class. According to historian Gerda Lerner, social class refers to the degree of access one has to resources and to power.[28] Resources can be defined culturally and in other ways, but they are real and quantifiable. A woman's social class determines her access to economic power, land acquisition, political power, education, technology, and entry to important social networks. Thus, social class sorts out positions in society along a continuum of economic success and social privilege. Social class creates multilayered locations, relations, and experiences that differ according to gender, race, and stage in the life cycle.[29]

In a woman's identity, these core elements of gender, race, and class are interdependent, interactive, and dynamic, rather than independent and static.

Gerda Lerner reminds us that "gender is constructed racially and through class and ethnicity."[30] Stuart Hall adds, "Race and gender are the modalities through which class is lived; disentangling them is impossible."[31] Scholars use the term "social location" to capture how the intersection of gender, race, and social class places a woman in a particular position within society.

Understanding women executives is predicated on recognizing this intersection. First, it helps us to understand why there is no such thing as a monolithic black woman manager or white woman manager. Certainly, there are powerful differences between these two groups of women, but social class also causes differences among women within the same racial group. Second, while black and white women's professional experiences vary, there are essential similarities. *Our Separate Ways* shows how the women's experiences are related in systematic ways.

In our framework the three interlocking elements are embedded within a larger context represented by two concentric circles. The first circle represents culture. "To say that two people belong to the same culture," says Stuart Hall, "is to say they interpret the world in roughly the same ways and can express themselves, their thoughts and feelings about the world, in ways which will be understood by each other."[32] Culture encompasses shared meanings between people, shared cultural practices, and the everyday effects of such practices in terms of power and social regulation. Women raised in the same culture have a common heritage with shared norms, values, and world views.[33] They also share a frame of reference in which their feminine identity is grounded, a sense of group identity and affiliation, and a sense of society and how to behave within it. Culture also influences the values a woman holds, the career choices she makes, and how she navigates the corporate arena.

The other concentric circle is history, a critical contextual factor in understanding the careers and lives of women managers. One of the most prominent thinkers on adult development, Erik H. Erikson, argued that "human life is inextricably interwoven with history."[34] The eminent sociologist C. Wright Mills coined the term "sociological imagination" to capture the same sentiment: "Neither the life of an individual or the history of a society can be understood without understanding both."[35] Mills was an ardent believer in exploring the relation between biography, social structure, and history in the social sciences. Social norms, societal beliefs, the structure of institutions, and cultural mores are reflective of particular historical periods. History shapes the landscape of a woman's life. It can open new avenues for growth and development, or conversely, erect roadblocks to opportunity.

The women executives in this book tell their individual stories of trials and triumphs, but the stories taken together also tell a collective story. It is the story of black and white women who came of age in the '60s, during the civil rights movement, when unprecedented educational and employment possibilities were made available to African-Americans. In turn, the civil rights movement helped usher in the women's movement, enabling women not only to increase their numbers in the workforce but also to enter nontraditional careers. In this historical moment, women gained the option of becoming career-oriented, able to devote more time and energy to developing their careers than ever before.

From this rather broad conceptual framework, we developed six questions to guide our research:

1. What are the women's early life stories?

2. How did race, gender, and social class affect key developmental aspects of their lives?

3. What are the effects of gender, race, and social class over the course of their lives?

4. What role conflicts do the African-American women experience as a result of their bicultural life structures?

5. How do gender, race, and social class affect the women's work experiences, upward mobility, and career satisfaction?

6. How do women managers negotiate their work, family, and community roles and the interrelationships among them?

Because we were dealing with a largely understudied phenomena at the time of this research, we found it very useful to think of our framework more as a set of assumptions guiding the research than as hypotheses to be tested.

Methodology of the Study

To address these questions, we conducted in-depth interviews with a targeted group of women executives and combined this material with a survey of a broader group of women managers. The primary tool for our research was the life history interview. Extensive life history interviews were held with eighty black women and forty white women for a sample total of 120 women. We purposely oversampled black women. Researchers typically take this approach when a group or phenomena has been underinvestigated.

The life history approach is defined by sociologist Norman Denzin as "a method for collecting life stories to capture the subjective meaning of experience over a person's life course which cannot be wholly represented by quantitative methods."[36] In other words, this method reveals how an individual views and interprets her life course. By life course, we mean the sequence of socially defined roles and events a woman enacts over time.[37] The life course concept allows for the incorporation of historical events and the sociocultural context as well as internal and psychological changes. It also allows us to gain a fuller and richer sense of a woman's total life.

Past research on women in management tends to strictly focus on their careers, dismissing other relevant dimensions of their lives. We call this "the parachute approach" to women's managerial research: Women dressed in business suits, armed with a briefcase in one hand and an M.B.A. in the other, infiltrate the white male bastion of corporate America. Once inside, they fight tenaciously to shatter the glass ceiling, so they can climb the steep ladder of the corporate hierarchy. But other than the barriers they face and the obstacles they overcome in the workplace, what do we know about female executives? Most of what is written about women managers gives scant attention to their early life and development. This occurs despite a considerable body of literature on adult development indicating that women experience more complexity in career choices and career experiences because of the effects of early sex-role socialization, when they learn what roles are and are not important for girls.[38] This tendency to study women managers at the point they enter managerial careers creates another shadow phenomenon. Their managerial careers are studied using the same lens used to study the careers of men. Researchers fail to probe how women's lives in their entirety, influence their behaviors, feelings, and choices as managers.

INTERVIEW PROCEDURES

The life history interviews were conducted in two parts. The first part focused on the women's early childhood through college experiences. Part two covered career experiences and personal lives to the present time. Each woman's interview averaged six to eight hours and was conducted in two or more sessions. By the completion of the interview, we had heard each woman's life story. We wanted to conduct the interviews in a way that would encourage the women to share their feelings about race and gender without feeling they were being evaluated or judged. To do this, we assembled a six-person team of black and white women to conduct the interviews. Graduate students whom we had trained assisted us. Black members of the research team interviewed the black women executives while white team members interviewed the white women executives.[39] The details of the interview procedures along with the interview protocol are described in Appendix B.

THE SURVEY

The life history interviews were supplemented by an in-depth survey of 825 black and white women managers across the country. The survey covered career dynamics, current work situation, career history, race and gender dynamics at work, personal life, personal dimensions of racial and ethnic identity, stress factors, and background information. The survey contents and sample are fully described in Appendix C.

The results of the survey were used to confirm some of the themes and patterns that emerged from the life history interviews. These findings are presented when relevant to the discussion of the narrative data. The life history interviews, though, are the main focus of this book. Women's stories, told in their own voices, best point to the complexity of the choices and challenges they face in their lives. In a book striving to bring black women managers out of the shadows, we did not want to silence the power of their voices.

THE WOMEN

Because our focus was the women themselves and not the organizations they worked within, we chose a sampling approach to reach the women directly. The women who participated in the interviews occupy a wide variety of executive and managerial positions in private sector corporations. Their job titles include: executive vice president, senior vice president, divisional president, divisional head, vice president, regional director, corporate treasurer, general counsel, and director. They are highly educated, sophisticated, achievement-oriented, and professionally accomplished. At the time of the life history interviews, 75 percent worked

in Fortune 500 companies. Table B-1 in Appendix B gives summary statistics about the women interviewed.

The women were born at roughly the same time and experienced
approximately the same historical events at a similar time in their lives. A
majority of the women are part of what Gail Sheehy identifies as the Vietnam Generation, born between 1945 and 1955, with a small number born
in the late 1950s as part of the Me Generation.[40] The women we interviewed were trailblazers, members of the first significant wave of women
to enter managerial positions in corporate America during the 1970s and
1980s. Their stories are noteworthy because at the time they entered the
workplace, the term "woman manager" was an oxymoron. Both the academic and popular business press were asking, "Can women be managers?" Our participants had on average about fifteen years of work
experience at the time of the interviews. Many, especially the black
women, were the first women in their companies to be in a management
position. They had to carve out paths where none existed.

Colleagues had told us there was little chance of getting busy women
executives to spend the time required by the interviews. We found just the
opposite. Once the women understood our goals and committed themselves to being involved, they were enormously generous with their time,
and even welcomed the opportunity to share their life stories. We sought
an open and intimate relationship, one that would enable us to explore
very private moments in their lives. In many instances, the women
revealed feelings and recollections they had not before shared publicly.
Throughout the interviews, we paid careful attention to each woman's
attempt at self-understanding and self-discovery. Telling their stories
enabled the women to see how the different threads of their lives came
together. We found that one of the effects of the life history method is the
self-reflection it triggers in participants.

Interpretation of life history data is challenging. While we offer a
detailed description of how we analyzed the women's interviews in
Appendix B, we want to underscore a few points here. As noted earlier,
we ended up with each woman's life story. While the person-centered
nature of life history interviews gives us rich and detailed portrayals, it
relies on what individuals recall and how they frame and perceive situations. Each life story narrator selects, from a wide array, those moments
deemed most significant. Life history scholars argue that life stories are a
way of fashioning identity, in both the private and public sense of that
word. Ultimately, what we learn is how individuals make sense of their

lives. The women's stories are recollections filled with flashbacks and significant memories. To mitigate the inherent subjectivity of the women's experiences, we placed their narratives within a broader historical and cultural framework, even though the women may not have acknowledged or mentioned this framework during their interviews. Our challenge was to hear and honor their life stories while bringing a researcher's eye to their possible meanings and significance.

PART I

Flashbacks

WHEN WE CONSIDER the subjects of this book—women managers and executives in corporate America—we are likely to make many assumptions about them. Whether they are black or white, we assume that successful professional women share not just impressive curricula vitae, but also formative life experiences. We assume that they are products of middle- or upper-class families and that they benefited from average American privileges: a solid education, financial security, and professional opportunity. But the life stories of the women we interviewed for this study upend all such assumptions.

Women whose lives defy stereotypes are often invisible, so in our account of their experiences we would like to start by making them clearly visible. We will let them tell their distinctly personal stories in their own words. We will let them shed light on the many different early-life experiences that shaped them: poverty as well as privilege, isolation as well as support, domineering as well as doting fathers, the clamoring of social movements, and the armoring provided to some by their families.

Out of the 120 professional women we interviewed, we have selected fourteen women—seven of them black, seven of them white—whose stories best illustrate the themes we found surfacing again and again among their contemporaries. We have grouped them in such a way as to highlight these important themes, and we follow their stories with an analysis of those themes. In the first chapter of this "Flashbacks" section, we focus on women who suffered lost childhoods—either because they were raised in what are today called "families at risk" or because they suffered traumatic losses as young girls that shaped their growing-up experiences. In the second chapter, "Their Fathers' Daughters," we have chosen women whose stories best illustrate the developmental role played by fathers—whether they were positive models or motivating adversaries for their daughters. In "Comfortable Families, Uncomfortable Times," we try to show how geographic and social location influenced a woman's future, whether that location was the community in which a girl was raised or the social upheaval she saw around her. Finally, in "Executives in Training," we show how some black families "armored" their daughters, raising them with a strong awareness of how to survive a racist society, how to surmount the obstacles it poses, and how to thrive in the corporate world.

Here, then, are their flashbacks—the poignant memories and salient stories they told us about their early years.

1

❖

LOST CHILDHOODS

Ruthie Mae White

Ruthie Mae White has always been a survivor. The eldest of eight children born to Johnnie Mae and Jonathan White, she grew up in the Carolinas in the 1950s in one of the poorest counties in the United States. Johnnie Mae tried to support her family by sharecropping and cooking and cleaning for whites. But in the rural South, black people trying to scrape out a living by sharecropping lived a mission impossible. Poverty that defied description was an everyday reality for Ruthie Mae and her family. The house the family rented was no larger than a small shed, with floors made of uneven plywood planks perched atop concrete cinder blocks. The roof was a combination of rusty tin and tarpaper. Ruthie Mae does not remember having indoor plumbing until she was in high school, but she does recall the fun she used to have chasing chickens out from underneath the house through the cracks between the worn-out floorboards.

Today, Ruthie Mae White is vice-president of mortgage originations for a vast metropolitan area in one of the country's largest financial institutions. Ruthie Mae's skin is the color of rich, dark chocolate, and she wears a short-cropped natural hairstyle that illuminates her chiseled

African facial features. She is a spunky, petite woman who does not hide her humble beginnings and is always dressed as if she were ready to attend a church service.

Ruthie Mae manages a team of fifteen loan officers. Her unit is responsible for generating new business, identifying new products, and providing a high level of service to customers. "The key to success in my role is balancing my time in the office with the need to be out in the field," she said. "I cover a pretty large area. Clients like to see you if they are going to give you their business. Then, of course, there's working with the back-office folks."

Ruthie Mae's parents, both of whom came from very poor backgrounds, separated when she was a baby. Having to leave school to work the tobacco fields as children, neither parent had completed elementary school. After the separation, her father lived with another woman in the community. However, her mother continued to have his children, even though he was fathering children with the other woman at the same time. Between the two women, Jonathan White fathered sixteen children. Ruthie Mae does not remember her father being around very much. Nor does she think her father provided any financial support to help raise her siblings and herself.

What does stand out in her mind, however, are the times her father would pile all eight of them in his car and take them for a joyride. Along the way he would always stop at the local dry goods store. Mr. White would go inside after telling his children to wait in the car. But Ruthie Mae, a child with a mind of her own, never listened. Instead, she would wait for a few minutes before following him into the store. Once inside, she would walk around the store, pick up bright red apples from a basket, grab a fistful of penny candies, and snatch up as many licorice sticks as her small hand could hold. She would then quietly put her bounty on the store's counter. The storekeeper would tally the price of her goodies on a brown bag. While he was adding things up, Ruthie Mae made sure to avoid eye contact with her father. Of course, she knew he would pay. He did not want people thinking he was not taking care of all his children. When the storekeeper would tell them the total cost of her pluckiness, Ruthie Mae would bolt through the store's door. Her father would come marching out of the store, holding the bounty, yelling and screaming all the way. Ruthie Mae, along with her brothers and sisters, did not mind hearing their father's rants, because they got to eat all the goodies on the way back home.

Ruthie Mae employed a number of tricks to get money out of her father; whatever small amounts he gave her she would always turn over to her mother. Lack of money was a big problem for the family. As a result, all the White children were working by the time they reached their eighth birthday. They toiled in tobacco fields, did yard work, cleaned white people's houses—whatever they could do to keep a roof over their heads. On occasion Ruthie Mae's paternal grandmother and uncle would help the family out, but they did not have much family stability either. Also, there seemed to be some estrangement between her mother and her father's family. Because of this tension, Ruthie Mae could not depend on her father's kinfolk for emotional or financial support.

Ruthie Mae often found herself in charge of her siblings, trying to take control of the chaos that surrounded them and the uncertainty life brought. When she was feeling overwhelmed by the circumstances, she would always sing the lyrics to her favorite gospel tune. That kept her going, especially the refrain, "and on thyself rely." At a young age she knew what it meant to rely on herself, and to have her six brothers and one sister depend on her as well. "I always thought of myself as the mother of my family, because I was the one who hugged and kissed them when they were sick or they got hurt or cried." Her own childhood, she remembers, was snuffed out by this added responsibility.

The elementary school Ruthie Mae attended was a one-room building with a stove in the middle. Pupils would sit on either side of it. There were no books, only a chalkboard that the teacher used infrequently. Most of the school day the children spent playing outside on a wooden swing set. Ruthie Mae recalled, "We didn't learn anything. I was in fourth grade when we transferred to a school in a building with rest rooms inside, and I was fascinated by that." In the new school the other students were reading. It was then that Ruthie Mae discovered she could not read. She did not master books until seventh grade, but by then her education faced a new impediment.

Rather than having Ruthie Mae attend classes when she was in junior high school, Mrs. White insisted that Ruthie stay home to take care of her three-year old brother. At the time, she did not believe her mother valued education. "Mama's priority was to make sure we ate regularly." This was increasingly upsetting to Ruthie Mae. Fortunately, though, Ruthie Mae's seventh grade teacher, Mrs. Garrett, came to her rescue. She made a home visit to find out why Ruthie Mae's attendance was so irregular and found Ruthie Mae home babysitting. In order to get Ruthie Mae to come to class every day, Mrs. Garrett told her to bring her younger brother with her. "He disrupted the whole class, but Mrs. Garrett never said anything about it," Ruthie Mae said in a tone softened by admiration and appreciation.

High school was a turning point in Ruthie Mae's life. The principal, a real taskmaster, took a special interest in her. "I worked harder in all four grades in high school than I have ever done in my life," Ruthie Mae declared. Thrilled at the discovery of her own intelligence, Ruthie Mae carried books home every evening, devouring them late into the night. She also became a leader, and was selected as senior class president. But despite such success, Ruthie Mae was conscious of being excluded from the more popular students in school. Skin color and economic status split the students into two "tribes": one made up of the working-class kids who happened to be light-skinned; and the other made up of the kids who were poor and dark-skinned. Ruthie Mae's story is a real-life manifestation of the social dynamic portrayed in Spike Lee's *School Daze*, with its light-skinned, straight-haired Wannabes and dark-skinned, nappy-headed Jigaboos. Ruthie Mae wore a tam everyday to hide her "kinky and natty" hair.

In the twelfth grade, however, the social order shifted. "It was the year where the poor, black, kinky-haired, dark-skinned people took charge of the school," she recalled with evident pride. Ruthie Mae was elected class president. She realized you didn't have to be light-skinned with long hair to do well. "We could make it without all that. . . . We were smart too," she added. "We had the highest scores on all the standardized tests because we studied hard." The principal broached the subject of college with Ruthie Mae. He talked her mother into letting her apply to colleges and paid the application fees.

By this time, Ruthie Mae had acquired another guardian angel. In ninth grade she began working as a babysitter for the family of Mr. Nelson, a white lawyer in town. The Nelson family lived in an impressive two-story brick house, and Mr. Nelson drove a Cadillac, a rare extravagance in those parts. He first approached Ruthie Mae about part-time baby-sitting; over time, he increased his requests until she was able to stop cleaning the houses of other white families.

But whenever she went to baby-sit, there was little for her to do. "Most of the time I would get over there, and everybody would be sitting around watching TV, including him and his wife," she said. For her services, he paid her fifty cents more than the two dollars a week she had earned cleaning. On some weekends Ruthie Mae was allowed to stay over at the

Nelson's to take care of the children. Occasionally, she accompanied them on family excursions. Instead of tiring household duties, Ruthie Mae was encouraged to do her homework.

At Ruthie Mae's house, her mother would turn off all the electric lights by eight o'clock in the evening to save on the electric bill. If Ruthie Mae had to study in the evening, Mr. Nelson would come to get Ruthie Mae so she could study at his house. Mr. Nelson would even help her with school assignments. The Nelson's home had a library filled with books. Ruthie Mae had never seen such a display of literature. Her mother was neither able to buy books, nor to read them. Ruthie Mae avidly devoured as many books as she could during her afternoons at the Nelsons. Her newly acquired knowledge was put to good use, as she began to get A's on all her assignments in school. Teachers commented in class about how she was blossoming intellectually.

Ruthie Mae's good grades enabled her to win full scholarships at four different colleges. She chose to attend a historically black college that also happened to be the college farthest away from her hometown. "I would have ended up being asked to come home to work on Saturdays picking tobacco to help out my family," she explained. Her initial plan was to major in education, so she could return to her rural community and teach. "I wanted to teach more than anything," she sadly admitted. However, family responsibilities took a toll on her college dream. Unable to student teach because she had to work part-time to help her mother provide for her younger siblings, Ruthie Mae changed her major to business. Attending classes and working, she still was on the honor roll all four years through college. Ruthie Mae married her college sweetheart the latter part of her sophomore year. But she divorced before graduating. A single parent at the age of twenty-two, she managed to graduate with honors that same year.

Immediately following graduation, she began her career in the financial industry as a bank teller.

Linda Butler

By the time Linda Butler turned sixteen, she was out on her own making a living. Linda's petite, fragile appearance is exaggerated by the high leather chair she sits in behind a massive dark mahogany desk. Her wood-paneled, classic but utilitarian office features a wall of windowpanes with a view of the other tall downtown buildings. Linda's pale, almost translucent white skin masks the resolve and perseverance it took to rise from a very poor and traumatic childhood to be the only woman at the senior executive level in a large utility company. She speaks with a strong and confident voice. She is finishing her first year as vice president of corporate affairs, a position held previously only by men; she is responsible for public information, public relations, and employee communications. "We're charged with reviewing everything that goes outside the company on a mass basis," she said, "to ensure employees adhere to company policy and company image."

Linda, an only child, was born in 1947 in rural Mississippi to poor working-class parents. Linda never knew her father. Her parents were divorced before she was born and her mother later remarried. Linda spent her childhood traveling from one small town to another with her mother and stepfather, an itinerant worker who found work where he could. They always lived in the poorest part of town, sometimes in a trailer. She has vivid memories of one of the small towns they lived in. "We stayed in a small cinder block house on the outskirts of town. We had no transportation. We had no telephone. We were poor. I remember the house because the floorboards had large cracks between them. If you dropped something, it would be gone forever. I lost a little five-and-dime bracelet in that house."

The rural communities in which Linda spent her early childhood were once part of the Cotton Belt that ran from Texas and southern Oklahoma to the Carolinas and northern Florida. Its hot weather was well suited to the growth of the cotton plant. But by the 1950s many rural whites were leaving farming to become industrial workers. Many with small farms had abandoned low-income farm life to work in local textile plants or other factories in the surrounding small towns. Mills offered an avenue of escape from the land that had failed them or that had been taken over by large-scale commercial companies. The textile industry became the bedrock of the Southern economy of the fifties and sixties.[1] Families of the factory workers often lived in mill houses or mill villages built by the companies. These villages were worlds unto themselves, with four-room cookie-cutter houses featuring sand-plastered interior walls and white exteriors.[2] But even this level of comfort was not available to Linda's family, as her stepfather could only find short-time jobs. Linda recalled one place where she lived: "There was a steel mill, a cotton plant, and a rubber plant. If you lived in that little town, that was all there was. It was a big union town and the workers would go on strike at the drop of hat."

Linda learned at an early age to take care of herself. "We moved a lot because of my stepfather's work. I like to refer to him as a 'tinker man.' I can remember one time moving over the Christmas holiday. When it came time to go to school on the first day after the holiday, my mother and stepfather were both working. So I stood outside our little house by myself and took the bus to school. I went into school and registered myself. I could read and I knew my numbers so they put me in first grade. I was five years old but told them I was six."

After her mother's death, seven-year-old Linda was left with her stepfather. Unable to care for her, he sent her off to live with relatives. She never saw him again. Linda grew up being shuttled between her grandparents and aunts and uncles. When she lived with her relatives, she did a lot of the household work: "I did most of the cooking, most of the washing, and most of the housekeeping. My aunt more or less had a holiday. I didn't really like it but these people were keeping me so I felt I should do something to repay them. I cannot remember after my mother died anyone in my family hugging me or showing emotion until many years after I was a married adult. We were a distant family. They took care of me when I was young because that was what you were supposed to do."

Linda had to grow up fast on her own. "I don't remember my mother much or my stepfather. All of my relatives were struggling, so I would stay with each one until they could no longer afford to take care of me. I don't remember getting encouragement to do anything. The entire time I was growing up, no one ever talked to me about college. No one even talked to me about finishing high school. A number of the women in my family had quit high school to get married and had children very, very early. So no one really said 'We expect you to do your homework. We expect you to finish school.' I've thought a lot about this, and I don't know if there's something you're born with inside that makes you want to be different, but I saw all of that and I said, 'I don't want this.' I wanted a better life. I wanted a decent house. And I never wanted to go back unless I did so on my own terms."

The itinerant life was hardly conducive to getting an education. In first grade alone, Linda went to four different schools. Most of her early education was in small, segregated rural schools. "I really don't remember the first time I saw a black child. In my early years, it was all whites." In the end, she attended sixteen different schools before she graduated from high school. She loved to read. "I would lose myself in books," she said. "I remember being so proud in the first grade right after that Christmas when I first started school. I was reading the thickest book in class while all the other children were in the 'skinny books.' Now looking back, it was an escape. The reading helped me realize there were different lifestyles out there and not just the one I was used to."

Linda went through school wearing a cloak of shame. "I was a loner. I had moved around so much and was always the new kid. I was always uncomfortable. I really didn't want them to know how poor I was; I didn't have what everybody else did and I couldn't go places they went. So it was just easier not to get involved. Nobody knew that. There really were no supports. I think if I had told them I would've possibly gotten some more support." She paused, then added, "This is hard for me to share."

"There was never any thought of saying, 'I don't have lunch money.' You did something else at lunchtime instead of eating. In my senior year a teacher took some girls to one of the women's colleges in the state, but I wasn't able to go. I didn't have the money for the weekend and I didn't want to tell anybody. So I didn't go." These experiences left an indelible impression upon Linda, a lesson she keeps with her today: "I just have a real hard time understanding somebody who doesn't want to get out of that. One thing I get from my family is that we will never accept welfare. We'll starve on our own."

Linda was an intellectually gifted child but was never in a school long enough for teachers or counselors—or her relatives—to recognize it. "I would have started senior high school at twelve if I hadn't moved around so much. It got rough financially for my grandparents, so an aunt and uncle in South Carolina said I could come live with them. I didn't even tell them I was going to skip ninth grade. I just went ahead and registered myself for tenth grade. Even though I knew I wanted a better life, I still didn't go to college because at the time I graduated I was in a small high school. We had no career counseling. No one to tell me there were actually scholarships you could get. There were no community colleges." Linda added, "My family expected me to get married early and have kids even after I decided I wasn't going to do that. I was going to finish school."

There were no guardian angels for Linda. She was on her own. At sixteen, after graduating from high school at the top of her class, she left her aunt and uncle's home and went off on her own to the first big city she could reach. "I found a job as a part-time clerk but when I got down to personnel to fill out the forms, they realized how old I was and told me I had to get my parents to sign working papers. My uncle signed for me. After I got a full-time job there, I found a lady with two rooms to rent and I went to live with her and work. I didn't have a car so everything I did was by bus. I had a ride to work and back every day. But I enjoyed it. I was on my own. I wasn't making much money—I think about $200 a month—but I survived."

Even though Linda had the second highest IQ in her high school when she graduated, it was eight years before she ended up attending a state college at night to earn her degree. She paid her tuition from her meager earnings. "I got my first two years out of the way and designated management as my major. The quarter I took my first management course was also the quarter I took my first accounting course. I had a boring management instructor. But I loved accounting. It was like a puzzle with all these pieces that you have to find to put together and when you get through you have got the puzzle solved. I liked that aspect of it. I switched my major to accounting and got my degree."

The flashbacks of Ruthie Mae White and Linda Butler shatter many assumptions we hold about the early life circumstances of successful women: that they must come from middle-class backgrounds, with nurturing, supportive and intact families; that their careers were launched after a straightforward educational progression. Ruthie Mae and Linda are hardly unusual; their stories are representative of a percentage of the other women we interviewed. Raised in what we would call today "families at risk," many professional women—especially women raised in the rural South—have experienced childhoods marked by two or more of the following conditions: family violence, overwhelmed mothers, parental abandonment, neglect and abuse, and dire poverty. These women may have taken on their mother's responsibilities at an early age.

Black women raised in families of risk, in most cases, were among the poorest of the working poor, those defined by Andrew Billingsley as "families where at least one member is employed . . . [with] median incomes below the poverty line due to low wages. . . . Even with multiple earners, they are not able to move out of poverty."[3] Their families, in most cases, were run by a single head of household, usually the mother. The median yearly income for rural blacks in 1960 was $845, compared to $2,484 for rural whites.[4] With only a few exceptions, the women's parents had received less than a high-school education. Such early life situations were made more daunting for the black women because they also had to cope with growing up in a racist, caste-like society. Carol Stack, in her elegantly written *Call to Home*, states that "conditions of life in the rural South for poor black people had to be either swallowed whole or abandoned; people literally had to take it or leave it."[5] Poor rural whites like Linda Butler, on the other hand, had the option of leaving the farms that failed them for low-paying mill jobs.

Yet Ruthie Mae and Linda share a profound sense of a lost childhood; both found that the freedom that flickers in childhood was soon extinguished. As another black interviewee said, "It seems like all of sudden I just grew up. I have to tell you, I can't remember much about my childhood. It seemed like I was always the one in charge of everything." Missing from narratives of such women are the tales of the usual activities girls engage in during adolescence. Instead, their accounts describe the adult roles and responsibilities assumed while still children. Self-parenting children—those in charge of taking care of themselves and their siblings—learned early on in their lives to be self-reliant, mature, and responsible.

The black women we interviewed often had outsiders—people from their community, church, or school system—who took an active interest in them and helped the girls cope with the harsh realities of everyday life. These "guardian angels" were not connected to the women through bloodlines or through family friendships. They offered support and provided them with resources. In some instances, they gave the young girls unconditional love. They helped to soften the conditions these women lived in throughout their childhoods, filling the void left by unavailable parents or extended family members unable to provide emotional support. Guardian angels may have swooped in to help at one critical moment, or they may have developed an ongoing relationship with the girl. Often the assistance they offered to the young woman gave the girl's family relief as well.

The white women who grew up poor did not talk about supportive guardian angels. Instead, many were like Linda, isolated and forced to fend for themselves. Unlike the black women, whose communities often cut across class lines because of racial segregation, poor white communities were often distant from middle-class white communities. The women talked of the shame of poverty and keeping it secret from others. Consequently, they had to cope differently with their circumstances. They knew they had to do it on their own. An important motivator among the women was a resolve to escape their impoverished environments.

The stories of Ruthie Mae White and Linda Butler convey the impact of gender, race, and social class on a young woman's life, but they also help us understand the two cultural contexts in which black and white women's lives are embedded: one the culture of resistance, and the other the culture of individualism. Like Ruthie Mae, the black women we interviewed were raised in a culture of resistance that has its genesis in the subordinate status of the African-American. Subordinate groups have consistently struggled to find ways to resist and fight systems of oppression in order to overcome dominance. Black women, in particular, according to historian Stephanie Shaw, "were encouraged and prepared to resist, wherever possible, the constraints the larger society sought to impose on them."[6] The culture of resistance left a powerful imprint on the women's identities. Sociologist Patricia Hill Collins broadly defines the characteristics of the culture of resistance as a legacy of struggle for family and community, an ethic of caring, self-definition, an oral tradition, and a dialectic of oppression and activism.[7] We will return to this concept later in the book.

By contrast, and in common with the other white women we interviewed, Linda was reared in a culture of individualism. The idea of American individualism first appeared in the writings of French sociologist Alexis de Tocqueville. While notions of individualism were historically rooted in patriarchy, early white feminists embraced individualism and leveraged it as an argument for their right to the vote and to self-actualization.[8] Though a constant feature of U.S. culture, the intensity of individualism has varied over time. White women in our study came of age during a period in which individualism enjoyed a resurgence: the postwar 1950s and 1960s that produced the Me Generation. Robert Bellah and his team describe the culture of individualism as one that "encourages us to cut free from the past, to define our own selves, and to choose the groups with which we wish to identify."[9]

The stories of Ruthie Mae White and Linda Butler bear out strikingly separate cultural orientations. A poor black girl is encircled with support and encouragement. She is not taught shame because of her poverty. Instead, the community affirms her self-worth. She survives because of the collective support she receives. And she recognizes that when she succeeds, she must reach back to help others in her community. On the other hand, a poor white girl is isolated from the community. She must fend for herself. Her poverty is secretive and shameful. She learns she is responsible for herself and must literally pull herself up by her own initiative and hard work.

Joyce Canton

As director of marketing for a Fortune 100 consumer products company, Joyce Canton has learned "to stick to her guns" in an often dynamic and volatile business. Joyce's youthful appearance, blond curly hair, and blouse with a soft, ruffled neck belie the fact that she is a seasoned marketing executive who also held a managerial-level position in her previous job with another company. She brings to mind a younger version of Dixie Carter, a honey-toned mixture of charming femininity and cool professionalism.

At the time of her interview, Joyce was contemplating an assignment in Asia and confident about her career future. "I know that by taking an international assignment now I could potentially end up running a company in two to three years. I would be competitive for a general manager's position. I could also be competitive for a vice president position here because I will have picked up experience that a lot of my peers here don't yet have."

Joyce's self-confidence stems from her early childhood. As an only child raised by her father after her mother's death, Joyce grew up in a solid middle-class neighborhood of Victorian homes in a town of only four or five major employers. Her hometown was in the western panhandle of Maryland, near the old Mason-Dixon line separating North from South and freedom from slavery. Joyce recalled, "My entire town was white. Very white. There was a minuscule black population and a minuscule Jewish population. The main division was whether you were Protestant or Catholic. Things were divided more by 'poor white trash from the wrong side of the tracks' than by racial lines. There just wasn't enough diversity in the town for race to even be an issue."

Not until Joyce took a trip to Mississippi as a young girl did she become aware of differences between blacks and whites. "Before that, I had the sense that most of the people who waited on you were black—whether it was the waiter at the country club or the housekeeper I saw at my parents' friends' house. In addition to seeing Mississippi's large proportion of black people, Joyce also recalled witnessing a civil rights riot. "We went down to where my grandmother lived—I guess around 1964 or 1965—and the National Guard was posted all over town. We thought this was a lot of fun, because we would see the big machine guns and the tanks. We raced around the tanks and jumped up and down. For a kid, this was exciting. I don't think I had any notion that there had been violence in the town or that windows had been smashed. I don't even remember if anyone was killed."

Her father's busy medical practice kept him away from home a great deal, especially after her mother's death. Joyce learned quickly to fend for herself. "I became fairly independent after my mother's death. I used to laugh that I had charge accounts when I was ten because my father didn't have an idea how to shop for clothes for me. I would go to Main Street, dawdle around, and buy my fall wardrobe. I signed the bill and they would send it to my father. I would take the clothes and when he got home, he would go through what I had purchased. If he really hated something, I'd take it back. I just took over at ten."

"I knew from that time I was never going to stay in my hometown. I truly do not have any one person I can point to or any one instance that made me realize that. It just became clear to me I was not going to stay there. I was not going to get married at eighteen to anybody that I knew in high school and have five babies, which probably 90 percent of the people I grew up with did. I knew I was going to college and that I would live in a big city."

Joyce doesn't remember receiving any messages about her gender from her parents while she was growing up. "It's hard to judge, but I really don't remember getting a sense that my parents had different expectations for me because I was a girl. The thing I remember was what I imposed upon myself as a little girl. I was very much a little girl. I was not a tomboy. I was vocal about not wanting to wear pants. I wanted to wear my little patent leather shoes. I wanted to wear dresses, especially sundresses. I wanted to be pretty. I wanted to have little outfits. So I don't know if my parents passed that on to me or if I just somehow rather decided I wanted to be a classic little girl."

Joyce attended the public schools in her small hometown. "The only other alternative was Catholic school. I attended fairly traditional schools. My elementary school was really truly the old traditional brick schoolhouse."

Joyce excelled in high school and became a leader in many school activities. "I was vice president of my class in my junior year and head of the newspaper for two years. I was in the band and in the French club. I was also in the honor society." She also worked part-time during her last two years of high school. "I wanted to go to work. I come from a family with a strong work ethic. Also, I had started looking at colleges and was pretty sure I was going to a private university. That was going to come with a fairly substantial price tag. I wanted to start to feel like I was going to put something toward maintaining myself."

She graduated salutatorian of her high school class. "There were two National Merit Scholars in my high school: I was one of them, and the other was a boy. So, for the most part, accomplishments—academic as well as who was class president or who ran for student council—were shared between boys and girls. It wasn't like the girls could only do certain things. There really wasn't much of a split. If anything, I got the impression that girls were smarter because other than the one boy, all of the other top students were girls." She went on to say, "I think I actually came out of high school with the impression that you could do a little bit of everything. I was probably naïve to believe there weren't any barriers. I knew I was going to to go to a good college, a private college. I was going to study communications and journalism and law."

Joyce didn't get much career counseling or help selecting a college from her high school counselors. "I remember going to my guidance counselor when I got my SAT scores. She handed me the *Barron's Guide to Colleges* and basically said, 'Match up your SATs with schools and that's where you should apply.' The way I ended up where I went was almost by a fluke. I truly did go through the *Barron's Guide* and looked for those colleges that had preparation for law school and any kind of journalism and communications programs." Joyce ended up attending an elite private college in the South. "I went to visit the campus and it was lovely, bucolic. It was very appealing to me."

College was an eye-opening experience for Joyce. "My college years were the most formative. I don't remember a lot about elementary school and high school. Probably there was something conscious about that, because I was determined put my small hometown behind me. In college, I became aware for probably the first time that people had grown up in various backgrounds and with varying degrees of privilege. I had gone to college thinking I had led a fairly privileged lifestyle because I was in a secure well-to-do professional family. Out in the big world I realized I had no clue what a prep school was before I went to college. I had never encountered people who had gone to one. It was a very different to find a class of people who had gone to such schools. They tended to be more white, especially white males."

"For the most part it was a fairly segregated environment. The university still had a fairly active fraternity and sorority system. There were black sororities and white sororities, black fraternities and white fraternities."

Not only did Joyce get exposure to more diversity, she became, in her words, "a political junkie. My courses in public policy dealt with major social issues. I mean there was Busing 101—desegregation issues. There were courses on public housing policy, and on arts funding policy. As an academic experience it was formative in many ways. And I developed strong ties to many of the faculty and to others involved in politics."

Joyce left college thinking "that whatever career I chose I would be successful by the time I was thirty. I thought these things happened all the time and would come together very quickly. If you're talented, you're going to make it. Yes, you're going to make it right out of the box."

Like Ruthie Mae White and Linda Butler, Joyce Canton had to grow up fast. Her childhood, too, was shortened because of her mother's premature death. But Joyce's middle-class status buffered her from many of the harsh conditions experienced by Ruthie Mae and Linda. She was able to attend good schools in her middle-class neighborhood and went on to a private university. We found generally that the effects of early life disruptions were lessened for women with middle-class backgrounds.

Psychologically, though, Joyce was as isolated, if not more so, than Ruthie Mae or Linda. She, too, had to learn to be independent and to fend for herself. Her relatives did not play a prominent role in raising her after her mother's death. "The loss of a mother," says writer Hope Edelman, "represents a developmental challenge [for the daughter] . . . forcing her to take on responsibility for herself very quickly; she has to advance rapidly in her development."[10] This was a continuing difference we found in the black and white women's early life narratives. White women, whether or not they survived at-risk environments, portrayed their families as largely insular; black women described much more expansive kinship ties and even what sociologist Carol Stack refers to as "fictive kin."[11] Fictive kin is a unique element of African-American culture where non–blood relatives are called to "play mother, brother, sister, aunt, uncle, or cousin."

Colleen Powell

Colleen Powell cuts a striking figure in a gray suit and pale pink cashmere sweater. This is complemented by her crisp, precise way of speaking. Her petite figure, brown shoulder-length hair, and fair skin convey gentleness. But her gold, wire-rimmed glasses let you know she is a serious woman. After twenty years working in finance, the last eight of them in a Fortune 50 company, she seems unfazed by her accomplishments. On an international assignment in Latin America as corporate treasurer, she reports to the president of the Latin American Division. When the phone in her office rings, she picks up the receiver and engages in conversation in Spanish. She is also fluent in Portuguese.

The oldest of five children and the only girl, Colleen grew up "real poor" in Arkansas. "I would not characterize my childhood as a particularly happy childhood. As a matter of fact, it was a struggle," she said.

Concentrating on getting out of poverty was the only way she could survive. Colleen's early life has proved to be the motivating force behind the goals she has established and risks she has taken as an adult. When she was twelve years old, her parents divorced. Her father was physically abusing her mother. Colleen's mother got as far from her husband as possible, but she was unable to take her children. Colleen learned about her mother's departure while at school. At the end of the school day, her seventh-grade teacher gave her a letter her mother had dropped off. Colleen was the only child her mother told. Colleen told her brothers, assuming an adult role as she did so, and effectively becoming their surrogate mother. Colleen did not see her mother again until she was eighteen years old.

"It was a very emotional experience for me," she somberly admitted. Soon after their father remarried a woman who also had five children from a previous marriage, she and her siblings found themselves living with their paternal grandmother. "It was difficult for him to take care of two households, so I think you can imagine which one he decided to take care of," she said. First abandoned by their mother, Colleen and her brothers were then abandoned by their father. "I was the one who took care of everybody, and I still do."

Colleen has fond memories of her grandmother: "She was the sweetest, most self-sacrificing, loving person I think I have ever met." Colleen's grandmother earned her living as a domestic, but she did not earn enough to take care of five children. To help her grandmother make ends meet, Colleen worked two jobs from the time she was thirteen years old, cleaning houses, taking in laundry, and working in a neighborhood youth program. "The money I made during the week I gave to my grandmother to help support my siblings. The money I made on the weekends was mine."

Colleen attended segregated schools. All her teachers were black. They were all supportive, pushing their students to do their very best and taking a personal interest in them. Colleen did well in elementary school, but the trauma in her personal life set her back for a while. "I sort of dropped back; then, when I got into high school, I refocused." Refocus she did. She made the top ten in her graduating class. Her favorite subject was math. She took all the accelerated courses. Not one to be a wallflower, Colleen was president of the Thespian Troupe, sang in the school choir, and was a member of the honor society.

An anchor of support for Colleen was her godmother, Donna Glover, a single, middle-aged woman who was a neighbor of Colleen's grandmother. Ms. Glover immediately "took a liking" to Colleen when she moved to her grandmother's house. First Ms. Glover invited Colleen to her home for Sunday supper. Not long afterward, she adopted Colleen as her goddaughter. She took her self-assigned job as the young woman's guardian angel quite seriously. She invited Colleen to different cultural events, exposing her to the opera, the symphony orchestra, and to what Colleen calls "the better things in life." Their relationship even continued after Ms. Glover moved to another state. Soon after she moved, she paid for a round-trip train ticket during Colleen's summer vacation. "My godmother's goal was to make me a very well-rounded person. I got exposed to a different kind of life, one that I ordinarily would have missed."

By her senior year in high school, Colleen was uncertain about what she was going to do. She needed to work. College was not on her radar screen, at least not for a couple of years. "I didn't think about it, not until twelfth grade. Who was I going to think about it with? Nobody!" There was no money for tuition. Shirley Ford, a high school counselor, encouraged her apply to a special work-study program in the local junior college geared toward preparing students to enroll in a four-year university. Colleen was easily accepted. After being in the program for a year, Ms. Glover decided it was time for a change. "Godmother told me flat out, 'You're just playing around here. This is no challenge for you. You are going somewhere else.'" While Colleen was thinking about possible colleges to attend, Ms. Glover suggested that she apply to her own alma mater, one of the historically black colleges. To support her goddaughter's application, she wrote a letter of recommendation. Colleen was accepted and received a full four-year scholarship.

Colleen returned home from college only for an occasional holiday, taking classes year round and completing her coursework a semester ahead of her classmates. Most of her time was spent studying, and it showed. She made the Dean's List every year. College courses gave her an opportunity to discover her intellectual passion: economics. She was the first woman to take courses in the college's Department of Business Administration and Economics. "Everybody told me how tough it was going to be, especially for a woman. I received an A on the first exam, an A on the second and an A on the third. I started thinking, 'Maybe this isn't quite so tough.'" She worked in the student enterprise group, where she learned how to develop her own business.

Attending a historically black school broadened Colleen's perspective. "I was exposed to black people who had money. I had never had this experience before; their outlook on life was very different from mine." In addition to learning about diversity among blacks, Colleen's social life took a new twist. Through her pre-med college roommate she met, fell in love with, and became engaged to a young man who was attending medical school. On weeknights they studied together. On weekends they went to movies, played cards, or attended parties given by other medical students. Colleen found herself having to decide between two potential lifestyles: being a doctor's wife and living life in relative comfort, or carving out a career for herself. In the end, she decided to concentrate on her own career, breaking off the engagement. In retrospect she is content: "I am fortunate that I did not get married at that time. I think I would have been very unhappy in the position of doctor's wife."

The dean of the college took an interest in Colleen, often talking to her about her future career. At the time, her plan was to continue with school and get a doctorate in economics. She was not sure of what she wanted to do after getting the doctorate. The dean had a different view. "I remember him saying, 'That is nice, but I can tell you that an M.B.A. is a more marketable degree than a doctorate in economics.'" Armed with an undergraduate degree in business economics and outstanding scores on the Graduate Record Exam, Colleen applied to several top-tier business schools. She was accepted to all of them. The Sloan School at M.I.T. even wrote asking her to apply. She attended her first choice, a top business school renowned for its program in finance.

Marilyn Paul

A marketing executive in the food division of a very large Fortune 100 consumer products company, Marilyn Paul markets household products common to many American cupboards. The formality of her corporate office is tempered by all kinds of colorful wind-up toys, gadgets, and trinkets, and packages of the products she has managed and marketed for the company. A slight, well-manicured, articulate woman, Marilyn described herself as "intellectually ferocious." She fills a room with her self-confidence and is being groomed to head the entire food division. "I manage $350 million of the business, I have twenty-seven people in my organization, and my position is three levels below the president. I'm sort of a functional specialist, with responsibility for all of the marketing of the brands in my division as well as some responsibility for a number of other functional areas in the division. My job consists of 50 percent marketing and 50 percent business management. I travel two to three weeks a month. I'm in the plants. I'm with my customers. I'm with consumers. I spend a lot of time with people who either make, use, or buy my products. A lot of my time is spent in meetings resolving issues. Four months out of the year, I'm doing serious planning, whether it be strategic plans for the next five years or short-term operating budget plans."

Marilyn grew up in the affluent suburbs of Connecticut during the early sixties. Because of her father's corporate career, Marilyn and her five brothers and sisters lived in many different suburbs while she was young. "My father was a corporate executive with an M.B.A. from Harvard Business School. We always belonged to a country club. Houses were on big lots. It was a very affluent community rife with conspicuous consumption, and enormously competitive." A family's vacation plans, routinely printed in the local newspaper, were another indicator of wealth and status. "There were very explicit expectations about behavior. It was a very small, insular world. There were Catholics and there were Protestants, but there was no one else. Very Waspy. Very preppie."

However affluent, Marilyn's early childhood was emotionally traumatic. She grew up watching a younger, beloved sister slowly die from polio. Her mother was consumed with the tragedy. At the same time, her father's rising corporate career necessitated frequent family moves. "I remember the time I spent in school from fourth to eighth grade as just horrible years in terms of external socialization. The towns we moved to weren't friendly. It was just enormously painful. I was suffering from having lost my sister. Going through that experience—losing a younger sister—made me forge a closer relationship with my other brothers and sisters. Having the experience of not being accepted by other children when we moved made me withdraw a lot. I began to accept what my mother had said about the world being harsh. I internalized that perspective. I knew if I couldn't be accepted socially, I'd have to be smarter. I'd have to be better. And for a long time I used my intelligence as a weapon. I could always outperform other people. I retreated to thinking, books, and learning."

Marilyn's mother, though college-educated, centered her life around her children. "My mother worked outside the home before she had her children but then, with six children, she was enormously busy. She is an extraordinarily intelligent woman, well educated. But she was close to shattered when my younger sister died." Marilyn believes she got her intellectual fervor from her mother but she did not want to be like her mother when she grew up. "My mother has good reason to be the way she is, but I did not want to be like her—always waiting for catastrophe. We moved many, many times when I was growing up. I'm not sure my mother wanted to move each time. But my father's career dictated a lot of moving."

It was Marilyn's father who was interested in her achievements when she was growing up. A celebrated World War II hero, her father graduated from business school and went on to an impressive but uneven corporate career. As a young girl, Marilyn rejected the passive attitude she witnessed in her mother and identified with her father's take-control, take-charge attitude. "My father got on with his life more, and he had more outside the home than my mother did. He was more upbeat. Even though he wasn't there much, he was more accessible emotionally. You know it surprises me, of all my siblings, I'm most like my father, who was a corporate executive." She added, "My father and I have always been very close. We became even closer when I was in college, when I had a difficult time."

Her dad also gave Marilyn her first awareness of business. "I remember my father always having the products around from companies he worked with and I would ask him questions about them. When I was in high school, my dad would have dinner and then work after dinner. I knew what my father did."

Marilyn doesn't remember getting any messages about being a woman when she was growing up. "My mother spoke very little about what it meant to be a woman. But I remember, though, my mother had enormous difficulty when my older sister went to law school. My father was as interested in his daughters' achievements as in his sons. But my mother was really taken aback when my sister wanted to become a lawyer—because it was so out of her context. I think in some ways it was a violation of what she thought as possible for her and so she couldn't understand it. My father never set limits. He never gender-typed his kids." Marilyn went on to say, "The most important thing my mother communicated to me was an enormous love for education. She placed a high value on it. What I cherish most about my mother is her intellectual curiosity and her love of books and of learning."

Growing up in an upper-middle-class family in the suburbs meant her neighbors were white and family activities and social events took place with other white friends and family members. Marilyn bluntly stated, "We were among the upper class—all white. I did not meet anybody who was even Jewish until I went to college." Her parents' lives away from home were also monoracial. Her father, as a corporate executive, worked with other white men in prestigious, well-paying firms. "Race just wasn't there. There were plenty of blacks in my town. We had a black maid, but racial interaction wasn't part of your life. I was never taught to think those people were equal, but I was also never taught to hate."

If race did not seem to play a significant role in the family's life and in Marilyn's identity, religion most certainly did. "I'm Irish German Catholic," Marilyn volunteered. "Even though Vatican II occurred in 1964, we were raised with strict classical Catholicism. My mother converted to Catholicism when she married my father. Everybody was Catholic in the town we lived in when I was very young. It was when I left that town that I became aware of being part of an ethnic group and of being Catholic. That's how I first identified myself, as a Catholic. My mother imbued in us a real respect for other people and a real sense of values. I also learned that there was right and there was wrong."

Marilyn attended parochial schools in the early years of elementary school. "I don't remember much about what I learned in school. I remember the nuns were just overwhelming, domineering." Later she attended public schools, because her mother felt Catholic schools were "intellectually stifling." The affluent public schools she attended in the neighborhood had only a sprinkling of black students.

"My academic performance was stronger than anybody's until I went to college. I was a phenomenal performer all through junior high and high school. I was always into books but in seventh and eighth grade I began to love school, to love learning. I went into history and social studies and I absolutely adored it. My teachers loved me because I was smart and responsive. I mean, I just sucked up the information. I finally came into my own."

Marilyn believes she paid a price for being too smart at a time when girls were not expected to excel academically. "It probably made me more of an anomaly to be this smart and as out front about it. I always knew there was this social cost, of not fitting in, but I couldn't *not* learn and excel. It was just too much fun to learn, and at some level, I just couldn't repress that kind of intellectual curiosity. I needed control and to be visible."

Marilyn was in advanced classes and graduated second in her high school class. She was also active in student government and school clubs. She remembers having two diametrically different visions for her life: "I always imagined that I would get married and have kids *or* that I would be president of the United States. Seriously, I never quite knew how that would all work. But I had these two kinds of conflicting visions, never putting them together. I really did think I could be president of the United States."

Going to college was taken for granted. There was also little debate about what college she would attend. Marilyn was accepted into every Ivy League school she applied to during her senior year. She attended her favorite of the schools and majored in sociology, which she loved. For the first time, she became conscious of gender-related issues in her life. The women at her newly coed college were excluded from some of the all-male campus clubs. Women were, in her words, "still being imported" on the weekends from other campuses. Similar to her high school, her college was predominantly white; she had little interaction with black students. "The lines were very hard to cross." Marilyn was never able to break through the cliques shaped by old prep school alliances. She was largely apolitical, and was not active in campus groups.

One bright spot during college was selling ads for a student publication. "When I was in college, there was a student-run publication and in it we placed ads from corporations. For two summers I went out and I knocked on doors and got business people to buy ads. I liked doing it very much." But it was not until the end of college that Marilyn fully realized she "really would have to work. I was probably a senior in college before it really occurred to me that I was going to have to support myself. That was clearly an expectation from my parents. And I wasn't dating anybody. But it really just sort of hit me like a ton of bricks. I had never internalized that fact." Her success in selling ads spawned an interest in business, but she still was not certain what she wanted to do.

Colleen Powell and Marilyn Paul are among the highest-ranking managers we interviewed. Educated at two of the top business schools in the country and at the peak of their careers, it would seem as if they have always been on a level playing field. Many whites often assume, when seeing two professional women at the same level, one black the other white, that they have traveled a similar path over the course of their lives. That race does not make a difference. We know better. These two women's backgrounds differ not just because of race, but because of the intersection of race and class. Colleen grew up poor in a family at risk, in the rural South, abandoned by her mother when she was quite young. Colleen's early life is reminiscent of Ruthie Mae White's experiences. Marilyn was raised in an affluent, upper-class family in the suburbs of the Northeast. Her father was a high-level business executive and prominent community figure. Her mother was a well-educated woman who decided to be a homemaker.

While the commonalities between Colleen's and Marilyn's professional lives are clear, what remain truly incongruent are their early life experiences. These two women's paths would not have crossed during their childhood. There would have been no friendships, no familiarity, and no common ground to prepare them to communicate and to be genuine colleagues as adults. Such a gap in frame of reference often exists among professional women who otherwise seem to be on a par. The different social locations of poor black women and upper-middle-class white women set up subordinate and superior self-perceptions—and relationships—among colleagues. We will return to this theme in later chapters.

2

THEIR FATHERS'
DAUGHTERS

IF SOCIAL CLASS often serves as a wedge between women, then gender acts as a common denominator. Likewise, women's relationships with fathers especially link them, even if the father-daughter relationships differed or left differing imprints. We found two typical patterns in the relationships between the women and their fathers, which we labeled "daddy's girl" and "domineered daughter." Daddy's girls have strong, deep, caring relationships with their fathers, based on mutual admiration and respect. These girls want to emulate their fathers. Domineered daughters grew up under authoritarian, controlling fathers with whom they had difficulty developing emotional intimacy. The daughters either gave in to these domineering fathers, or rebelled and struggled to find their own identity. These relationships influenced what lessons the women learned about what it means to be a woman and also shaped the ways they approached relationships with men in their later professional and personal lives.

Jean Hendrick

Jean Hendrick's imposing, confident manner during her interview is exactly what might be expected from a top executive in the razzle-dazzle cosmetics industry. Her tall, slim, but broad-shouldered figure is accentuated by the charcoal gray, man-tailored pantsuit she wears. Its belted waist projects "conservative but stylish." In her office, everything has a place. When she speaks, every word and every gesture showcases her communication skills. A senior vice president at a Fortune 100 company, Jean has over fifty staff members reporting to her. After nineteen years with her company, she is now responsible for worldwide communications, including advertising, public affairs, public relations, and employee communications. It is her job to create communication strategies and programs for both internal and external consumption. As Jean puts it, "Even though I have people working for me as writers, art directors, planners, and strategists, I am still the person who ensures good writing and production in film, video, or print. I tacitly persuade somebody to do something they might not otherwise do, whether a commercial or a motivational event for our sales force." Jean exudes energy. She is assertive and highly animated as she talks about her life and managerial career. She knows how to hold court and clearly enjoys doing so.

The youngest child in a close-knit family of three children, Jean grew up in the suburbs of Chicago. "We had a really wonderful house, a beautiful house—one of the nicest houses in a very nice, very white neighborhood. It was certainly upper-middle-class, with a lot of Jewish kids and some Catholics. The Catholic kids all went to Catholic schools." The only black people Jean encountered in her childhood were maids and country club workers. "The blacks that I knew at that time were the people who worked for my parents, usually cleaning women. In those days everybody had help; nobody thought it was a big deal. My grandparents always had a black woman who lived with them. They were her family, and they treated her well, with the love and respect and caring they would extend to anybody else in the family. My mother and father treated the people who worked for them the same way."

Growing up in an affluent neighborhood meant tennis, ballet, music, and swimming lessons as a routine part of daily life. Jean grew up in a two-parent home with a stay-at-home mother—the idyllic nuclear family. She remembers her family being the envy of many of her friends at the time. The family was "extremely close knit, loving but self-contained and self-sufficient," Jean said, adding that she adored her older brothers. "I didn't get the habit as a child of really reaching out. I was friendly and had plenty of friends, but my family never really worked at being friends with a lot of people or relatives. We were self-contained."

Her mother worked as a secretary in a publishing company until she married Jean's father. "I don't think she was 'relegated' to raising a family but rather she had a full, rich life. My mother played golf in the summer, and bowled in the winter. My parents always belonged to a country club and my mother was head of the woman's golf association. She participated in the PTA. She helped with the Brownies and the Boy Scouts. She definitely wasn't the garden-club-type woman. She was what was described in those days as more of a 'man's woman.' She always got along well with men and never sought to have lots of female friends around her."

An entrepreneur, Jean's father started and ran a number of successful businesses with her grandfather. "I come from an enterprising, risk-taking family. At times my father did extremely well and at times the entire rug might have been pulled out from under him. Growing up, I never knew which times we were in because there was an evenness about the way he conducted his life and a very up spirit he always had even in difficult times. My father was a stunning athlete, gifted in football; in the thirties he almost made it to the Olympics. We grew up in an achievement-oriented atmosphere where being competitive was emphasized. It was very important to my father to do your best—not so much to beat everyone else but to do your best."

Jean wanted to meet her father's expectations. "'Daddy's girl,' that's what I was. My father was the absolute force in my life," Jean exclaims. "He encouraged me. I always wanted to make sure I was as terrific as he always thought I was. My father would always tell me, 'There's nobody like you in the world. Do you understand how terrific you are? Look at how you did that.' He made me believe I could do anything. It was just a wonderful way to grow up." It was Jean, rather than her brothers, who seemed to inherit her father's athletic talent. "I was a girl's champion tennis player and spent a good part of my early life as a competitive player. For a number of years I was one of the top ten girl players in the country."

Her mother was very supportive of Jean's father's career. "My mother didn't work, but she really was a tremendous support to my father in his work. Every night when he came home he would bounce ideas off her. They were both charismatic people but very different from each other. Yet they were very much equals. Her opinion was probably the one he respected the most."

Jean doesn't remember receiving any messages about her gender when she was growing up. "I never got advice about being a woman. I got advice about being a person. I was brought up with the belief that there was nothing I couldn't accomplish, that I had all the qualities that I needed to succeed if I were willing to work hard. There was nothing I lacked. My job was to understand that I was capable. I might need to work. I might need to focus. But the capability was there, as opposed to 'Well, you don't know if you'll be able to make it or not!' I was *expected* to make it. In my family we were expected to make the very best effort, to be goal oriented and achievement oriented. It was natural that I would do something in my life that would allow me to be a success. That's why I knew that I would have some kind of career, do some kind of work." Jean accepted and assimilated the idea that if one works hard, one will be successful.

Jean's upper-middle-class status gave her access to privileges, making it possible to attend the very best schools and participate in a host of social and cultural activities, from private lessons to trips to the theater. Jean attended public schools in her suburban neighborhood, walking to school with her friends. Jean remembers elementary school as "terrific for the most part, encouraging, helpful but not terribly strict *or* lenient." The schools Jean attended tended to be all-white schools except for a "sprinkling of black students in high school." All her teachers were white. "Nobody defined themselves as 'white Protestant.' Nobody thought about it. We were just people."

An honor student in high school, Jean remembers studying "without exaggeration, five hours every night. I only came out of my room for dinner. I got very good grades. The thing to do was to get A's. The people who got the good grades were the most respected, and you wanted to be one of those kids." Ninety-nine percent of the students in her high school went on to college, many attending Ivy League schools. Even though she had no idea what she wanted to be, Jean never doubted she would go to college. It was an expected path for those in her community. "I didn't really think about what my career would be. I knew I liked to write and I liked to act but I didn't really think of what I would be. I never thought, for example, of being a teacher or a doctor or anything like that." In high school she was a very active student. "I joined the art club, the drama club, student government, and whatever sports teams there were. I did a lot of activities. I participated a lot in the various clubs and stuff but not the academic clubs like math or chemistry."

During high school, Jean decided she wanted to attend a women's college. "I wanted to go to a women's college and applied to Wellesley, Smith, Skidmore, and several other smaller women's institutions. I wasn't interested in going coed. When I went to visit coed schools, I didn't really like them. They seemed a little too rah-rah. The women's colleges seemed quieter and more sophisticated. I liked the idea of men coming from the men's schools on the weekends but the rest of the time being able study and not having to worry about them." Jean ended up attending a small private women's college in the Southeast, where she majored in art and English. She didn't select a major with a career in mind but majored in the subjects she enjoyed.

Being a Yankee in an elite Southern school suddenly made Jean feel different, not as special. "I didn't realize that this wasn't the place for me until I got there. It was the first time in my life that I felt I had come from the wrong side of the tracks. That's when I understood what ostracism was. I was a Yankee, and the Southern boys only dated Southern girls." Jean almost left but decided to "tough it out." As she had no preconceived ideas about what she would do when she completed school, when a professor suggested she go to graduate school to study drama, she did so; she was accepted to an Ivy League university. "I had no idea what a big deal it was to be accepted there. It just happened so quickly. I found myself there without a passion for doing it, but it seemed like the next logical thing to do."

Jean only lasted a year in the program. "I didn't like acting. I was not able to subjugate myself so easily into other people's parts. The only parts I was really good at were the ones with a lot of humor. I was a comedienne. I figured out I was a performer rather than an actor." After leaving the program, Jean went to secretarial school. "I went to Katherine Gibbs, one of those business schools where you learned the basic secretarial skills. I knew that if I were going to go somewhere and get a job, I had to know that stuff. So I learned typing, shorthand, and business etiquette." Jean was twenty-two years old and had no idea what she would do. "It never occurred to me to map out an absolute route with a definite goal."

Sandra Martin

A senior vice president of human resources for a large and important bank, Sandra Martin spends her days developing human resource policies and strategies to help make her company the number one bank in the country. She is also responsible for executive compensation and handles the personnel side of the bank's recent mergers. Succession planning and recruitment of officers are also part of her position. "It's a demanding job, but it's a good job. I'm also responsible for leadership development—focusing on the talent we have in the bank and how to develop it."

Sandra did not start her corporate career until she was thirty-four. In less than ten years with the bank, she has risen rapidly and expects to be "on the executive team one day." She is a perky, aggressive woman with surprisingly bright red hair. Her descriptions are vivid and frank. Sandra's infectious energy comes across as she shares her life story. She can't seem to sit still during the interview. Instead, she paces or sits atop her desk. This is a woman used to making her point in a no-nonsense fashion. She told us she wanted to be like "Sheena, Queen of the Jungle" when she grew up.

The oldest of three girls, Sandra grew up on a farm in the flat spartan landscape of western Kansas. She was born just before her father went off to fight in World War II. When he returned, he bought a farm. "Out there in western Kansas it was a half-mile to our nearest neighbor. The world looked like one big sky. You could drive forever past field after field of soybeans, wheat, or corn. The horizon went on for miles, uninterrupted by buildings or mountains."

Like other women in our study raised in rural settings, for Sandra a trip to town was a real treat, a chance to roam Main Street and visit the small stores and shops. She speaks fondly of her grandparents. "When Daddy was at war, I spent a lot of time with my grandparents, who lived in town. My grandfather ran a small hardware store. I would sit around with him while he chewed the fat with all the guys in town. He'd drag me around town with him and show me off because I could read the newspaper at age five." If she wasn't visiting her grandfather in town, she was with her grandmother. "Nanny didn't get dressed in the morning. She read *True Confessions*. And she was great. I loved her. I'd go stay with her, and she'd feed me Pepsi and M&Ms. I'd get to hang around on the couch with her."

Friendships with other children were often made at school because the farms were so far apart. A favorite pastime for young Sandra and her friends was staging impromptu talent shows in their farmyards. Saturday nights and holidays occasionally brought a chance for them to wander around a county fair, to see a movie in the town hall, or to watch a second-run movie on the side of an old barn.

Sandra doesn't remember getting any messages about her gender or what it meant to be a woman. On the contrary: "My dad raised my sisters and me as if we were boys, which had a good side to it because he took us everywhere he went. If we wanted to go, we could go. No matter where it was—to the grain elevator to take wheat, or to ride the combine. He also demanded a lot of us. We loaded hay. If it was hard physical work, he expected us to be able to do it. So my sisters and I grew up knowing much work was expected of us. Daddy taught us to shoot guns. He let us do things that boys would normally get a chance to do. Now, as I look back on that, I think it was valuable."

Sandra described her mother as a typical western Kansas farmwoman. "She took care of the chickens, she canned and baked, and she was a member of a home demonstration club—all those things farmwomen did. She was smart and she had graduated from high school and started college when she was sixteen. My mom put herself through college during the Depression. She married my father after she finished college. And when my father went away on a big construction job for a couple of years, she started her own real estate business in town. She did very well on her own."

Sandra's father left an indelible imprint upon her. "Looking back I don't think my mother influenced me like my dad. Now that's funny, because Mother is as smart and competent as anybody ever was, but I think Daddy was much more of an influence on us. He just dominated the family. When he needed to get work done, it was my sisters and me he asked. We were his work crew."

Sandra learned to take on challenges at a very early age. "When I was eleven, my daddy had a broken arm. That's a disaster if you're a farmer. We lived on a long muddy road. We had a John Deere tractor, one of those big tractors. My parents needed to get to town for something but Daddy could not drive the tractor. So he hooked his car up to the tractor. He made me drive the tractor while my Mom steered the car. I had to pull the car down the muddy road to the highway. I had to do this because Daddy couldn't. Think about being a girl and doing things like that."

Unable to make a living by farming alone, her father often left home to do construction work. Her mother ran her business in addition to working on the farm. Sandra and her sisters kept the farm running. So Sandra learned to be independent at a young age.

"My parents expected me to be responsible for whatever I did. I had a lot of freedom, but when I got into trouble they would expect me to accept the consequences. They never covered up or tried to get me out of anything. As work and life have gone on, I realize that most of the things I get myself into are my doing and so I'm responsible for them. I just accept that. In the eighth grade I was like a boy, in a way. I got into fights and I did all sorts of things, but I didn't expect my parents to take up for me. I expected to handle it myself. I don't remember getting any academic or athletic pressure. But I just knew that whatever I did was my own responsibility. That's the main thing I remember. You break it, you fix it."

Sandra attended small rural schools. "I went to a school that had eight grades and three teachers. I rode the bus for miles just to get to that school in the morning and many more miles just to get home in the afternoon because the geographic area that our school district represented was incredible. We had four kids in the eighth grade and not one was closer to me than five miles. We probably had a total of maybe forty-five kids in that school."

Sandra had a positive school experience. "I remember liking my teachers a lot. It was great—almost like a big family. We were smart and well prepared." Even though she attended small rural schools, Sandra was determined to get her fill of everything available. She loved competitive sports. "I was smart and I was treated well in school. I played tennis and basketball. I did all the sports well. I participated in everything I could. I was on the basketball team and the track team, even though we didn't have a girl's track team. Now that was funny: nobody was interested enough to coach a girl's track team so we just did it on our own. We'd run track events not even knowing what we were doing. I was a cheerleader. I was in the band. I was in the pep club. I was in my church group. There wasn't anything that went on in school that I didn't participate in."

Not only was Sandra adventurous and competitive but she was also rebellious. She knew at an early age that she wanted more than her hometown could offer. "I just developed this real 'I'm going to show you' streak. I got into a lot of trouble. I would go out and we would have drag races out in the country. I drove cars when I wasn't supposed to drive cars. I did all these things and my parents didn't have a clue."

"All of a sudden I was just in the midst of all this stuff and I liked it. I don't know why. I can't put my finger on it except that it could have been because my daddy was such a strong person. He influenced us so much that I guess I just had to break away. I think I did the things I did to get away from my hometown. There wasn't anything in that town that I didn't do. I was in every organization. I played every sport. I participated in everything they had and to me it just wasn't enough."

The year before she was to graduate from high school, Sandra became pregnant. "When my mother found out, she went to bed for a week. I think it was just a total shock because they just never dreamed that it would ever happen to me. I don't even know why I got involved. I liked risk and I was ignorant. I didn't have a clue as to what happened or how you got pregnant because Mother never talked about any of those things. With Daddy being the strong one and raising us as if we were boys, there was no need. We were thought of as boys. But I was a girl so I got pregnant." Her father's response was, "Sandra's gotten herself into a mess. It's her responsibility to get herself out. Now just get up and go on with life." So Sandra did. She got married at sixteen.

Sandra took correspondence courses to finish her requirements for graduation. It was the 1950s. Girls had to quit school if they became pregnant. By eighteen, Sandra had two children, but that did not stop her from going to college. "The only thing I remember thinking was that if I didn't finish my college degree, I would never have anything. I thought of college more as an insurance policy than as having a career. My thought was, 'I have to finish college. If I don't finish college, I'm doomed.' "

So she left her hometown with her husband and they both attended a state college. Sandra decided to major in math because "I like to know if I'm right or wrong. If I was right, then nobody could do anything to make me wrong." Sandra did finish college but spent the next fifteen years of her life raising children and supporting her husband's successful career.

Jean Hendrick and Sandra Martin's stories exemplify the contrasting types of father/daughter relationships we found among the women we interviewed. Jean's description epitomizes what we generally heard from the women who described themselves as daddy's girls. The relationships they described with their fathers came close to what our culture often envisions as the ideal father/daughter relationship—a father who genuinely loves and supports his daughter. A majority of the women we interviewed identified much more with their fathers than their mothers, especially when it came to career models. Several studies have found that women in nontraditional careers have had atypical relationships with their fathers, who were unusually involved and supportive.[1] Researchers also point out that girls often identify with their fathers because of their greater freedom and independence, their access to the external world, and their right to say what they think.

It was their fathers who taught the daddy's girls self-reliance, independence, and courage. It was their fathers who first gave them glimpses of the world of work. For many of the white women, their fathers were the ones in the family with a career: their influence and expectations seem to have had a major impact on their daughters' career aspirations. Explicitly and implicitly the women received messages about being a *person*, not being a *girl* or a *woman*. These messages made them feel unconstrained by their gender. The white women did not remember being made aware that they might face discrimination and sexism because of their gender. Instead what they seemed to have taken away from their relationships with fathers was a gender-neutral message, that they could be anything they desired. They did have positive memories of their relationships with their mothers, and these relationships with their mothers may have mitigated some of the possible negative effects of being strongly influenced by their fathers, especially when their father's behavior was overbearing and controlling.[2]

Many women who talked of being daddy's girl described their mothers as Jean did. Jean talked about her mother as "a man's woman." These women's strong identification with fathers seemed to affect their perceptions of how their mothers related to men. All characterized their mothers as women who were "comfortable around men"; none describe them as being controlled by men. Many of the white women in our study were clearly influenced by observations of how their mothers related to men. One lesson the women learned was how to establish comfortable relationships with professional men. But more important, they believed being a "man's woman" did not place women in a subservient role. A significant number of the women described themselves as having developed professional styles in their organizations with which their male colleagues were comfortable, much as their mothers had developed relationships that made men comfortable.

Women who had domineering daddies like Sandra Martin spoke of a different experience. Although they identified with their fathers, the women in this group described less positive relationships. The influence of their fathers stemmed from their sheer dominance in the family. Curiously, there was a tendency among the women to rationalize, not criticize, their father's behavior. Sandra's father was strict and demanding, raising them like boys. The lesson of gender women in this group received was the need to take on masculine traits—to learn to be tough and competitive.

Some of the black women, too, learned what it meant to be a woman from their fathers, but their relational stories with their fathers ended differently. They learned about sexism by observing the relationship between their fathers and their mothers, and resolved never to let themselves be so controlled by the men in their lives. Other illustrations of black women's relationships with their fathers are in chapter 4.

Brenda Boyd

The position of vice president of corporate giving for a Fortune 100 company requires Brenda Boyd to move beyond the normal boundaries of her company and to form alliances with public-sector organizations. In the corporate world, she is the interpreter, facilitator, and social conscience of the company. In the world of grass-root organizations, she is a fairy godmother. Brenda seems to relish both dimensions of her role. She is a woman of medium stature, with a porcelain-smooth honey complexion, dark shoulder-length hair, and an air of wisdom, grace and, serenity.

The earliest years of Brenda's life were spent in Englewood, New Jersey, just south of New York City. There, she, her mother, and her younger sister shared a two-family house with her maternal grandparents. She has no recollection of her parents living together. Edward and Joanette Boyd divorced before Brenda was two years old; her sister was still an infant.

Brenda describes her mother, a paralegal professional, as highly intelligent, generous, caring, and eccentric. When asked what she learned from her mother about womanhood, Brenda responded sadly, "I got the message that being an intelligent, assertive black woman meant that you had to be prepared to not be liked or loved by a whole lot of people. She knew classical music, art, and philosophy, and she was attractive, yet there was no one for her to talk to." Another influential female model for Brenda was her grandmother. "She was the littlest person around, but somehow she was always running the show. She never raised her voice, and she never did anything that wasn't gracious, but when Grandma spoke we all stopped and listened." From her grandfather, an avid reader, Brenda gained an awareness of African-American history. "He would talk about people like Marion Anderson and Paul Robeson, all the great black musicians and scientists. He was so full of us [black people]! He loved our literature, our music, our science and our work." Together, Brenda's grandparents gave her a wonderful model for marriage, one built on true affection and a deep-rooted love.

When Brenda was twelve years old, Mrs. Boyd moved her two daughters into an apartment just far enough away from the house where her parents lived. Apparently there was tension between Brenda's mother and grandmother. But the move left the two children unsupervised during the day because Mrs. Boyd had to work. This situation did not make Mrs.

Boyd happy. On the one hand, she did not wish to leave the girls with their grandmother because her mother was not strict enough with them. On the other hand, they had no supervision after school. "Now I am old enough, I think about what it must have been like to work in New York City and then come home to take care of two little girls. There was so little support." Under these circumstances, Mrs. Boyd made what must have been a very difficult decision: she sent Brenda and her sister to live with their father. "She really did not like the idea," said Brenda, "but she just felt our father would provide us with a better environment than she could."

The transition was tough. Brenda missed her mother deeply, although they corresponded regularly and spent summer vacations together. Her father had remarried and started a second family. Brenda was now the eldest of four children. Father and daughter had spent so little time together that they were almost strangers. But over time they developed a relationship. "Dad was a very caring person toward his children. He provided us with this great environment and he saw to it that we had all the creature comforts. I didn't have to worry about clothes or having money to buy things. The only thing I had to worry about was getting my education; doing well in school was my job."

Bonding with her stepmother was an entirely different story. Brenda was never comfortable with their relationship; at best it was awkward. A subtle tension existed between them. "Dorothy never was completely secure with me and my sister in her house, although she worked very hard at it," recalled Brenda. But it was Brenda's father, Mr. Boyd, who made the decisions in the family.

A lawyer with his own practice, Mr. Boyd implicitly gave Brenda messages on the role women assumed in marriage. He expected his wife to be submissive and dependent. He did not allow her to work. Instead, he gave her an allowance to manage the household; but there was little left to indulge her needs. When she surreptitiously worked as a substitute teacher, and he found out about it, he met her at school and forced her to go home. After that experience, she never attempted to work outside the home again. Observing her father and stepmother at such close range left Brenda feeling that her stepmother was being "beat up psychologically" by her father.

Living with her father and stepmother created other transitions for Brenda, who had to deal not only with a new household, but also with a new city. Before settling in Cincinnati, the family lived in Memphis for a brief period. The difference in the three cities of her youth gave Brenda culture shock. "Parents never sit you down and explain to you that you are getting ready to go into a new world," she said, "and that in the new world the rules are different."

In Englewood, Brenda and her friends jumped double Dutch in front of the houses. In Cincinnati, little girls did not jump double Dutch. They skated, but they skated inside in skating rinks. In Englewood she was taught classical music; in Memphis she was taught gospel. Raised Episcopalian, Brenda belonged to a church in Englewood that was reflective, with peaceful music. In Memphis, the church choir was jamming, and people shouted when possessed with the Holy Spirit. In Englewood, the majority of the teachers were white. In Memphis, the teachers and students were all black. In Memphis, the teachers expected all the children to read and they were caring and supportive. Teachers took pride in their students. In Cincinnati, where the teachers were white and the students all black, teacher's expectations for students did not seem to be very high.

Throughout high school, regardless of the city, Brenda received great grades, never dropping below an A. "I was one of those kids teachers wanted." The Cincinnati high school Brenda attended had over 4,000 students. She took academic-track classes, was in the honor society and on the track team. She spent most of her time reading, going to basketball games, and listening to music. A shy girl, dating was not big on her list of activities. Academically, Brenda was not challenged. Many of her classmates were behind grade level. "I had never seen kids who could not read. I remember saying to my father, 'Thank God I didn't start school in Cincinnati because I never would have learned anything.'"

Teachers and administrators did not put much emphasis on attending college, and counselors were too overwhelmed to spend time with individual students. Brenda was left to her own devices. "I knew I was going to college. My father had gone, my mother had gone, what else was I supposed to do? But I didn't know *why* I was going; it was not about finding a career." Mr. Boyd wanted his daughters to attend college, as long as the college was not too far from home. He discouraged Brenda from selecting a historically black college where he believed the students did more partying than studying. So Brenda applied to a state university and was accepted. The university was far enough away so that she did not have to come home on the weekends.

College was exciting. It was the sixties. There were students who used drugs, free sex was in, and flower children abounded. The campus was volatile, with race a hot issue. Some black students criticized Brenda for being too bourgeois and acting too middle class, but Brenda did not let their opinions get to her. Her independent nature bloomed. She decided to major in psychology, and by her junior year, Brenda was paying her own college tuition and expenses by working as a head resident in her dorm.

Then, in Brenda's senior year, her mother died unexpectedly. The news of her death devastated Brenda. She continued with her classes, but remembers little from September through January of that final year. "I just went through the paces. I finished up the semester by just going to class after class, but I really wasn't there." Brenda did not have a clue about what she was going to do after graduation. She was still in shock over the loss of her mother. "I was still in this daze and didn't care much about what I would be doing."

In the law school library one day, Brenda started talking with a professor, who turned out to be dean of the law school. He encouraged her to apply to law school. She thought it sounded interesting. Lacking any other agenda, she applied and was accepted. Brenda started law school the next fall, but she soon dropped out. "I decided I needed a place to rest. I was between things, but I didn't even know *what* I was between."

At this time, Brenda was dating a man who "adored" her. Their relationship became serious, and after a few months they got married. Soon, Brenda realized the marriage was a mistake. By this time, she wanted to continue her education. At the age of twenty-four, married and now pregnant, Brenda began studying for a doctorate in higher education administration.

Like Brenda Boyd, several of the black women interviewed recalled that their earliest exposure to sexism occurred within the confines of their own families. These women characterized their fathers as chauvinistic and authoritarian. As one woman put it, "My father always spoke down to my mother. He dictated exactly who could be in the house, who was going to do what in the house, and how it was going to be done. It was like my mother was a child in the house, too." Other black women made a different point, expressing how unsupportive their fathers were toward their mothers. The burden of household chores rested entirely on their mother's shoulders, even though their mothers were working just as hard outside the home as their fathers.

By paying attention to everyday interactions between their parents, the girls gradually learned how men sometimes dominate women by abusing their authority. As Brenda Boyd told us, "I watched my stepmother just go way down emotionally because she was totally dependent on my father. She became very submissive around him after giving up her profession." Determined not to follow in her stepmother's footsteps, Brenda vowed to support herself. She had no intention of letting a man dictate to her what she could or could not do. She was not the only black woman determined not to repeat the experience of her mother. Many of the women flatly stated that they would never tolerate the kind of emotional abuse or lack of support from their spouses that their mothers suffered with their fathers. Nor did they intend to assume a subordinate role in relationships with men. To manage overbearing males, both in their personal and professional lives, many black women assume a no-nonsense, take-charge attitude.

Still, a daughter's relationship with her father is different from a wife's relationship with her husband. Like Brenda, black women raised by domineering fathers expressed a great deal of empathy toward their fathers. "My father is an extremely hardworking person, a very intelligent man. He wanted to be a first violinist, but he did not think that was a very practical aspiration since they were so poor. At seven years old, he was cleaning bathrooms for lunch money. I think he figured out a way not to ever have to clean bathrooms again. He worked his way through to law school." Brenda acknowledged her father as a good provider and a loving man.

Often in an interview a woman would concede, "My life is different from my mother's and father's; theirs was a different time." However, complex factors were at work. Within black families men often feel the need to exert control. Home is a place where black men feel that they can be in charge. Feeling under siege by white culture, especially by white men, black men may vent their rage and their frustration on those people who are closest to them: their wives and children. Home becomes the safest place to show their anger about racism and about their continual state of forced underachievement in the workforce.[3]

3

❖

COMFORTABLE FAMILIES, UNCOMFORTABLE TIMES

Maxine Schneider

Maxine Schneider likes to describe her corporate position as the "best job in the whole wide world." Articulate and charismatic, Maxine is well aware of the effect she has on others. Tall and sophisticated, she eschews the dress for success navy blue suit in favor of a fawn-colored two-piece Armani set. A perfect mix of accessories gives a hint of femininity without compromising her polished, professional look. Her personal style reflects the self-image she has built since high school. "I wanted to be like Katie Keane, a model in the comic books when I was young. She lived in New York and was a real sophisticate. Katie was a really neat, strong woman, and she wasn't married."

Maxine is passionate when she talks about her corporate career. Currently director of corporate affairs for a large communications and publishing conglomerate, Maxine describes her job as having three components: creating awareness, added-value opportunities, and ancillary projects. "A lot of my work goes on behind the scenes, where I generate contacts and projects for the company that may eventually lead to revenue either through subscriptions to our magazines or through the purchase of advertising space." She spends a lot of time with the publishers on the business side of the company, keeping abreast of what they have in the works for their magazines and other products so she can incorporate such plans into the speeches she makes around the country at conferences and corporate events as well as at government hearings and political meetings. "I've been in this job for two years," she said, "and I've already been to the White House four times."

The oldest of five children, Maxine remembers the feeling of community and connectedness found in her neighborhood in Chicago. She paints a picture of an idyllic urban middle-class neighborhood where on hot summer evenings parents would sit on front porches with kids playing close by. Their laughter and prattle would mix with the sounds of cars passing by, kids roller-skating or playing hopscotch and jacks games, or girls twirling hula hoops around their waists while a chorus of others kept count. There was a sense of well-being because everyone was known in the neighborhood or the block. "It was wonderful. You could walk to school passing all the rosebushes and flowers outside the houses. You really had neighbors. It was the fifties but it wasn't suburban. It was the city, with house after house on the block. Each house was different, though. We lived in a great brick house with a front porch. When you sold Girl Scout cookies, you just knocked on your neighbor's door and they were supportive. On Halloween you ran from house to house. It was just perfect growing up. There were lots of kids in the neighborhood but you also had wonderful older people. It was great. There was a feeling of camaraderie."

"We were German-Austrian, which I knew from an early age because my mother's German grandparents had heavy accents." Yet there were few traditions in her home that celebrated her ethnic heritage. "We always just felt like we were American. We didn't do traditions. There were no special foods we ate on holidays." While Maxine grew up amidst rich ethnic diversity in her neighborhood, she had little contact with blacks and other nonwhite groups. Her neighborhood was all white, far removed from the black sections of the city. "My neighborhood was a combination of WASP and Irish residents—there were the Mulligans across the street and the Bradys with their seven children." She added, "I did not go to school with one black person until I went to college."

Maxine matured quickly and was independent at a very early age. Her father was a successful entrepreneur who owned a number of businesses, while her mother worked as a realtor. "I was naturally independent, if there is such a thing. When I was starting kindergarten my pediatrician said, 'Maxine is like a little old lady getting ready to go to school.' I was the one telling the other kids to line up."

Her father's businesses often kept him away from home, but Maxine was still a daddy's girl. "My father is truly the salt of the earth. He is just a good, good person for all the right reasons. He'll do something just because it's the right thing to do. He's just nice. Ever since I was little I could sit down and talk with him. My mother was a screamer and my father was a talker. Dad was busy with his career and wasn't around much when I was little—but any attention from Dad was great." There was tension in her parents' marriage, and Maxine grew up always on edge, thinking her parents would divorce. "My mother was domineering, constantly degrading my Dad."

She doesn't remember receiving any messages about what it meant to be a girl. "My mother always said to aim for the highest. My parents never really said little girls play this way or little boys play that way. Never. None of that at all." Maxine felt equally comfortable doing boy things as girl things. "I could just as easily sit on the steps and play with dolls as I could go to the backyard and play horses. There were lots of boys in my neighborhood. I remember playing hockey and being on the ice rink with them. I didn't feel alienated."

Maxine's mother wasn't her role model, she said—either for traditional homemaking or for less traditional activities. "My mother didn't teach me to cook. Nor did she talk with me about what I wanted to do. My mother always wanted to be a stewardess and she was accepted, in the late forties or early fifties. But her older sister convinced my grandmother not to allow my mother to do it. For years and years my mother has harbored a feeling that she never really had a chance do what she chose to do."

During first through eighth grades, Maxine attended a Catholic school in her neighborhood. "I really liked the regimentation. I liked the uniform and the structure. You went to church in the morning and on certain days we had communion. I loved the nuns. I think every Catholic girl goes through this at some point. I thought I'd become a nun. Parochial school was just a wonderful experience. My school was part of the community. We had homecoming and the entire neighborhood would get involved."

Maxine was a gifted student and very active in high school. "I always have been able to set my own goals. Now, I don't know if it was because of my parents or if I just naturally did it. All the activities I joined in high school I did on my own. I was on the debating team. I was in the theater group. I've always been very extroverted and very vocal. I was always in the honor society." Maxine also played sports and was on the cheerleading squad. Even though she did not go to a Catholic high school, Maxine still thought about becoming a nun. "I was going to become a Carmelite nun. They were the only ones that could pray for the world. They don't ever talk. Obviously I could never have done that!"

Maxine doesn't remember her parents being actively involved in steering her toward college or a career. "Never once did either of my parents ask any of us what classes we were taking in school, what our curriculum was, or what we planned to major in during college. There was no direction. They never really asked, 'What's your project on?' We had to have our homework done and there were definite routines at home, but there never was any direct help, even when you were sitting down to decide on college. They never said, 'Let's take a look at those brochures.' " It was her high school teachers that influenced young Maxine. "Janet Cross, the drama teacher, influenced me. She was a great, strong woman. She would pick me up for the plays and once asked me to be student director."

"I always just assumed that of course I would go to college and then I would get a job." When it came time to go to college, Maxine applied to a number of schools including Skidmore and the University of Michigan. She ended up at one of the Big Ten schools where there were separate dorms for women and strongly enforced curfews. "When I first started college, women had to be in by midnight on weeknights, and by 1 a.m. on the weekends, and we couldn't have men in our dorm rooms. Luckily after the first semester the rules were changed. Men could visit but the door had to be open and all four feet had to be on the floor at the same time." Maxine started out as a sociology major, then moved to drama, and eventually became a business major. She described herself as both a "hippie" and "sorority sister." "I had the string of sunshine beads around my neck, bangs, real long hair, ripped jeans with the fringes, and a blue work shirt. But I also pledged to a sorority."

She continued, "There weren't a whole lot of us who were hippies in the sorority but those of us who were would be going to rallies against the Vietnam War or posting signs of protest. I would say that half of the women in our sorority had hats and white gloves. They were worried about whether they were going to have a date on Friday and Saturday night. I mean, there were boys being killed in Vietnam. I wasn't a fanatic but I was definitely aware and involved. However, I was not the least bit aware of the women's movement."

Maxine found it easy to get good part-time jobs while she was in college, so when it came time to find a job after graduation she wasn't worried about her future. "I had all these positive experiences so I didn't expect anything different, and no one ever said 'It's going to be hard or difficult.'"

Karen Brown

Karen Brown currently resides in New York City, but she grew up in Los Angeles, in Watts. She is a senior human resource executive responsible for corporate recruitment, compensation, and benefits. A petite woman, on the day of our interview she was wearing a soft pastel three-piece suit tastefully accented with bold pieces of gold jewelry. Her efficient manner at work is offset by her soft voice, gentle humor, and graciousness. Underneath her mild demeanor, however, she harbors a deeply buried rage over the state of race relations in America and the inability of corporations to recognize the talents of competent African-Americans. This is a subject about which Karen knows a great deal, for she is also responsible for implementing the company's diversity initiative. On a table in the corner of her medium-size office lies a copy of Jeanne Noble's book, *Beautiful, Also, Are the Souls of My Black Sisters.*

During our interview, Karen burst into laughter when she reflected on the racial mix of her childhood haunts. "White people didn't come into Watts; the community was ours." Her tone turned somber as she recalled the Pacific Electric Railroad that formed the dividing line between blacks and whites. On the black side of the tracks, the streets were cracked and broken, and in need of repair. Garbage pickup ran on a hit-and-miss schedule, and as a result, litter was left to pile up on the streets. On the white side of the tracks, the streets were paved, the garbage was regularly picked up, and the sidewalks were clean. It was a constant visual reminder to those living in both communities that the life circumstances of blacks and whites were worlds apart. This separateness was punctuated by the 1965 Los Angeles riot in Watts. The riot broke out in Karen's neighborhood, just four blocks from her house, causing her street to be sealed off by police. Karen was sixteen, and she remembers nights filled with the nerve-racking sounds of screaming police sirens and fire engines.

Karen's parents, George and Ellen Brown, rented an apartment in the public housing projects when they married. By Karen's first birthday, the family had moved into its first house, only three blocks away from the projects. Their house was a single-family California bungalow with a large front porch, complete with a swing, on a tree-lined street. The neighborhood cut across the middle and working classes, including those on welfare as well as professionals and service workers, and homeowners as well as renters. On the same square block where the Browns lived there were also businessmen, a doctor, a lawyer, and several educators. Mr. Wilkens, who worked for the post office, and Mrs. Wilkens, who was a social worker, owned the house next door. The Dowd family, the Brown's neighbors to the right, owned and managed a small insurance company. Mr. Williams, whose family lived across the street, was a junior high school principal whose wife was a teacher.

Karen tells anyone who asks that she had a great childhood. She can talk for hours about the good times she had with her family. But there were also troubled times, marked by the turbulence and disruption caused by her parents' divorce. She recalls being awakened by loud arguing late at night. There were two saving graces in Karen's life at the time. Church was one. "Our church supported family life, which in our neighborhood meant two working parents. Our minister made sure church was a gathering place for young people; there were always activities going on." Karen was involved in church-sponsored activities at least twice a week.

The other saving grace for Karen was her large and loving extended family; her grandparents, aunts, uncles, and cousins were always available and never failed to give Karen and her sisters support.

In fact, after the divorce, her mother sent Karen and her older sister off to live with their grandparents in the Southwest, so she could complete her education. The unsettling physical displacement lasted for one year. Nonetheless, what Karen remembered most about that year was the emotional security and guidance her grandparents provided, especially her grandmother. "She was very caring and at the same time she was firm, intelligent, and balanced. She was my inspiration."

Mrs. Jones, Karen's grandmother, was the home economics teacher at the school the girls attended. She had a reputation for being a tough disciplinarian. For her granddaughters, Mrs. Jones created a routine structure. Every day after school, Karen and her sister would meet in her grandmother's classroom to help her prepare for the next day. There were pins to pick up, fabric to fold, and patterns to file. Once at home, they had household chores to attend to. In the evenings, Grandmother Jones worked with the girls as they did their homework. Next came an extra hour devoted to studying different subjects under her tutelage. Karen was amazed at her grandmother's vast knowledge. "She was a woman who loved education, who loved to learn. She instilled that value in me," Karen fondly remembers. Not surprisingly, Karen maintained straight A's during the sixth grade. From her grandmother, Karen learned that it was acceptable for women to be wise, tough, and clear about what they wanted out of life.

Karen was about ten years old when she reached the conclusion that women worked in order to take care of themselves. Karen's mother, Pauline, finished college and worked as a school guidance counselor after her divorce. (She remarried when Karen was in her early teens.) All of Karen's aunts and both of her grandmothers worked. Mrs. Brown also instilled in her daughter the die-hard value of black womanhood: black women are strong. "My mother had some very strong views on being a woman," reflects Karen. "She believed black women had additional crosses to bear in life." Karen's mother made it her life mission to prepare her daughter to cope with life's extra burdens.

Once back in Los Angeles, Karen attended geographically segregated schools, with a handful of Mexican-American kids. She was always at the top of her class academically, but feels she did not work very hard. "I didn't push myself. I'm a lazy person." Still, in high school she was placed on the college prep track. Math was her favorite subject throughout high school. "I liked it; it was very logical." An extroverted adolescent, she was very social and became involved in lots of activities both at school and in the community.

Even then, Karen was aware of issues of social equity and racism. She took a proactive stand. Along with several other students, Karen helped organize a group called the Student Committee for Improvement in Watts. "We were very active in it, trying to clean up Watts, and working with local civic organizations who were doing all kinds of things to improve the area." It was the summer of 1965, the summer after the riot in Watts. Much was changing in the community. "Our science and math books were always old, shabby books. In 1965 we received all brand-new books. I will never forget that: going to school and seeing brand-new books. The riot shone a real spotlight on the community."

One day when Karen was in eleventh grade, she started to menstruate during her morning class. She had terrible cramps accompanied by a bad case of nausea. Between classes Karen went to see the school nurse. The nurse called Mrs. Brown at work to get permission to send Karen home. Mrs. Brown informed the school nurse that just because Karen got her period or was having a few cramps, she should not be sent home, not then and not any time in the future. Mrs. Brown then requested that her daughter be sent back to class. Karen spent the rest of the day running back and forth to the bathroom. By the time Karen returned home, her mother was solemnly sitting in the kitchen. Mrs. Brown told her to sit down. Next she explained to her daughter why girls did not come home just because they got their period. As far as her mother was concerned, a period was a normal bodily function and a little pain was to be expected. It was nothing earth-shattering. Business was to go on as usual, with no acting foolish or whining. "Girl, you're just going to have to adjust like the rest of us do." Those were, Karen remembers, her mother's last words on the subject.

From a very early age, Karen knew she was going to college. Both her parents and her stepfather had graduate degrees. Even her grandmother had a graduate degree in education. Karen knew exactly which college she wanted to attend—the all-women's historically black school her aunt had attended. Aunt Faye was one of her favorite role models, because she had such a fabulous style. The summer before leaving for college, Karen emulated her when she found a great pattern for a sleeveless dress with a jacket, picked a raw silk fabric in a beautiful shade of turquoise, and sewed her own version of an Aunt Faye outfit. Grandmother Jones's contribution was a matching pillbox hat.

On the night before she left for college, Aunt Faye came over with a homemade cake for her to take with her, a little reminder of the taste of home. The next day, wearing little white gloves, Aunt Faye's cake in hand, and dressed in a new outfit, Karen boarded a plane headed to the Southeast. "I was Miss Prim and Proper, and scared to death." She was seventeen years old. Initial fears soon melted away as she entered college and began to make friends. The love of her life was in college in Arizona. She spent her days attending classes, hanging out with her girlfriends, and writing him love letters. Not taking her course work too seriously, in her freshman year she flunked one course, and made C's in the others. For the first time in her life, she was forced to develop study skills and to push herself intellectually.

With the exception of her father, who had a law degree, teaching was the family profession. Not only were Karen's mother and grandmother educators, but so were all her aunts and several of her uncles. So, it was a pretty safe assumption that Karen would take up teaching as a career. "What else could you do? There was law, but not many women studied law then. We did not have any doctors in our family." But Karen discovered during her first year that she disliked her education course. In fact, she dropped the course and decided majoring in education was not for her. Laughing, she recalled, "My mother went ape shit on me when I told her I was changing my major."

The faculty at the college Karen attended was outstanding, studded with well-known black intellectuals. From them Karen developed an interest in history and economics. She grew intellectually, making the Dean's List in both her junior and senior years. She also fell in love several more times, until she met Kevin in her junior year. "He was a lot of fun and a kind man. I thought he was real smart and I just enjoyed being with him." After doing several on-campus interviews, Karen accepted an offer to join a management-training program at a major retail company. She graduated with a degree in history and a minor in economics. Six months after graduation she and Kevin married.

Dawn Stanley

With her dark olive complexion, deep blue eyes, and dark-brown silky hair, Dawn Stanley's colleagues often believe she is of Italian or Greek origin. They think she is white. But this high-ranking marketing executive in the manufacturing industry is African-American. "I've been in meetings and the whites will start telling racial jokes thinking I am one of them. I'm real cool and let them play their stuff out. I don't get thrown by that ... I don't get intimidated. Later on someone will hear that I am a sister, and then one by one they come running into my office checking to see if everything is all right." Dawn has a husky, sensual voice that gives her an air of both being sassy and laid-back. This woman is very clear about who she is, and she does not feel it is necessary to make a whole lot of fuss.

Dawn is the younger of William and Sylvia Stanley's two children. Their other child, Howard, is four years older than Dawn. When Dawn's father completed his dentistry degree on the East Coast, the family packed up all of their belongings and headed off to Seattle. Dawn was very young when the family resettled. But the family did not make this transition alone. A small caravan of the family's closest friends—classmates of Dr. Stanley from dental school, their wives and their children, and a few other couples whom they had known since childhood—all made the journey together. This group assumed the role of extended family for the Stanleys. Dawn remembers holiday dinners, birthday parties, and special celebrations spent together. The group formed a Jack and Jill Club. An organization for middle-class families, Jack and Jill of America provides their children with opportunities to socialize and to participate in cultural activities that foster healthy identities. This connection is particularly important for black families living in mostly white neighborhoods.

Raised in a white, middle-class, professional community, Dawn knew all the children on the street where she lived. They played together. Parents welcomed the children into their homes. Dawn never felt different because of her race. But she also believes that her family's physical appearance—fair-complexioned with light eyes and aquiline facial features—buffered them from experiencing racial discrimination. The fact that her father was a dentist also contributed to the family's acceptance. Dawn describes her family as being very traditional, with a lot of love and respect between her parents. "It was just a very healthy, wholesome, loving family environment." Both parents taught Dawn the value of education, and they made sure their children were equipped to lead successful lives.

Dawn was a daddy's girl. She looked just like her father. They were buddies, spending time together whenever possible. On special days, she would accompany him to his office. However, when Dawn was in fourth grade tragedy hit: Dr. Stanley died. He had been sick for some time, but had kept the severity of his illness from his daughter. Dawn never got to say good-bye to him. His sudden death created a huge hole in her heart that has yet to heal. "I have really missed him, and I often wonder as I've gone through one phase or another how would I be different if my father had lived."

Dr. Stanley's death altered everything in Dawn's life. Her mother uprooted her children, moving back to the Northeast, where she had the support of her family and friends. Once they relocated, Mrs. Stanley returned to the nursing career she had had before the birth of her son and Dawn's grandmother came to live with the family. All this change was a tremendous shock for Dawn, who felt betrayed by her mother and abandoned by her father. Additionally, the trauma sparked tension between Dawn and her mother, who had never shared the kind of close relationship Dawn enjoyed with her father. This tension continued to grow between them throughout Dawn's adolescence. The tension centered on Mrs. Stanley's tight control over her daughter. Dawn felt her mother did not give her space to make her own mistakes and to learn from them. She often felt judged by her mother. This situation left Dawn feeling alone. "There wasn't anybody at home that I could really talk to or share my emotions with."

Despite their differences, Mrs. Stanley gave Dawn a strong foundation on which to build her life. She taught Dawn the importance of self-reliance, of getting an education, of choosing a career path, and of building financial security. Dawn remembers her mother saying, "You are married to someone and one day you look up and he's gone. You are left with children or just yourself; either way you always have to be in a position to take care of yourself."

When the tension between Dawn and her mother grew to be too great, Auntie Sharon intervened. Auntie Sharon, her mother's best friend from college, was a lawyer. She also served as a real role model for Dawn. Both mother and daughter depended on her to help ease their frustration with each other. This was particularly true during one of Dawn's more stressful periods with her mother, a period she dubs "the junior high school wars." Dawn believed her aunt really understood her feelings and was interested in what she had to say. Auntie Sharon would sit Dawn down and very caringly ask, "Okay now sweetie, what's your side of the story?" After listening to Dawn's interpretation of the problem, her aunt would usually respond with, "Now you know you're wrong, you're acting like a fool, and this just won't do." Since her aunt was emotionally distant from the situation, it was easier for Dawn to listen to her and reconsider her behavior.

Dawn went from an upper-middle-class, all-white elementary school in Seattle to a black urban school with a mixture of socioeconomic levels in Baltimore. She had fit into the former but now stood out in the latter because of her fair skin, silky hair, and blue eyes. In junior high school, Dawn faced a new challenge: trying to prove her blackness to her class mates, who treated her "like a white girl," threatening to beat her up. Dawn's response was to prove her blackness. She did everything she could think of to show how black she was, starting with wearing her hair in a big Afro. As for her schoolwork, she did the minimum required, while still maintaining excellent grades in all her classes. "I always made sure that there were never going to be any problems coming from school." Of course, her mother noticed the change both in Dawn's behavior and in her appearance. She did not like what she saw.

With much coaxing, Dawn applied to one of the top private schools in the city. "My mother made me take a couple of tests and go on a couple of interviews. I would always say, 'I'm not going to do it.' She would say, 'Just do it, let's see if you get in. I won't make you do anything you don't want to do.'" Dawn passed all the tests and was accepted into the school. Under great pressure from her mother and under even greater protest, Dawn began private high school. It was a mostly white, upper-class, all-girl's school. Dawn made up her mind to "go there to do what I have to do. But I hated being at that school. I hated being with those white girls. I always was being kept from being with my people. I couldn't wait to get the hell out of there."

When it came time for college, Dawn selected a large liberal arts college in New York City. The college was far enough away from her mother, but in the same city as Auntie Sharon; it was a simple compromise between mother and daughter. "I did not want to be in another girl's school. I was sick and tired of looking at women," she said, laughing. Dawn was not a star student in college, but academically she held her own. "I was never one who had to get the best grades. I got a good mix of A's and B's, and that was fine with me." She declared elementary education as her major at the end of freshman year. "I was much too squeamish to think about medicine and I didn't like biology."

At the time Dawn was modeling her career after Maria Montessori, with the intention of being the next educational pioneer in early childhood learning. She dreamed of starting her own school, but it did not take long for her dream to die. The bottom line was that she really did not enjoy teaching full-time. And there was the issue of money, given the reality of a teacher's salary. Her mother's words of advice on self-sufficiency echoing in her head, Dawn began to think about other career options. Her roommate was majoring in business and enjoying her classes. In her junior year, Dawn switched her major to business. She started taking courses in marketing, management, and finance. It did not take long for her to get hooked. By her senior year she was "really toying with managing when finishing undergraduate school."

When Dawn made her intentions known to her mother, "she hit the roof." Mrs. Stanley thought her daughter better suited to being a lawyer. Her intention was for Dawn to go to law school immediately following graduation. Dawn's response was, "Whoever said anything about going to law school?" Dawn's plan was to work for a couple of years to get some experience before entering an M.B.A. program. She had thought about going to one of the business schools in the city. After hearing Dawn's plan, Mrs. Stanley decided to do a little investigating of her own. She talked to some friends, several of whom had children who had attended or were attending M.B.A. programs. Mrs. Stanley discovered that an M.B.A. was one of the hottest degrees to receive. From there she went on to research the top M.B.A. programs in the country. She was determined that if Dawn was going to get an M.B.A., she was going to do so in a top program. It was Mrs. Stanley who insisted that Dawn apply to four of the top-ranked programs and that she apply while still in her senior year of college. Even without any solid work experience, Dawn was accepted into two of the schools. She chose one. Three months later she was off to a new city and entering business school. Dawn was about to work harder in school than she had ever worked before.

Gloria Goldberg

During her interview, Gloria Goldberg described herself as having absolutely "no flinch mechanism." If she weren't in her present job, she joked, she would be a fighter pilot. "If I say I am going to do something, by the time I'm verbalizing it I'm already ready to do it. It took me a long time to realize that other people were *just* talking. It was just hot air." Initially, her pony-tailed auburn hair and flamboyant manner of dress, including the fur coat draped behind her chair, seem at odds with her decisive management style. That style has served her well in a career that demands risk-taking, entrepreneurial thinking, and fast action. But the hectic pace of her job hasn't erased the gracefulness and poise she developed as a promising young dancer.

A vice president and investment banker for one of the top capital management firms in the country, Gloria spends her days negotiating and financing equity deals, buying and selling companies, and developing turnaround strategies for start-ups. "My job is about making sure things happen. It's like being a traffic cop—you're out there to make sure other stuff happens. It's about finding projects, finding financing, finding equity, dealing with the outside world. A certain amount of things must get done for each deal but for the rest of it, who knows what's going to happen? Meetings and presentations take an unbelievable amount of preparation and time." She is the lone woman in the top echelon of the company.

Gloria, the oldest of three children, grew up in an upper-middle-class Jewish family in Westchester County, New York. Her family lived in the house her father inherited from his parents. A housekeeper cared for the children and maintained the house while Gloria's mother attended school. Westchester County was a picturesque world of broad, sloping green lawns and tree-shaded, somnolent streets and cul-de-sacs. Neatly trimmed boxwood hedges stood like sentries at the entrance to homes, guarding a hard-earned privacy.[1] Few streetlights or fences marred the beauty of Gloria's suburban neighborhood. This was no Levittown-type tract suburb with long rows of uniformly built single-family homes for the middle class of the '50s. Westchester County was much more deeply rooted. Executives, doctors, lawyers, scientists, professors, and artists had long inhabited this wealthy county. It had the largest number of *Who's Who* listings in the country.[2] Gloria remembers it as a "well-educated community. It's where all of corporate America lived." She recalled the exodus of fathers each morning, dropped off at the rail station by their wives. The wealthiest of the group traveled in the comfort of private club cars attended by black porters. Gloria and her brothers were each day loaded into the family station wagon for the trip to school and then shuttled to a myriad of after-school activities.

Gloria described her neighborhood as "99.9 percent Jewish." There were a few blacks living in her neighborhood but for the most part, she said, they were "token blacks." "I mean I can still tell you their names. There was Whitney Young and there was Ossie Davis and Ruby Dee, all well-bred blacks." She described her father as "a die-hard FDR liberal" who taught her to treat blacks—especially those who worked for him— the same as whites. "We were color blind. My father did not allow us to say anything racist. If you did, your mouth was washed out with soap."

She went on to say, "It's funny. Race was never an issue. I never really thought about it one way or the other. Religion was much more important because my parents had a Jewish preference. If there were blacks in my elementary school, then they were 'Oreos' and acted white and thought white. This was before black power."

The affluence of her family and the community in which she was raised greatly influenced Gloria's early development and expectations. "My father was a capitalist. He had a tool-and-die business and it was his little fiefdom. There were years when it was extraordinarily profitable, and years when there were risks; but generally it was very successful. "Gloria grew up hearing stories about doing business and making deals from her father. Entrepreneurs surrounded Gloria throughout her childhood. She recalled, "I had great-aunts who ran their own companies or who were top managers in others. It was not unusual for women to do something in business. I remember that a lot of my relatives didn't work for other people."

Gloria's mother was a well-educated woman. "My mother got married right before her senior exams in college because she didn't know what she would need them for. So she didn't even graduate. When I was about eleven or twelve, she decided to go back to school. She first finished her bachelor's degree, then she got her master's, and then eventually a doctorate."

Independence was stressed in Gloria's family. She remembers her parents' expectations clearly. "Just recently I was thinking about my family and my parents. It was like a house with five different people who happened to live together. I realized later that we were all encouraged to do what it was we wanted to do, to be very, very independent and just do it, to a point. But my sister wanted to be a housewife with two kids and there my father put his foot down. He said, 'Damn it, she's going to go to college. She is not going to waste her brains. Then if she wants a husband and two kids, that's fine but she damn well better do something with her brain.'"

One of Gloria's passions in her early life was ballet. A talented dancer, she dreamed of being a ballerina one day. "I think I saw my first ballet when I was six. It was my birthday and my mother had made me a pretty velvet dress with beautiful little ribbon bands. We went into the city and it was the Kirov's first appearance in America. It was probably one of the world's best casts, dancing *Don Quixote*. And it was magic. I can still close my eyes and see the steps in the scene, absolutely intact, like a photograph. That's when I knew I wanted to be a ballerina."

Another daddy's girl, Gloria had a close relationship with her father. It was he, not her mother, who encouraged her to pursue her dream to be a ballerina. "He thought it was marvelous. My mother was violently opposed to it and thought I should have some form of practical job with some useful skill. She hated his encouraging me to dance. But he thought, 'No, if she wants to dance, why not dance? What a lovely thing.' I was going to be a dancer in marvelous costumes on stage. It was really quite fun up on stage. I would be a peasant in one performance and an aristocrat in another. I wanted to shoot for the moon!"

Gloria doesn't remember being taught that her gender could be an issue. "I grew up believing that you could do pretty much what you wanted to. There could be some hassles, but if you were willing to put the effort in you could do the things you wanted. I was always encouraged to believe that the world was going to be very fair. There was a rather abrupt awakening when I realized how stacked the deck was. Oddly, I would have preferred to have been made more aware of it. I sometimes wonder if it may have been more helpful if I had been told what to expect."

Gloria attended the excellent public schools in her suburban neighborhood. She was in all of the advanced placement classes and threw herself into everything, from cheerleading to drama. But her passion remained the ballet. Every afternoon she went off for several hours of ballet practice. "By time I was twelve I was doing the master ballet class. By the time I was fourteen I was practicing with the dancers of the American Ballet Theater." But injuries later prevented Gloria from realizing her dream to dance.

Gloria always knew she would attend college. "You didn't think about it. You were going to go. You had no options. Suburban Westchester County was your college-bound, high-SAT community. You were expected to go to college." Gloria and other white women who grew up in affluent suburban communities chose prestigious colleges such as Wellesley, Radcliffe, or Smith. So when she realized she would not realize her dream to be a ballet dancer, Gloria went off to an elite women's college in the Northeast. After a couple of false starts, Gloria finally settled on political science as her undergraduate major. Gloria attended law school at a prestigious public university after completing her undergraduate education.

The flashbacks of Maxine Schneider, Karen Brown, Dawn Stanley, and Gloria Goldberg reveal the power of geography and social location when combined with race. The places where the women grew up added a critical dimension to their identity formation and their access to material resources. These places served as the backdrop to the early portion of their lives. These places include the community where the women's families lived and where the women shared a common history and culture with those around them. The community was also the place where they gained their earliest sense of self and of belonging in the world. In addition, place also represents home. According to Linda McDowell, director of the Graduate School of Geography of Cambridge University, "Home is much more than a physical structure. The house is the site of lived relationships, especially those of kinship and sexuality, and is a key link in the relationship between material culture and sociality: a concrete marker of social position and status."[3] But place is even more than home. These four stories challenge assumptions we have about the places professional women come from and the relationships between them. As McDowell suggests, "Places are made through power relations which construct rules which define boundaries. These boundaries are both social and spatial—they define who belongs to a place and who may be excluded, as well as the location or site of experience."[4]

Even though Maxine and Karen both grew up in cities, the experience of their early lives demonstrates the depth of the boundaries between their communities. Because many of the white women's families did not live near blacks, their knowledge of blacks came from observing them at a distance. Even this indirect contact left a negative impression. It was only on family excursions to downtown Chicago that Maxine Schneider's parents had to drive through the Southside. In this inner-city neighborhood, Maxine's mother cautioned her to check that car doors were locked and not to stare at black people on the street so as not to attract their attention. Avoiding all interaction with black people was a way of making them invisible. "You always tried to look down and not look." Maxine remarked. "I was always thinking, 'Please don't do anything.' Yes, I do remember the fear of getting caught in the wrong section of town." Putting up blinders to the conditions in which black people lived was an act of self-protection, but also an act of self-aggrandizement. Turning a blind eye to societal inequities allowed whites to believe that blacks had not only different, but undesirable, values.

Likewise, Karen Brown remembers white people passing through Watts but never stopping. This made them remote; it made her neighborhood a place where they did not belong. White people passed through, but they lived in a separate world.

Childhood geographic locations have a complex effect on women's understandings of race and their own racial identities. Growing up in the suburbs of Seattle, Dawn's physical appearance—her fair complexion, straight hair, blue eyes, and fine facial features—didn't distinguish her from others in her Seattle community. For her, race was neutral; it had no special significance. She was accepted within the family, the extended family sphere, and the immediate community. At school the children were oblivious to Dawn's race or class. This situation changed dramatically when Dawn relocated to an urban area in the Northeast. All of a sudden, Dawn discovered that race mattered. Because the black children perceived her as being white, Dawn became determined to prove she was one of them. Her blackness became both socially and culturally charged. In the context of the political African-American community, Dawn developed a black consciousness unavailable to her in the white suburbs. Psychologist William Cross would explain that when Dawn moved she had an "immersion" experience, becoming aware of her "black self, developing a sense of pride in black people and black culture."[5]

As an adult, Dawn still struggles with race at work, but not in the way one may imagine. The racial context—the place—where she works is white and race is invisible. But Dawn rejects being "incog-Negro," pretending she is not black in order to fit into the company. If anything, she is very clear about her racial identity. "The hardest thing for me is not white people who don't know I am black," she acknowledges with evident sadness, "It is black people who don't know I am black. When there's a meeting for black people exclusively and I walk in, it hits them that I am black." Such black-on-black prejudice within the black community—between light- and brown-skinned blacks—is rarely discussed openly. Beverly Daniel Tatum discusses the negative impact of "colorism," the "societal preference for light skin and the relative advantage historically bestowed on light-skinned blacks,"[6] within the black community. A by-product of the plantation hierarchy, which privileged the light-skinned children of African slave women and white slave owners, colorism has created a post-slavery class system based on color.[7] Darker-skinned black women perceive that they will be subjected to greater scrutiny and feel that whites are more comfortable with black women of lighter skin hues. This awareness causes deep pain. Skin-color prejudice, Tatum argues, is a form of internalized oppression; it can be toxic to black children and detrimental to black adults.

Gloria, like the other white women who grew up in affluent, predominantly white, suburban neighborhoods, lived in open spaces surrounded by beautiful landscapes and attended elite schools. During the era in which these women were growing up, suburbia was an exclusive domain, both socially and politically conservative. Conspicuous consumption was a prime activity that shaped one's identity and sense of belonging. Monoracial and monocultural childhoods were the norm, in the physical environments and the major institutions. Children like Gloria, engulfed in whiteness, failed to develop a racial identity or an awareness of how race structured not just the lives of black people but also their own lives. Race was something black people or other people of color possessed. As another interviewee, Marilyn Paul, succinctly put it, "Race just wasn't there. It just wasn't a subject. I've got to tell you it's a sin of omission rather than a sin of commission. It just wasn't on my radar screen." They were not socially conscious of the cultural and economic advantages afforded them because of their skin color. If anything, they learned to be color blind—to believe that race doesn't make a difference. For if blacks and whites are the same under the skin, the implication is there is no racism in the United States and blacks have the same chance as whites to make it in society. We found this belief permeated many of the white women's adult views of the workplaces they entered.

Yet below the surface, the "all-white" childhood experiences often *did* include knowledge of and interactions with people of other races, most often blacks. But black people were on the periphery of their lives, out of direct vision, only entering in the margins of their families' lives as maids, helpers, employees, people who lived a safe distance away, or, as Gloria believed, were "Oreos." Seeing black people in subordinate roles, or as tokens, did inform their perceptions of African-Americans.

Even when women like Gloria were aware of their ethnic lineage, family life was not centered on ethnicity. Because ethnic identification was minimized in their families, a majority of the women developed what we call a flat ethnicity. When we asked about their ethnicity, many identified themselves with a religious label rather than an ethnic one. There are at least two dimensions to the flatness we heard. First, there was a sense of themselves as not being "ethnic," that ethnicity was not part of their childhood. For the majority of the women, ethnicity had been leveled to a single identity that was difficult for them to articulate. One woman talked about the ethnicity of the place where she grew up as "kind of general nothing." Second, there was a lack of knowledge about other ethnic groups. Part of this resulted from growing up in relatively homogenous physical and social environments. They describe parents whose social circles were largely monocultural. It was often a move away from these homogenous environments that led to the realization of the existence of diverse ethnic groups.

4

❖

Executives in
Training

Julia Smith

Julia Smith is a tall and striking figure with deep dimples and a warm
smile; she could easily be mistaken for a model. In fact, however, she is a
mover and a shaker in the financial industry, where she became the first
black woman to be brought into her company's executive ranks. This
sophisticated, intellectually strong woman's origins can be traced to the
deep South. Julia began her life in a small rural community in the Mississippi Delta, with a population of 875. Her family had lived there for
generations. Her maternal grandfather, considered a pillar of the community, owned the grocery store and gas station on the black side of town.
He was also a skilled mason. Grandfather Thomas worked with stone,
concrete, and brick, and shared his gift by teaching young black men the
trade. All of these accomplishments were rare, because a majority of black
men in town barely carved out an existence for themselves and their families by sharecropping. Julia feels tremendous pride in family's heritage;
this has, in return, helped her to develop a positive self-concept, and given
her a sense of place in the world. "I look at portraits of my grandfather's
family: they aren't dressed shabbily. There is one picture of him and his

87

younger sister, and they are dressed beautifully. He must have been four or five years old at the time. Hanging from his pocket is a gold watch that he still has today."

Julia's parents met while both were attending the same college. Theirs was a storybook romance. Mrs. Smith, Julia's mother, was the homecoming queen of her senior class and her father was the captain of the football team. They married shortly after her mother graduated from college. Both began their careers as teachers, working their way into administration. Each obtained graduate degrees. "I am not saying there were no trials and tribulations, but the steps were all in place," Julia said. "It was just like *The Donna Reed Show*, except that the circumstances were much more modest because of the reality of race." Over the years, Julia's parents built a close and loving relationship. Julia was their only child.

It was Edna Smith, Julia's mother, who orchestrated the family's move from Mississippi to Detroit. When Julia was asked how she was most like her mother, she cited her mother's determination combined with her ability to take risks. "I am result-oriented like my mother," Julia said. She continued, "We move ahead and get things done." Julia also expressed the differences between them in terms of her generation's exposure to the white world and the resulting confidence gained from interacting with whites on a professional level. "My mom, I think, very often lacks the kind of self-confidence that she was able to give me. At a distance, she can analyze issues related to racism very cleanly. When she is in it, she is very intimidated. That is a function of exposure." She continued by adding, "I have benefited from being in a generation that has not only an easier row to hoe, but also the self-confidence that goes along with being a well-educated third-generation professional."

Julia described her father as the foundation of the family. Unlike Edna, Earl Smith is more cautious, and weighs the pros and cons of a situation before taking a risk. Father and daughter both "look for affirmation from inside ourselves, not from outsiders," Julia said. Julia also pointed out how her father shaped her career aspirations, overtly encouraging her to follow her dreams. The important issue was to find a *career* that would provide financial security, rather than a *job*. Julia recalled going through the typical stages of what she wanted to be when she grew up. There was the wanting-to-be-a-nurse stage, which developed into the wanting-to-be-an-engineer stage, which eventually turned into the wanting-to-be-an-architect stage. Her father, she said, never argued for her to be a writer or poet. Both of her parents were high achievers, so they expected Julia to

have a career doing something reasonably substantial in one of the professions traditionally open to African-Americans. This meant education,
law, or medicine. In the '60s the world of business was not an option.

Being a girl child living in the South in the '50s meant that Julia
learned very early in her life about racism. Julia remembers going to the
voting poll on Election Day with her grandparents. Although a poll tax
prevented a lot of the black people from voting (Julia could not recall seeing other black people at the poll), her grandfather had the money to pay
it. A white boy, who appeared to be younger than Julia, was standing near
the entrance. He looked up at her grandfather with a snicker on his face,
and said, "What are you doing here, nigger?" Grandfather Thomas looked
right past the boy as he walked through the door. Inside, Grandmother
Thomas was the first to vote. Julia had never heard anyone, black or white,
talk to her grandparents in such a humiliating way. In looking back at the
situation now, she said, "How dare this little white kid, with mud up to his
knees, call my grandfather a nigger?"

When they returned to her grandparents' home later that afternoon,
Julia overheard the adults talking. Although her grandfather was annoyed
over the ways white people were intimidating black people and keeping
them from the election poll, he never mentioned being called a nigger.
Julia learned some very important racial lessons this day. It was clear to
her that being able to vote was the most important thing. "Going, paying
your money, filling out the ballot, and putting it in the box was the point."
The other racial lessons were very basic: never let white people stop you
from doing what is important; when confronted with racial hostility, do
not overreact, and always be vigilant never letting your guard down in the
presence of white people.

It was the summer just before Julia entered the fourth grade when her
family made their northern migration. They made their first home in
Black Bottom, a black urban community in Detroit. Julia saw a distinct
difference between the rural Southern community where she had lived
and her new urban neighborhood. Gone were the outhouses and the out-
right poverty. In both places the community was black, but blacks had a
greater degree of freedom to move in and out of the white world in
Detroit. Of course, there were still racial boundaries. For example, black
people had to sit in the balcony at the local movie house, so Julia's parents refused to let her go.

Three years after arriving in Detroit, the family moved to the "promised
land," a lily-white Jewish neighborhood in the suburbs. The dismantling of

housing discrimination and the sale of property to blacks with the passage of the Civil Rights Act of 1964 gave black families greater choice as to where they could live. Julia's family was the first black family to reside not only on their street, but also in their immediate neighborhood. Julia had just turned twelve and she was beginning junior high school. In her new school setting, she was popular with her classmates and she developed friendships with several of the girls. It was not unusual for her to be invited to their homes for sleepovers. Or she would entertain them with the latest Motown sounds at her house.

The social backdrop in Julia's life had a bicultural flavor, in that she moved between two worlds: her black working-class community and her white, Jewish, middle-class school. Although living in the suburbs, Mr. and Mrs. Smith maintained close ties with Detroit's black community— their church, her sorority, and his fraternity. Their church provided the social fabric for the family; it gave the family a way to cope with the racial isolation that came from living among whites. Julia learned quickly how to move gracefully between these two worlds. On weekdays she interacted with her white classmates and on weekends she reconnected with her black friends.

Living in the Midwest, away from strict racial boundaries, Julia's parents took the opportunity to selectively expose her to the world of white culture. It was not by coincidence the leading ballerina in the first ballet Julia saw was the Native American dancer Maria Tallchief. Julia recalls her as "nonballerina-ish," because Ms. Tallchief had brown skin and a commanding physical presence. Nor was it by coincidence that the first opera her parents took her to see was *Madame Butterfly*. The production she saw featured a rising young black diva named Leontyne Price. Both of these experiences allowed Julia to discover that being black and female were not handicaps. It also created an alternative standard of femininity and beauty through which Julia could see herself.

The racial landscape of the junior high school Julia attended was a reflection of the community she lived in. Julia was one of ten black children attending the school. Bright and articulate, she was placed in the honors program. Academically she excelled. Socially, she was well liked by both her teachers and peers. By the time Julia entered high school the racial landscape of the community was slowly changing. "When I started high school it was probably about 50 percent black and the other 50 percent was overwhelmingly Jewish. By my senior year the percentage of Jewish students had dropped to one third."

In high school, Julia was in the honors program taking college prep courses. Because of her academic placement she found herself the only black student in most of her classes. Julia's extracurricular activities centered on the school newspaper and yearbook, where she was the production manager. She was one of two black students involved in these activities. Most of the other black students opted for athletics and cheerleading. So Julia was racially cut off from the other black students. She did not think of this as a detriment to her social life, since she was involved with black teenagers in her church group.

While most of her teachers were supportive, she did encounter subtle racism from one algebra teacher. "I was not doing well; I was bringing home C's. This was in the eleventh grade, a tough year for me. It was also important because it was the last year before the SATs. My mother went over to school and asked the teacher, 'What's the deal?' And the teacher said, 'These kids can't learn algebra,' meaning these black kids. Enraged, my mother confronted the woman." Getting Julia a tutor, a math teacher who was Mrs. Smith's friend, took care of the algebra problem. From then on, Julia excelled in math and science.

There was never any doubt in Julia's mind that she would attend college. She came from a high-achieving, well-educated family. In her junior year she was deluged with information about colleges. She finished high school at the age of sixteen. All of her classmates went to Big Ten Schools, but Julia chose one of the Seven Sisters in the Northeast. She wanted to leave home, but it was important to her to be at a small school. At the time of her graduation she was thinking of becoming an architect or engineer.

There were only a handful of African-American women at her college when she arrived. They became a tight knit group, studying together, sharing the "black table" in the cafeteria, and dating black men from a nearby men's college. Many of these women would become Julia's lifelong friends. She was active in the Black Student Union on campus. The campus was relatively small, but there was a large gulf between white and black students. Although she and the other African-American women felt socially isolated, she learned to cope because, in her words, "All of us had come out of similar experiences where we had learned to compete with white people." However, some of the faculty did not expect her or the other black women to perform well. Julia remembers an adviser saying, "You aren't expected to make it here." She felt at times it was hard for her to receive a fair grade. There was only one black professor on the faculty.

In time Julia lost interest in engineering. She discovered a new passion: economics. She decided on a double major in economics and government. She chose her major because "social issues were important and learning about Africa was important. In my mind everything fit nicely into a neo-colonial model." Julia graduated from college with plans to study economics in graduate school. Although she was not certain about a career, she wanted to do something that was socially relevant. It was the mid-'70s, a time when young, college-educated African-Americans thought they could do anything and really make a difference in the world. "Frankly, I didn't have the whole career orientation. I think it came largely from a very naïve presumption that things would just sort of fall into place in some kind of way."

Patricia Triggs

Patricia Triggs is a substantial woman, in terms of her wit, intelligence, and size. Her sentences are vividly spiked with profanity. She is a woman who is comfortable with herself. In her role as a strategist for a Fortune 100 company, Patricia consults on product marketing with the company's top-ranking executives. She is disciplined and knowledgeable, especially on start-up operations in Asia.

Patricia is the elder of Arthur and Iris Triggs' two daughters. The Triggs lived in an apartment in a black working-class neighborhood on the south side of Chicago. Arthur Triggs, a salesman for a black-owned company, was a very determined man. Never content with his current salary or position, he seized every opportunity for promotion. All his hard work paid off, allowing the family to buy a modest, three-bedroom house in one of Chicago's newly integrated suburbs in 1966. Patricia was eleven years old.

"The neighborhood was calm, nice and clean. You could go up the block and play baseball and softball. There was a pond and in the winter it froze so we could ice skate." Patricia discovered a small cluster of black families, all with children in her age range. These families lived only one or two streets away from each other, making it easy for the children to play together. Patricia did not remember building any close relationships with the white children in the area.

Patricia credits her mother for playing a large role in her success. Patricia has wonderful mother stories. "Everything my sister and I did, my mother did. We did Girl Scouts; she was a Girl Scout leader. We did ballet class; she sat there and watched us doing our pirouettes and pliés. When we had music lessons, she listened to us practice the scales."

Patricia was one of two black children in her suburban elementary school, in which students were well behaved and expected to excel. All of her teachers were white. A smart and highly motivated student, she remembers being treated differently in elementary school because of her race. Being a rarity meant she got a great deal of attention from her teachers, which made her feel special, "They always knew who you were," she said. "I liked school. I liked learning. I liked it so much, I often sought out additional help. I was not only special as a black student, but also as a student they liked teaching. You didn't have to pull me along. I was wanting more all the time."

Family rituals were a way of life in the Triggs household. One ritual that took place every Sunday afternoon was the family meeting, when her father brought family members together to share their experiences of the past week, discuss the upcoming week, talk about any problems involving the family as a whole, and plan family events. At these meetings, Patricia and her younger sister were assigned chores for the week. Patricia liked to tell her parents about special school projects, and show off the A's she received on her weekly math and spelling tests. As Patricia and her sister grew older, they would take turns running the family meeting. From this ritual Patricia learned how to talk and interact with authority figures. Perhaps an even more valuable lesson was the early recognition that her parents were interested in her thoughts and feelings regarding family matters; they wanted to hear her voice.

In our interview Patricia, a daddy's girl, proudly declared, "I was told by my father that I was a person of the world, and I was entitled to experience what the world had to offer." Arthur Triggs knew exactly what it took to prepare his girl child for the changing world that awaited her. He took an extremely supportive role in nurturing his daughter's intellect and curiosity. When Patricia was in sixth grade, she was already helping him sort out his sales records. On Saturdays, he took both his daughters to his office. Father worked while the girls occupied themselves by playing office. Patricia always insisted her sister be the secretary. Needless to say, Patricia was the boss. By the time she was in high school, father and daughter continually practiced negotiation skills. One weekend there was a school dance Patricia wanted to attend. She asked her father's permission, but he told her she was too young to go. Patricia argued that his decision was not fair. Mr. Triggs countered by asking her to prepare an argument on why it was not fair. He suggested she come up with a reason for being allowed to attend the dance, and then they would talk again. "Imagine me trying to lay out my argument and then come back to this imposing man," laughed Patricia. But she did.

The following night Patricia pleaded her case. Her argument was simple: The dance was a school function, she attended the school, and therefore, she was of proper age to participate. To support her case, she had already made arrangements for transportation with a classmate whose mother was driving. Finally, she pointed out to her father, she would be with a group of her friends, all of whom he knew and liked. Mr. Triggs listened carefully to her argument, and in the end, Patricia won—she got to go to the dance. Now she had gained the confidence to use her voice.

When Patricia was a sophomore in high school, she expressed an interest in following in her father's career footsteps, pursing a career in management. Tapping into his professional network, Mr. Triggs scheduled a series of lunch meetings with his black colleagues, selecting men and women who were employed both in large white corporations and black-owned companies. Patricia, dressed in her Sunday best, accompanied her father to lunch with a branch manager, a vice president of marketing, and a district sales manager. During each lunch she was able to ask questions about their careers: how they got started, what they did in their jobs, and anything else she wanted to know. These lunches expanded Patricia's career horizons. Mr. Triggs literally guided her earliest career aspirations, and in doing so gave her a vision of what her life could be, fueling the fire of her dream.

During her high school years, Patricia attended two different schools. She thrived academically at both. Patricia found herself in the predominately white college preparatory classes while many of her black friends were not. Her extracurricular activities included participating in sports, the marching band, and several academic clubs. Because of her successes, she had a lot of visibility. Patricia was a highly recruited National Merit Scholar. She knew she was going to college. Her parents had instilled that in her early on.

At each school, the percentage of black students kept climbing. During her freshman year, 3 percent of the students were black; later in high school that percentage reached 20 percent. As the composition of her schools changed, so did the tensions between black and white students. Patricia walked a delicate line, navigating between black and white schoolmates. It was her first striking experience with racial discrimination and the pressure to choose sides. "You had to identify whom you were with," she recalled. "Are you with the sisters and brothers, or are you with the white folks? There were labels like Toms and Sallies. The black kids would be quick to point out, 'Oh, she's with white folks.'" A test of allegiance was an everyday battle for her. "I never hung with black and white kids together; I tended to relate more one on one with individuals from each group. With the whites, I would go bowling and have a good time. With the black kids, I would go skating. I didn't like going to white parties. With the black kids there was a sense of community and I could go home and study with them. We might have sleepovers. I never felt the same about the white kids; I didn't want to go to sleepovers at their homes."

When it came time to select a college, Patricia could have attended any school she wanted. She chose a historically black college in the South because in her words, "The blackness was important to me. . . . I felt I was missing something." After pausing to think, she then added, "I had gone to an all-white elementary school, and an all-white high school for my fresh-man year. My sophomore, junior, and senior years were eye-openers in terms of ethnic diversity. But I always wondered if I could really hang with the sisters and brothers." Patricia majored in business, something she had become interested in during high school. College years for her were an affirmation of her cultural identity. She developed lifelong friendships with some of her fellow students, and remembers feeling comfortable and secure in the all-black environment. Of course, she maintained an excel-lent academic record and was active in student government. On the eve of her graduation, Patricia's dream was to become a marketing executive.

We purposely end the Flashback section with the stories of two black women raised to be powerful. Julia Smith and Patricia Triggs counter the stereotypic image of the black experience. They represent the opposite of what white America usually hears about black women: that black women are raised in unstable families headed by uneducated women and absent fathers who do not provide for their children, that they live in inner-city neighborhoods where they receive inadequate education, and that they are not prepared to interact socially in the white world. There has been a tendency, at least in the popular culture, to obscure the fact that func-tional and stable black families have always existed. Julia and Patricia are hardly exceptions among the black women we interviewed. Both repre-sent a prototypical segment of black women who were raised in solid middle-class families, with educated parents, and a loving, supportive extended family. Many of the women in our study in this segment were

second- or third-generation educated, with their parents having graduate education. And as sociologist Linda McDowell points out, their suburban lifestyles gave them "access to clean air and more open space than in the
city center, as well as a range of educational opportunities in local schools."[1]

Their flashbacks give us wonderful examples of the ways black women
can be armored as young girls to withstand racial oppression and to possess the strength and courage to move forward into the world.[2] Armoring is a "political strategy for self-protection," whereby a girl "develops a
psychological resistance" to defy both racism and sexism.[3] We believe the
armoring process is a critical element of the black woman's psychosocial
development. Both Julia and Patricia were taught by their parents to
dance to the beat of their own drum. They instilled in their daughters an
individualistic sense of beauty, grace, style, and intellect. These parents
also gave their daughters the message that they could conquer the white
world. As a result, these women developed a protective shield that
buffered them against the unsavory elements of the outside world—a
world where they quickly discovered that black women are often invisible,
devalued, and dishonored because of their race and gender.

Julia's and Patricia's parents had financial resources and personal connections at the time overt segregation was being dismantled. Consequently, they could expose their daughters to the arts, to historical
monuments, and to finer restaurants within white America. However,
they were highly selective of the place and events they chose. We call this
"selective exposure." These parents intentionally chose only those activities that would reinforce their daughter's positive self-images. At a time
when black girls were growing up in segregated communities or were
among a tiny handful of blacks living in otherwise exclusively white suburbs, selective exposure enabled them to gain deep insight into the social
norms, behaviors, and attitudes of the white world. This element of their
armor increased their self-confidence, enhanced their social skills and
grace, and gave them the courage to comfortably move back and forth
between the two cultural contexts. That is, they learned early in their lives
how to be bicultural, interacting and engaging in both the white dominant culture and their own culture.

The flashbacks of Karen Brown and Dawn Stanley in chapter 3 reveal
another dimension of how the armoring process works. Self-reliance, a
woman's ability to take care of herself, is instilled in her at a young age.
Both of these women's stories illuminate how black girls are socialized
early on to be independent, not to rely on anyone for support. They are

taught to be strong. Being strong is a habit of survival for black women.[4] Such habits are "responses to pain and suffering that help to lessen anger, give a sense of self-control, and offer hope."[5] A disturbing silence exists when it comes to black women talking about their pain, whether emotional or physical. Silence is one way black women have adapted to living in a world of interlocking oppressions.

One last point needs to be made concerning the flashbacks of our black women subjects. They learned the importance of being responsible to the black community—part of the culture of resistance. There was the expectation of giving back to the community; it was an attitude of service. Julia Smith and Patricia Triggs were not the only ones in our group of black women to receive this message. Imbued with a strong sense of ancestry through stories shared by parents and grandparents of the struggles of black people, these middle-class black women developed a strong sense of duty and responsibility. They learned that success is not based on individual achievement but rather on a collective upraising of others who are less fortunate in the community. This ethic was not just confined to the black women raised in middle-class families, such as Julia Smith, Patricia Triggs, Karen Brown, Dawn Stanley, and Brenda Boyd. It was also a dominant theme in the early lives of poor and working-class black women. You hear it as well in the words of Ruthie Mae White, where it seems to emanate from a desire not to have others experience the harsh conditions she had been subjected to during her childhood. "I feel like I have to do something. I share what I have, but I wish I could reach back and grab more people. I stay in touch because it is where I derive my strength."

As these flashbacks reveal, women's early life experiences are shaped by history, culture, race, gender, and social class; these experiences in turn shape quite different values, standpoints, and identities, not only across racial lines, but also within the same racial groups. The next part of our book illustrates how early life lessons greatly influence their professional identities in the workplace.

Part II

Flashpoints

MUCH OF WHAT has been written about women in managerial careers leaves the impression that all women make similar journeys to the doors of corporate America. And that once in the doors, they face common obstacles and choose common strategies for overcoming them. Our research shows, however, that black and white women travel separate paths and make different choices about how to persevere in their professional careers. Black women, in particular, have had to break away from traditional career choices as teachers and social workers, occupations historically available to college-educated black women. Having entered careers traditionally dominated by white males, black women have had to contend with both sexism and racism. These experiences contribute to separate approaches toward both navigating their careers and making change in the workplace.

In this section of the book, we organize the women's journeys thematically, around critical "flashpoints" in their life paths. These watershed moments lead not only to opportunities but also often to considerable frustration and struggle. The flashpoints we've selected were identified by the women we interviewed as critical junctures in their adult lives. The flashpoints often defined breakthroughs or moments in which lessons were crystallized. Into the life stories of the women you met in "Flash-backs" we weave important findings from our national survey of professional women.

The first chapter of this section, "Breaking In," traces the paths of these women from college to their first managerial job; we explore influences on their career choices and their career entry. In "Fitting In," we describe the women's perceptions of the corporate cultures they entered and focus on the various choices they made that enabled them to cope and adjust. "Barriers to Advancement" details the obstacles to upward mobility encountered by each group of women. In "Climbing over the Barriers," the women explain the ways they approached the barriers encountered and reveal their perceptions of their career progress. To a certain degree, all of the women in our study employed strategies to get ahead and to continue to ascend the corporate ladder. At the same time, they all grappled with whether they should take up the challenge of changing the workplaces they entered. In "Making Change," we explore this very issue, focusing on the differences in how black and white women perceive their role in tackling race- and gender-related injustice in their companies. As women chart their careers and navigate the corporate waters, they must repeatedly make choices about their personal lives. In the last chapter of this section, "Work Isn't Everything," we describe these choices and the women's mixed feelings and poignant perceptions about the quality and meaning of their personal lives.

5

❖

Breaking In

In "Flashbacks," we let our subjects tell us their life stories up to the point of their education. But how did these women get from college to the corporate life? How did they begin their managerial careers? Did they take similar or separate paths? A key question in our research was how women gained entry to a field that was dominated primarily by whites and males at the time these women were ready to break in.

We found that racial differences played a role in determining the way black and white women entered managerial careers. But gender played an even more powerful role. Understanding gender issues is a prerequisite to understanding these women's experiences; because managerial careers have traditionally been a male domain, as young women our subjects found their career choices restrained by societal notions of appropriate female careers.

One of the most striking similarities among the women was that few of them aspired, in the early years of their adult lives, to a career in management. While part of this can be explained by their early-life experiences, the historical moment in which the women reached the career entry stage played a major role in their early career paths. This larger social context, defining different roles and expectations for men and women, made the processes of choosing a career and entering a career distinctly different for women.[1] Traditional career theory defines "career choice" as a process of simply matching one's assets and liabilities with occupational needs in the environment, and defines the "life stage" model as a process of reevaluating career issues at different stages in one's life. But such traditional career development theories are based on research with men, whose socialization and gender support active career involvement and offer a wider range of careers from which to choose. Recently, management scholars have proposed alternative career development theories that explicitly take gender into account.[2] According to these theories, a woman must overcome gender role expectations, stereotyping of occupations, gender and race discrimination, and multiple role expectations before she even chooses a career.[3]

Therefore, our discussion of how the women entered their managerial careers must be placed within the context of prevailing social norms and beliefs about women's roles and abilities. At the time these women embarked upon their careers, there were well-prescribed societal beliefs about gender roles. Additionally, there was both race- and gender-related segregation in occupations. Understanding this historical period helps explain the women's early career choices as well as their subsequent experiences once they entered corporations.

Historical and Social Influences on Women's Career Choices

Women's Traditional Roles

The entrance of women into the managerial ranks of corporate America has a long and complex history. A majority of the women presented in the first part of this book began their careers in corporate America in the 1970s, a time when managerial positions were still dominated by whites and men. To break into corporate careers, they were up against two major structural constraints. First, they entered their careers at a time when American society still comfortably believed in the traditional domestic roles of women. Since the early nineteenth century in the United States, women's work lives have been defined by a social ideal that proclaimed home as a woman's place and the workplace as a man's place.[4]

Despite Betty Friedan's revolutionary 1966 book, *The Feminine Mystique*, which challenged the idea that women belonged in the home and is credited as the spark for the women's movement, women at the time were still largely expected to spend much of their adult lives as homemakers.[5] Even if they did attend college, young women were socialized to the idea that they would one day marry and their adult lives would be spent raising and caring for a family. For example, in the 1960s, only about a third of white women were in the paid labor force.[6] If white women did choose to work outside of the home, they were viewed as mere casual workers who entered the workplace only until they married and had children. However, this was not the case of all women. The imposed domesticity of the time had a different consequence for black women.[7] In contrast to white women, married black women were much more likely to be gainfully employed outside the home. Over 40 percent of black women were in the paid labor force during the same period.[8] Yet they were mostly confined to domestic and service work. Phyllis Wallace, in her seminal study of African-American women in the labor market, pointed out that the higher participation rate of African-American women was due to the long-term inadequacy of the earnings of African-American men.[9]

We were surprised to find in our data that few of the white women we interviewed identified the women's movement as a significant influence in their lives. Thus, the white women in our study may be part of a group of women who did not embrace or identify with the values of the feminist movement of the late '60s. A possible explanation for this finding is self-selection. Perhaps the women who did identify with the ideas of the women's movement did not end up in corporate America or had exited by the time of our interviews. Another possibility is that they may have believed or supported the women's movement as young women but now in the workforce have come to believe that issues of women and discrimination are no longer salient. In contrast, the African-American women we interviewed talked a great deal about the influence and impact of the civil rights movement on their lives.

Sex and Race Segregation in the Workplace

The second major constraint on women's career opportunities in management was sex and race segregation in the labor market.[10] Since a majority of the women in our study were born between 1945 and 1955, most would have reached the career entry stage in the late 1960s and early 1970s. In 1970, only 3.9 percent of white women workers and 1.4 percent of black women workers were employed in managerial and administrative jobs.[11] And the majority of this group were managers or supervisors in the public sector. Sex segregation and race segregation were remarkably stable features of the U.S. workplace during the twentieth century until about the mid-1970s. The best jobs, in what labor economists refer to as the primary sector, were reserved for white males. White women and racial minorities were relegated to lower paying jobs in secondary labor markets.

Consequently, the majority of the women who worked outside of the home were relegated to low-status, female-dominated occupations— service, secretarial, or caretaker positions. African-American women were overrepresented in domestic service jobs.[12] Even when sex segregation lessened and white women gained some access to better-paying factory jobs in the aftermath of World War II, African-American women continued to face discrimination and prejudice. One study reported that black women were only able to make minor entry in factories because, "industry as a whole never accepted them."[13] College-educated African-American women could only aspire to careers as teachers or social workers. Middle-class white women with college educations who applied for jobs in corporate America were likely to be channeled into secretarial and other clerical positions. Ironically, at one time secretarial and office jobs had been the gateway to managerial jobs for white men. However, when the typewriter was introduced into the office, middle-class white women were hired to operate it. Soon clerical jobs became feminized (female dominated) and no longer represented a path to managerial careers. Instead they became low-level jobs to support male managers.[14] This feminization process affected strictly white women.[15] Black women were virtually absent from secretarial and clerical jobs because of their race. This trend of white women gaining access to better jobs while black women and other women of color were barred has been a repetitive theme in analyses of the career opportunities of women.[16]

It is important to understand that gender stereotyping reinforced the sex and race structuring of managerial jobs. At the time the women entered the workplace, it was not generally accepted that a woman had the requisite skills and abilities to be an effective manager. A number of studies of women executives done in the late 1960s portrayed them as unsuitable for managerial careers. It was not unusual to find research studies and magazine headlines that asked: Can Women Be Managers? *Harvard Business Review*'s 1965 survey of its subscribers and a sample of professional business organizations found only 9 percent of male managers were favorable toward female managers. The percentage agreeing that they personally would feel comfortable working for a woman was 27 percent. Fifty-four percent of the male managers believed that women rarely expected or wanted authority.[17]

Another factor that contributed to keeping women out of the corporate suite at the time was their lack of access to an M.B.A. degree, the coveted passport to corporate success for men. During the 1960s an M.B.A. was all but unavailable to women. Many business schools did not admit women. In 1970 a mere 1,038 women earned M.B.A.'s, compared to 25,506 men.[18] For black women the numbers were far lower.[19] Antidiscrimination legislation prohibiting race and sex discrimination in the workplace did not begin to significantly affect opportunities for women until the late 1970s. It was only in the mid- to late 1980s that larger numbers of women began moving into the skilled crafts, managerial positions, and other jobs traditionally held by men.[20] The proportion of women in management positions in the United States grew from 16 percent in 1970 to 26 percent in 1980.[21]

Thus, the women in our study met both structural and cultural resistance to entering a management career. At the structural level, managerial jobs were "white male" jobs and not for women of any race. Culturally, there was the general belief that women did not possess the traits, abilities, or capacities for management.[22] Women were first expected to be homemakers; if they did venture into the workplace, they were more suited to female stereotyped jobs as teachers, librarians, social workers, nurses, or secretaries.

For black women, it was more complicated. An additional cultural factor that discouraged African-American women from entering business was the pressure to pursue a career that their parents and relatives understood and believed their daughters could be successful in. At the time these women came of age, middle-class professional African-Americans were either teachers, doctors, or lawyers—not managers. Dawn Stanley recalls her mother's indignation when she told the family she wanted to get an M.B.A. and work in business. "I called my mom to discuss my decision, and she was not impressed. She wanted to know why I wasn't going to law school. She told me since I didn't want to go to medical school, I should consider law school. Top black professionals in our community were lawyers or doctors." Part of this stemmed from their parent's unawareness of management as a career in which black women could succeed. Historically, the careers proven to be successful paths for blacks were medicine, law, and education. These were also paths with fewer entry limitations relative to management. This is a point that was not lost on the black women's parents. Consequently, they tended to socialize their daughters to select careers in familiar fields in which they could gain entry and also be successful. Black parents, especially those in the middle class, wanted to ensure that their daughters could be self-reliant.

Meandering versus Direct Paths

So how did the women in our study end up in their managerial careers? Our analysis of the early career history of the black and white women indicated two dominant paths of entry into their managerial positions: meandering and direct. These terms capture the two basic routes taken by women from the moment they completed their education to the moment they began their first managerial position in corporate America. A "managerial position" is one in which they became responsible for supervising a group of employees, managing a functional area of the business, or having responsibility for an area of the budget. A majority of the women— both black and white—took the meandering path to their careers (see Table 5-1). They did not have well-crystallized aspirations toward a career in management. They held jobs in other fields before getting into a managerial career or delayed pursuing a career because of marriage. Several of the women in this group changed their career paths by getting an M.B.A. Gloria Goldberg's experience is typical: after stints in two different law firms, she says, "getting an M.B.A. was the way to get your ticket punched to get into investment banking." About 56 percent of women in each group earned graduate degrees, but a significantly larger percentage of the black women interviewed had an M.B.A. degree (67.6 percent vs. 55 percent). This difference probably reflects black women's sense that they would need the credentials to enter a career previously closed to black women.

The few women who took a direct path typically began their business careers early in their adult lives. Early on they set their sights on entering management. Leaving nothing to chance, they laid plans and systematically followed strategies for reaching their goal. They pursued education suitable for a managerial career. They followed well-defined career tracks. They worked solely in business management. Once they entered a company, they followed traditional career ladders in their companies to reach a management position.

EARLY LIFE INFLUENCES ON CAREER CHOICE

There were three recurrent themes in the women's narratives, regardless of the path they traveled to their managerial career. First, few women reported receiving career counseling or guidance during high school. Most didn't remember talking with a guidance counselor; those who did portrayed the encounter in a negative light. Guidance counselors offered them little help in either college choice or career counseling.

Second, a majority of the women in both paths reported having parents, friends, or relatives as sources of encouragement not specifically for a managerial career but for achievement. Several research studies have demonstrated that parental encouragement is one of the most important factors in girls' career motivation.[23] The relative influence of family, relatives, and friends varied by a woman's socioeconomic class. In the case of working-class and poor African-American women many had fictive kin or guardian angels (often teachers) who provided critical social support during high school that helped them attend college. This was especially important for women whose parents did not have the material resources to pay for a college education or the knowledge or time to assist their daughters.

TABLE 5-1 *Key Characteristics of Interviewees' Managerial Career Entry*

Characteristic	Black Women	White Women
Meandering path[a]	60 percent	70 percent
Direct path[a]	40 percent	30 percent
M.B.A. degree[b]	67.6 percent	55 percent
Average number of years to first management position: Meandering path	6.5 years	6.7 years
Average number of years to first management position: Direct path[c]	3.6 years	2.1 years

[a] This was computed by examining information on career history given by interviewees, who were asked for a chronology of positions held, including job title, years in each job, and level of responsibility. We also had to rely on their narratives to build a complete chronology of their careers from the time they completed their education.
[b] These figures represent the percentage of each group with M.B.A. degrees.
[c] There was a statistically significant difference in the average number of years.

Several described in detail black teachers who turned their lives around or who bolstered their self-confidence and self-esteem. Mamie Jefferson feels strongly that she would not be in her position as vice president of merchandising for a large discount retailer if it were not for one of her black teachers. Mamie grew up in rural Texas, in what she described as "turpentine country": an area supported by turpentine extract harvested from the surrounding pine trees until the supply diminished and Mamie's family, like the other poor blacks who had settled in the area, were left to scratch out a living by other means. The segregated high school she attended had little to offer. "The school overall was not very challenging. There were no foreign languages, just a very basic curriculum." For Mamie, the only good academic program in her high school was home economics. Indeed, it was her home economics teacher who convinced her that "you can go as far as you want to go." This teacher first encouraged Mamie to pursue her interest in fashion and designing, praising her early sewing designs and prodding her to take on leadership roles during high school. Mamie went on to be valedictorian of her small rural high school. By the time she graduated from college, she knew she wanted a career in the retail fashion industry.

Black teachers were often the only role models for career-oriented young black women. Predictably, large number of the African-American women wanted to become teachers. It was this career dream that helped Eliza Washington leave behind the days she spent picking tobacco in eastern North Carolina when she was seven years old. Now in her mid-forties, she is a regional branch manager for one of the top banks in the county. Eliza described an influential teacher and the effect she had on her: "She had material signs of success—and I mean wealth that I had never seen a black person in our community have. She had a husband and two children. She was happily married and had fun on the weekends. I got to baby-sit for her. I got to sleep over in her house. I got to live in her world for a little while. She introduced me to a world of things that I had never known about. She was the first person I saw who just lived a totally different lifestyle." Her teacher paid for Eliza to visit different colleges during her senior year in high school.

By contrast, many of the middle- and upper-class women found role models in fathers who were successful in their business careers. Ours is not the only study to find that fathers act as a source of occupational identification for daughters who end up pursuing nontraditional careers.[24] Yet our study also found that many successful women grew up with mothers who were themselves employed and highly educated. This was particularly true for the middle-class black women; as a group, they had highly educated mothers with active careers as teachers, nurses, and social workers.

The final common thread in the women's life stories has to do with personality and motivation. Many of these women stressed their desire to be independent. Although the majority had no idea of what profession they would choose, having a career was viewed as a way of breaking away. This theme emerged when we asked the women to recall the visions they had for their lives as they graduated from high school and when they were twenty. Deborah Jones, who is today a senior production executive in the entertainment industry, grew up in the Bedford-Stuyvesant neighborhood of Brooklyn in a family torn apart by divorce. The tensions between her parents and her mother's subsequent decline into alcoholism left an indelible imprint upon Deborah. Her desire to be independent reflects what we heard from a number of the women, both black and white: "I knew I wanted to be able to take care of myself, to live my own life. That's really what I wanted. I had to have my own life."

MEANDERING PATHS

Sixty percent of the African-American women and 70 percent of the white women we interviewed took a meandering path to their managerial careers. As one woman put it, "I sort of wandered into it." We examined chronologies of the women's careers to determine the average number of years it took for them to achieve the first management position. On average, it took 6.5 years for black women and 6.7 years for the white women. Many of the women started in other fields. It was only later in their adult lives that they ended up in business management. Other women delayed entry because of an early marriage or postponement of undergraduate education. Their actual entry into management positions was often serendipitous. They did not engage in elaborate career strategies or tactics. Often these women just reacted to fortuitous events. The narratives of Brenda Boyd and Joyce Canton demonstrate the similarities and the differences in the meandering paths of the black and white women.

Brenda Boyd's Path. If she was uncertain about a career, Brenda Boyd was absolutely certain about one thing: she was going to take care of herself. "When I think back, I see that I always wanted to make sure that I could take care of myself. I didn't really understand what that meant, but I knew I didn't want to be dependent." Although she expected to marry one day, she also expected to work. But when she graduated from college she still had no idea what she would do. She was, in her own words, "in a complete fog." A chance meeting with the dean of the law school had sent her off to law school. But after two semesters she knew it was not the career for her. Marriage came next. Although her marriage was faltering and she was pregnant, Brenda decided to pursue a doctorate in higher education administration. She wanted a career in which she could help people improve their lives. It was something her father had instilled in her and something he strived for in his own life.

After earning her doctorate, she did a stint in the administration of a state department of higher education. Brenda realized there that she "did not have the temperament to put up with the bureaucracy and the kinds of limits placed on what could be done to help people. So I decided at that point I needed to work someplace where one could make a difference without all the red tape. I wanted to be in charge of some kind of corporate philanthropy. I wasn't sure at the time exactly what it was called, but I knew I wanted to be in that type of position." Through a fortuitous call to a friend, Brenda learned of a large company that happened to be creating a department of corporate affairs that was to have a charitable contributions program. She was hired as the department's first director and was responsible for establishing its charitable contributions programs. Seven years later, she went on to assume a senior-level position in public relations in the company.

Joyce Canton's Path. Joyce Canton was highly motivated to have a career, to leave her "little town," and to live in a big city. "I was not going to get married to anybody that I knew in high school. I was going to go on to college and one day live in a big city." Joyce worked assisting her father in his ophthalmologist office but she knew she didn't want to become an eye doctor or optician. "I never thought I would get married right after college but I had in mind that somewhere around twenty-seven or twenty-eight I'd get married. I'd go to graduate school then go to work for a few years and then I'd end up being married. I'd probably have kids by the time I was in my early thirties."

After graduating from college with a degree in political science, Joyce took off for New York City. First, she worked as a waitress. When she finally got a job as a secretary, she had to keep waiting tables to supplement her meager paycheck. After about a year, Joyce became press secretary to a congressman. Even though she liked her work, she said, "At some point along the way, I decided I did not want to be a starving journalist in the back woods of Alabama for *x* amount of years. I came to the conclusion that some financial security and flexibility were of value to me. I did not have the temperament or the lifestyle to be a starving artist and to make it in journalism." Joyce decided to go to graduate school but was uncertain about what exactly to pursue.

The lead staff person in the congressman's office had an M.B.A. and after a conversation with him, Joyce decided to get that graduate degree. "I'm not sure I had any good reasons for going to business school except that it involved one year less than law school. When I actually got to business school and was trying to figure out what aspect of this was going to make sense for me, I remember not having a clue as to what most people did after business school." During her graduate education, she figured out that marketing tapped her talent and her interests. When Joyce graduated with her degree, she interviewed with several firms and landed a job as an assistant manager in the marketing area of a Fortune 500 pharmaceutical company. Two years later, she moved to another consumer products company as a marketing manager, a position that put her on track to be a vice president.

The examples of Brenda and Joyce are typical of the women who took meandering paths to their managerial careers. Both came from middle-class backgrounds. Middle-class parents in the '50s and '60s expected their children to be well educated, whether they were male and female or whether they went on to have a "career" or not. Children of the middle class were socialized to value intellectual challenge or, as the renowned sociologist Pierre Bourdieu would put it, to build their "cultural capital."[25]

Yet neither Brenda nor Joyce received career information or career counseling during high school. As we pointed out earlier, most of the women in our study graduated from high school with little help from school counselors. This is the case even though so many of the women we interviewed were exceptional students—national merit scholars, valedictorians, salutatorians, and class leaders. Both Brenda and Joyce were star students in high school. Both went to college and graduate school. Yet Brenda and Joyce were given little help in translating their intellect and drive into professional careers. Jean Hendrick's experience echoed that of Brenda and Joyce, and she nicely summed up what we heard time after time when we asked the women to recall their plans when they finished high school: "I knew I was going to college but I didn't really think about what my career would be. I knew I liked to write and I liked acting but I didn't really think of what I would be. I never thought, for example, of being a teacher or a doctor or anything like that."

For the women in our study who grew up in poor and working-class families, however, college was not a foregone conclusion. We did not hear the kind of unqualified certainty about college that we heard in the narratives of Brenda and Joyce and of other women raised in middle-class families. Nor did all of the women from poor and working-class backgrounds attend college right after high school. As a poor young white girl, Cecilia Monroe traveled by school bus from her rural South Carolina homeland to attend elementary school and high school. She told us, "I never felt I would go to college, even though I really wanted to attend. It was really a big want in my heart. I felt like I was intelligent enough to go, but my parents were poor and they had three others to get through high school. They didn't need me to burden them, so I didn't. It was 1963. There weren't the alternatives like you have now—at least no one told me about them." So instead of going to college after high school, Cecilia went to work in a textile mill alongside her mother. It would be several years later before she attended college and earned the degree in computer programming that opened the door to a corporate job. Today Cecilia is a senior-level manager of computer applications for marketing operations at a large financial institution.

Likewise, Ruthie Mae White had little hope of going to college, having grown up in a poor black family in the segregated south. But she knew she wanted out of a life controlled by the cycle of planting and picking tobacco. She was valedictorian of her high school class and received a scholarship that enabled her to attend a historically black college, but she had to work throughout college to send money home to help support her single mother and her brothers and sisters. She had little time to plot out the arc of her career.

Both Brenda and Joyce factored in marriage when thinking about their futures. Both tended to place their occupational plans in the larger context of family and life aspirations. Other research has shown that women generally consider the implications of their occupational choice for their present and future family lives.[26] By contrast, men generally take for granted that they can consider careers without worrying about the impact of marriage. Marriage and relationships, however, have a primary role in the dreams and self-identities of many women.[27]

Serendipity, or what Mary Catherine Bateson refers to as "semidirected happenstance" in her book *Composing a Life*, played a large role for the black and white women on meandering paths.[28] These women were not systematic in their career choices but rather took an incremental approach, responding to fortuitous events and gradually learning along the way what they did or did not like. Brenda went to law school because of a chance conversation with a dean, only to realize later that she didn't like law. She got her job in corporate America through a timely call to a friend whose company just happened to be thinking about a new position. Likewise, Joyce Canton gained clarity about her career goals gradually and by happenstance. A chance conversation with an acquaintance sparked Julia Smith's interest in business. "She started me thinking about it. I said, 'Well maybe I ought take the GMAT'—the aptitude test for admission to business school. So I sort of just walked in two weeks later and took the test." Scoring in the ninety-seventh percentile, she was accepted by an Ivy League business school. From there she was recruited into her first corporate position as a financial analyst.

College itself did not clarify career goals for either Brenda or Joyce. This was typical of the women on a meandering path. Julia Smith speaks with incredulity as she talks about her life after graduating from a prestigious women's college with a degree in economics. "I had no idea of the kind of active assessment that needs to go into choosing a career. It's not that I dismissed it. I didn't even realize that it needed to be done." She describes herself as "drifting aimlessly" in the years right after college. Two masters degrees and seven years after undergraduate school, Julia Smith finally identified what she wanted to do: have a career in business.

But there are also distinct differences in the meandering paths of various women. Typically, the women who took a meandering path pursued or tried other careers before moving into management. Like many of the black women who took a meandering path, Brenda initially wanted a career that would allow her to help others. "I felt that my responsibility in life was not just to selfishly take advantage of the luck of the draw that I had in life," she said, "but instead was for me to use the luck of the draw and also my intellectual ability and leadership to help the black community as a whole." Anchoring many of the African-American women's ideas about their careers was what we call an *ethic of giving back* to the African-American community. Career anchor is a term coined by organizational scholar Edgar Schein to describe a basic value or motive that plays a significant role in forming the direction of a career. The critical feature of the career anchor is that it "serves to guide, constrain, stabilize, and integrate a person's career."[29] We did not find such a consistent career anchor among the white women.

The ethic of giving back first surfaced when we asked the women about the visions they had for their lives after high school and about the basic values they espoused at age twenty for their lives. A significant number of the African-American women wanted to be in socially relevant careers, careers that would allow them to lift up their communities. A business career did not serve this goal. As Julia Smith said, "It was the early 1970s, 1973 to be exact. Business school? I hardly knew what it was, and what little I knew indicated that it was pro-establishment, something that was going to be detrimental to black folks. It was not something I thought I would enjoy. I was an economics major and to me that was socially relevant." By the time Julia entered business school, her early impression of business had changed. But she never abandoned her desire to give to the community. "I guess somewhere along the way I realized that you could do both. One gave you the resources to do the other. There was a place for role models and if nothing else you made money you could donate. The whole notion of revolution and all that sort of business had died down. It was pretty obvious that it wasn't going to happen the way I had envisioned it."

Likewise Ruthie Mae White remembers wanting to teach "because I needed to go back and re-teach. I needed to tell people that we've got to rise above this. I needed to go back for my brothers and sisters—to reach back and grab them so they would not be lost, so it would not be tobacco farming time again. I wanted to teach more than anything, and I wanted to be a good teacher." Soon after graduating from college and getting a teaching position, however, pragmatism forced Ruthie Mae to take a job as a bank teller: "I could not earn enough teaching to send home money to help my family."

The ethic of giving back, a dimension of the culture of resistance, has a long tradition in the African-American community. In her highly original study of professional African-American women from the 1880s to the 1950s, sociologist Stephanie Shaw traces the roots of what she calls an ethic of socially responsible individualism that directed the women's lives. During a time when few African-American women achieved much formal education, those few who did were encouraged and expected to help those in their community who were less able.[30] Shaw convincingly shows that community and educational mentors joined with families to imbue African-American women with a determination to use their education in a socially responsible way.[31] This ethic is embodied in the phrase "lifting as we climb"—using individual achievement to uplift others in one's community.[32]

It may appear paradoxical that the African-American women who embraced the ethic of giving back ended up in business careers rather than sticking with their initial orientations toward helping careers. However, these women did not abandon the ethic of giving back but instead found ways to enact their commitment through the positions they hold in their corporations. In chapter 9 we demonstrate how these African-American women consciously practice the ethic of giving back by using the power and authority of their jobs.

Another difference illustrated by the narratives of Brenda and Joyce is that unlike the African-American women, a larger number of the white women started out in organizations as secretaries or clerk-typists. Even though Joyce had graduated from college, she initially worked as a secretary. Some of the women, like Abby Zeigler, a vice president of finance in a financial services company who had majored in psychology at an Ivy League college, were given typing tests during their employment interviews, even though they were applying for nonsecretarial work. Abby remembers having "absolutely no clue" about what she was going to do with her life on the day she graduated from college. She wanted to work but ended up as a secretary—a job she found incredibly boring. After four years of secretarial jobs, she changed the trajectory of her career by getting an M.B.A.

Still other white women took secretarial positions because of their understanding of the types of jobs available to women. Jean Hendrick, despite being well educated and from an upper-middle-class family, knew all too well the options available to women. She enrolled in a secretarial school after college so that she could learn to type. After a couple years as a secretary, Jean decided that the only way she would be able to dramatically alter her career was to get an M.B.A. Several of the white women who did not attend college directly after high school also began their corporate lives as secretaries. Many worked as secretaries while going to college at night. It was only after earning their undergraduate degrees in business that these women were able to move out of their secretarial positions onto paths leading to management positions.

This was the route taken by Linda Butler. At sixteen Linda was on her own. Despite her academic ability, she did not have the money to attend college after high school. So she went to work as a secretary for a large oil company, taking college courses at night. Although she completed her degree in record time for a night student, Linda worked as a secretary for several years after graduation before she had a chance to move into a supervisory position at the oil company.

DIRECT PATHS

Forty percent of the African-American women and 30 percent of the white women in our study took direct paths to their managerial careers, beginning their trek toward a managerial career early in their adult lives. Critical turning points in their careers were a result not of happenstance but of calculated strategy. Patricia Triggs and Marilyn Paul typify the women who followed direct paths.

Patricia Triggs's Path. Patricia embarked upon a management career like an arrow on its way to a bull's-eye. She set her sights on being a marketing executive during her freshman year in high school. Patricia had a vision for her life: "I saw myself being independent, having my own apartment, managing myself, doing what I wanted to when I wanted to because I wanted to do it." During her senior year in college, she signed up early for campus interviews because she wanted to be certain she had a job in marketing by the time she graduated.

Patricia landed a job on the bottom rung in marketing at a Fortune 500 consumer products company. She progressed quickly on a career path designed to lead from an assistant to a managerial post in the company. But living as a single African-American woman in a Midwest city was, in Patricia's words, "the pits." After weighing her options, she decided to pursue a different strategy, one she had observed being used by "the smarter white men in her company." She decided to pursue a job in consulting that would enable her to sharpen her analytical skills. Patricia believed the synergy between her consulting skills and her marketing experience would catapult her onto a faster management track. There was one problem: she needed an M.B.A. to work in consulting in the 1970s. So she applied to and was accepted into an M.B.A. program in an urban city. Early in her M.B.A. program, she began attending career fairs, targeting the consulting firms she had previously identified. "My strategy was to get an internship during that first summer and then be invited back into a full-time position." Her strategy worked perfectly. With an M.B.A. degree in hand, she joined one of the most prominent consulting companies in the country as a full-time associate—the only black woman associate in the company. She intended to stay there long enough to sharpen her analytical skills. After a tumultuous and trying tenure at the firm, Patricia left to take a position as a marketing manager in another large consumer products company, exactly as she had set out to do.

Marilyn Paul's Path. Marilyn grew up very much aware of her father's career as a corporate executive. Her father had an Ivy League M.B.A. and she wanted to have one herself. Her interest in business had been confirmed by a great experience selling ads for her college newspaper. She liked both selling and talking with businessmen. "I still marvel that I knocked on a fifty-year-old businessman's door and got him to buy an ad from me." So when she graduated from college she decided to work in business first and acquire hands-on experience before going to graduate school. But she did not want to go to New York and be a banker like everybody else. "I found it just stultifying," she said, "and not very challenging." A college friend suggested Marilyn contact her father, who was a corporate executive with a national retailer. Marilyn did well in her job interview with the company and was hired as an assistant buyer. In only a year, Marilyn was promoted to sales manager. She found herself managing twenty people at age twenty-two. But the position was not "intellectual enough" for Marilyn, so she decided to return to school for her M.B.A. sooner than planned. After graduating at the top of her business school class, she did not return to retailing. "It's an interesting business, but it takes a while to get to a point where you use your mind." Instead, she interviewed with consumer marketing companies and took a job as an assistant product manager in the marketing division of a Fortune 100 company. Her early career progressed like clockwork. A year and a half after joining the company, she moved up to associate product manager; a year and a half after that, she was named product manager for a major food product.

The early career paths of Patricia and Marilyn reveal critical features of the direct path. Both were interested in a career in management or business early on. Patricia had made her decision during high school and majored in business during college. Marilyn's career goal had crystallized by the time she received her undergraduate degree. Once they had a degree in hand, these women remained focused on a managerial career. Dawn Stanley also made a choice about a career in business early on. "It was during my junior year that I switched my major to business," she recalled. "I started talking to professors about being in business and wanting to manage a product or a service or something. I became real focused on working in one industry." Dawn entered the consumer products industry as an assistant product manager. She has continued on that path, rising to the level of vice president.

Because this group of women was so focused, they developed strategies to assure that they would attain their goals. When Patricia was told by campus placement that she could not interview with a certain company because she was an undergraduate, she was not deterred. Patricia describes in animated detail how she got both the interview and the job. "I knew I wanted that job—that was all I wanted. It wasn't like well, 'I'll just go on another interview or just change my career plans.' That was what I wanted, and I felt I had to have it. On the day the company came to the campus, I went to where they were holding the interviews—all suited up, résumé in hand—and just sat outside the reception area. When the interviewer came out to let one student go and pick up the next one, I intercepted him and said, 'I know you're not here to interview under-graduate students, but I have a particular interest in your company and here's why. Here's my résumé. I live on campus and I will be at this num-ber all day so if somebody is five or ten minutes late or you want a cup of coffee, call me and I'll be over here in five minutes.' He said okay. I went back to my room and sat by the phone. He called me. I was there in five minutes. We interviewed and he invited me to visit the company's head-quarters. I went to corporate headquarters and had dinner with a brand manager and two other managers. The next day they made me an offer on the spot." Similarly, Marilyn impressed her friend's dad with her desire to get into business. She, too, had her first job by the end of the interview.

Another salient characteristic of the women who followed the direct path is that they started out in a position in which they could move up in a well-defined way. All of the women in this group landed positions that were in traditional corporate career tracks. Patricia's first position was in marketing in a consumer products company, which "was the hub of the business. My company was a leading-edge company and my job was in the career I had chosen for myself. I planned to make a career there." The usual track in her company was explicit: first you were promoted to brand assistant, then to assistant brand manager, and eventually to brand man-ager. For Marilyn, an equally defined track lay before her: from assistant product manager to marketing director and eventually to vice president.

The major difference we found between black and white women who took a direct path was in the number of years it took them to advance from an entry-level position to their first management position. On aver-age it took white women 2.1 years to be promoted to management; for African-American women it took 3.6 years. In other words, on average African-American women spent 1.5 years longer in nonmanagerial jobs when they entered their companies. (See Table 5-1.) This is an important comparison because it is between black and white women who took a direct path, those who were the most motivated early on to a career in management. They entered right after college or upon completion of an M.B.A. degree. The different time frame for achieving a management position may help to explain why the white women in this study had progressed farther than African-American women in the managerial hierarchy. Of the women we interviewed, 45 percent of the white women were in upper-level management positions, compared to 19 percent of the African-American women. Previous research has shown that even small differences in upward mobility at the early stage of a managerial career can have a heavy impact on the later stages.[33]

This relatively slower pace reflects, we believe, the different obstacles the women encountered as they entered corporations. All women met resistance—whether they entered a bank, a consumer products corporation, a manufacturing firm, or a high-tech company. The commonalities in the resistance encountered tell us something about the strength of gender in the workplace and the extent to which managerial careers are steeped in patriarchal ideology. But black women met more resistance. As Cynthia Cockburn points out in her book on sex equality in organizations: "Despite social legislation for equal opportunity for women and racial minorities, white men were not about to let down the drawbridge on their castles."[34] But this was just one of the challenges women confronted in the early stages of their careers.

6

❖

FITTING IN

REGARDLESS OF THE PATH they took to their careers, all of the women we interviewed had to adjust to the organizational cultures they encountered.[1] Not only did they have to learn how to be a manager, but they also had the extra burden of coping with organizational cultures that were largely white male domains. What were the women's perceptions of the corporate environments and cultures they entered? What were their expectations? What conflicts did they experience because of their gender, race, and class of origin? How did they respond to the cultures they found? What lessons did they take away from these early career experiences? Such questions address what is known as *organization socialization,* defined by organization studies scholars as the ways in which newcomers change and adjust to an organization.[2] Ultimately, organization socialization involves the match between individuals and the organizations in which they work.[3] A complex process, socialization includes achieving role clarity, confronting and accepting organizational reality, fitting in with the norms and values of the organization, and locating oneself in the organizational context.[4]

According to scholars, the socialization process hinges on what is known as the "unique dynamic of conflict," which sets socialization apart from other types of learning that newcomers acquire after entering an organization.[5] Conflicts can occur between the newcomer's expectations and values and those of the organization. The rate at which newcomers become socialized is determined by the amount of interaction between newcomers and insiders, because these interactions allow the conflicts over expectations and values to play out. Naturally, the potential for conflict is a function of the number of differences between newcomers and insiders.

Although much has been written about the organization socialization process, it has not been systematically examined through the lenses of race, gender, and class.[6] Our analyses of women's socialization must incorporate these lenses, because their entrance into the corporate world created an interface between people of different genders and races. A majority of the women we interviewed were either the first woman in their company to enter a managerial position or part of a very small cadre of women managers. African-American women were often not only the first of a different gender but also the first of a different race. In addition, not all of the women had a middle-class background, with its associated indoctrination to the cultural and social conventions of the managerial profession. White women from poor and working-class backgrounds had to cross both gender and class lines; while black women from poor and working-class backgrounds had to cross three lines—gender, race, and class—as they entered a middle-class profession dominated by white men. While there were a number of similarities in the way our subjects perceived adjustment conflicts, we found significant differences between the experiences of black and white women, especially with respect to how quickly organizational fit was achieved. We also found differences in how the two groups of women chose to respond to the organizational cultures they entered.

Solos and Tokens

"I had never felt so disadvantaged as a black woman," said Brenda Boyd as she reflected upon what it was like to be the lone black woman manager in the manufacturing plant of a Fortune 500 company. "It was very difficult. I entered a company where the whole world was the world of men. Everything was male culture. That's when I knew the feminists were right. There's a woman's culture and a man's culture. They used different language, had different mores. I had to learn white male culture. I had to learn the culture of baseball and football. None of my analogies, none of my metaphors were appropriate. They didn't understand what I said. They could not believe I was good for the business. It was just a brutal environment. It was sometimes a lonely, demoralizing experience. I never had peers to talk with. So I had to learn how to be particularly diplomatic so as not to be misunderstood." Although Brenda projects utter confidence today, sitting in her large, well-furnished office, she admits that, "it wasn't easy for me to have lunch with women friends in those days. I was at a [manufacturing] plant. It was not downtown. We had an executive dining room for a good reason—because we weren't near a lot of restaurants. So, most days, I'd go into the executive dining room. Imagine a big room, full of big tables, full of big white men—all of whom, every day, would greet me with that stoic, stony blue-eyed look. Then they'd drop their eyes back to their plates and continue eating. I mean, there might be seventy-five people in there eating and of that seventy-five, there might be one or two friendly faces."

Maxine Schneider found herself described as the first woman buyer in the large retail company she joined after graduating from college. It began the day she entered the company. "One week into my training program they called me in and said, 'We'll let you be the guinea pig. We're going to make you an assistant buyer in furniture but you're going to fail. The competition was between thirty-two men and me. All the buyers were male and all the assistant buyers were male. You had all male salespersons except for two women. The only female at a high level was in interior decoration."

Two important points are found in Maxine's story. First, she was put into an area of the company that was purely a male domain. Buyers had power; buyers made decisions about what stock the company would carry and sell. Second, not only was she breaking new ground for women in her company, but the male buyers in the company did not expect her to do well. If Maxine were to fail, it would "prove" that women can't be buyers.

Like Brenda Boyd and Maxine Schneider, a majority of the women we interviewed entered corporations where there were few if any women managers in their departments or in the entire company. One of the first shocks for these women was simply being the first or one of the first in a white male domain. Brenda perceived the culture as alien; none of her previous experiences and ways of being helped her fit in. She felt she did not even know the language. And her white male colleagues failed to understand her. Well-known organization scholar Rosabeth Moss Kanter, in her theory of proportional representation, labeled this phenomenon "tokenism"—a generalized person phenomenon that results from being rare and scarce within a dominant group. In Kanter's theory tokens are "the few of a different type in an organization with a numerically dominant type."[7] Within the set of tokens there is a subset, the "solos"—"the only one of their kind present."[8] (Kanter's theory focused primarily on gender tokenism, and looking through the gender lens helps us to understand one layer of the issues the women in our study faced as they adjusted to corporate life. In our study, however, race added another layer that Kanter's theory does not address.)

Kanter's theory suggests that women who hold token positions will experience distinct problems at work compared to peers working in settings whose gender composition is balanced. According to Kanter, tokens experience three special sources of pressure in the workplace: visibility, contrast, and assimilation. As tokens, Brenda Boyd and Maxine Schneider were subjected to high visibility. Rather than benefiting them in a positive way, visibility tends to create performance pressures on tokens. Dominant group members can perceive that tokens have been preferentially selected and are not truly qualified.[9] The women's token status meant they had to perform under a different set of expectations and conditions than male managers. Maxine was even referred to as the "guinea pig" and was fully not expected to meet the performance expectations. Brenda's white male colleagues could not believe she "was good for the business." As tokens, they were viewed not as individuals but as representatives of all professional women of their kind. Maxine's placement in a nontraditional department for women made her a floor piece much like the furniture she had to sell to prove her competence. Her performance would be taken as a sign of how all women could perform.

Another effect of tokenism that the women in our study experienced is the exaggeration of their differences from white male managers. Kanter argues that the presence of a different type causes the dominant group to underline its culture, thereby heightening boundaries between themselves and tokens. Brenda was kept outside the circle of men eating in the cafeteria. She was not invited to sit and join them for lunch. She could not break into the camaraderie of the men. They had a different language, a different culture (of "baseball and football"). If the women were to become insiders, they were expected to assimilate to the culture of the dominant group.

Many of the women also talked of the sheer loneliness and isolation of being the only one of their kind. Gloria Goldberg, who joined an investment-banking firm after completing her M.B.A., said, "This may sound obnoxious, but I was fairly sure of my abilities. But it gets lonely when you're the first woman banker in a place. All the top people in the firm were white men, most were Catholic, and 95 percent of them came from the same college."

Double Tokenism

Like Brenda, many of the African-American women described the overwhelming sense of isolation they felt as the lone African-American woman. Brenda's isolation was compounded by the fact that her work site was physically distant from a more diverse location where perhaps she might have encountered other African-Americans. In a real sense, she was simultaneously a racial token and a gender token. This kind of double tokenism created a unique set of challenges for the African-American women as they started their managerial careers.[10] Our national survey data reveals sharp differences between the African-American women and white women when it comes to the experience of being solos and tokens. While 41 percent of the African-American women managers felt they had to always perform better than their male colleagues, only 15 percent of the white women felt this way. Nearly 40 percent of the African-American women reported they did not have other black women who could serve as role models. Only 17 percent of the white women reported they did not have white women who could serve as role models.

Other research has reported that racial tokenism increases stress on workers.[11] Living with a double token status proved especially daunting to the African-American women managers in our study. One critical issue the African-American women described was whether to confront racism or to ignore it. Deborah Jones recalled the seminal incident in her job as a consultant with a prominent national firm that forced her to deal with racism: "This one was painful, definitely painful. I was working on a very hard, complex, and demanding consulting assignment where most of the contact was by telephone. I was dealing with this woman on the phone and we were chatting. We start laying out what she wants to do. She was really representing her boss. We go through all of this stuff, and I tell her we need to meet. At the meeting, she discovers that I am black. She then tells my firm that she doesn't want to work with me and asks whether they can put somebody else on this. My boss comes to me. Now, he is trying to find a way to tell me this without it coming out that she doesn't want to work with a black person. My boss is squirming in his chair and bouncing all around in my office. He never could actually come out and say it that day. The next day the manager of our office talks to me, because I had told my boss that I wasn't getting off the client. I absolutely refused. Eventually they did take me off the project, and they had to tell me it was because I was black."

"It is the only time in the whole time I was at the company or since that time that I cried. It was so painful to me because I felt they didn't want to back me up. I felt betrayed. It told me something about the company. I learned a real good lesson. I figured out how I was going to start dealing with my company, what I would give for the company and what I wouldn't give. And I came to understand how I would deal with white people, because up until that point I hadn't seriously thought about it. I was just dealing with them the way I would deal with anybody. After that incident, I always questioned. I would ask them up front if it was going to be a problem. I would say, 'Don't bullshit me, because I've had enough experiences in here to know that this is obviously an issue for some clients, so I want to know if my race is a problem before I get started.'"

In Deborah Jones' case, confronting racism head on, forcing her colleagues to confront racism was her way to survive in her company. (This mode of survival will be explored further in chapter 8.)

Karen Brown also found confrontation important to maintaining her sense of competency and not internalizing racism. After her boss had sent Karen at the last minute to represent the department at an important meeting, Karen chose to spell out what it meant to be the only black woman. "I went to my boss's office and I said to her: 'You know, I was not only embarrassed because I was late, but it was really awful as the only black woman—the only black person—in that room among all middle-aged white men in horn-rimmed glasses, for me to walk in late.' I told her I didn't appreciate her letting me know at the last minute because I should have been better prepared. I was not able to say anything at the meeting. Of course, they looked at me as if I was an ass, which I was. Now, I didn't do this in an angry way. I did it in a very direct way. What I found from that experience made me feel good. I didn't carry it around with me, and I didn't bottle the anger up inside. When I can figure out a way to articulate things in a business setting and get it out, then I am far better off emotionally. It doesn't drag me down. I don't get shut down."

Not all of the African-American women used a confrontational style to cope with the racism they encountered. Julia Smith much more subtly bolstered her sense of worth and dignity. She strategically placed all of her award plaques, diplomas, and special citations, including an invitation to the White House, on the wall behind her desk so they will be visible to whoever is sitting in the chair facing her. Her actions can be viewed as a form of self-protection. During the interview she tells us this is her way of reminding those who enter her office that she is an accomplished woman. Julia also has expensive, beautiful African-American art displayed on the shelves in her office. The African-American art keeps her grounded and in touch with her racial identity and cultural legacy. For African-American women, coming to terms with how they would respond to these racial hurdles was critical to remaining resolute and confident throughout their careers.

Fitting In versus Not Fitting In

One of the lessons the African-American women seem to take away from their early career experiences is the realization that they would probably never truly fit in their organizations. The survey data also support this conclusion. When asked whether they agreed with the statement "I feel accepted and a member of my company's team," only 51 percent of the African-American women agreed, compared to 81 percent of the white women. (In the next chapter we will discuss the constant reminders African-American women received that they did not belong.) The African-American women had to find a way to maintain a sense of worth and psychological well-being in an environment that constantly reminded them they didn't belong.

What comes through strongly in the descriptions of African-Americans' early years in corporate America was their ability to distinguish between what around them was a result of their own capabilities and what reflected racism or other external causes. We define this ability as "defensive efficacy."[12] It is clearly an outgrowth of the armoring they received as young black girls. A strong racial identity also helped the women have a firm sense of self-efficacy (belief in one's own competency) and helped them not internalize negative perceptions of their competence.[13] Defensive efficacy helped them to maintain self-confidence in the face of both the subtle and the sometimes blatant acts of racism they encountered in the early years of their corporate careers. Without defensive efficacy, such messages might have diminished their personal agency and derailed their managerial careers at an early stage.

The black women talked a good deal about coming to understand the

inherent hierarchical, competitive, and political nature of most of the corporations they entered. It also meant coming to terms with the fact there
was not always a direct relationship between ability and upward mobility. This realization was crucial to their surviving setbacks or low points
early in their careers. A case in point is the experience of Patricia Triggs,
who had resolutely set her goal of becoming a marketing executive while
she was still in school. "I must have done seven or eight projects the first
year," Patricia Triggs told us. "Each for a different partner, a different team,
a different client, and a different issue. I did extremely well on all the jobs.
I knew this because I got detailed written reviews after each project. So I
could prove I had done extremely well. I could even show I started from
a point of doing very good work to having everything in the excellent column. The notation on my evaluation was 'she is extremely promotable
and should be groomed.' So I'm feeling pretty good, working eighty to
ninety hours a week. I have no social life but I'm busting out, learning
loads. I am expecting that when I get my annual review I'll not only get a
good review but also an incredibly huge raise. Well, the two partners on
my review committee—who by design have never worked with the person
being reviewed—gave me an awful appraisal. It basically said, 'You can't
even think and chew gum at the same time.'"

"I got a very small raise. I was utterly and totally devastated. I wasn't
upset or irate. I was just taken aback, thrown off guard. I just felt hurt. 'How
could they?' and 'Why me?' I asked. I realized later that they just liked to
down people. This was a consulting firm. Consulting firms are not public
entities. They are privately held firms. The money belongs to the partners.
There's no human resource department. I was dogged because it was kind
of a partner's game and everybody's a pawn. I don't think it was all racially
driven. They dogged people big time. So I could look around at my peers,
people who were interns with me, and see that they had been dogged badly
on different scales. So I just regrouped. That's what saved me, saved my own
sense of pride and humanity as a black woman. I thought about why I was
there. I was there for quick salary appreciation, which was obviously not
forthcoming at the company. But I knew I would get it when I left. I was
there for industry exposure and I was getting that. I said to myself 'Well,
you're getting what you came for.' But my plan was to eventually leave."

Colleen Powell used similar terms to describe the lessons she learned
as a managerial trainee in a large bank. "Basically the learning that sticks
in my mind as a black person is that you must respect yourself. You must
respect your capabilities. You must make others respect you. You should

never let anybody trample upon you, regardless of who they are. I know who I am and I feel very comfortable with who I am. I have learned to have confidence in myself."

Thus, in forming a professional identity within their organizations, African-American women worked from the understanding that they would never truly fit in. Instead of becoming a position of weakness, this understanding became an energizing force, giving them what sociologist Patricia Hill Collins refers to as outsider-within status.[14] Outsider-within status exists when one is located on the boundary between two groups statuses—one with potential power and the other with little power. Thus, black women managers technically have membership in a high-status group—they are powerful by virtue of their credentials and titles—yet as black women they are members of a group that has traditionally had low power and status in society. So despite their access to insider culture, African-American women managers remain outsiders. They can never gain the full insider power accorded white male executives because of their race and gender. As a consequence, they do not feel fully accepted. The overall sense we got from the women's narratives was that they felt tolerated but not fully accepted. As one interviewee succinctly put it, "I feel like a guest in somebody's house." One factor that contributes to commitment to an organization is feeling comfortable in your relationship to it.[15] Feeling more tolerated than accepted undermines feelings of comfort and commitment for African-American women managers.

In contrast, we found that white women responded differently to the cultures they encountered. The white women as a group entered corporations with a certain amount of ingenuousness. Most admitted not being prepared for the corporate cultures they entered and most did not expect to have difficulty fitting in. Maxine Schneider spoke in a slightly embarrassed tone about her early career days. "No one ever said to me: 'It's going be difficult.' I didn't go in thinking it was going to be hard. I came in with this real positive, open mind. I didn't have on a gray flannel suit. In 1972, no one was telling us what we had to look like or not look like." Jean Hendrick was no less naïve in her expectations: "The day I arrived at the company I knew I wanted to become one of the very few female officers. There was no question in my mind that that's what I wanted, and I was positive that I was capable of doing it. To me it was only a matter of time before they realized that's what I should be." She laughed, hearing herself. "It didn't occur to me that it was going to be a process of making many different moves and proving many different things." For Gloria Goldberg, it was the office politics she hadn't anticipated. "The politics and sabotage were difficult to deal with at the time," Gloria told us. "The work, oddly, once you gained confidence, was hard but always doable. I was capable. The sheer stabbing in the back—what people would do—was something I wasn't ready for and wasn't good at."

We believe the women's naïve expectations stem from the messages they received as young girls. The overwhelming message, especially to middle-class white women, was a gender-neutral message—"You can be anything you want to be."[16] Most were not prepared for gender discrimination. As Jean Hendrick told us, "My mother never gave me advice about being a woman. She gave me advice about being a person." The messages they received made many feel they were not constrained by their gender. While this had the positive effect of bolstering their drive, it also created a certain amount of naïveté about what to expect once they entered their managerial careers.

Unlike the white women, the black women were socialized by parents and relatives to be prepared to encounter racism. While they were encouraged to achieve, they were also armored and cautioned about the obstacles they might encounter. We believe this armoring did not immobilize them but rather allowed them to persevere in spite of the racism and sexism they encountered. The black women also received encouragement to reach beyond society's racist constraints, which helped them to reach beyond traditional career restraints as well. As Julia Smith remembers, "My mother and father told me that I would experience racism; but they taught me not to be paralyzed because I was a black girl. They pushed me and said that I could do whatever I wanted to do and I could go beyond." So while both black and white women received similar messages about "being anything they wanted to be," black women learned either from their parents or through early life experiences to expect discrimination.

It did not take the white women in our study long to feel intimidated by the male-dominated environments they entered. Consequently, they had to learn to overcome the uncertainty they felt. Gloria Goldberg recalled how she quietly developed confidence. "At the brokerage firm when I was working as a runner, it was just amusing to observe men. At that point I was still in awe of them—their cleverness and power. I was also a bit scared of them. It didn't take long for me to realize that these guys were no smarter than me. In my next job, I was suppose to sit at meetings and take notes and not say anything. I remember sitting there thinking, 'I could have thought up this stuff.' It was a very funny revelation. I realized I was as good as any of the other guys out there. I could do this stuff and maybe do it even better than they could. I was good no matter what somebody said. I was good." Jean Hendrick had to overcome feeling intimidated when making presentations to her male colleagues. "However frightening it was, you could get through it. They weren't going to ask you every single thing I was terrified they would ask; they were basically on my side and wanting to like the idea rather than wanting to criticize or rip it to shreds. It was not as hard as I feared it would be. Preparing thoroughly, intricately, was absolutely necessary. I memorized my stuff. I remember saying to my mother at one point on the phone, 'Well, I'll tell you one thing. I could never work at this company and have a baby because it takes up so much—it takes up every ounce of energy I have."

What difficulty the white women encountered did not necessarily lead to outrage. Typically, the women accepted the cultures they entered and tried to fit in. Ann Gilbert, who knew she wanted a career in business early on, told us, "I was very fortunate to have the father I had, and I attribute a lot of my success to him. But there was a certain naïveté too; it took me a long time in the workforce before I realized there was discrimination and before I realized that's just the way it was. I wasn't going to fight the system." Marilyn Paul, whose career has progressed steadily in the company she first entered over twenty years ago, told us, "This is an incredibly open organization for women. I am sure being a black woman entering a company in 1982 was very different from me joining the company in 1982. But I never really found being a woman to be an issue here."

How the two groups of women responded to the corporate environments they entered is a major source of disjuncture between the women. African-American women expressed much more awareness of racism and sexism in their companies and seemed much more willing to speak out against injustices. The white women as a group were relatively less vocal about injustices.[17] Even though they encountered exclusionary practices and often hostile corporate environments because of their gender, they seemed to believe they could fit in by doing the right things. Again, we believe these differences can best be explained by the intersection of race and gender. White women managers in organizations share the same race as the men who dominate managerial positions. This seems to create an unconscious expectation that racial commonality would afford them some of the privileges and benefits enjoyed by white male managers. Race privilege is not a bargain for white women, however. It comes with the price of gender subordination. As sociologist Aida Hurtado points out, "The invitation to power is only a pretended choice for white women because, as in all cases of tokens, their inclusion is dependent on complete and constant submission."[18] Black women managers have neither race privilege nor gender privilege in organizations. Thus, their struggle is not trying to fit in but finding a different way to claim a professional identity in their organizations. Our conclusions are consistent with another study that found that white female managers reported levels of organizational fit comparable to their male counterparts. African-American managers—both male and female—reported achieving less fit.[19]

One way the women learned "the right things" was through white male role models. Because there were so few women in corporations at the time these women began their careers, men became their managerial role models. Sandra Martin, who today is perched to assume a top management position in her company, revealed, "One of the things I noticed when I came to work was that there were no female role models at all. The only woman I ran across in my division was the worst person I could have modeled myself after. She was the only vice president I knew and all I learned from her was what never to be. So I really took my cue from men. I was surprised because the woman's movement was going on, and I thought I would be the last woman to get in this company. That was not true. Instead I was one of the first women to start up through the ranks."

Likewise, Linda Butler spoke about the very supportive male mentors who helped her during the early part of her career. She credits them with helping her move from a secretarial position to a line position in the company and eventually into management. "While they still saw me as a little girl or somebody to pamper and bring candy and flowers to when I did something special for them, the men didn't mind answering the questions I had. They were a tremendous influence on me in my early time at the company. I don't know whether they realized that's what they were doing. Perhaps they did, but they were very supportive. As a matter of fact, one of them really helped me over the years by explaining the technical aspects of the work. I don't know whether they thought I was the daughter they didn't have or the granddaughter or whatever."

None of the black women interviewed related stories about white male managers treating them "like daughters." Nor did the black women speak of white male managers as role models. African-American women were more likely to tell stories that indicated a lack of support, and none described a father-daughter type relationship with white males.

Learning to Be a Manager

Beyond fit issues, what lessons did these women learn about being a manager as they attempted to launch their careers? There appear to be four important ones: how to develop good relationships with others, how to figure out their own "managerial style," how to face tough issues, and how to work through their employees. Male managers must follow the same learning curve, but can do so without the double burden faced by women. Black and white women managers must learn to be a manager while simultaneously dealing with gender issues. Black women managers have to contend with racism as well as sexism.

A dominant theme in learning to be a manager was the importance of developing relationships with others in the company. Sandra Martin describes how she came to understand the importance of having good relationships: "One of my early bosses, James, made a deal with me. He said, 'If you stay for one more year, I'll let you go.' And I made that deal. It was no advantage to me at the time, but in the long run it paid off." The performance of Sandra's division was excellent that year, and she was promoted into the line side of the business. "I believe a lot of your success, your long-term success, depends on your relationships with people. You do people favors sometimes when there is no payback to you immediately. At first I thought I had stayed a year too long in a job that did nothing for my career but in reality it was a good decision."

All of the women, both black and white, talked about coming into their own managerial styles. "My first managerial job was as a branch manager," Ann Gilbert recalled. "I learned about managing a team effort." Alice Booth, who today is a vice president in a large utility company, told us, "I learned that one person can't do it all and how important it is to delegate in order for the other person to learn—even when it's much easier for you to do it yourself."

Sandra Martin said she learned that facing tough issues was part of being a good manager. "I felt like I had a knack for it. I learned from my early work experience that you have to face the tough issues. You cannot let them go. I also learned that I liked the decision process involved in being a manager." Mamie Jefferson learned quickly as an assistant buyer in her first managerial position, "You get what you want by motivating other people in a positive way. I knew I couldn't do all the work myself. I needed other people." Sometimes the women learned how to work through employees' early mistakes. Ruthie Mae White recalled that one day, soon after she'd been made a manager, the bank tellers purposely came to work thirty minutes after opening time. "Although I loved management, I realized how unequipped I was to be a manager. I had learned the technical aspects of the job but I had never learned the management aspects. And that was a valuable lesson at the time." Karen Brown recalled, "I remember wanting to have people do it exactly the way I wanted it done. I figured out soon enough that those people who had been working there a long time probably knew a little bit more than I did because I had just walked in on the scene."

Career Turning Points

Early in their careers, all of the women had to clear the hurdle from an entry-level position to a full-fledged managerial position. A majority of the women identified a significant turning point in their early careers that pushed them to a new level of performance and responsibility. It was often a make-or-break situation. For the majority of the women, that turning point was either doing well in a particularly challenging job assignment or being placed in a position where they were no longer in a "learning mode" but in one that required them to produce results. A turning point for Patricia Triggs came when she was made marketing manager. "It was the first time I had control. I was driving as opposed to following." Colleen Powell's turning point came when she was placed in charge of financial operations for a foreign subsidiary. "This was learning something entirely new, a much more risky situation because of all the nuances of doing business in a foreign country. It was dealing with field operations. It was dealing with a different culture and trying to learn the operations of the business." The turning point in Anna Smalls' career came in an investment company when she realized she had to ask her clients for their business. "Although I had been visiting clients and sending them information, they weren't giving me their business. I wasn't making them feel guilty about not giving us the business." Once she learned to ask for the business, she was successful in increasing the number of deals she brought to the company. For Sandra Martin the turning point was being aggressive and asking for a higher-level job she wanted. "I came to work with the bank making nothing. I was doing analyst work for the company. One of the two people in my department had a job I coveted.

The person in the job did not like the job and wanted to transfer out of it. So the day I heard that he was getting transferred I put a note on my boss's desk that said, 'I want his job.' Now I had only been there six months and I wanted to beat everybody else to the punch. So I made sure my boss knew that I wanted the job. Then I was in there early the next morning and I said, 'I'm serious. I want to do that job.' I got it, which made me the senior person in the department."

For Gloria Goldberg a turning point came when she starting putting together deals. "It was my decision what a company was valued at, how it was negotiated, and how it was presented."

Linda Butler's challenge came when she was put in an assistant manager position. "I think the biggest challenge was when I went to one of our local offices as a manager. I had been in a staff department for several years and then went to an office as assistant manager. It was a new program. We had not had assistant managers before. So the current manager did not know why I was there. I think he might have felt threatened. He didn't know what to do with me so his solution was to let me handle all the safety matters and all the training, then watch him do everything else. About the only time I really got any good management experience is when he was gone and something happened that I was able to take care of myself. My vice president could see that I could handle things. So when my manager moved on, I was made manager. I was the first female manager at the company's largest metropolitan office."

Marilyn Paul's turning point came "when I became a category manager. I had spent five years in new product development, and I had a lot of responsibility but I didn't have the intense pressure of a brand being mine. As a category manager, I became responsible for the brand's success or failure."

These turning points were key to advancing our subjects' careers. When the women finally understood that meeting these challenges or demonstrating performance meant success in their positions, their careers took off. From then on, challenges could be put before them and they would use those to move themselves from entry-level positions to high-level positions. A key to advancement for the women was to be put in a challenging position and to grasp the measure of performance.

Perhaps Dawn Stanley best captured what we heard from a number of the women about the transition from a nonmanagerial to a managerial position when she said: "Coming up the line you have to manage relationships and getting the work done with other resource groups. But once you get into a managerial role you have your own assistants and associates reporting to you. It was big. It was scary. A nonmanagerial position had to do with knowing your own capabilities. You know you can get the work done and get it done right. But in a managerial position you have to worry about your staff doing what they're supposed to be doing. You don't have time to go through all of the details. So you learn to ask questions, set priorities, and trust people to get things done with enough guidance. It's very different. I think I did a reasonable job, but I know I had a lot of things I could have done much better. But you learn."

Having an opportunity to produce tangible results was a critical experience for all of the women in the early years of their careers. What almost all of these women discovered after getting their foot in the door was that simply doing the job was not enough. It would take much more to move up the managerial ladder and successfully navigate their way in corporate America. The race- and gender-related dynamics they encountered early in their careers did not disappear but continued to surface and affect their career progress.

7

❖

BARRIERS TO
ADVANCEMENT

MUCH HAS BEEN WRITTEN both in the popular press and in academic circles about the glass ceiling blocking women's advancement to top-level positions in corporate America.[1] The metaphor aptly captures the dilemma of women managers trying to rise to the top.[2] However, when the effects of race and gender are taken into account, the metaphor is insufficient.

The obstacles to advancement perceived by the black women managers were different both in degree and kind from the obstacles perceived by white women managers. As black women, they were subjected to a particular form of sexism shaped by racism and racial stereotyping.[3] The theoretical concept of *racialized sexism* also captures the idea that the experience of gender discrimination in the workplace depends on a woman's race.[4] For black women managers, sexism is entwined with racism. To understand the perceptions of black women managers regarding the barriers they encountered, we must imagine a two-dimensional structure: a concrete wall topped by a glass ceiling.

National Survey Results

Our survey data offers a quantitative picture of the differences we found. First and foremost, the white women managers in our national survey made greater progress in reaching upper-level management positions. Thirty-two percent of the white women managers were in top-level management positions compared to 14 percent of the African-American women managers surveyed. When we analyzed the respondents' employment histories, we found important differences. The proportion of jobs held that were demotions for black women was considerably greater than for white women. Similarly, black women tended to make more lateral moves in their companies than white women. The difference in managerial levels is also reflected in salary level differences. Twenty-seven percent of the white women were earning $100,000 or more, compared to 10 percent of the African-American women. A larger percentage of the white women managers (67 percent) were satisfied with their career progress; only 58 percent of African-American women managers were satisfied. One of the important keys to career advancement is proving one's ability in "line positions"—jobs that have direct impact on a company's bottom line. The white women surveyed had an edge over the black women in gaining experience in line positions (70 percent versus 61 percent).

As a consequence, we found less satisfaction among the African-American women with their present positions. Sixty-two percent of the African American women managers surveyed agreed with the statement, "I am satisfied with my current position," compared to 75 percent of the white women. While 74 percent of the white women agreed with the statement, "I have considerable decision-making power in my position," only 59 percent of the African-American women agreed. White women managers perceived their current responsibilities to be more significant than African-American women did, and they also believed to a much greater degree that their jobs allowed them to use their skills and knowledge. These differences existed even though there were no differences in the educational levels of the black and white women managers in our sample.

There were also significant differences in perceptions of relationships with colleagues. The African-American women managers were more inclined to feel that they had to outperform their white colleagues—both male and female—to succeed. African-American women had less positive perceptions of their relationships with their bosses and colleagues. Consequently, they reported receiving less collegial support than did the white women managers in the survey. Generally, the white women surveyed were more positive than African-American women about their organizations' overall management of race and gender relations and commitment to the advancement of women and people of color. African-American women did not feel their companies were implementing policies that would advance people of color.

Perceptions of the Concrete Wall

Our interviews supported much of what we found in our national survey. We asked women about obstacles to their career advancement, about how they saw the road to the top in their corporations, and about how they felt about the progress of their careers. While there were some similarities between how black and white women perceived obstacles to career advancement, there were also a number of striking differences in their perceptions. Our goal here is not to suggest that one group of women experienced greater or lesser challenges in the workplace, but rather to illuminate the specific nature of the barriers as perceived by the women themselves. The stories of Karen Brown and Jean Hendrick give depth to the responses we heard during our interviews.

Karen Brown's career moved smoothly upward for the first eight years after college. She had advanced well beyond her initial position as a management trainee with a large retailer, and her career showed steady progress, with promotions every two years like clockwork. But she hit a wall in her fourth position as sales manager, a position "reserved only for men" where "there certainly weren't any blacks." The white men she worked with, in her words, "treated me with such disrespect." She faced constant challenges to her authority and almost daily incidents of racism. Her boss ignored her but constantly complained about her poor performance to the personnel department. "He never even came to my office. He never talked to me—never said one word to me. There was one incident where I had a lot of work to prepare for something and did all of it but two things. I had arranged for two of the guys I worked with to do these two things while I was away, but they didn't do them." Karen was blamed for the incomplete work. Then she was asked to return to her old position as an assistant sales manager. It was a demotion. To advance her career, Karen had to leave the company.

The day she arrived at the company where she has spent nineteen years, Jean Hendrick knew she wanted to become one of the few female officers. "There was no question in my mind that's what I wanted. I was positive I was capable of doing it. To me it was only a matter of time before *they* realized that's what I should be doing." But her climb up the corporate ladder wasn't that simple. She became an officer after eight years, which she describes as "a big deal, especially for women." Less than two years later, she was promoted to vice president. At the time she had her baby, she was the first female officer to have a child. Then the promotions slowed, and she languished between lateral moves. Finally, seven years later, she was promoted to a group vice president position. Jean has been told by more than one male colleague to dress less colorfully and to talk less about her children. "I've been criticized for being too dramatic, too emotional, whatever. In other words, I was asked to be more like them, more like the men." She wonders if she will be able to move higher, into the very top echelon of the company. "The company has become suddenly chauvinistic. In the past they were, and then they weren't. Maybe it's just a little bit of a growing pain. I'm trying to be optimistic. A lot of women are feeling it now."

While the glass ceiling represents the inability of women like Jean Hendrick to rise above a certain level in the corporate hierarchy, the concrete wall facing African-American women managers is more persistent and more pernicious. It manifests itself in six ways: daily doses of racism, being held to a higher standard, the invisibility vise, exclusion from informal networks, challenges to authority, and hollow company commitment to the advancement of minorities.

DAILY DOSES OF RACISM

One of the most distinctive elements of the concrete wall is what we call "daily doses of racism." The everyday occurrence of such incidents almost renders them mundane.[5] Any one dose, taken alone, might be viewed as inconsequential. But cumulatively they take their toll, marginalizing and humiliating black women managers. White colleagues, both male and female, often downplayed the racial element of the incidents, offering race-neutral explanations. Black women managers were invariably admonished by dominant group colleagues that the incidents were a "joke," a "mistake," "not important," or an occurrence that "had nothing to do with their race" that "could have happened to anyone."

Our interviews with African-American women were full of vivid descriptions of daily doses of racism. Deborah Jones, a senior-level human resources executive, remembers an episode that still angers her today: "At the consulting company I worked for, we held an annual partners meeting. I was a principal by then, and we had the meeting at our office. We were having a very big reception and then a dinner. We were all there, including partners from all over the world. Besides me, the only other blacks present were a black guy, Kenneth, who was also a principal, and the receptionist. Everybody was having a very wonderful time. The partner who ran one of the European offices and I were talking. He told me they had lunch every day in his office. I said, 'That's a really nice perk.' He asked, 'Do you serve lunch here?' I said, 'No, we don't do that.' He said, 'No, I mean do you serve the lunch to the consultants every day?' Again, I said, 'No, we don't do that,' and he asked me again. Then I realized that this man was asking me if I personally made lunch for the consultants. So when it dawned on me, when the lightbulb went on, I said, 'No. However, should we ever require that consultants serve lunch to each other every day, I'll be delighted to take my turn.' He kind of looked at me, turned red as a beet, and didn't know what else to say. Two other principals heard the exchange. One said, 'Deborah, I'm so sorry.' I just left the room. Later, I spoke with the head of our office, who wanted to tell me that's not what the partner meant. I said, 'Oh yes, that's what he meant.' Then he said, 'Oh, well he must have been joking.' I said 'No, he wasn't joking.' Then he said, 'Oh, I bet you he would have said that to my wife.' I said, 'I seriously doubt that he would have said that to your wife.'" Deborah's experience is not unusual. The partner assumed she was not a consultant despite the setting and the purpose of the event. We heard similar stories from other interviewees who were mistaken by whites as secretaries, as assistants, or as anyone other than the manager in charge.

Sometimes the dose of racism was more blatant. Anna Smalls, who at the time of the interview was the highest ranking African-American woman manager in her investment-banking company, remembered being stunned by an incident. "We were at an off-site business meeting. I was the only black woman present. It was evening. The formal portion of the meeting for the day was over. After the meeting, a small group from my work team went to the bar for drinks. There were four white males, all managers. They asked me if I wanted to join them. I thought it would be best to go to my room and not get involved in socializing, but then I figured it was important for me to act like I was part of the team. So I went. Everybody gathered around the bar for drinks. The five of us were standing in a circle. One of the guys said to me, 'My, this was a good year for you; you did like 187 percent for the year.' I said, 'Yes, I had a good year.' Then one of the other guys looks me right in the face and jokingly says, 'You little black bitch.' I couldn't believe it was coming out of his mouth. It was very insulting. The other guys dropped their jaws. I mean, they looked at him as if they couldn't believe what he'd said. I'd been called a black bitch before, but not in my work environment. It's been on the streets with a cab driver, that kind of thing. But this was a peer. This was a business environment. This was where people were supposed to be professional." When we asked Anna, "What did the other men say or do?" she answered, "Nothing."

An African-American woman can be undercut by white men either because of her race or because of her gender. The two are so often fused that it is difficult for African-American women to determine whether they are experiencing racism or sexism or both. In this incident the words of the white male colleague are significant. He did not simply say "bitch" but "black bitch." U.S. courts have held that the use of "bitch" is a form of sex discrimination as it is a derogatory word used to denigrate women. In a 1977 sex-discrimination case on the question of whether the word "bitch" used by a male in reference to a woman constitutes prejudice, the court agreed with the plaintiff's argument that "a bitch is a female dog, which when in heat, actively seeks insemination; judged by the cultural standards of the time, such a dog is considered lewd—one of the meanings of bitch when applied to women."[6] Historically, the sexuality of black women has been portrayed as wanton.[7] When the word "black" is combined with "bitch," it relegates a black woman to a profoundly inferior position, grounded in the devalued status of being both black and female. It is a poignant reminder of her societal status, despite outstanding performance.

The women spoke as well of racial incidents that cropped up in everyday business interactions. They were not so much directed at the women personally but directed at black people as a group. Mamie Jefferson, the only African-American among the top management of her retail company, notices such slips in everyday conversations or at meetings. "We

were having a buyers' meeting—me and the other senior-level vice presidents—and the candy buyer, an older white woman who was in charge of
candy, cookies, and things like that, had brought in some cookies for the
meeting and had put them on a side table. One of the cookies was a vanilla
wafer. People were standing around the table and someone made a comment about vanilla wafers, whether or not they should eat one. I'm sure she
didn't know I was in the room; her back was to me. And she turned to the
other white managers and said something to the effect, 'Well, you'd better
be careful or people will think you're black.' There's a notion that the primary consumers of vanilla wafers are black people. It was just like somebody making a statement about black people eating watermelon. The
whole thing was just one of those ill-thought, ill-spoken phrases that happen in conversations in a company." Mamie told us the woman making the
comment was oblivious to her presence. Sometimes the comments were
more harsh and direct. Brenda Boyd, now a mid-level communications
executive, remembered the head of corporate communications saying during a meeting discussing advertising budgets that "he didn't know why we
advertise in black newspapers because black people don't read."

We detected a sense of bewilderment from the women as they spoke
about these doses of racism. But what was most striking to us were the
reactions of the women. As one woman told us, "I've had some tough situations in my company because of racism, not blatant, but the normal
kind." Racism described as "normal" was a theme pervading many of our
interviews. Sometimes it was perceived as so "normal" that several women
responded "No" when directly asked, "Have you ever experienced discrimination because of your race?" Yet during the course of their interviews they recounted personal, overt, and negative racial experiences.
Perhaps their perceptions reflect the extent to which African-American
women face racism in their everyday work lives. Daily doses of racism are
so common that women become inured to them; they become almost a
backdrop to their daily work environment. Additionally, African-American women often sublimate such experiences in order to cope with the
frustration, humiliation, and anger caused by being targets of racial incidents, thereby lessening their sting. Other researchers have found that
often members of minority groups minimize personal discrimination as
a form of self-protection.[8]

Nonetheless, the women were not devoid of feelings about these
episodes. Patricia Triggs said she just "carries it." "I come home some days

and I'm real unhappy because of somebody's ignorance. I remember at one site there was a guy who had an office right beside mine, separated only by glass. This white man could not part his lips. He walked by me every morning and afternoon to get coffee but he never spoke. The first couple of times I said, 'Good morning.' He said nothing. After a while I knew this man could not speak to me. I really knew it when I was walking down the hall with a white woman colleague, and he spoke to her but not me. It's stuff like that I carry with me, and it's hard to get rid of how it makes me feel."

HELD TO A HIGHER STANDARD

Often the discriminatory barriers the African-American women managers experienced manifested themselves more subtly. Being stereotyped as incompetent and unqualified for the jobs they held is one example. Julia Smith, recounting her early experiences at a Fortune 500 manufacturing company, told us that she "clawed" her way to vice president in the financial division of her company. "During my first year at the company they apparently thought I was God's gift. I had this fabulous background academically. I had an Ivy League M.B.A. I worked for this guy who was a comer in the organization. We worked well together. He was nice and gave me a lot of visibility because I was sort of his favorite. I worked my ass off. I did great work. I made him look good. I really worked hard because I thought that at last they were ready not to let race be a factor. They had gone to great lengths to bring in people who were well qualified and black. I was going to give it my best shot. This is my career and reputation, I thought. I got my first review, which was very high. I had been identified as high potential in absolute terms."

"But when it came to the next job, I ended up in a staff position in the chairman's office supporting the board of directors and the executive committees, including the strategic planning groups, both national and international. But it wasn't crunching numbers in the strictest sense. I complained that I wasn't crunching numbers and wanted to know what was happening. They said not to worry because the job had visibility with the chairman and it was important work. But when it came time to move to the next level, they said, 'She's unproven with the numbers.' I said, 'Wait, you guys put me here. You told me it was important, and I believed you and worked my tail off.' They said, 'Well you know we need to put you in another numbers job before we can move you to the next level.' I said,

'I asked you for that originally. At the very least I'm sitting here with a degree from a prestigious women's college, a master's degree in economics, an M.B.A. from an Ivy League school, and a great track record. Don't I deserve the presumption that I can crunch a few numbers?'"

Many of the African-American women we interviewed believed they were held to higher and often different standards than their white colleagues, even when their credentials were extraordinary. Sixty-five percent of the African-American women managers who participated in our national survey believed they had to outperform their white colleagues for the same rewards. Said Julia, "You have to be 1,000 percent on top of stuff to move ahead at the same level."

Whitney Hamilton remembered a similar challenge at her newspaper. "I saw, when I was coming along, white guys go from reporters to editors overnight—literally overnight. One even went from reporter to being an assistant managing editor overnight. But when it came time for me to become an editor, I was told there were things I needed to do first." As a result, the women often felt they were in the spotlight where they could not dare underperform. "Black women need to do work that is sterling— not good work, but sterling work—on a consistent basis," Patricia Triggs told us. "Because I was black and female I always felt like there was a judge out there. There was a lot of weight on me. I thought, 'If I don't do this, will they never let anybody else [black] come and do it?'"

The African-American women felt they were held to higher standard because they were always fighting the stereotype of being incompetent, despite having the right educational and experience credentials. On one hand they are held to a higher standard, having to jump additional hurdles to advance in their jobs. On the other hand, when they display competence, their colleagues often express surprise. Deborah Jones recalled one of her white male colleagues asking her, "Where did you learn to speak like that?" Even though she expressed confusion about the question, her colleague persisted in wanting to know if she had taken a special speech course to learn how to speak. Psychologists refer to this as the "flower blooming in winter" effect.[9] When majority group members set lower standards for a black woman and she exceeds the standards, then the black woman's performance becomes remarkable. Or they treat the woman as an exception to her race and gender, leaving intact the general stereotype of black women as incompetent and unqualified. "They were surprised that I was smart, competent, and capable because they didn't expect that," said Whitney Hamilton. "People have preconceived notions about black women. I get high praise sometimes because I think they didn't expect anything. When I can speak English and do whatever I am supposed to do, people are just overwhelmed. I then become the exception."

Patricia Triggs found it was often difficult for some of the white male managers whom she encountered to accept that she could do things as well as they could. "I do not fault them for their ignorance, but it just offends their egos if you can do it and are black. They don't know it offends their ego. They sit there making objective decisions like you're not quite ready, you have to work on this, or you have to work on that."

Psychologists suggest that stereotyping occurs as a way of filling information voids about people. Again, at the time these women entered corporate America, there were few if any models or examples of successful African-American women managers. In a decade when male-dominated corporations openly questioned whether women could even be managers, African-American women presented an altogether different challenge. There were no reference points, no models of them in authority positions for white colleagues to draw upon. Rather, the most pervasive images of African-American women ingrained into society were either negative images or images of African-American women in subservient roles.[10] The language and actions of white colleagues suggest they define black women first as black and female before seeing them as managers and executives.[11] The women we interviewed were faced with the dual challenge of transforming negative stereotypical images and simultaneously creating new professional roles.

Julia Smith's story is instructive about another dimension of the issues black women managers face. She was placed in a highly visible position in her company that was not a position that would lead to a higher level of responsibility. African-American women managers often find themselves in this predicament—placed in highly visible positions that benefit the company but not necessarily their careers. They can be unwittingly used as "affirmative action cover girls." Sociologist Sharon Collins found in her study of black mobility in white corporations that black executives are sometimes placed in positions that present an image of diversity to external audiences to serve race-related purposes.[12] Instead of Julia advancing to the next level of management, she ended up having to prove her ability once again in a position with the same level of responsibility. Our national survey data indicated that black women managers experienced a higher level of lateral moves and demotions within their organizations than did white women managers. Thomas and Gabarro, in their recent study of minority executive career paths, reported a similar pattern. Minorities had longer proving periods compared to the dominant group executives in the sample.[13]

We need to point out here that the white women we interviewed also talked about stereotyping as the major obstacle to their corporate mobility.[14] However, the stereotyping they describe centered on gender differences: male colleagues believing they could not have a career and a family, for example, or male colleagues criticizing "feminine style of behavior." Gender stereotyping, not surprisingly, was perceived to be more prevalent among older men—the men at the highest ranks of the organization. Gina Davidson, who today manages a large power plant, a rare position for a woman, stated "White guys over fifty-five are the biggest pain in life. For whatever reasons, as a group they are just Neanderthals."

Not only did the women have to confront negative stereotypes, they also came up against resistance to the very idea of women in the corporate suite. Gloria Goldberg, who has reached a senior level in investment banking, talked about how foreign the idea of a woman at the officer level was at the time of her promotion. "It took me probably a year to make vice president, a year and a half longer than the other guys. I know I was bringing in more business than half of them. It was not overt sexism you were fighting but something else. It was the decision by an old-line investment company to move a woman up. The question wasn't can she do the work as well as a guy, but do we really want a female officer? You were fighting a different battle than any of the guys who just had to do the work well."

Sylvia Whitaker, who is the most senior woman executive at the southern corporate headquarters of the insurance company she works for, told us: "I just wish someone could wave their magic wand and put away all this Southern male traditional mind-set that they're born with. They can't help it. I wish that I could take the environment I was in and the years that I've spent and project it twenty years down the road where it would all fit together nicely. It's just that women are before their time in the South. It's just the way it is. And it's not out of badness. I haven't really run into what I call pure male chauvinism in the ugliest form. It's just there."

Gender stereotyping made the women fear they would be seen as too emotional, too unassertive, and not committed enough to their careers; in addition, they feel viewed as helpers and not as primary breadwinners. Such stereotyping becomes justification for differential treatment. Sylvia Whitaker was taken aback when she encountered such stereotyping in her boss. "I was trying to tell him about an agreement we had made when I started working for him. I was giving him some feedback about how he wasn't meeting that agreement. He wasn't being defensive about the feedback, but what he said to me as he looked me in the eye was, 'You know what you just sounded like don't you?' I said, 'No.' He said, 'A jealous female.' Something in my head went 'Warning, warning. You've worked for this guy for a year now and you had no clue. When you least expected it, that ugly thing showed its face.' I've been accused of a lot of things in my life, but this was the first time anyone had ever called me a jealous female." Earlier in her career when she revealed that she was pregnant, another boss told her "You will never be successful doing both. You cannot be a good parent and be a successful manager here."

Sometimes the gender stereotyping goes beyond words. Jean Hendrick recounted being told several times by male colleagues not to use her hands when she spoke; they said she was too demonstrative. "I remember going into a meeting with a senior-level white male. Two of my assistants were also in the meeting. We had met to discuss a pretty significant problem that would require action. We were in discussion, and I was animatedly describing a solution to a problem that he had presented. I was using my hands as I spoke. He went over to the drapes on the window and removed the tieback. He came over to me and tied my hands together. Then he said, 'Jean, let's see if you can talk now.' I was a senior officer and my subordinates were in that room. I immediately locked my jaw and pretended that I wasn't able to pronounce my words with my hands tied together in order to make everyone laugh. I was making a joke to protect him from being embarrassed for being so dumb."

Jean's story underscores the nature of the gender stereotyping white women faced entering male-dominated environments. Research has demonstrated that women managers are expected to adopt masculine personality traits rather than maintaining feminine qualities in order to be accepted and to succeed in the corporate environment.[15] Additionally, research has shown that women are more likely to be verbally interrupted than men.[16] But Jean's story illustrates more than the denigrating effect of gender stereotypes. The behavior of the senior white male reflects the ways in which some white men resist gender equality in the workplace. According to Cynthia Cockburn, one way men resisted women's invasion into spaces of male domination was through the reassertion of male supremacy. She further suggests that male opposition can range from the administrative to the physical.[17] It is hard to imagine a man who speaks in an animated manner having his hands tied by a colleague. Jean was not just a victim of stereotyping but also of harassment. The tying of her hands demonstrates how a potentially powerful woman can be cut down to size by sexual means. Tying her hands can be viewed as a controlling gesture designed to diminish any power Jean may have had in the meeting and even in the organization. His comment, "Let's see if you can talk now," can be taken as a direct challenge to her power and a reminder that she was not conforming to proper managerial behavior.

Another rationale used to block promotion opportunities and justify lower wages was that these women were not the primary wage earners in their families. A number of women told stories of pay discrimination based on such reasoning. As one interviewee remembered, "Six years ago I had a peer, we both worked for the same boss. He had five people reporting to him, I had twenty-five. He was paid $15,000 more a year than I was. When I confronted my manager about it, he said, 'Well, he's got a family to support.'"

Gender stereotyping was also perceived to affect the types of work assignments and positions available to women. Investment banker Gloria Goldberg remembered, "When they handed out the random walk-in-the-door assignments, the women were always given the absolute garbage deals. There were never real deals assigned to them. The men were given the sure things." She went on to point out that "the key to promotion in investment banking is making big deals." Women were often excluded from jobs that led most directly to the senior ranks. They were usually assigned to human resources or communications, positions of far less status and rank. Ann Gilbert, who is now a vice president in her investment-banking firm, observed, "I think women still tend to be viewed as being technically incompetent. Or as adding value in more of a staff support role, more than in a line position."

THE INVISIBILITY VISE

Another barrier that surfaced in the black women's narratives is what we label the "invisibility vise." Black women perceive that their white colleagues feel more comfortable with blacks whose racial identity is suppressed, yet African-American women managers often want to maintain a strong, "visible" racial identity at work. This clash catches African-American women in a vise. Karen Brown, one of the highest level African-American women managers in corporate America today, talked eloquently about certain objects she keeps in her office: "See that book sitting over

there," she said, pointing to a table. "A colleague looked at the book a couple months ago and he said, 'Why do you have that book here?' I said, 'I
want to remind people that the person in this office is a black woman.' I
want no doubt about that because, guess what? They forget sometimes.
You ought to hear the stuff that comes out of their mouths. They forget
I'm a black woman. It's like I'm invisible. It's amazing to me. When they
get comfortable with you, you become invisible." She continued to explain
how her boss had compared her to another black employee. "He said
'Karen, you know Kent just wears his blackness.' I said, 'What about me?'
And he said, 'You don't wear your blackness.' I told him this enrages me
because it means two things have happened. One is that I have made him
awfully comfortable with me because I am black. Second, there's something wrong here if I have to be seen as nonblack. I was really upset. . . . I
mean I was shut down for weeks behind that."

Deborah Jones had a similar experience as the only black woman in her
company. "I found out that my boss used to tell people that I was black, but
if you didn't know that I was black, you didn't think about it. What bothered me was that Jim had to create a rationale in his mind for my blackness. That's what he had to do to make me acceptable to clients. There is no
way that I could ever walk around thinking that I'm not black."

To be accepted, African-American women are expected to assimilate.
They have to literally lose their blackness for white colleagues to feel comfortable with them. White-dominated organizations often make cultural
assimilation the price of acceptability for racial minorities.[18] This, of
course, is a condition impossible for the African-American women to fulfill. They take this as an affront to their identity, but it is also a threat to
their ambition, as maintaining a strong racial identity at work is an
important grounding and coping mechanism. Most of the African-American women we interviewed were not willing to leave that part of themselves, learned from their family and educational experiences, outside of
the corporation. This makes sense, since armoring—the socialization
from family early in life—helped these women withstand the racism and
sexism they encountered in their later years. This armoring is indeed one
of the major reasons why the black women in our study have been successful in corporate America despite the challenges they face daily.

It may seem puzzling that the black women had such a negative
response to being made raceless by their white colleagues. Isn't this a positive result, as it meant they were viewed simply as individuals? It may
appear black women want it both ways. On the one hand they are upset

because their colleagues cannot get beyond race and gender and accept them as managers, yet at the same time they do not want colleagues to ignore their racial identity. How can these apparently contradictory perceptions be reconciled? Without question, having a clear sense of their racial identity helped them to maintain self-esteem and confidence in the face of racism and sexism in their work environments. But the implication that they acted in a way to conceal their racial identity (i.e., "acting white") or that they were focused on making white people comfortable was disturbing to the black women we interviewed.

This notion of comfort also surfaced in the narratives of the white women. They talked of what we refer to as sexual tension—men feeling "uncomfortable" working with women. Although not explicitly stated, it was clear these women were talking about white men working with white women as their equals. "All it boils down to is being comfortable," Sylvia Whitakers said. "Men and women, side by side working together. For some reason low in the ranks, that's very comfortable and no one has a problem with it. There's something that happens on that top floor. Something about it is not comfortable. Up to this point all of their life experiences with top people have been with all men." Judy Rosener refers to this phenomenon as sexual static.[19]

A significant part of this sexual tension arises from the newness of women in nontraditional roles. When women leave the home and enter the public sphere, they violate the original, if tacit, sexual contract. In the original terms of this contract, a woman's place was in the home, not the boardroom. Jean Hendrick offered this observation, "I think there are men who are very easily intimidated by smart, strong women because in their experience women are not like that; plus, they're not attracted to women like that. So they don't know how to handle them. . . . Men who are used to thinking of women as sexual partners or as potential relationships don't really know how to deal when they're presented with an intelligent, opinionated, forceful woman. It is very awkward."

Again, we point to the historical period during which these women entered their corporate careers. The introduction of women into jobs traditionally reserved for men changed social relations in organizations. Noted organizational scholars Hearn and Parkin argue that the presence of women in nontraditional places in organizations creates charged sexualized social relations.[20] "For a lot of men," Jean Hendrick observed, "their first thought about women is sexual, and that makes them uncomfortable. And men don't like to be uncomfortable. They're under enough pressure and so they'll find all kinds of other things to say that are negative about this gal. She's too this, she doesn't understand finance—never mind they hired her for a creative position—or she waves her hand around too much when she talks, or I heard she went out with one of the guys. What they're really saying is, 'She makes me uncomfortable and I don't know how to deal with it. Therefore, I don't want her around.'"

On the Outside: Exclusion from Informal Networks

Another barrier experienced by the black women is limited access to informal and social networks in their organizations. The African-American women we interviewed felt they had less access to these networks in their organizations than white men and white women. As a result, they felt cut off from important organizational information, and less accepted as full members of the organization. Many of the women spoke of the critical importance of informal networks in career advancement. In most corporations, excellent performance is necessary for advancement but is not the sole criterion. Getting ahead also depends on access to informal networks and the relationships those networks can foster—mentorships, sponsorships, and help from colleagues. Building these relationships requires that the women be part of the social networks within the company. In our national survey, we found that having white men in their network and being accepted by white men on the job helped African-American women managers attain higher management levels. Yet, only 59 percent of the African-American women reported having white men in their networks, compared to 91 percent of the white women managers.[21] As we pointed out in the previous chapter, African-American women often feel as if they are outsiders in their own organizations.

Julia Smith told us how networks affect job opportunities in her Fortune 100 company, "When you network, you find a new job much as you would if you were out in the world looking. Once you have good results in one place, you have visibility; you will be hired away. When someone in your network gets a new set of responsibilities, he or she usually brings people along that he knows, trusts, or has worked with in the past." Black folks, Julia Smith says, just don't have the kind of extensive networks that allow for repeated quid pro quos. "It means that black folks who do not have those relationships don't move." Anna Smalls, a vice president in a Wall Street investment-banking firm, confirmed that view. "The firm is just like a fraternity. That's how it's run. My white male colleagues are very socially connected. It's a great big kind of brotherly thing. They like to deal with certain clients. They have the old boy network and the old lines of communication. That's how they do business." Formal and informal networks can serve to reinforce the dominance of white men, thereby institutionalizing inequality.

Similarly, the white women managers also believed that exclusion from the "old boy network" was one of the barriers to women's advancement. Sylvia Whitaker calls it the armpit phenomenon: "They put you under their armpit and say come fly with me up to the executive suite. They (the men) are earmarked from day one. I truly believe that unless you have been lucky enough to get into the 'armpit' track, your chances of advancing may still be real but it's going to take a lot longer." Likewise, Ann Gilbert told us, "I think women are still coming of age in the business world. Some men don't quite know how to deal with it. Some men still resent women being there. There's kind of an intrinsic good old boy system or network in place that you have to work around. If you don't go golfing with the guys on Saturday or you don't shoot a few hoops with the guys after work, you don't ever get to be a full-fledged member of the team. And men relate very differently to women than they do to men. Men are still the primary power force in businesses."

Informal social functions and networks, on and off the job, are said to foster collegiality and strengthen working relationships. But for many of our black interviewees, such events served as a source of anxiety. First, many of the black women we interviewed rejected the idea of using informal networks to advance because such settings could engender negative experiences, like Anna Small's experience when she joined colleagues at a bar only to be called a "black bitch." Other black women shared stories of painful rejection when they tried to participate in social activities. One interviewee explained her reluctance to socialize outside of work. "One of my colleagues invited me to a party, but she apparently didn't let her in-laws know that a black couple was coming. When we walked up to the door, we could hear everybody having a good time. I rang the doorbell, but nobody came. The door was open so my husband and I walked in and everybody stopped, just froze. I guess they were saying to themselves, 'These black people are at the wrong party.' But the woman who invited me said, 'Oh, come on in.' My husband said, 'Let's get out of here.' I said, 'No, we're going to stay.' We go in there and sure enough the first thing someone asks my husband is 'What do you do?' He tells them he's a supervisor with the public transit system. They walk off to another couple. My husband said, 'Don't you ever ask me to go to another one of these functions.' I didn't even pressure him after that experience. But it's just hard. In order to move up you've got to participate in all those things. My marriage is important to me and my family is important. But I'm not going to allow a job to make him uncomfortable in order for me to move. I'd rather not have it if I have to go through all that just to get the title of vice president."

CHALLENGES TO AUTHORITY

African-American women managers—but not their white counterparts—expressed frustration over the lack of control and authority in their managerial roles. The African-American women in our national survey sample reported challenges to their authority from bosses, subordinates, and colleagues.[22] These challenges may well emanate from a lack of acceptance of black women in authority positions. Consequently, these challenges created an obstacle to their ability to demonstrate competence.

After having tough but supportive bosses in the early part of her career, Karen Brown was almost devastated when a new boss "appointed this guy who worked for him and who was my peer to be over me and to check up on the work I was doing. He never told me that but I found out about it. I just remember it was awful. I'll never forget it because my friend came to town and she sat in my office and said I looked like I was in a lot of pain. I didn't understand it. I was being watched. I was being set up."

Colleen Powell, an upper-level executive in corporate treasury, recounted how a white female supervisor at a much lower level challenged her authority by attempting to take away her secretarial support. She believed this would never have happened to another officer at her level. "Without consulting with me, she calls my secretary and tells her to report to human resources to interview for another job in the company. She also told my secretary not to tell anybody that she was going to human resources. Well, my secretary calls me. I tell her to do what she says, and we will deal with it. I had put a lot of time and effort in training my secretary. When I checked with human resources, they said this supervisor had told them she had cleared this action with me. I said, 'I assure you, she did not clear it with me.' The situation escalated and there was a meeting of this supervisor, a human resources representative, my boss, and myself. During the meeting, the supervisor tells me she doesn't think I need anybody with the skills I had outlined. I said, 'Wait a minute.' She had the unmitigated gall to tell me what I need, when she is there not to tell me what I need but to accommodate my needs. After the meeting was over, I stayed to talk with my boss. I told him I considered it deceitful, disrespectful, and unprofessional. I said to him, 'Well, what do you think?' He then says, 'Well, I have never known her to be deceitful or disrespectful.' He then goes on to say, 'She may have told me and I may have forgotten to tell you.' I realized then the situation was graver than I had thought. The two of them had conspired. It made me angry. I don't think she would have done this to a man or to a white woman. Perhaps she felt she could get away with it with me for some reason."

Hollow Commitment to the Advancement of Women and Minorities

The final barrier the black women perceived was hollow company commitment to advancing women and minorities in companies. Our survey data echo what we heard from women we interviewed: skepticism about their companies' efforts to affect real change. Patricia Triggs was of the opinion that top management in her company wants diversity and multiculturalism, and yet fears it. "The classic mind-set preventing progress is, 'Power is a zero-sum game, and right now I own it and those I parcel it out to are like me and do what I say, so I know I will always own the power. If I have to share the power with people who are not like me and do not do what I say, I may have to give up some of it.'" Dawn Stanley told us that black men and women in her manufacturing company feel there's "no corporate commitment to supporting or promoting them. There is no commitment in terms of getting managers to promote blacks who work with them." Another interviewee was even more explicit in talking about her experience: "If you don't have a senior management person who says this is the approach we're going to take, you're never going to get there. It will be the same ten white men on the staff going around to all the plants saying we're getting serious about our diversity this year. It'll be the same ten white men who have been here for the last ten years. They do the same dog-and-pony show. But it doesn't change." We found that only 21 percent of the African-American women who completed our national survey felt their companies were committed to the advancement of people of color in management. In contrast, white women were much more positive about the efforts of their companies to advance women and minorities. The women's perceptions point to the fact that African-American women need a commitment beyond mere words issued by top management. Careers can be blocked at lower levels of an organization when managers are not held accountable for the advancement of African-American women.

Perceptions of Career Progress

An obvious questions remains: How did the women feel about their overall career progress in corporate America? A large percentage of the black women felt they were *behind* where they should be while about the same percentage of white women felt they were *ahead* of where they expected to be. (See Table 7-1.) When we analyzed the black women's reasons for feeling they were behind in their career progress, we found that the majority attributed the lack of progress to being stalled in their companies. Karen Brown, a senior human resource executive, told us bluntly, "I am blocked here. Right now it doesn't trouble me. . . . But in two years it will." Deborah Jones, a production executive, told us, "I think I'm a little bit behind in two ways. First, I think I should be making more money. I make a lot of money, but I think I should be making more for somebody who has my years of experience at my age with the kind of exposure that I've had and with my ability. Second, I think I should be at a different level and have a different title. That's where I see the glass ceiling, by the way." Brenda Boyd too, expected to have made better progress in her company, which she had thought was more receptive to women. "Well, I'm behind where I expected to be in my career. I would have thought I'd be vice president by now. I thought this company would be a very likely place to be a vice president. There's a receptivity to women and there are black officers, whereas at my last company it was inconceivable for a woman or for a black person."

TABLE 7-1   *Interviewees' Perceptions of Career Progress*

Level of Progress	Black Women	White Women
Ahead of expectations	23 percent	38 percent
Where expected	28	21
Behind	39	25
No opinion or did not answer	10	16

White women explained their lack of progress differently. Few attributed their slow progress to gender discrimination or company failure. A majority of the women offered explanations related to the nature of the work, cited things they had not done to assure their promotion, or suggested they were not "really behind." For example, Ann Gilbert attributed her slow career progress to changes in the banking industry. "The job I'm in now is a less management-oriented and more project-oriented position. I probably would have imagined more management responsibility now although this change has been very positive in terms of broadening my perspective on banking and in general." Marketing director Joyce Canton said of her feeling of being behind, "I'm not particularly impatient about the fact that I am overdue for a promotion to vice president. This assignment, while it's lateral, feels like a completely different job." Jean Hendrick assessed her career progress in this way: "I'm a little behind where I should be. I don't mean I'm behind in my accomplishments. But I should have gotten myself to one of the top positions. I don't know that I ever will, for two reasons. First, I don't know what's going to happen to the company. Second, I just still don't know if I am willing to come across in the way that will get me there. So while I feel that I should really be at the top, there's a step that I haven't taken. It may be that I'm just not perceived as enough of a business person—a real, real business person."

The white women who felt they were ahead of their expectations for their careers expressed surprise and amazement at how far they had progressed. For the most part, they were not comparing themselves to white men but to their early lives. This was true of women from both humble and privileged backgrounds. Sandra Martin told us, "I'm ahead and I don't really know what to do about it. I told my boss when I got promoted to senior vice president, 'I don't know what to ask for next. I'm stunned.' And he grinned and said, 'Don't worry about it. Tomorrow you'll think of something.'" Cecilia Monroe said, "I am so much ahead of wherever I thought I would be career wise and money wise that I'm just in awe sometimes." Gloria Goldberg, who grew up in an elite suburb of Westchester County, was no less exuberant in describing her progress: "I'm not just ahead. I think I'm beyond anything I ever imagined other than in daydreams."

We heard some of this sentiment in the voices of the black women. Many made it clear that they had achieved far more than what they thought their early backgrounds and race would allow. Yet, most were careful to distinguish that from where they should be compared to the white men in their companies. Typical of this expression is what we heard from Colleen Powell. Being a mid-level executive in a Fortune 500 company far exceeds what Colleen Powell expected in terms of career or professional prospects. As a young girl, she had to grow up incredibly fast after her mother left home to escape an abusive relationship. "But it does not mean I am where I should be. I cannot complain. I live a very good life. I can take care of myself. I am relatively independent . . . I have been very fortunate in comparison to many other people, in comparison to most people in this country. Look, I can get on a plane and ride first class. If I get tired of the situation here, I can make a reservation on a plane and fly first class to our international sites. Not many people can do that. I am extremely appreciative of all this because, except by the grace of God, I could be some place else." But when it comes to measuring her progress against white men in her company, Colleen made it clear that she is behind. "Based on what I contribute in comparison to what others contribute I deserve something else."

The women in our study encountered formidable barriers to their careers. If the barriers described by the white women seem less daunting, it may be because they have indeed made greater progress in attaining high-level management positions. Yet, despite these barriers, all of the women in our study have attained a measure of career success. How did these women crack the glass ceilings and scale the concrete walls they encountered? How do they make sense of their mobility? As we will show in the next chapter, how they perceived these barriers resulted in very different strategies for overcoming them.

8

❖

CLIMBING OVER
THE BARRIERS

THE MOST SUCCESSFUL women in our study, both black and white, were able to attain top-level positions in their organizations. How do these women explain their upward mobility? How did they overcome the barriers we described in the previous chapter? We found that the women were adept at taking lessons from their early lives and developing strategies for navigating the corporate environment. We focus in this chapter on the successful strategies these women developed.

When asked what their companies had done to help them achieve success, only a small percentage of the women we interviewed pointed to instrumental company policies. The women were more likely to identify helpful individuals than helpful organizational practices. "I cannot say my company has helped me, because in fact it has not," said Patricia Triggs in a typical response. "There have been individuals who have helped make the environment conducive to my success. The reason I'm careful to distinguish between the two is that so many people have been treated so poorly it would be unfair for me to characterize my company as one that does all these wonderful things. I have remained unscathed, partly because of the way I manage it and partly because of the people I have worked for, who have helped me to succeed."

Likewise, Joyce Canton told us, "I don't know if it's so much what the company has provided as that I've been fortunate enough to have had a few people in fairly influential positions give me support."

Perseverance

One word seemed to crop up again and again in each woman's narrative—perseverance. As these women attempted to carve out their identities as managers, they had to have staying power and a determination to succeed. While organizational practices deeply embedded in an elite male culture significantly shaped the women's experiences, we should not overlook the significance of personal agency.

No one in our study was more focused on a career in business than Patricia Triggs. She was determined to succeed from the time she was an undergraduate college student talking her way into an interview reserved only for graduate students. That perseverance has never left Patricia. Throughout her career, she always knew when it was time to stretch. One critical turning point of her career came when she took a new job as a brand manager in the marketing division of a consumer products company. "In all my previous jobs all I had to do was do well in relation to the needs of others. In this job I had to determine what doing well meant and make sure it happened. I had to define the requirements and work with people to fulfill the requirements. I wound up working 110 hours a week and gaining eighty pounds. There was no such thing as working out. There was no such thing as eating healthful food. When you're there until 2 a.m., you order in all the food you need. There's no kitchen. You eat dinner out of candy and pop machines. I just wasn't worried about it. I was singularly focused on my ability to perform because now it was of critical importance. It wasn't like when you were training and you didn't do well. Then it could be said you just hadn't learned enough and that was okay because you weren't in charge. But now I realized that if I didn't succeed personally, a lot of people were going to pay for it. I knew I had to come through." And Patricia did come through. Seven short months later she was promoted to a director—a promotion that usually takes fifteen years of service with her company.

Gloria Goldberg, who rose to be the only woman in the top levels of a prominent old-line investment company, shared a similar experience: "My personal life bit the dust at times. I was sure I wanted to get this thing done, to close a deal, to get a promotion, or to do whatever. Something was propelling me to succeed. I made the trade-offs: just the sheer hours I worked, and the traveling all over." Patricia's and Gloria's stories exemplify what we found generally among the women, both black and white: As a group they all demonstrated high resolve and resilience in the face of numerous obstacles. We could also see that a good deal of their motivation and personal agency stemmed from distinctive early life lessons and experiences.

Out-Spiraling Moves

In addition to the perseverance and determination revealed in the stories of Patricia Triggs and Gloria Goldberg, a common element in the women's career paths was a willingness to change employers or functions to gain upward mobility, a technique known as "out-spiraling career moves."[1] This is a pretty consistent finding in the literature on women's career advancement.[2] Out-spiraling moves add breadth to job skills. Such moves often turn into quantum leaps, propelling the women to a job with greater responsibility and visibility or putting them on a faster career path. A move from the domestic side of her company to the international side fueled Karen Brown's rise in her company. "When I moved from the U.S. business to the international business, it was a big leap. I had never been in a job where after six months I didn't have it pretty much down. I have a pretty quick learning ability, but going to international was tough. It took me a year to sort it all out." After she did sort it out, she moved from director to vice president.

We found two major prompts for out-spiraling moves among our interviewees. One prompt was the realization that the potential for promotion in a present job was limited. As Dawn Stanley puts it, "When promotion opportunities haven't been there, I've left. If I was ready and the company couldn't make it happen, I've left." When her career stalled as a product manager in one company, she moved on to the director level position she wanted at another company. When Patricia Triggs could not get a fair review despite her outstanding performance, she left. She joined a Fortune 500 consumer products company in a move that doubled her salary. "At that point I was making more than I ever thought I would see in my life. I finally had my dream job. I was in charge. I was reporting to the head guy. He was taking my advice. I was traveling around the world doing marketing strategy. I had realized my plan."

Another prompt we found among several of the women was working with a manager they perceived as racist or sexist. Out-spiraling moves allowed them to find a more hospitable work environment. When Karen Brown was offered a demotion, she refused to take the job. "Taking that job was a clear railroad out of there. I knew I could recover in the company, even with the refusal, but I would never recover if I worked under this guy." Karen Brown's rapid rise from management trainee to assistant sales manager was cut short, and she eventually left that company to make a significant career gain in her next position.

For Gloria Goldberg, the prompt was constantly hitting the glass ceiling. "I not only hit the glass ceiling, I kept bouncing into it so brutally that it was either get out or do it for yourself." She left the company and went to another investment brokerage house she felt was more conducive to women's success.

While these women gained from out-spiraling moves, our national survey data suggest that out-spiraling moves did not always result in equal benefits for black and white women. The national survey data indicate that even though black women may have received promotions when they moved to a new company, they also experienced significantly more demotions in other companies compared to white women. How do we interpret this finding? Once the black women got to their new companies, they often had to prove themselves all over again in order to advance.[3] Some of the same issues they faced in the companies they left (i.e., prejudice, stereotyping, etc.) resurfaced in their new settings.

Climbing the Concrete Wall

While there were common denominators in their experiences, we also found important differences in the ways the women plotted their advancement. Generally, the black women were much more outspoken and unwilling to acquiesce to the white male–dominated environments they encountered. They recognized more readily than did white women the race- and gender-conscious system of upward mobility in their organizations. On the whole, white women did not hold the same perceptions and were not as quick to perceive their relative disadvantage and the presence of discrimination in their organizations.[4]

We also found that as a group the black women were more critical observers of the social-structural barriers in their companies than the white women. Intergroup theory holds that the way we perceive our social reality is significantly determined by our group memberships, such as gender and race.[5] The black women's narratives were filled with critical observations of corporate cultures in their organizations and what they learned from them. Dawn Stanley told us, "You start to see some of the dynamics and the inter-relationships going on. The power struggles, the ego struggles. It's of value in the sense that you really start to understand that the higher you go the more political things become. The more important relationships become, the less important the actual business at hand becomes. You can see an arbitrary business decision being made because of relationships." Julia Smith had a similar take on the organizational cultures she had worked in: "One of the things that you learn is how strong the old boy network is. Just to see it in action is awesome. You are close enough to see what it confers in terms of privilege, power, position, and all that. You realize how locked up the stuff is, and it makes me look back with amusement to the conspiracy theories of the sixties. There doesn't need to be a conspiracy; a conspiracy would be redundant. The power structures are the same and yield the same outcome, even more subtly than it if were well thought out and organized. The way in which the power dynamics work in organizations to buffer the position of white males couldn't have been scripted any better than the reality. As an outsider you ask, 'How could all this fall so neatly into place?'"

The black women's outsider-within status, it seemed to us, bolstered their willingness and ability to tread a delicate line. Even as they were inside their companies, able to observe corporate culture, they remained outsiders as well. "Sometimes I get caught up in all of this, without real-izing that I have," said Colleen Powell. "Then I have to bring myself back to reality and say, 'Look, this is their world; they are giving me a little piece of it.'" A mutually reinforcing dynamic seems to be operating. Because the black women feel they have never been fully embraced by their compa-nies, they do not become fully vested in them. Experiences of racism and exclusion leave the women no choice but to operate from a "border" posi-tion. The black women in our study learned how to maneuver within their corporate cultures without totally sacrificing their identities.

Black women's managerial advancement is best characterized as "climbing over" and not "breaking down" the concrete walls in their organizations. More than one woman literally described her effort as "clawing my way to the top." Even though they successfully "climbed" over the wall, they were careful to point out that the wall remained. The women used creative strategies to climb over the obstacles they faced.

Here we must note again a fundamental difference in the experiences of black and white women. The image of a glass ceiling that is often used to describe the difficulty women face in rising to the top of organizations is an inadequate metaphor for what black women experience. Glass implies that the barrier faced is fragile and can be broken. A glass ceiling is also clear. Thus, it is possible for a white woman to observe all that is happening above her. She can gain some access to how the organization works. She can identify the company's key players and future advocates. More important, while she is observing organizational life, those at the top also have an opportunity to observe her. On the other hand, a concrete wall is a hard, solid dividing mass. Unlike the glass ceiling, the concrete wall is not transparent. An African-American woman manager remains outside the wall, cut off from the mainstream of organizational life. She is isolated from her colleagues and marginalized. There is even the possibility that the executives on the other side are not aware she is waiting behind the wall. Her existence is largely invisible to them. If she is lucky and possesses abundant perseverance, a black woman manager can only slowly chip away at the wall or climb over it.

SASSINESS

Over time the top-level African-American women developed a refined sassiness as part of their business persona or style. By sassiness we mean a posture of speaking out that allowed them to give voice to their views without being perceived as impertinent. This finding is not surprising. Historically, African-American women have a long history of "speaking up" to transform their work sites and conditions.[6] Such strong voices could have derailed these women. But they developed a knack for tempering this outspokenness. In chapter 9 we elaborate on African-American women's posture toward change. A vice president of marketing described her style in this way: "I'm not callous about saying things and I don't get flip. But I also won't allow my opinion not to be heard. I won't sit back if I have a different opinion. I may sit back while I'm listening to hear how people are going and then come out with something different. But I will be heard. I'm not afraid." An overriding sentiment we heard from the women was a refusal to play what they describe as "the game." "I'll never move up if that is what it takes," said Mamie Jefferson. "I've always felt that my qualifications and my experience and my ability should be enough, but I've learned that is not always true." The women placed a high value on being honest and forthright, not out of political naïveté, but out of conscious choice. Julia Smith perhaps articulated this the most clearly: "One of the reasons they like me is that I can go along with people. I'm conversant with the world, and I tell people the truth. Someone called me the other day and told me some people wanted our business—in an area I happen to control. He said, 'You really wowed So-and-So, and they said you are really one smart lady.' I said, 'That's very nice. I wish I could reciprocate.' That was the truth. To have gotten where I am, there is a point at which you call a spade a spade. That can be attractive to senior people—to be able to depend on somebody to tell them the truth."

Colleen Powell echoed Julia's sassiness. "I am not the kind of person to sit back and let it happen, to take it," she said in a no-nonsense voice. "If they think for one minute I'm going to sit back and permit them to walk on me . . . Never. Never. Never. Especially when it is clearly wrong."

Sociologists have described African-American women's assertive style as an adaptive response to their shared history of oppression.[7] Yet we found that while the women's sassiness was a source of strength and empowerment, it could also become an invitation for additional oppression and eventual derailment.[8] In other words, outspokenness could be a double-edged sword. The African-American women who had reached the highest levels of management in our study were able to tread a fine line so that their colorful style was not perceived as a threat. Even when she was very angry at a challenge to her authority by a white woman at a lower level of management, Colleen Powell's style of resolution was refined rather than angry. "I went to her office and said, in an attempt to be positive, 'Look, I don't want to fight with you. I will fight with you only if I have to. But we can work together to make this a positive working experience for everybody because I cannot work in this kind of negative environment. Together we can change it. I think we will get better results if you come to me if there is a problem with my secretary before going to my boss! My secretary handles my work.' I told my boss that the day my secretary was taken, I would write a memo to the head of the division outlining the risk associated with removing my secretary, who processed financial transactions with huge sums of money. I reminded him that I had put a great deal of time into training her. I also let him know that it was his department and he could move her if he made that decision. That's when things changed."

But for others in the early years of their careers, such candidness derailed their advancement. Speaking out was perceived as being militant or overly aggressive. It was clearly not a strategy to employ in the early stages of a career. One of our interviewees talked about how her sassiness affected her career advancement: "I'm up front. That's the part that got me in trouble. You've got to learn to be political. I've probably screwed myself more times by being what I consider honest and straightforward." She had been at the company for three years when her mentor put her on a high-profile corporate advisory panel that met with the president of the company. "I wasn't very good on the panel and it was because I ticked off the president with a statement that was absolutely true but which he didn't want to hear. I made statements about some processes that we were using that weren't working. I got the feeling he didn't like the fact that I criticized something he had put together. After that point, he couldn't have cared less about my career."

FORMAL "INFORMAL" INTERACTIONS

One of the barriers encountered by the African-American women managers we interviewed was exclusion from the informal company networks. They found themselves often cut off from the supportive networks and important information that are critical to performing well and advancing one's career. We discovered that the most successful African-American women found other ways to tap into important organizational information without being part of the informal network. Since they were less likely to encounter their colleagues on the golf course or at a country club social, these women relied more on formal settings to network with colleagues, to gain access to information needed for their jobs, and to garner support for accomplishing work goals. This, of course, was not a perfect substitute for the kind of informal sharing that occurs in many organizations. But the women reported it was a strategy they employed with success.

Typical of such strategies is one used by Karen Brown in her job as a senior-level human resource executive. Karen holds a regular luncheon with a group of white line officers. "I need information. I also need some alliances in order to accomplish the things I'm doing here. With any changes I want to make, I've got to have these officers buying in. I'm not going to walk into a room and present something to a group of officers and not have them with me." Karen's luncheons give her a chance to build those alliances. Deborah Jones, a senior human resources executive in the entertainment industry, employs a similar strategy, "What I try to do is understand what they're interested in, to find out their agenda and understand how it is going to relate to whatever it is I want to do. Then I think about how I am going to make them see that what I want to do is important. It takes a lot of listening and it takes asking questions. Then it takes processing what you're getting back."

Getting Sponsorship, Not Mentoring

We found that very few of the African-American women managers in our study had mentors.[9] Extensive research suggests that mentors provide protégés with two types of support that can be helpful to advancement: career support and psychosocial support.[10] In describing their relationships with their bosses, even those identified as supportive, the women were careful to not characterize them as mentors. "I had one boss, I'll never forget him," recalled Karen Brown. "He really pushed me a lot. I hated working for him because he was one of these guys that didn't even say good morning. He was not a kind man. But he always challenged me, and I always thought he saw potential in me. I wouldn't call it mentoring but I would say there was mutual respect." What was missing in the relationship she describes with her white boss was psychosocial support. "I would have liked more support; I would have liked to be able to talk about things that troubled me. But black women have to take whatever they can get out of relationships." Julia Smith, too, described a boss who is far from a mentor: "I get support *in my job* from my boss. But in terms of *moving ahead*, which is equally important, I don't get support."

What was critical to their advancement was gaining sponsorship. A majority of the successful women identified supportive bosses who championed their careers, not just by being good bosses but actively fighting for their advancement. "There was a guy who had been in the company a year and half before me," recalled Patricia Triggs. "Senior management was going to promote him to the director level. But my boss went to senior management and said, 'There is no way you're going to promote this man unless you promote this woman because her work is equal to if not better than his. I don't give a damn how old she is or how long she's been here.' I didn't know any of this until later. He just walked into my office one day and said, 'I want you to know we're making you a director.' My boss made sure I was promoted. He explained my promotion and why it was appropriate to his whole regional staff, and everybody was pleased. I became very committed to him." Patricia went on to add, "Black women have to be lucky or astute enough to work for people who make sure they get credit for their work and make sure the value of their work is understood among their peers. Many times the black woman's work is credited to her white male boss. So you have to work for a special individual who says, 'Excuse me, but So-and-So did this, not helped me but drove me. Did it, presented it.' Working for somebody who is honest and fair isn't enough. Bosses have to go to bat to get the black woman what she has due."

African-American women managers did not talk, as white women managers did, of "mentors" or "father figures." They did not get the kind of psychosocial support mentoring suggests. However, they were adamant about how important it had been to their careers to find a sponsor, someone in the organization who championed their interests and publicly endorsed and advocated for their movement to higher positions.

Self-Generated Developmental Opportunities

Another strategy for advancement used by the black women was to initiate their own developmental opportunities. One of the keys to advancement in most organizations is gaining experience and building one's skill set. When the women found they were stalled in their positions or that their bosses were not providing developmental activities, often they took it upon themselves to seek opportunities outside their current positions. During the course of her corporate career in finance, Colleen Powell has used this strategy many times. It ensured that she received the developmental experiences needed to build her skills and visibility. "I have had to develop myself by expanding my job. I went to department heads in other departments and said to them, 'I would like to work on one of your projects. I would like to work in, let us say, mergers and acquisitions.' Then it becomes mine. For example, I went to a group president's office and helped him do things and as a result I was asked to represent the company on a big negotiation."

Staying Culturally Grounded

Advancing in a predominantly white setting can go against one's cultural heritage and can feel tantamount to abandoning core aspects of identity, family, and community.[11] Successful African-American women managers refused to abandon their cultural and racial identities in order to be accepted in their organizations. Having to be seen as "not black" by their colleagues was intolerable; it would undermine their self-esteem and self-efficacy. Keeping in touch with their culture helped the women prevail in spite of the obstacles they encountered. In fact, behind the scenes, many of these successful African-American women supported other blacks in their companies, and formed or headed black network groups in their organizations.[12]

The women also found subtle ways to display markers of their cultural identities in their work settings: a petite, gold Nubian mask pin on the lapel of a fashionable blue suit; a Romare Bearden original gracing an office wall, an ebony wood African sculpture on a window sill; a copy of Gordon Parks' photographic-essay book *Songs of My People* alongside a stack of *Fortune* magazines; a brightly patterned Kente cloth scarf draped on a classic black wool dress; or the signature black-and-white cameo earrings of the Coalition of 100 Black Women flashing beneath a stylish haircut. These markers were as much for the women themselves, to reaffirm their own sense of identity, as they were for their white colleagues. But the black women managers we interviewed carry more than visible signs of their culture with them into the workplace. They use their cultural histories as a lens through which to understand and survive their workplace.

Breaking the Glass Ceiling

A theme permeating the white women's narratives was that many entered corporate America largely unprepared for the discrimination they would experience because of their gender. We believe the women's naïveté may have helped the women continue in spite of the obstacles they encountered when they entered their managerial careers. But at the same time we found most believed they had to work particularly hard to prove they were as good as the men in their companies. Unlike the black women, who were more likely to point to social structural barriers and the need for institutional changes, the white women found more individualistic ways of understanding the barriers. A majority of the white women managers were reluctant to label the obstacles as discrimination. Sandra Martin shared a belief with other women who argued that what they were facing was not discrimination per se. "If I felt it, I'd say so. But I don't feel that way. I feel like I'm sort of gender neutral in here." Said Marilyn Paul of her consumer products company: "I probably have been manipulated some because I've allowed myself to be manipulated. But I don't think that's discrimination. That's just a good tactic for somebody to use. I never really found being a woman an issue here."

This resistance to the notion of discrimination shaped the way white women confronted the barriers they encountered. As Linda Butler told us, "I guess I just accepted that that's how it was, and it was up to me to change perceptions of women and what we could do." Linda has proven herself more than once, often by just demanding more of herself. The only woman at the senior level of a large utility company, she comments, "I don't want them to say, 'Look, a woman can't handle it—that's what happens when you put her into a position of power.'"

Even women who acknowledged discrimination in their companies were cautious in their responses. Gloria Goldberg reflected, "You learn to keep your mouth shut a little longer. You learn who to trust. Sometimes you're right and sometimes you're wrong. As you rise up through the company, you learn to use your power to overcome it." Marilyn Paul told us, "I give up a lot, sometimes. I don't argue about everything. I have more respect for hierarchy." Even when there was a blatant case of sex discrimination, white women muted their response. After the episode in which a senior male tied her hands to stop her from talking with them, Jean Hendrick told us, "I didn't yell, because he actually was the one making the mistake, and I wanted to protect him from it. That was really dumb."

Many of the women believed speaking out would do more harm than good to their careers. "When I first starting working, my first boss made propositions," said Ann Gilbert, an investment banker who grew up in a middle-class family in rural Virginia. "I didn't know at the time what exactly he was proposing. I was naïve and I just kind of made a joke about it. Then it sank in that he had propositioned me. I was shocked and horrified. Luckily for me, I was working for another guy as well, and he asked me, 'You seem like something's upset you. What is it?' I just said, 'I'm having a hard time with this. I'm really trying to understand what I have done. I've always considered that I've acted professionally in my job.' And he said, 'What do you do about it? Nothing. He has been with the company for ten years and you have been here for one. So if you try to raise this as a sexual discrimination issue, it's not going to get you anywhere.' It was good that I had somebody like that to talk to, because he was exactly right. Even though I knew it was wrong and that there was nothing I had done to solicit his behavior, making a big deal out of it would only have hurt my career." Because Ann had less seniority and was a woman, she was less likely to prevail in presenting her complaint.

The women stressed the importance of learning to play by the rules and adjusting to well-entrenched performance requirements—work hard, they told themselves, and you will succeed. Their perceptions mirror the meritocracy ideal of the dominant culture, which holds that success and rewards come from individual talent and effort. The idea of meritocracy was imbued in these women, especially the middle-class women, at an early age. Many were, after all, socialized by parents to think of themselves as "a person" and not as "a woman."

All of the white women agreed that getting experience in the major areas of the company's business was key to their future mobility. They also stressed the importance of aligning their language and behavior with that of male peers. Other studies of women above the glass ceiling have found that women modify speech and behavior to better fit in with male-dominated corporate cultures.[13] Sylvia Whitaker told us, "You need to understand that companies are bottom-line driven. Everything needs to get sold or presented in terms of earnings. You need to be able to speak that language. Basically, you need to be able to speak all the languages in the company."

A number of the most successful women in our group emphasized the significance of getting into jobs that are part of a career track to power.[14] Maxine Schneider, for example, understood that her company was sales-driven. Her success as a divisional sales manager ensured her rise in the ranks. Now director of public affairs for a Fortune 100 communications company, Maxine has earned credibility at her company because of her success in sales. Building credibility was a critical accomplishment cited over and over by the women we talked to. "You have to produce," Sandra Martin said. "They don't care how you do it, as long as you deliver the goods." She added, "When you grow with a company you learn this: In the long haul, what matters is excellent work, developing good relationships and credibility with people everywhere you go in your company. Once you develop credibility, when you help them, they help you."

A few white women emphasized the importance of a relational managerial style to their success. No one believes this more than Marilyn Paul. As marketing manager of the food division of a Fortune 100 consumer products company, she earned a reputation for turning around ailing products. She told us during her interview, "So much of doing well in business is eliciting ways people do well and making them want to work more than anything else in the world. I spend a lot of time pulling work from people and trying to make them understand that they're masters of their own destiny. People want to work for me because they feel I have their best interests at heart; that has been something that has made me successful. And when you get more senior in the organization that becomes even more valuable." Three levels removed from the top of the company, Marilyn is being groomed to take over an entire division.

Like their African-American counterparts, a majority of the white women who had attained the highest executive positions stressed the importance of a supportive boss. But the white managers had had much more success in finding not just good bosses, but also mentors and coaches. Linda Butler credited her rise to the senior executive level—she is the only woman at the corporate level of her company—to the support she received from her bosses. "For whatever reason—whether they thought I was the daughter they didn't have or the granddaughter or whatever—they were very supportive. I think they took real pleasure in letting people know that I could do things and making sure that I got the credit for it." Marilyn Paul said of her boss, "He really wanted me in this position; he really pulled my career." Another interviewee told us, "I had this one boss for whom I worked for seven years. I am a very hard worker; he saw that and he saw that I had potential. He took me under his wing. I was privy to things that other people weren't. He also gave me advice and constructive criticism and worked with me on many things. He was very supportive of my career moves."

We found that the white women managers in our study exhibited two postures that were not shared by black women managers. Some saw discriminatory barriers for women but were reluctant to speak out. They accepted discrimination as part of the organizational culture. Others believed their companies allowed them to be *gender neutral*. For this group, individual achievement was proof that gender was not a problem. These women were more likely to echo normative corporate rules for advancement. Our findings suggest that white women managers can feel more compelled to acquiesce to the norms of a male-dominated environment.

The price of membership in executive careers extracts a high price for black women and white women, albeit in a different ways.[15] To understand these differences we refer back to one of the frameworks guiding our study. Aida Hurtado asserts that black and white women experience exclusion differently because of their relative positions to white men. Black women believe rejection is the state of affairs and they refuse to shed their identities to fit in. Day-to-day interactions in their organizations often reinforce their beliefs. White women believe they can gain access and try to fit in. In race- and gender-conscious organizations, being white carries advantages not just for white men but also for white women. A larger percentage of the white women had attained top-level management positions compared to the black women. Yet, in the end, white women managers still must contend with gender discrimination, which usually takes the form of overprotection, subordination, and sexualization.[16] This is a point not lost on some of the white women we interviewed. As Jean Hendrick reluctantly admitted, "I normally don't think this way. But it's occurred to me, finally, out of all my naïveté —which has served me very well when you think of it—that the fact that I am a woman, in the end, will have held me back."

9

❖

MAKING CHANGE

OUR STUDY FOUND that many women use their agency at work to fulfill their commitment to social change in their communities. They also have found ways to engage the corporate hierarchy in the name of social equity within their own companies. We discussed earlier the importance many of the black women placed on giving back to their communities. Do white women, as well, have a similar need to change perceived racial and gender injustice in their companies? We found profound differences between black and white women on this score and explored the reasons for these differences.[1]

All the women interviewed know how to play by the rules to get ahead in their companies. However, we found that many of the black women are determined to change the status quo of their white male–dominated organizations. Their determination is based in part on their perceptions of workplace injustice. Such perceptions were evident in our national survey data. Only 22 percent of the black women believed that race relations within their company were good, compared to 78 percent of the white women. Additionally, 78 percent of the white women had faith that their companies were truly committed to the advancement of people of color, while only 21 percent of the black women did.[2]

Frustrated and angered by such social injustices, black women have learned to put their energy to work in proactive ways, maintaining membership in their organizations without withdrawing or taking a back seat. As the late activist and poet Audre Lorde suggests, these women use anger so "it becomes a powerful source of energy serving progress in change."

We think of these women as "tempered radicals," a term coined by organization management researchers Debra Meyerson and Maureen Scully to describe individuals whose "values and beliefs associated with a professional or organizational identity violate values and beliefs associated with personal, extra-organizational, and political sources of identity."[3] Tempered radicals, Meyerson and Scully explain, are "individuals who identify with and are committed to their organizations and also to a cause, community, or ideology that is fundamentally different from, and possibly at odds with, the dominant culture of their organization."[4] While such women are radical in their desire to change the system, they temper their rage enough to constructively intervene within the system, influencing their colleagues, bosses, and subordinates to move beyond the status quo.

Women's Expressions of Tempered Radicalism

Based on the women's narratives, we found two distinct types of tempered radicals among black women: (1) internally oriented tempered radicals who channel their efforts toward social change within their companies, and (2) externally oriented tempered radicals who direct their energy toward working in the black community for change. Internally driven tempered radicals are usually high-level women who have regular access to top executives.

INTERNAL FOCUS

Patricia Triggs' story is that of an internally oriented tempered radical: "I play a number of roles in this company. One is helping black people get ahead and trying to help anybody out of a bad situation. Another role I play is making sure money from this company keeps going into the black community. Money is allocated to the Black Graduate Consortium. I make sure the director of the consortium meets with our chairman to ensure that there is a relationship between them and us. I make sure we buy tables at fund-raising events for the black community. The farther up I go, the more I will push for these kinds of corporate contributions."

Patricia also leverages her power in other ways: "I also play an active role in creating policies that will work for the betterment of black folks even without the white boys realizing what they are doing. I actively work to make things better. When I am asked my opinion, I vocalize it. When I have an opportunity to push for something that is good for black people in my company, I move right ahead and jump on it. I feel no guilt. I feel pleased to be able to fulfill what I consider my obligation as one black person who has been allowed to slip through the cracks—for whatever reasons. I mean, there aren't but so many of us and it helps to know who I am."

She continued: "It also helps being a black woman and not a black man. A white man's ignorance doesn't allow him to feel as vulnerable to a black woman, so he'll let you through the cracks and give you that promotion, figuring, 'She is never going to hurt me because she can't get my job. She can't outdo me.' A white man's sense of confidence remains intact with a black woman. But his ignorance allows me to outdo him every time."

Like Patricia Triggs, Karen Brown is an internally oriented tempered radical. Recently Karen's company went through a merger that resulted in downsizing. The company had laid off a very successful and well-qualified black man as part of the downsizing effort. A subsequent reorganization in Europe resulted in a white European man being tapped to fill the position the black man had just left, a position that had supposedly been eliminated. Karen felt strongly that the company should not bring the European man to the United States for this position and urged her boss to talk with a senior manager. "I said to Susan, 'Absolutely not—the roof is going to come off this building. I can't support it.' Two days later, Susan comes back from having her talk with the senior manager. He absolutely has to bring this guy here. I said, 'Put him in France, put him someplace. I don't care where you put him. Find a job for him outside the company. But do not bring him into this job.' Finally Susan calls me and says, 'Karen, they're going to announce the filling of the position on Friday.' I thought about this all weekend. On Monday, I called her and I said, 'Susan, I've thought about this. I've tried to work this out with you, but it's not working. I cannot support this move at all, on any level. I cannot support it professionally, and I can in no way support it personally.' I added that it made the company vulnerable. We could have ended up with a lawsuit, and my downsized former colleague would have a very good case."

Karen was balancing her commitment to the company as an insider with her strong sense of injustice over this move. She was also aware of her accountability to the black community. "I told Susan that I have to look the Black Professional Association in the face, and I'm the one that is going to have to answer the questions in the BPA meeting, not the people who made the decision. It ruins my personal credibility. Susan comes back with, 'Well, I'm going to have to help you work this out.' I said, 'Susan, you know me real well and you know how I think through things. I've thought this out every way possible. I have tried to work it out. I can't work it out. There is nothing that gets me there. You have never heard me say that before.'"

Patricia and Karen share two goals that reflect more generally the objectives of black women who try to make change from within: to make the company more receptive to hiring people of color and, once people of color are on board, to make the work life better for minorities. These women cleverly use their position and relationships with the powers-that-be to garner support, broker resources, and influence policies affecting minority employees—whether professionals or secretaries—as well as the larger African-American community. In doing so, they build bridges between the affluent corporate world and African-American communities that are struggling for survival.

External Focus

The externally oriented tempered radicals use membership within a traditional system to advance a cause or ideology outside of the organization's boundaries. Black women devote time, energy, and skills to advance minority communities. Keenly aware that they have managed to crack the ranks of white corporate America, these women feel that now it is their duty to help others who are less fortunate.

Julia Smith, for example, serves on the board of the Studio Museum, a premier showcase for African-American art. "I've always enjoyed art, and I've never been talented enough to do anything on the creative side. But bringing a business sense to an African-American museum allows me to contribute in my way to my community. Our kids in New York don't have a whole lot else culturally; I am giving to them."

Serving on boards of cultural institutions has been a long-standing and even conservative path for the elite, but what distinguishes women like Julia is the political and social agenda that shapes their choice of how, why, and where to give their service.[5] High-ranking black corporate women such as Julia Smith, Colleen Powell, and Karen Brown serve on the boards of political and educational organizations, charitable associations, and major cultural institutions in black communities, where they can lend their expertise and technological savvy. They do so even after working grueling eighty-hour weeks. There is, for them, a two-pronged benefit. Affiliation with these women's companies allows black cultural organizations such as the Studio Museum in Harlem to expand their funding network and to heighten their prestige in the broader society. At the same time, companies benefit from socially responsible employees; this enhances the company's public image as an organization that cares about the welfare of society, as well as demonstrating a commitment to the social and economic advancement of the black community.

Shawn White worked in the entertainment industry and has recently become the president of a small spin-off company that is owned by the company where she began her career. Shawn was very specific in expressing how she will contribute and how she links the personal and the political, "I see myself funding a school, getting my friends together, forming a network of people who not only raise money, but who directly finance the operation of the school. We pay a teacher $65,000 to educate ten black kids. We start from there, start with a teeny-weeny base and expand from there."

Shawn has a clear agenda, though she may have to defer her radical objectives until later. However, because she so clearly articulates her agenda, she is less likely to let it disappear as she advances. This clarity of purpose proved to be a differentiator between the black and white women we interviewed.

Black women's narratives suggest that even those who did not feel they had power to advocate within the company for racial justice found ways to channel their commitment to service at the grassroots level. Some feel the first step is to make *themselves* as strong and economically independent as possible. Shawn White said: "The only way that I can really help other people is to make myself as strong as possible. You make yourself strong so as not to depend on other people economically, because if you do, you will constantly be at their mercy. So in order for me to give back to the community, I have to be as strong as I possibly can." Beyond herself, Shawn recognizes her responsibility to try to improve the destructive dynamics that exist within the black community. She described her concerns, "Until black people are educated about our history and traditions, until we start reducing inequality, our own children will be on the outside . . . we will never gain the economic power and social strength to move ahead."

Some black women targeted their involvement to meet a specific need that they felt was particularly troublesome, such as programs for inner-city youth or senior citizens. Much of this work is done during weekends and nights, particularly for women such as Eliza Washington, who are in lower to middle management positions and who may have less capacity to redirect the corporation's resources.

Nonetheless, Eliza links her project to the work world inasmuch as it enhances young people's career aspirations. "We've talked about the dream long enough," she said. "We can dream all we want but unless we wake up and go about our business making the dream come true, all its ever going to be is a dream." Eliza spends every Saturday morning and Thursday night at church counseling a youth group. "I'm really involved in that, and it takes a lot of planning. When I stopped doing it for about two years, I missed the kids. Some of them now have started working, and they come back. They take me to dinner and say neat little things that I introduced them to years ago. You say what you can say; you reach who you can reach. You get comfortable with the idea that your job is to plant the seed and let God do the growing."

White Women: Where Are the Tempered Radicals?

When white women speak about trying to change their companies from within, they rarely focus on injustice—racial or otherwise.

After Jean Hendrick's company brought in a "diversity" consultant, Jean got involved in her company's diversity task force, both as part of a broader corporate effort and because the related training programs fit with her job responsibilities. When asked if she sees a role for herself in improving race relations, she responded, "I'm working right now on sort of an executive committee task force on managing diversity," and then went on to explain her vision for this work: "My aim is to bring to life for employees an appreciation of diversity that goes beyond race, color, sex—a diversity of approaches, a diversity of right brain/left brain, operational/creating, nurturing/managing, leading/following." She looks forward to this work: "It will be very interactive and a fun sort of thing, too, because I think that's what makes a corporation strong—a diversity of skills and talents and approaches to problems that cut across color or sex. I think it's going to be very exciting, because it's really taking the whole idea of diversity to a much higher place."

While we heard black women appealing to the deep roots of problems in society at large, Jean sets her vision higher. She sees herself soaring above the painful landscape of racism, sexism, and oppression. She focuses instead on diversity in cognitive style. While beneficial, this focus neutralizes the deeper cultural and historical dimensions of "diversity"— it ignores issues of race and gender. It also averts her attention from the inequities her colleagues of color are likely to feel working in the company (presumably the reason a diversity consultant was brought into the company in the first place). Jean has watered down her own ability to make effective change.

When asked about race relations, the white women sometimes described how they counter racist and sexist jokes in the professional setting. Linda Butler confessed that she does not expect to "ever take an active role . . . but I do feel that I don't like to see people discriminated against. While I sometimes don't jump down somebody's throat for making an ethnic remark, I do let them know that I don't appreciate it. I think it's a put-down. So, while I'm not going to go out and march for civil rights or anything, I think that in my own rather quiet way I let people know where I stand. I don't know whether or not they respect me for it or not. I don't really care."

The white women's stories suggest a much more quiet and understated tempered radicalism than what we see among black women, who are much more engaged in trying to make change in the name of social justice. Linda's risk-averse disclaimer about 'not marching for civil rights' suggests a concern about issues on a much smaller scale. Seventy-nine percent of the white women in our national survey felt ashamed and embarrassed upon hearing their white colleagues tell racial jokes or make racial slurs, but we did not hear the kind of desire to make policy changes that we heard from Patricia Triggs or Karen Brown. Linda's way is reactive and personal. It is a way of making small wins. It is extra-tempered.

Externally oriented tempered radicalism was difficult to find in the white women's narratives. White women, like black women, do donate their time and talents to community groups, cultural institutions, and charitable associations, but they did not speak of their involvement in terms of a collective identity or cause. Most viewed community involvement as a "civic duty" or extracurricular activity, rather than a moral obligation to raise the prospects of an entire community or challenge an oppressive social system.

A Contrast of Needs

Black women interviewees express their tempered radicalism via calculated strategies aimed at making a difference by uplifting the black community. They are "radical" in their ideals and the struggle to eliminate oppression. They are "tempered" in that they work within the confines of the corporate world, which is not accustomed to the emotional expression of frustration. They are also radical simply by being minority women in the corporate world; their very presence contradicts the status quo of the canonical white male manager. Also, they are radical in the sense of generating a new vision of what it means to be "race women," as defined by St. Clair Drake and Horace R. Cayton: "A race man refers to any person who has a reputation as an uncompromising fighter against attempts to subordinate Negroes. The race woman is sometimes described as forceful, outspoken, fearless, a great advocate of race pride, devoted to the race, and one who studies the conditions of the people."[6]

We looked for parallel evidence of white women's tempered radicalism on race and gender injustices, but found few examples in their narratives. White women do not express nearly the same degree of anger or frustration about sexism in the workplace as the black women do about racism and its intersections with sexism. They wrestle with how to play along and do not rock the boat. Even in modest moves, such as not laughing at a racist joke, they are cautious and concerned about career implications. This tells us that white women we studied may not have a larger discourse about righting injustice in society that underlies talk about pragmatic moves at work. By using a racial lens in exploring the contrasts between black and white women we begin to understand why black and white women have differing ways of tempering their radicalism.

Influences on Black Women's Tempered Radicalism

Raised in a culture of resistance that had its beginning in the subordinate status of the African-American community brought on by racism, classism, and sexism, black women have historically been encouraged and prepared to resist, wherever possible, the constraints the larger society sought to impose on them.[7] So, the root of black women's tempered radicalism is a sense of injustice that black women do not deny or try to soften.

This culture of resistance leaves a powerful imprint on the women's identities. Sociologist Patricia Hill Collins broadly defines this culture of resistance as a legacy of struggle for family and community, an ethic of caring and self-definition, an oral tradition, and a dialectic of oppression and activism.[8] While parents served as the main socialization agents, preparing their daughters to cope and benefit from the culture of resistance, there were other factors at work as well. In the late nineteenth and early twentieth century, "Black institutions of higher learning . . . stressed the development of black and female leaders who would return to their communities and serve as successful examples of the 'bootstrap' philosophy while working to provide similar opportunities for others."[9] Institutions of higher education reinforced the idea of social responsibility.

At the very heart of the culture of resistance lies a black woman's "homeland," or community of origin—the geographic, social, and psychological space where African-Americans lived, shared a collective history, and held a common understanding of the way of life in the black community.[10] Homelands consisted of teachers, ministers, social workers, neighbors, and shopkeepers. Black women's families joined with people in the homeland to give these women unconditional love, armored them to go out into world and to do their best, and told them stories of black people's painful struggles to achieve racial equality. Thus a resounding theme plays throughout the black women's narratives: They were expected to use their talents, skills, and education in order to give back to their homelands, especially to those who were less fortunate.

The black women in this study frequently cite their deep interconnectedness with their communities of origin—their homelands—and their nested circles of community inside and outside the corporation. The shared historical experiences of blacks as a group in the United States, and their ability to relate readily to others' plights (especially true of women raised during the civil rights movement), makes them see and want to tackle structural sources of inequality. Retaining a collective identity keeps black women connected even as they ascend the corporation in what might otherwise become an individualistic quest for success. Their personal mobility is experienced as part of the mobility of their whole group. Under these circumstances, the adage "you lift as you climb," resonates for black women managers. Julia Smith talked about how the importance of giving back is deeply rooted in her family legacy: "I spend time away from my job doing volunteer work in the community. That's motivated by the fact that my family has always—at least for the last two generations that I know of—been involved in the community. My mother and father were models—they always said, 'You've got to give something back. You cannot be content just to rest on your laurels.' My grandmother and grandfather, as a matter of survival, support, and a sort of deep religious conviction, always gave something back to the community. Their need to contribute is motivated very much by an understanding of the racial dynamics in the United States, the fact that black folks are only as strong as their weakest link. It is this belief that has generated a family tradition." Julia explained with pride that, on holidays, her grandfather provided small bonuses for his workers and made sure that each of their families received a ham, which made him one of the most respected black men in the county.

Because of such socializing forces, black women may not interpret their behavior as being "radical." For them it is simply a way of life that they were taught from childhood. They would tell you that caring about other people, having a social obligation, having a racial obligation, and speaking out against social injustice do not amount to any big deal; they come with the territory of being black and female. Deidre Gainey's words when she responded to the question, "Do you see a role for yourself in the black community?" illuminate this very point. In a slightly sarcastic tone she answered, "That seems a little too 'highfalutin' to me! I can see doing a little bit of what I can when I can, taking two weeks once a year to teach and be a mentor at a black college, talking with educators, working with One Hundred Black Women. Things like that I can do when I can. I try to help as much as I can." Deidre would not call herself a "tempered radical." For black women, being tempered radicals is a natural mode, undeserving of any "highfalutin'" name.

Obstacles to White Women's Tempered Radicalism

A number of factors inhibit white women from acting as tempered radicals. The most important is that white women see themselves fitting into the corporation, at least more so than their black female counterparts. Another factor is their belief in meritocracy. "Meritocracy is a 'taken-for-granted ideal,'" writes organization scholar Maureen Scully, "a social system in which merit or talent is the basis for sorting people into positions and distributing rewards, such that the positions of highest authority are occupied by those of the greatest merit."[11] A belief in meritocracy is based on the assumption that the playing field is equal for all the players. And as long as the workplace is perceived as a fair game, there is less of a driving urge to make changes. The question becomes how to play the game artfully and credibly, rather than how to contest the game. From this position, the self rather than the system becomes the target of change.[12] It is tempting for white women to believe in meritocracy and to follow the individualist course that this ideal prescribes. The mentality of "I'll show them" is based on the belief, and hope, that talent will triumph in the end and that hard work will ultimately be recognized and rewarded. As cases of individual white women advancing to the top become more numerous, this belief is validated. The promise of meritocracy appears to be realized, even if, as Rosabeth Moss Kanter long ago observed, women at the top can block as much as enable other women's advancement.[13]

The white women participants were raised to embrace meritocratic opportunities. Jean Hendrick explains how clear this message was for her in her family. "I was brought up with a spirit that there was nothing I couldn't accomplish, that I had all the qualities I needed to succeed as long as I was willing to work hard." Her middle-class upbringing provided her with the resources and cultural capital that would bolster her success. However, these structural sources of privilege were not central in her story. She focused instead on the importance of talent and hard work, traits that will ultimately enable her to attribute her success mostly to herself. Her success itself becomes a testimony to the inherent fairness of the company where she works.

Several black women in the sample also describe an upbringing that subscribed to the idea of meritocracy, if with a subtly different twist. Whitney Hamilton described parents who "gave me the feeling that I could do whatever I wanted in the world, as long as I put forth the effort." Her family vacations followed the U.S. Open, where her father was one of the few black men to play; this was "his way of showing his children there were no limits." But this message came with a spin: it was clear to Whitney that for her father, such achievements by his black daughters would be a radical challenge to society's racist restrictions; he was almost daring the system to hold them back. Likewise, black women's advancement in corporations shakes up, rather than confirms, the cherished meritocracy. These women approach the meritocracy by simultaneously getting on board and critiquing it. This is tempered radicalism. By contrast, white women, who were raised only to get on board, accept meritocracy without a dose of skepticism about its promises; they are usually defenders of the status quo, not tempered radicals.

White women's status in corporations is another factor that contributes to their muted tempered radicalism when it comes to social injustice. Since white women are more fully invited into the corporation, it is harder for them to push back and decline privilege. One of the white women in our study directly articulated this relative ease of membership. "We're a traditional company, and up until the seventies, we had no black people at all in management positions," Linda Butler observed. "It's been easier for me, because I am a white woman. I was accepted more easily. They're used to dealing with me or with my type."

The prospect of belonging may be difficult to resist.[14] Linda Butler's account shows how she is aware of her privilege. She spoke about her stoicism in hanging in there to win the presumed rewards. She tolerated rather than contested discrimination. "I just accepted that that's the way it was and it was up to me to change those people's perceptions of women and what we could do. As a result, I've probably been harder on myself, because, you know, I'd rather die before I cry. I don't want them to say, 'Look, a woman can't handle it—that's what happens when you put her into a position of power.'" When the prize is big enough and likely enough, white women remain in the game and reshape themselves to fit in. They swallow any hurt: "I'd rather die before I cry." Reframed this way, small moves may take more courage than they initially appear to. Because temptation is dangled more fully in front of white women in corporations, their renunciations, even if small, may take more courage than those of black women.

Our analysis suggests black women feel they bear most of the cost of being advocates for racial justice in their companies. And they feel abandoned by white women. They have reduced their expectations of white women so as to not expect comradeship at all, especially in the name of social justice. They do not fit into images of everyday corporate reality, and, even unwittingly, they take on the role of tempered radicalism: Why? Their communities sustain black women in their work—not just the community that sustains them today, but the community of yesterday, their community of origin, their homeland. Memories of childhood guardian angels and inspirational grandparents continue to feed their ongoing community affiliations. The intergenerational passing of the baton focuses their efforts on giving back to a collectivity.

White women may feel they are unfairly chided for their lack of strategy or voice when it comes to being radicals for social change in their companies. They may truly believe that their small moves result in a big impact on their companies. They may explain how they are downplaying or deferring their radicalism as part of a strategy. However, black women like Shawn White who are deferring their radicalism for a more fruitful moment in their careers are able to explain their cause and to keep the vision alive. In the white women's narratives, we hear no such descriptions of an underlying and self-conscious strategy. They do not describe being inactive now as they wait to activate change tomorrow. Rather, they describe individual—not collective—agency. They describe the strategies and machinations meant to advance their careers. Only once they secure a position of power and status do they consider how to make their companies better for all.

10

❖

Work Isn't
Everything

We have focused, in the previous chapters, on the public lives of the women in our study. But what about the ways the women's private choices have intersected with their career choices? Whether the decision was about marriage, children, or relationships, we found that when the women talked about their professional and personal lives, racial differences mostly melted away. Race may have meant separate journeys through childhood and separate career paths, but regardless of actual marital and family status, all of the women we interviewed faced the same turbulence when work intersected with family and femininity.

The gender dividing line and its assignment of different standards for personal relationships for men and women trumps race in determining the choices the women made for their personal lives.[1] Both black and white women are subjected to strong societal pressures to make marriage and family a central part in their lives. Daniel Levinson, the renowned scholar of adult development, has pointed out the power of gender splitting—the rigid division between male and female, masculine and feminine—in human life.[2] The whole notion of careers in organizations has been traditionally predicated on the life cycle of men, and the expectation that personal dimensions of life will take a backstage to career.[3] But the expectation for women—whether or not they enter traditionally male careers—is that family will remain a paramount priority. So professional women, whether black or white, face a dilemma unknown to their male peers: they must constantly negotiate conflicts between career and family or personal life.

Nonetheless, we did find some significant differences in the issues black and white women grappled with. Our survey data show that a significantly higher percentage of the white women were married (60 percent, versus 44 percent of the black women). A larger percentage of the black women had never married (43 percent, versus 25 percent of the white women). Only about a third of each group had children. African-American women were significantly less likely to report that they were involved in a fulfilling relationship with a spouse or significant other. Indeed, we found that more white women managers reported receiving support for their career aspirations from spouses and significant others. Perhaps the most striking difference was the anxiety expressed by the African-American women about the lack of fulfilling relationships with men in their lives. In fact, it was one of the top three personal life stressors for the black women. It was not among the top three stressors for white women, whose most frequently cited stressor was a shortage of personal time.

All the black women we interviewed spoke of the isolation they experienced in the workplace. They often found themselves the only person of color working in a sea of whiteness. Over time, such isolation takes its toll: their personal lives became flat and nondescript. Time spent with family and friends was reduced as they advanced professionally, heightening their sense of vulnerability. So much of their energy was spent trying to cope with the day-to-day challenges of working in a white male–dominated environment that little time was left to invest in a personal life.

Black women also suffered by having to be the Rock of Gibraltar in their family of origin. This was especially true for the women who were raised in poor or working-class families—more so than for white women from less-privileged backgrounds. Their education, professional status, and income often caused relatives to call on the black women to intervene in family problems. Some black women talked about having to intervene in family situations when a younger sibling was arrested or found to be on drugs. In some cases, the women had to assume financial responsibility for their family members—elderly parents, aunts and uncles, or nieces and nephews—who still lived in inner-city areas. This may be the reason more black women reported that not having enough money was a major life stressor: assisting their families economically often strained their financial resources.

Despite the high emotional toll caring for their families exacts on black women, the literature is largely silent on the work and family conflicts faced by professional black women.[4] Our black interviewees told us they never shared their personal problems with colleagues, for fear it would trigger negative racial stereotypes about themselves, their backgrounds, and their families. They paid their family dues quietly, viewing the need to be supportive or help out as their duty, as they were the fortunate ones. Yet, such a role presented a double burden: while these women could not share the difficulties they were having with family members with their workmates, neither could they turn homeward for instrumental career support. Their families simply did not know how to respond, and frequently were at a loss to offer concrete suggestions for dealing with difficult problems. Very often, these black professionals had no one to talk with or turn to.

Personal Life Choices

Much of the literature on career and family/personal life frames the dilemma between career and personal life as an either/or choice.[5] The literature assumes that time and emotion can be placed in only one sphere at a time and that intense involvement in one role may interfere with full participation in the other. Thus, like all women who choose to work outside of the home, the women in our study had to confront whether they were to be defined primarily by their career or by their family/personal life. These two separate orientations represent the extremes of choices available to women. However, we found the choices they made were neither dichotomous nor static. Their choice sometimes changed over the course of their career. Three patterns emerged in the women's narratives that capture the choices they have made in their personal lives. The women we interviewed sometimes shifted to a family/personal life orientation after an initial intense focus on career. We labeled this a shifting orientation. We also found women who made their personal and family life central and other women who gave their career primacy. These two patterns we labeled family/personal orientation and career orientation, respectively.

How can we account for the choices the women made for their personal lives? The women's career and personal life orientations developed from a number of influences. Early childhood experiences, imprints from the roles assumed by their mothers and fathers, and societal conceptions of gender roles all seem to have profoundly affected the choices available to them and ultimately the choices they made in their personal lives. The constraints and expectations placed on them from the corporate environment—an environment that demanded long hours, total commitment, and loyalty as prerequisites for advancement and success—also influenced their choices. Without a doubt, managing their time—or their lack of it—was a struggle for all the women, black and white, no matter their orientation. In the life of a career woman, time is a most precious commodity.

SHIFTING ORIENTATION: THE WAKE-UP CALL

In many ways, the women in our study represent a generation of women who for the first time could single-mindedly focus on a career to the exclusion of finding a mate or raising children. As a result, these women were far more independent than women of their mothers' generation. And, unlike their mothers, they grew up in the changing social context of both the women's movement and the civil rights movement. They have careers in male-dominated professions. They were well educated, became well paid, and are now well positioned in some of the best companies in this country. In the early stages of their careers, the women in this group typically followed masculine models of career development. Their careers were the first priority in their lives. They made heavy investments in their careers, obtaining professional degrees, assuming professional risk, and working long and tedious hours. They did whatever it took to advance their careers.

Somewhere along this life journey, the women with a shifting orientation got a wake-up call that made them notice something was missing in their lives. Only then did they become aware of the sacrifices they had made in life, and the social and emotional ramifications of those sacrifices. The wake-up call took many different forms. Whatever form it took, it caused these women to make a conscious decision to shift the focus of their energy and to emphasize personal relationships—relationships they had given little attention to as they pursued their careers. The catalyst for this choice may have been a change in marital status, an introduction to the right man, a realization of the enormous personal sacrifices entailed in a career, or a sudden sense of having aged. We center on the stories of four women to illustrate the shifting orientation among black and white women in this group.

Julia Smith. Black women of Julia's mother's generation seem to have had an easier time finding suitable mates. Their lives unfolded before the advent of the feminist movement. Both men and women believed marriage was an inescapable dimension of life. It was expected that women would marry in early adulthood. Courtships started earlier, and unmarried women over the age of twenty-five were considered old maids. This was true even in middle- and working-class black communities, where black women were traditionally in the labor force to offset the low wages made by their husbands. There was never any question, however, that they were also expected to be good homemakers.

The pre–civil rights movement lifestyle also affected black women of Julia's mother's generation. Segregation resulted in closely knit black communities. Available young black men lived in the same neighborhoods, attended the same churches, and went to the same high schools or colleges as available young black women. In many ways, segregation made it simpler to meet and socialize with black men. Segregation also legally outlawed and socially stigmatized cross-racial dating, reinforcing the social connections between black men and women. "It just sort of fell into place for my mother, in a way that was not unusual for women of her generation," said Julia Smith in a moment of reflection about her mother's storybook courtship with her father while they were in college and their marriage shortly thereafter. "I guess I expected it would be the same for me."

Julia's wake-up call came in her mid-thirties. She found herself feeling isolated, frustrated and vulnerable—and less able to carry on her usual cool, focused, and above-the-fray demeanor at work. "All at once it dawns on you how difficult life is. Shit happens, as the saying goes. Parents get sick and start needing support, your own body starts wearing down, friends die, and at the same time you are being squeezed by the company. The deeper you get the more you realize the frustration and the more isolated you become."

While life was pulling Julia in many directions, she felt she was facing her problems alone, without an emotional anchor. "Until recently, I never thought that having a relationship was or was not a choice. My personal life has ended up without a major male presence, but I'm not sure that that was an affirmative choice."

And yet for Julia today—as for many black professional women—the issue is no longer on the back burner. "I hate to break the news to you," she said to us, laughing, "The thing that's on every single black woman's mind is the whole issue of relationships." The statistics back her up. For professional, career-oriented black women, finding a compatible mate is a major life challenge. A *Wall Street Journal* article reported that single black women outnumber single black men in every adult age bracket.[6] There are also fewer well-educated, economically stable black men in positions of authority. Why? Too many black men get caught up in a web of crime and drugs, with statistics showing that more black men are in jail than in college.[7] More young black men die from homicide than from any other cause. Those whose lives have not fallen into disarray and despair make other choices—whether opting to build personal relationships with white women or choosing a gay lifestyle—that result in a diminishing number of eligible black men. While eligible black men date white women, black women have fewer opportunities to date white men, finding that white men have not expressed an interest in them.

For black women seeking suitable black mates, pickings are slim. While white women have a chance of meeting white men in comparable positions at work; black women find few unmarried black men there. The percentage of black women employed in executive, administrative, and managerial occupations is greater than the percentage of black men.[8] "Certainly in my work there aren't a lot of black people, let alone black men," Julia pointed out. "The guys I do meet tend to be too young or are hooked up with somebody. And a giblet will not do," Julia flatly conceded, referring to black men who just seem unable to get their act together professionally and personally. Like giblets, black men who are irresponsible, immature, womanizers, or noncommittal—with no get up and go—are viewed as something you discard.

Black women who have been successful in their careers desire men who have the skills, knowledge, and savvy to be equally successful. What the women we spoke with found attractive were intelligent men who are able to take control of their lives and can carry their own weight in a relationship. Their expectations for what they want in a man and in a relationship are high: "I'm not saying a man has to be a doctor or lawyer, but somewhere along the way there needs to be a commonality of experience," said Julia. "I want somebody who can share my world, who is able to empathize and give me support."

A few of these women also admit they feel they lack the ability to attract the black men who are available. They do not have a successful track record in their relationships with men. Missing from their repertoires are skills in the feminine wiles. Demureness and patience are behaviors they have to work hard at. Julia Smith underscored this point when she confessed, "Some of the sisters out there are like sharks—or maybe like serious fishermen—they know how to cast the fishing line and reel a man in. I don't know how to do it." But Julia continues to hope to one day have a fulfilling relationship with a man and it has become a priority in her life.

Patricia Triggs. As we've seen in Patricia Triggs's life story, Patricia had been concentrated on becoming an executive since she was in high school. Some fifteen years later, Patricia had achieved her dream. She had just returned to the United States after completing an international assignment, during which she put in 110-hour work weeks. The last thing on her mind was starting a relationship. Her wake-up call came out of the blue. She and two of her girlfriends were sitting in the company's cafeteria when she first saw Peter. "The boy was fine. We're talking about real fine," Patricia recalled of her first impression.

Patricia soon discovered that Peter was a manager employed in another area of the company. He was also single, and the word on the company's grapevine was that he was very eligible. Until Peter, Patricia's main interests in life were work and her parents. Like Julia, she was unsure of what to do. As it turned out, a little encouragement and assistance from her girlfriends was all that was needed. Together they concocted a plan to host a cocktail party at one of the women's homes. Each woman invited a "target" man, and the rest of the guests consisted of married couples and single men. They invited no single women so none would be available to talk to the eligible men, and yet invited enough people so they could socialize with others while approaching their special guests.

That night signaled the start of a relationship between Patricia and Peter. "He just knows so much about everything," she gushed with genuine pleasure. "It's fascinating listening to him. He's very well read, so he talks about politics, geography, history, and art." Peter introduced Patricia to a new way of living that meant spending time away from work to build a relationship and enjoy life. Together they attended jazz concerts, went to movies, and spent long hours talking into the night. In addition, he was a kind, patient, and sincere man who was family oriented, very much like her father.

Shortly after meeting, Patricia and Peter married. As a couple, they have a strong sense of "us against the world," in that they are extremely supportive of each other. Marrying Peter and having a child triggered a major shift in Patricia's life, especially her orientation toward her career.

When asked what she envisions for herself in five years, Patricia articulated a role for herself that is more homemaker than CEO. "It's a fantasy. I expect to be home. I expect my house to be neat, orderly, and efficient. I expect to be doing things with my child—finger painting, going to the zoo, attending Boy Scout meetings, and horseback riding. I want us to do a lot of things together. I want to keep my husband intellectually stimulated, well fed, happy, and sexually fulfilled."

For the time being, Patricia is not concerned about her career or where it is heading.

Sylvia Whitaker. Sylvia's career focus was greatly influenced by her early home experiences. "I knew I wanted to get out of my home environment as quickly as possible. I believe that observing the financial difficulty of my parents, my dad's lack of education, and my mother's traditional female career certainly helped steer me away from the more traditional roles that many women had. I wanted to do something that was challenging but I also wanted to make some money." A career was a way to achieve financial independence.

In the early part of her career, Sylvia Whitaker exhibited the same workaholism shown by her fellow CPAs. After completing her accounting degree, she joined a public accounting firm and threw herself into the demanding, fast-paced work environment. Sylvia focused on her career, thriving in the environment and accepting new challenges. Although she married her childhood sweetheart, "I formulated exactly what I wanted to do. I wanted to become a CPA, to become professionally positioned, and to move up through the ranks of public accounting." And she sped along the fast track, advancing quickly in her firm. "In my early twenties to survive the male playpen I was in, I made the mistake of trying to match behavior. That translated into becoming a hard-nosed, cold, abrupt bitch." Poised to be the first female partner in her firm, however, she decided one day that she "didn't want the money. I wanted more of a balance in my life. I wanted to get out into industry. I wanted a balance where I could have career advancement opportunities but also have time for a family and personal interests." Although she found a new job in the insurance industry, she quickly found herself once again focused on her career, working long hours and traveling frequently.

As her career advanced, her marriage faltered, and she found herself divorced. That divorce was Sylvia's wake-up call. "In the early part of my career, I was so focused and so enthusiastic about my work and my job, so motivated to advance, that I think I missed a lot of communication with my first spouse." Now in her second marriage, Sylvia has chosen to make her family more of a priority.

Sylvia Whitaker's shift from a career focus to a more personal focus epitomizes the experiences of other white women and shows how similar black and white women are when it comes to the rich family experience they crave.

Gloria Goldberg. Other single white women also shifted from an early focus on their career to a greater emphasis on family and personal relationships. In the early part of her adult life, career was paramount in Gloria Goldberg's life. Gloria, who remains single today, had her first significant relationship just out of law school. When it got serious, however, she realized she wasn't sure she was looking for something permanent and the relationship ended. "I would say probably in my early thirties something was propelling me. I wanted to succeed, so I made the trade-off. And then there were the sheer hours of my job. I had a dysfunctional existence—there were lots of dinners and all sorts of surface friends, but it was very hard to link into a stable social life."

Gloria's Goldberg self-described "no-flinch mechanism" served her well in the charged, ruthlessly competitive environment of investment banking, where deal making required not only wit but also daring behavior. "I liked the idea of doing deals. I liked the lifestyle." This work style for many of the women spilled over into their personal relationships. For the single women in this group like Gloria Goldberg, it meant making little time for personal relationships or dating.

Hitting forty was a catalyst for Gloria and other single white women in this group. With a twinge of sadness, Gloria related: "I wouldn't mind being married and having a family and that seems to have gotten crunched in the process. I wish I'd been more social. I was very careful about not getting involved. I didn't find anybody I was madly in love with, and I kept very much to myself. You look back and you realize you closed people off. I was fairly sure at the time I wasn't ready to get married, and I didn't want to be tied down because I wanted to shoot for the moon, just to go off and do bunches of extraordinary things. If you got married to someone, it was going to be a compromise decision, then you'd never get to just float freely." In retrospect, she said, "While I was doing it, it was fascinating. But my personal life paid the price at times. I remember once canceling a week-long trip with a boyfriend because a deal just kept rolling. I lost that boyfriend. That is where it took a toll."

How did the women's relationships and orientations change after the shift? The married women in this group describe simple, family-centered activities that give them satisfaction. When we interviewed Patricia Triggs, she was still adjusting to motherhood with a fourteen-month-old son. She manages her work schedule by going into the office extra early in the morning and by not taking lunch. This allows her to get home by late afternoon, enabling her to devote a couple hours totally to her son, although during hectic work periods she cannot always adhere to this schedule. Under no circumstances does she bring work home. This is a woman who once spent the majority of her time absorbed in professional endeavors. Patricia described the time she spends with her son with a look of absolute delight. "There's no music, no TV, nobody else around, just the two of us. We do what he wants to do. I get on my hands and knees and crawl around with him from room to room. I chase him around the house, I giggle with him, and we make each other laugh." Even Patricia is somewhat taken aback by her behavior, because prior to having a child, she never felt comfortable around babies.

But vestiges of her managerial style remain intact, even at home. Patricia manages her home—which includes her parents—very much like a company. She uses three systems. System one is a computerized family calendar that marks the times, dates, and places family members are scheduled to be. Everyone has input and each week everyone gets a printout. System two is a schedule charting the baby's daily routine. Designed by Patricia, it keeps track of his meals, the hours and the amount of time he sleeps, his regularity, and any physical problems he may experience. The third system is a regularly held family meeting that includes Peter, Patricia, their son, and Patricia's parents. Meetings are usually held every Sunday and serve as an opportunity for family members to catch up with one another. They discuss family priorities, upcoming obligations, and the baby's development, and Patricia assigns everyone weekly duties. Interestingly enough, this is a family ritual carried over from Patricia's childhood. Such rituals really do make indelible marks on our lives, and can affect how we structure our adult lives.

"We like to spend time together," Sylvia Whitaker said about her family. "We have a little place at the lake that becomes our little home away from home—away from the telephones and everything else. We like to travel. I love bridge and play a few times a month. We love sports. We love basketball." Time together as family is a precious commodity. The majority of the married white women in our study, regardless of their career-family orientation, were married to professional men. For the women in second marriages, families were often complex combinations of children from former marriages. The married women we interviewed strive to balance career and family, but balance is most often achieved at the expense of time for themselves. As Sylvia Whitaker said, "The constraints are twenty-four hours a day, three hundred sixty-five days a year. The biggest dilemma I have is giving myself priority time. I give it freely to my children, and I give it freely to my husband, but 'Sylvia time' is nonexistent. Not that I need a lot of it, but I'd like to think if I wanted it I could have it."

How do they negotiate career and family? In describing her household management, Sylvia Whitaker says, "We pay for someone to come and do the cleaning. Everything gets factored into the schedule. If it's Monday and it's piano lessons and my husband's out of town—or if it's time for a doctor's appointment or so forth—you just have to work around all that. You just have to be as creative as you can be and just set priorities like you do for anything else. You'd better have some good organizational skills and you'd better not need a lot of sleep. If you are one of those people who needs eight hours of sleep at night, then forget it. It just means being able to make choices and make plans."

The way these women see their lives five years in the future also reflects their shift in focus. "Hopefully, it'll be kind of like it is now," says Sylvia Whitaker. "The youngest will be almost a senior in high school. We're all still living. We're healthy. We will be two years away from no child support. We may be ready to get into that next dream house. We'll be having fun traveling and doing whatever."

The single women in this group think about marriage and often about children. Gloria admitted for the first time that she is thinking about having children. "I would absolutely love to be married with two or three little kids and just hopping along and working maybe two or three days a week. It sounds sort of funny but one would just work more or less time and there would probably be a housekeeper or a nanny or whatever. I don't find that unusual." Time remains a major constraint. "I would like to go out more socially and have a boyfriend or a husband. The biggest constraint has been just sheer time. The level and hours you have to work are the single biggest constraint." She said of her future career plans, "I am thinking of retiring and doing something else."

Despite not yet having found a mate, Julia still hopes that she will be successful one day.

So complete was the reorientation of the women in this group that when asked if they were forced to choose between their family and their career or between their personal life and their career, they would all clearly choose their family. Many gave examples of recent choices in their careers that showed the significance family and personal relationships have taken on in their lives. Sylvia Whitaker said no to a last-minute business trip with the CEO and three other top managers that was needed to close an important deal. "We had already planned our family vacation and had put down thousands of dollars on a trip . . . I knew I ran a risk my decision would reflect negatively on me. But I chose the family."

Family/Personal Orientation: When Family/Personal Relationships Have Always Come First

The women in this group have always placed family and relationships foremost. Their career is viewed as something to be integrated into their family life, instead of integrating their family life into their career. Although these women embarked upon careers, career was not the center of their lives or how they defined themselves. From their early adult lives, these women expressed a clear desire to marry. While they plan to continue their careers on some level, they have no intention of sacrificing their marriage. They intend to have a family and to maintain strong extended family bonds. Their careers do not control their lives. Several of the women spoke of their intent to take jobs within their companies that were more flexible and less demanding after they had children. Their approach toward work is reminiscent of what Felice Schwartz, the former president of Catalyst, called the "mommy track."[9]

Dannette Brown. "This might sound strange," said Dannette Brown, an African-American executive, "but I think I have an old soul that is untarnished and extremely feminine. When I'm with a man I want him to be the man, so I can be all woman." In her position as a sales manager for a Fortune 500 high-tech company, Dannette trusts her intuition in making decisions. She places great value on building solid relationships with her colleagues, and her style of management is interactive rather than authoritarian.

Dannette is representative of the black women in our study who described themselves as "a family person," "a man's woman," and "not a take-charge woman at home." Make no mistake; they too have consciously invested enormous energy into establishing their careers. But their relationships, their goals, and their expectations are "traditional." Dannette was emphatic when she said, "Once I am married, I will be married, period. That's it for me. I know that is a horrible thing to say in this day and age, but that's the way I want it."

"The one thing that's most important to me is having a family and having kids," she said, adding that her model of family life is the one she grew up with in Atlanta. "My parents have been married for forty-two years and they are friends." Other women in this group talked of wanting men who treated them the way their fathers treated their mothers. "I didn't get married early because I never found anybody who, over the length of the relationship, made me feel special. I wanted somebody who was going to be there for me, who could carry his own weight in a relationship—just like Dad did in our family."

Some of the black women who were raised in families of stress and struggle, who did not have positive male role models in their childhoods, had given up their dreams of being married and having children. However, these women refocused their energies on their parents and on siblings and their children, lavishing their nieces and nephews with love, attention, and support.

Dawn Stanley. "I don't think I go to work and try to compete with the boys. I'm me! Part of what allows me to be me is that I have no interest in being my boss. I'm not after power within this corporation and I don't want to spend the rest of my life in one," Dawn Stanley told us. For Dawn, a career was merely a means to financial security—a lesson her mother drilled into her early in life—not the goal itself. Having a "real good relationship" was always important to her. After she married, she gave up a promising position in New York to relocate to the Midwest, where her husband worked, but where opportunities were not as great. Eventually they returned to the East Coast, and Dawn's career became recharged. But at the same time, her marriage of eight years unraveled. At the time of our interview, she and her husband had filed for separation. Dawn was in the process of trying to understand what had gone wrong.

"It's a failed marriage," she conceded with a hint of sadness in her eyes. "Whether it was all him or all me, or fifty-fifty, or eighty-twenty, I now question my ability to have a good relationship with a guy. I don't think the problems were a result of my career. I don't think I've become so obsessive in management and so career-oriented that I don't have time to be a woman and to take care of a man. Yet, by virtue of the fact that I do spend 90 percent of my day managing people, it is something for me to think about."

Dawn was not the only woman absorbing the pain of a failed marriage.

In fact, the number of divorced and separated women in the group was high. Many of them were coming out of dual-career marriages. Often, the women complained of loss of energy from trying to juggle their careers while maintaining some aspect of a traditional family life—a struggle that wears many professional women out. Part of the problem is that men are not equal partners in domestic chores, and as a result, the woman has to run the household while managing a full-time career. Several research studies show that women still bear the brunt of the responsibility for homemaking and child care. Although husbands of employed women do more housework than husbands of homemakers, they still perform significantly fewer household duties than their working spouses.[10]

But trying to juggle work with family life was not the heart of the problem for the black women in this group. Like Dawn, they worried more that they had so successfully absorbed their managerial roles that they had become overly domineering at home. This seemed to be a more serious issue for black professional women than for their white female counterparts. Black women haven't been socialized to be submissive, docile, or fragile. For them this is one of the enduring legacies of slavery, and a result of another century and a half of race, gender, and class oppression. Historically, they have often assumed the role of family provider in addition to family caretaker, carrying both the traditional male and female gender roles in the household. Black women are consequently accused by black men of being matriarchs—and of thereby diminishing the authority of black men. Black women are often very conscious of this and work hard to temper their behavior so as not to be perceived as domineering and controlling at home.

Black men are susceptible to feeling emasculated in a society where, because of racism and inequality, they are often not able to adequately provide for their families. Black men express a desire to feel they have equal, if not greater, control in their households.[11] Even a professional black man who is successful in his career may bridle at a black woman who is financially independent, intellectually competent, and recognized in the public sphere of her life. Her ambition, drive, and expectations can unintentionally be an additional threat to his masculinity in a society that constantly undermines and questions his identity and his manhood. Thus, the culture of racism creates an additional tension black women must manage in dual-career marriages.

For these women, being in the spotlight at work came naturally. Yet being in the spotlight in one's profession at times accentuated the need to dim the spotlight at home. When a woman's earning power was more than her husband's, communication was key. The women we interviewed stressed how careful they were not to rub their financial security in their husband faces.

Competition was another issue the women brought up in our interviews. There is a belief in the black community that black women have it easier than black men advancing professionally in white-dominated corporations. And black women have successfully made inroads in managerial positions, while black men lag behind. Some black women spoke of turning down promotions in their careers because they feared it would create stress in their marriages, especially when the promotions would require the women to relocate. Marriages usually became most vulnerable right after a woman received a promotion. Thus, as a black woman moved up the corporate ladder, her marriage could begin to crumble beneath her.

Dawn was taking time to figure out what she wanted to do with the rest of her life. One fact was very clear to her, however: "I really want a relationship. Some days, some weeks, it really bothers me a whole lot more than at other times. So, I'm just generally down and depressed. My enthusiasm isn't quite there. I'm getting what I need to get done, but . . . there are plenty of days I come home from work and just sit and cry to myself."

Marilyn Paul. When she was in her early twenties, Marilyn Paul wanted to marry and have children, much like her mother. "I always wanted to get married and have a big house and four kids. I never thought I'd be working at thirty five. I used to think I'd get married and stop working. Or I'd have a kid and stop working." She didn't see any contradiction between her aspiration to be married and her desire to remain intellectually active. Marilyn had seen her mother, a college-educated woman, stay home and raise a family. She envisioned herself at home, still having an intellectual life. It was only on the eve of her college graduation that she realized that she would have to work. As Marilyn liked to say, "It took a while to click that I had to earn money." She planned to work only until she had children. But her life did not unfold as she planned. She described her eight-year marriage as "happy," and her husband as "just brilliant—a really smart, sweet man—kind and gentle." They have one child, but other than a short maternity leave, she is still working. Her successful career in marketing is demanding, and keeps her from spending the kind of time she would like with her husband and young daughter. Marilyn continues in her career not out of choice but out of necessity, as her husband lost his job during a corporate takeover. She plans to have another child when her husband's situation stabilizes.

Marilyn's career-family pattern was the dominant pattern we found among the white women we interviewed. Despite successful careers in corporate America, family and personal relationships have always been important parts of their identities. Most of the white women in this group were married with children, thought some did postpone having children until their careers were established. The importance of relationships was even evident in their work styles. When Marilyn said, "People want to work for me because they feel I have their best interests at heart," or when she described herself as a natural leader who "elicits what people do well, making them want to work more than anything else in the world," she is drawing from resources she developed in the family sphere. "I think I have a strong maternal streak," she adds.

Jean Hendrick. When Jean married her husband twenty-five years ago, she tells us that "romance was still popular and you thought of being swept up, taken off on a white horse." Many of the married white women like Jean and Marilyn value family time over personal time. Personal satisfaction and joy rest in the simple opportunity to be together as a family. The mother of two adolescent boys, Jean stated unequivocally during her interview, "I am first a mother. The fact that I am a professional woman—that I have a good job and that I make a decent living—is something I'm very proud of, but not as proud of as I am of my children." She went on to speak of the adjustments she has made at work to accommodate her family. "I try not to travel. I try to have people travel who are less tied down than I am. I have been extremely careful about devoting myself publicly as well as privately to my family so that I'll have the same kind of family I came from. Whenever there is a choice to be made, it's my family that will win."

Several of the white women who have placed a premium on family feel their mobility has been adversely affected. Jean said her choice "probably held me back and slowed me up in some ways," but she doesn't regret it at all. The price of opting for family time has also meant that these women could not participate extensively in formal and informal social activities after work. Jean pointed out, "I don't play golf. There was no way in the world I was going to take five hours to play golf on a weekend when I had already spent all that time during the week. I bet I would be the president of my company today if I were the only one I ever had to worry about. I feel I have the basic raw talent, and I have the energy level and the drive.

However, I would never ever want to do anything that would take more time away from my children. So yes, I have turned down jobs that required travel or jobs that required prolonged fourteen- or eighteen-hour days. I simply wouldn't do it."

All of the married white women in this group describe supportive husbands. Having a supportive spouse seems to help the women better cope with the dual pressures of career and family. Marilyn Paul believes her husband's less demanding schedule has helped her meet the more extensive demands of her own career. "He doesn't travel like he used to. We really have an equal share in the child responsibilities, and he's a wonderful man. So he's been enormously supportive." Likewise, Jean Hendrick spoke enthusiastically of the support she receives from her spouse. "My husband took over all the cooking and the shopping right after our first child was born. He started doing all of that and changed diapers and gave baths. He just did every bit as much as I did."

Their narratives suggest marriages in which the women and their husbands have become what have been described in the dual-career couple literature as superordinate partners.[12] "Jean says, "For both of us, the number one priority is the children. It's not that we think less of each other but we make a lot of assumptions about each other—that we'll be okay. We have been married a long time. He's not someone who goes off with the guys. He doesn't require time for himself, and I don't require time for myself. We spend time together as a family. That is our priority." Another dual-career profile we found among the women was what we called "synchronized partners," where the career and family orientation of each partner complement one another. Marilyn Paul and her husband are able to manage their home life successfully because his career is presently less demanding than hers. None of the women felt they were in competition with their husbands. Their major concern was the limited time they had for intimacy. We did not hear the same kinds of tensions in relationships we heard from the black women.

Overall, the white women in our study seemed to express greater stress from handling dual roles as a parent and professional. (For the African-American women the greater stress was not even having the relationship; paradoxically, they have already learned to manage dual roles by watching their mothers.) Balancing work and family seemed to be a prominent stressor for them. Marilyn lamented, "I miss my husband and my son when I travel. I have to travel, and I'm away from my child more than I would like to be. I really wish I didn't travel." During her interview, Marilyn made it clear she would opt for the mommy track if her husband's job situation permitted. "I would have another child if I could stop working for a while. I just don't think I can do both. I know that my engine is revved as far as I can take it."

We heard repeatedly from the white women about the lack of time for themselves. "I have sacrificed myself," Jean Hendrick told us. "I sacrifice attention to myself because I have my work, and I have my family. I am the one who won't have time to work out or won't have time to have a massage or won't have time to have my nails done or sit and do nothing or read a book or take a bath. Those are the things I've sacrificed. I'm on the edge—but not over the edge—nine out of ten days." How do the women cope with the overwhelming demands on their time? A key to their survival is trying to set priorities. As Jean Hendrick explained, "I feel pulled in many directions all the time. I look at my priorities all the time and reprioritize almost every day. I ask what is most important right now, not what is most important in the world. Is it the fact that my child doesn't feel well? Is it the fact I have to get to an early meeting? Is it the piano recital I have later this afternoon with my daughter? Or is it the fact my father is in the hospital?" Limited time also had implications for friendships. As another woman with children stated, "I think probably the greatest personal sacrifice is a lack of even a few close friends. You don't have much time to devote to outside activities."

All of the women with this orientation pattern—whether single or married—share a vision of a life five years down the road that places relationships ahead of career. Dawn told us, "I very definitely want to get married. I want kids. I want a stable sort of grounded family life and career will be integrated into that. My fantasy is living in a house on the water with my boat docked out back, in a really pretty area, with a wonderful husband who adores me and whom I adore and with a little baby running around, maybe two." "It sounds sort of funny, but I would adjust my time at work and I would have a housekeeper or a nanny." Marilyn said, without any hesitation: "I will have another child, and I will have taken two years off. I will be working in a job that is satisfying but one that has fewer requirements for travel." Jean Hendrick told us she would like to simply "have more control than I have now over my personal life. I would like to be more of the conductor than the orchestrated. One objective is to be in a position to spend more meaningful time with my child." Some women had dreams of partnering a family business with their husbands.

CAREER ORIENTATION: WHEN CAREER COMES FIRST

We found a group of black and white women who had decided to make their career the primary force of their lives, putting their family/personal lives in the background. These women focused foremost on achieving career goals, with personal lives fitted in any space left over. A dominant theme in these women's choices was ambition and taking delight in new work challenges. "Work is my womb," said one of the women who fell into this pattern. To say they were driven by their careers would be an understatement. Most acknowledged wanting to become a CEO. Their fantasies of what their lives would be like in five years were revealing: to be more independent and in control of their destiny, to leave their mark on the world, and to achieve some degree of power and status. Less important were relationships, family, and other dimensions of personal life. This finding clearly speaks to the fact that some women, both black and white, are perfectly comfortable carving out life paths without feeling torn between their professional and personal lives. While some might consider this approach to life abnormal, these women were quite satisfied with their choice. We found this choice among both single and married women. Including married women in this group may seem implausible, but it was clear even with some married women that their career was central. Either their spouses had taken on the primary responsibility for child care, or the couple had purposely decided not to have children.

In a society that may still expect women to be defined by family, placing career first can take courage, even more so for the black women in our study. Such emphasis on career could be viewed as selfish—or "contrary"—behavior in the African-American community. *Contrary* is a term often used in African-American culture to denote a woman's attempt at self-definition.[13] Psychologists Lillian Comas-Diaz and Beverly Greene point out that a black woman is perceived as contrary if she makes her own self-development or own needs a priority, ahead of the many needs of her family or of the African-American community.[14]

Colleen Powell. "I won't rest. I have these milestones that I reevaluate every four years," declared Colleen Powell. Her ultimate goal is to become so affluent that she can retire without obligations or worry. "Down the road, if my stock keeps doing well, I'll evaluate the situation, and if I am still enjoying work or having new challenges, then I will go another four years." Married for the second time, with three children, Colleen has been able to maintain a career orientation with the help of her family. "My husband has a heart of pure gold," she admitted. They struggle to determine what it means for both partners to be highly committed to their careers while also trying to raise a family. Ben, Colleen's husband, is a lawyer with a thriving practice. Their jobs call for both of them to travel, with Colleen shuttling back and forth between Europe and Latin America. As a result, Ben fulfills many of the day-to-day household routines. Colleen called this a "role reversal in their family" and admitted that Ben is her "humanistic" side.

There is, however, a certain degree of tension in their relationship stemming from both being consumed by professional responsibilities. Occasionally Ben is overloaded in his own work and reneges on his share of domestic obligations. Not one known for her patience, Colleen is quick to draw the line. "I accept him because this is him, to the extent it does not infringe on me too much. When it infringes on me too much, then I'm not making any more accommodations," she said matter-of-factly. If someone in their household is going to make a sacrifice concerning their career, the odds are it will not be Colleen. And while she is aware that she may be infringing on Ben's ego and overstepping her boundary by calling some of the shots at home, her behavior has not changed. So how does she go about making the choice between work and family? "It depends upon what the choice is. If it means moving to another country, I would have to give that up. I cannot relocate because my husband has his business here. If it means putting in time at the office, I have to do what is required of me so that I can help keep food on the table. We have to moderate our schedules. I have to adjust to his to the extent that I can. He has to adjust to mine and the children have to adjust as well." There is no confusion in her mind about what comes first, nor are there any apologies.

Part of Colleen's response is shaped by her difficult childhood. She learned to be in control and independent before she reached adolescence. "My husband will tell you that I could retire today, that he would take care of me. But then I might have to be dependent on him. When I don't have to work any more, it will mean that I won't have to depend on him or anybody else. I have calculated how secure I will be based on my investments. I'm not talking about our investments, I'm talking about mine. You may think this is extremely selfish, but ours is one thing, mine is another. Those are my plans." Colleen made it happen for herself, successfully carving out a career and building a secure life.

Deidre White. Deidre White, a senior-ranking executive in the consumer products industry, was asked what she had sacrificed in her life.

"Oh, probably having a personal life for the last ten years or so," she answered, laughing. But not having a personal life was not a major issue for her. "It didn't even faze me, I was so busy working my tail off and enjoying it to the hilt." So Deidre feels no remorse or regrets about it. "If I had woken up earlier, it might have made my life a lot more difficult. It's real easy when you're singularly focused and you can make all the decisions for yourself and not worry about anybody else. I realize there is something about me which is very selfish." With so few public role models and stories of black women who have chosen to focus exclusively on career, women like Deidre, who have concentrated their creative and intellectual energies on their jobs, often attribute their choices to "selfishness." This is especially true of black women, who are taught very early on in life to be the anchor for their family and the emotional wellspring for men, and who often watched their mothers surrender their dreams.

While some women feel a deep need to have it all—marriage, children and career—women with career aspirations are realistic in their recognition that this is almost impossible. "I don't know if I would have been able to do it all," Deidre said. "I marvel at women who are able to juggle family and career. I just think of all of what I did, all of what it took for me to do what I did without any involvement or any of that other stuff . . . it made it much simpler for me." Not long ago, Deidre became involved in a long-distance relationship. She and her partner commute back and forth whenever one of them can arrange it. "It requires a lot more than I have been giving to anything," she said with a giggle in her voice. Meanwhile, she is dreaming up her next assignment along with the CEO of the Fortune 100 company where she works. Somewhere in the near future she wants to take on the challenge of managing a major overseas division of the company.

Cecilia Monroe. When she was young, Cecilia Monroe rejected her mother's attempts to make her become more feminine. "I was my father's only son most of my life. I grew up with a more male perspective on life and how things work." This masculine orientation has never left Cecilia and is evident in her current focus on career. She decided early in her life "to be a hero of the world. I was going to be a professional person." It is a choice she has never regretted. Cecilia has remained focused on her career, working her way steadily up the managerial ranks of her company. Marriage and family remain distant. While she has had significant relationships with men, she has chosen to remain single and childless. Single white women like Cecilia who gave primacy to career do have fulfilling personal lives, but having a family is not as important to them. Cecilia told us, "I've never thought about family, about having a husband and children. I was grateful when my sister and brothers got married and had children so I didn't have to do that!" Her personal life is not empty, though. Cecilia spends her time away from work with a small circle of friends and family. "I cherish being a single woman, and I cherish being able to do pretty much what I want to do." For white women with strong career aspirations, independence was a central theme in their lives. When asked where she wanted to be in five years, Cecilia responded, "I'll have my pilot's license. I will be a woman in charge of her life and everything around her. I'll have a master's degree, and I'll be making $150,000 a year."

Linda Butler. Linda Butler married her husband twenty-four years ago. "I was barely eighteen when we married. He thought he could mold me into what he wanted. I think somewhere along the way he found out that he could do that only to a certain point." Throughout her marriage, Linda's career has remained paramount. Linda confessed, "If I were forced to choose between family and career, that's a hard one since I only have a husband. If I had kids, I don't think there would be any question. I admit that if my husband were to get another job in another state for whatever reason, I would have a hard, hard time giving up my job because it identifies me. I think I would opt for a commuter marriage. I hate to say it, but I think I probably would." Linda's workday does not end at the office. It spills over to home, with Linda frequently bringing work home to do during the evenings and weekends. Even after putting in a twelve-hour work day, Linda leaves the office with paperwork and works late into the night. "It has taken its toll," she said. "You just get more and more frustrated and more tired. There are many, many nights when I'd just as soon roll over and go to sleep." But she is driven by her career goals. "I have never felt that I had to have a child to be fulfilled."

Regardless of the particular choices the women in our study made in regard to their personal lives, each had confronted the issues somewhere along their journeys. A resounding theme in the personal lives of the single black women was an overwhelming frustration with the absence of a fulfilling intimate relationship with a man. It was not uncommon for some to admit that if the right man came along they would definitely consider reordering their lives. For the married white women, we heard greater frustration around seeking balance between work and family. We believe that because so much of the research on women managers has been collected on samples of white women, the issue of work and family balance unfairly dominates discussions of women's careers. However, as this chapter has illustrated, black women must grapple with an additional set of issues. Clearly, though, when it comes to choices about their careers that impact their personal life choices, black and white women alike face dilemmas their male colleagues can barely imagine.

PART III

The Self and
The Other

BLACK AND WHITE WOMEN share a common gender, and, as we showed in Part II, both groups of women crossed significant boundaries to enter a professional sphere long dominated by white males. We might assume such experiences create a foundation for strong bonds between the women. We would expect that struggling within an arena where men hold the seat of power would forge an unusual camaraderie, a base of mutual understanding, among women. Yet, we found just the contrary. Race and the many ways it shapes the separateness of the women's early lives—as well as their experiences in the workplace—creates deep fault lines in relationships between black and white women. One fault line is a differing perception of race and its significance to their identity. While race amplifies a black woman's voice and bolsters her sense of self, we found it plays little role in how the white women in our study perceive themselves. Perhaps an even more painful fault line is created by the distorted images black and white women have of one another. We found that stereotypes grounded in a history of inequality were alive and well in the corporate world.

This last section, in breaking the silence about relationships between black and white women, makes for uncomfortable reading. When we have presented papers to audiences of women about the images black and white women have of one another, we are often greeted with fierce denial. And yet we have also seen that as the material sinks in, as our audiences slowly come to terms with their own experiences of this phenomenon, something exciting begins to happen. As one woman wrote to us after hearing a presentation, "I must admit that I have struggled with the models you presented. Since I have not been able to simply dismiss this information, I have been forced to reflect on its applicability to my own situation. It's been a bitter pill to swallow, but I've accepted the validity, faced the reality, and adjusted my behavior accordingly."

In "The Racialized Self," we explore black and white women's racial self-perceptions, since an understanding of how women of different races perceive one another begins with an understanding of how they perceive themselves. Specifically, we focus on the ways in which race shapes a woman's identity, her sense of self, and her worldview. We show how many aspects of the racial self are formed through childhood experiences. Next, we turn to their images of one another and the nature of the women's mutual relationships. "Images of Other" captures the stereotypes women bring to bear upon each other and the misjudgments that impair their relationships. Its goal, of course, is to replace prejudice with perspicacity and to replace alienation with new, mutually beneficial alliances.

11

❖

THE RACIALIZED SELF

THROUGHOUT THIS BOOK we have illustrated the separateness of the life experiences and careers of black and white women. Black women do not feel they are welcomed into corporations. But their sense of outsider status helps them engage and spurs them to challenge the status quo of the companies in which they work. Yet, behind this urgent pushing back on the system is a deep reservoir of hurt and rejection. By contrast, white women are more likely to feel as if they are invited into the workplace, so they do not feel the need to push back. Instead, they believe good job performance will lead to rewards and career advancement.

Stories in Part I revealed that black and white women come from differing cultural, social, and economic geographies. One of the widest gulfs between them results from their disparate experiences of race. This chapter explores the perception of a woman's racialized self: the ways in which race shapes a woman's identity, influences her overall sense of self, and informs her life. While race unleashes a black woman's voice, it silences a white woman's. Take, for example, the following two narratives, which in their respective lengths underscore this point.

Brenda Boyd: "I experience myself as being exotic and mysterious to most white people. It is both the thing I enjoy the most and the most difficult part of my life. Being a black woman enables me—in spite of not having the right degrees, of not being the right color, of failing to be the right gender—to be what I am today. On the other hand, being a black woman is the thing that probably keeps me from moving ahead, because in a white world black women are simply unfathomable. That we have managed to get as far as we've gotten is unnerving to many whites.

"Part of the majesty about being a black woman is that we have a great strength to draw from our grandmothers and our great-grandmothers all through our history. At some fundamental level, we always know our way home. Home is our anchor, our center. Our strength runs in our veins. As long as we keep dusting off, as long as we do not let the dust stay on us, then we realize that there is something quite extraordinary about being a black woman."

Gloria Goldberg: "I have never thought particularly about what it means to be a white woman. Instead I have focused on what it means to be a woman, because it was clearly in my way. So being female came into my awareness."

Brenda and Gloria repeat what we heard from the other women. Black women's voices were resoundingly clear in stating what they cherish about their racial identity. But white women's voices were strikingly muted. Black women embraced what we call their racialized selves; white women did not. Black women also revealed a powerful like-mindedness when it came to their self-characterizations. Most, if not all, described an internal fortitude of mind and spirit. This inner strength and self-empowerment came up again and again in describing what they cherished about being black women. They saw their inner strength as something passed down from female ancestors, both those who were of blood-kin or those whose strength and achievement were legendary; thus, they often invoked such names as Sojourner Truth, Harriet Tubman, Lorraine Hansberry, Ella Baker, and Madame T. J. Walker. These foremothers stood tall against the challenge of racial, gender, and class oppression, giving younger black women a reconstructed definition of womanhood. There is an old saying in the black community that younger blacks stand on the shoulders of blacks who have walked before and have made a way for them in a hostile world. Our interviewees' comments suggest they are aware of standing on the shoulders of earlier generations of black women; they get strength and courage to move forward from doing so.

What these women did *not* express was regret, envy, or anger about being black and female. They were extremely proud to be black women.

Many took obvious delight in describing themselves as "mystical," "sassy," "provocative," "soulful," "full," and "spiritual." "I do feel truly blessed to be both black and female; it is very special indeed," Patricia Triggs told us. "It means being able to contribute to my family, to my community, to my company, and to other black women in a very unique way. I would never want to be a man. I would never want to be a white woman. I like being a black woman, even if it means you have a hard time in some circumstances."

These black women have learned to develop and to nurture positive self-images in spite of everyday messages that portray black women as manipulative, controlling, angry, harsh, aggressive, and everything from sexually lascivious to unappealing. These old, stereotypic images are hardly fading away in today's society: take a look at typical depictions of black women in music videos, the media, and in film. From Hattie McDaniel's Mammy in *Gone With the Wind* to the provocative and demeaning images in "Thong" by R&B artist Sisqo to "Back That Ass Up" by hip-hop's Juvenile. Such disturbing images appear in the works of both white and black directors and artists. Black women are besieged from all fronts. The positive self-image these women cultivate serve as a coping mechanism, a way to counter the derogatory attacks on their self-esteem. The armoring they received as young girls also enables them not to internalize restrictive self-images, but to claim positive ones. Under these circumstances, claiming the legacies of powerful, beautiful, achieving, and self-actualizing black women from past generations is critical to a black woman's fully developed sense of self, to her importance to community, and her to value in the broader society. Ancestral legacies underscore a deeply held belief that being black did not warrant settling for a position of subordination in life.

White women disclosed an entirely different set of sentiments. Far from being proud, they expressed confusion, ambivalence, and frustration when asked what they cherished about being a white woman. These feelings are difficult to represent in succinct quotes because the conversations involved stumbling, requests that we rephrase the question, evasions, silences, changes of topic, and anecdotes about the race of others. It was not being asked about being a woman that the women found baffling. They spoke about being a woman and about the varying dimensions of womanhood, such as being a mother, a wife, and a professional woman. They also talked about the pain of being female in male-dominated companies. Sandra Martin confessed her "horror of walking into a pinstripe world," where she would have to give up her female attributes. Jean Hendrick was just as adamant about bringing her femininity into the office, even though her male bosses suggested that she tone down her style of dress, hand gestures, and displays of emotions.

No, their silence did not originate from thoughts about being female; it followed their contemplations about race. "White" was the trigger word. For example, Sandra Martin offered, "I just think being white doesn't mean anything—one way or another, you're not aware of it or you don't think about it much." Or think about Jean Hendrick's response: "I've got to tell you, being white is not something I think about. I don't think about cherishing being white. There are qualities across all kinds of people to be cherished—integrity, humor, and generosity. The things that make a person or a group wonderful haven't anything to do with color or race or sex." They had a limited framework for understanding whiteness and it prevented them from being able to embrace being a white woman. In their experience, femaleness is separate from whiteness, making race an invisible or uncomfortable component of personhood. The white women, unlike the black women, made no mention of any connection to white foremothers, kin or otherwise. If white women such as Susan B. Anthony, Eleanor Roosevelt, and Amelia Earhart were the women's heroines or existed as models for actions, aspirations, or hoped-for legacies, they certainly gave no hint.

Indeed whiteness, for our participants, seemed empty of association. They share this perception with other prominent white women. *New York Times* columnist Margo Jefferson refers to "All-American whiteness," making her race as bland as Wonder Bread. Ruth Frankenberg, an author and sociologist who is one of the leading scholars of White Studies, refers to whiteness as "unmarked" and normative, referring to the improbability of white women bringing whiteness to the foreground of their identity.[1] White men have noticed this as well. Maurice Berger, racial commentator and author of *White Lies: Race and the Myths of Whiteness*, describes whiteness as implying "not a color of skin, per se, but usually an unexamined state of mind and body. Whiteness was a powerful norm that had been so constant and persistent in society that white people never needed to name it."[2] "Whiteness is culturally, socially, politically, and economically diverse," he continues. "It has multiple meanings, ethnicities."[3]

On the other hand, claiming whiteness occurs when a white woman embraces her racial identity and the significance race has in her life. This is difficult for many white women who perceive race as a characteristic of Otherness: something only Blacks, Asians, and Latinos have. White women attach race to people of color, but they cannot do the same for their own racial affiliation. Ruth Frankenberg believes "whiteness makes itself invisible precisely by asserting its normalcy; its transparency, in contrast with the marking of others on which its transparency depends."[4]

Why is this the case? One reason is that whites have traditionally been the dominant racial group in America. Gloria Goldberg made reference to this point when she sadly asked, "Do I need to have my consciousness raised? I've just not thought about any of this: I guess it is a function of being in the majority." Whites have never been forced to liberate themselves from racial oppression, and they never had to fight for civil rights in the name of their race like blacks and other minority groups. When you are perceived to be at the top of the racial hierarchy, race—especially your own race—recedes in importance. White women *have* had to struggle—and still do—to free themselves from gender discrimination, sexual harassment, and other forms of gender-related oppression. This might heighten their perception and understanding of the racial dimensions of oppression. Yet such struggles by themselves do not guarantee adequate understanding or appreciation of other dimensions of oppression.

White women did bring class oppression into the definition of their racialized selves. The white women who came from working-class backgrounds acknowledged that being black probably makes life more difficult, but felt that racism was no more detrimental than other forms of discrimination. These women equated their own experiences of living in poverty with the racism blacks experienced. They saw a connection between themselves and black women; as they had also traveled on rough roads to achieve their accomplishments in their careers and personal lives. Despite parallels and interconnections between social class and racism, each has different historical roots, and manifests differently among racial groups. A poor black woman struggles against not only her own poverty, but also against racism coming from both poor and upper-class whites. When a white woman sees the discrimination brought by her humble beginning as equivalent to racism, she psychologically distances herself from the actual effects of racism on black people, and she does not have to examine how being white, even though poor, is still a benefit in some ways in our society.

Curiously, ethnicity figured no more in white women's self-descriptions than did race. Although many of the women were aware of their ethnic lineage in terms of the places of origins of grandparents, family life did not center on ethnic customs and traditions. Ethnicity—defined by psychologist Beverly Daniel Tatum as "a socially defined group based on cultural criteria such as language, customs, and shared history"[5]—was minimized and there was little socializing with children from other cultural backgrounds. We refer to the elusiveness of the white women's ethnic identity as "flat ethnicity." There are at least two dimensions of flatness we heard. First, there was a sense of themselves as not being "ethnic," that ethnicity was not part of their childhood. Second, there was a lack of knowledge of other ethnic groups. Maxine Schneider underscores the first point in chapter 3 when she declares her German-Austrian ethnic background but confesses it doesn't mean much to her because it "felt like we were American." For Jean Hendrick, being a white Protestant meant being "just people." Joyce Canton lived in a very Waspish world—void of other ethnic groups.

Women who were Jewish were an exception. This is not surprising; as Beverly Tatum points out, "ethnic identities remain most salient to individuals of racial groups that have been historically disadvantaged or marginalized."[6] The Jewish women were more likely to have been socialized to their ethnicity by their parents during childhood, although none grew up in Orthodox Jewish homes. What they remembered was not necessarily the religiousness of their ethnicity but an awareness of the meaning of being a member of an ethnic minority. Their stories told of families gathering to light Hanukkah candles and to celebrate Passover dinners. In some instances, even though parents were not religious, they made sure their daughters learned important Jewish values and attended synagogue. Gloria Goldberg was taught by her parents "to be charitable, to be educated, to be a leader, and to play a role in the community. It was very important to do good deeds and support the institutions of the community."

Perhaps the most consistent theme we heard from the Jewish women about growing up was a sense of being different from other whites. Some even talked about their grandparents having faced tremendous discrimination because they were Jewish survivors of the Holocaust. Their parents prepared them to expect differential treatment. "I learned that if you're Jewish, you can assimilate all you want, but you can't ever pretend that you're not Jewish because no one else will let you forget it. So, you better not forget it," recalled Abby Zeigler.

Whiteness, until very recently, was a topic rarely discussed among white people. But with national dramas such as the riots in South-Central Los Angeles, the Clarence Thomas hearing, and the O. J. Simpson murder trial, race is a topic that is coming up more around white dinner tables and in executive offices. Still, we agree with Maurice Berger's observation that "while the social implications of whiteness remain mostly unspoken today, race is no less meaningful to white people who continually reinforce their own authority and social standing by seeing themselves in positive contrast to an inferior, negative, or even dangerous blackness."[7] Whiteness becomes even harder to discuss in a society that purports color blindness and pretends that race no longer matters. Such ideologies attempt to mask contemporary racism, but also limit whites from exploring their own racial identities.

In white women's narratives another response frequently surfaced in the women's narratives. Jean Hendrick's statement is a good case in point: "I don't cherish things about being white. I tell you one thing though, I feel lucky I happen to be born white rather than black or some other race." In her book *White Women, Race Matters: The Social Construction of Whiteness*, Ruth Frankenberg offers insight on the first part of Jean's response of not cherishing "things about being white." "Women's insistence that they did not see differences of race or color can be understood, at least in part, as an attempt to distance themselves from essentialist racism, the idea of white superiority based on biological and genetic differences."[8] Put differently, not cherishing whiteness allows some white women to believe they are not racists or that they do not buy into racist ideology.

As for Jean's statement of feeling lucky to be born white rather than black, she was not alone in expressing this sentiment. Many of the interviewees could talk more to the problems of being black rather than staying focused on their own race. Whiteness alone provided little space for the women to define themselves and claim their voices. But, when they contrasted being white with being black, the white women found their voices. They clearly understood being white in this society was better than being black. White women knew, in some respects, that they were better off because they lived their lives free from the day-to-day burdens of being black. Unwittingly, however, feelings of not wanting to be black implicitly correspond with being white and privileged, a topic we will discuss further on in this chapter.

What we found in both the black and white women's narratives was reinforced by the responses from our national survey data. While 81 percent of black women surveyed said they were conscious of their racial identity at work, only 19 percent of the white women claimed such awareness. Only 27 percent of the white women saw themselves as being members of the dominant group. Eighty-four percent of the white women reported downplaying their ethnic identity at work. However, black women were more accepting of their minority status (73 percent).

The racialized self-perceptions of black and white women are as different as night and day. Juxtaposing their perceptions illuminates one difference that keeps them apart. It also helps us comprehend how the infusion of race complicates or enhances the meaning of self for these women.

Learning Whiteliness

This division is rooted in their childhoods, starting in their families. Young girls are socialized on "whiteliness," or the ways of being white, by their parents, the other significant adults in their lives, the neighborhoods they grow up in, and the churches and schools they attend. They learn the scripts that dictate the roles, attitudes, and behaviors they should perform when around people of color. Philosopher Marilyn Frye has coined the term "whitely" to describe a deeply ingrained way of being in the world.[9] Allison Bailey, also a philosopher, builds on Frye's concept, and combines it with sociologist Judith Butler's notion of racial scripts, expanding on the idea of race being "performed attitudes and behaviors."[10] Butler proposed that "race may in part be thought of in terms of the repeated stylization of the body, a set of repeated acts within a highly rigid regulatory frame that congeal over time to produce the appearance of substance, of a natural sort of being."[11] Thus, whitely scripts reveal the everyday behavioral performances, rituals, and attitudes of "whiteliness."

During their childhoods, the majority of the white women's lives were surrounded by whiteness. "The place I grew up absolutely had no blacks. It was college before I really had friends that were black or Jewish or anything other than white, Anglo-Saxon American." "The town I grew up in was so white—even the cleaning ladies were white!" "My neighborhood was all white, Jewish." "I didn't even know what a black person looked like." "My grandmother used to read me the story 'Little Brown Cocoa.' It was about a little black child. It was like a fairy tale to me. It wasn't real." "There weren't any blacks at our school. I didn't have any black friends." This kind of racial isolation results in what feminist poet Adrienne Rich refers to as "white solipsism," the tendency to "think, imagine, and speak as if whiteness described the world."[12]

The white women from the Northeast and Midwest grew up in virtually all-white neighborhoods or towns, while the women from the South lived in the segregated spaces created by Jim Crow laws. Not only were their physical environments separate, but the major institutions they encountered in their early years were also monoracial. Being white meant attending virtually all-white schools and churches. Family circles and social networks were also white. Whatever the childhood activity, whether it was play or a cultural event, it took place in a same-race context. These monoracial childhoods contributed to the women's low consciousness and awareness of race, even of their own racial selves. Whiteness was the norm and the standard in every aspect of their lives. In this context, the whitely script dictated that these women stay within the confines of their own group by maintaining both a social distance and a geographic space from blacks.

But below the surface, what appeared to be all-white childhood experiences among the women often did include knowledge of and interactions with people of other races, most often blacks. Marilyn Paul said, "There were plenty of black people in my town. We had a black maid, but it wasn't part of your life." Black people were on the periphery of white women's lives, out of their direct vision. They remained in the margins of their families' lives as maids, helpers, and employees, or as people who lived a safe distance away. A number of white women we interviewed had black domestic help in their homes during childhood. In Marilyn's case, having a "black cleaning lady" allowed her mother to cope with the inordinate stress placed on the family because of her sister's protracted illness. Perhaps it is a reflection of the time period but we found this to be true across all the family structures and across class lines. Even women from working-class backgrounds, particularly those who grew up in the South, had black help (usually black women) in their homes at some point during their childhood. Here the whitely scripts impart to young white girls that one of the roles they perform in relation to blacks is that of mistress, the woman with authority, while blacks perform servitude roles. Indirectly, the women learned that blacks were less powerful individuals who required direction and instruction to do work. Finally, there was the lesson that it was a white person's responsibility to see to it that the job was done right.

Whitely scripts prescribe and justify appropriate behavior white girls should engage in when interacting with blacks. Such interactions were based on the race relations in that historical moment. For our interviewees, the historical moment was framed by the political, social, and economic context of the 1950s and 1960s, the collision of black demands for equality and an old racial order that had kept blacks locked in an inferior, second-class status in all spheres of society. It is not surprising that white women learned they could not be friends with blacks. For the most parts this lesson was learned from observing their parents' social networks. The women did not remember parents having friends of other races. There were also instances when the lesson was made explicit.

Cecilia Monroe told us, "I was playing with a couple of boys my age one day when I was about five years old. There was a little white boy, Charlie, and a little black boy, Tom. I enjoyed playing with both of them. My mother explained to me there was a difference—that Tom was black and that I shouldn't really be playing with him. She told me that black folks were not compatible with whites, and that, more or less, white girls do not play with black boys. I remember I didn't understand it." Growing up in a working-class family in the rural South meant that white women like Cecilia were more likely to live in closer proximity to blacks than whites in middle-class families. Poor and working-class white neighborhoods were often near the edges of black neighborhoods. Her mother's admonishment may have been an effort to make clear the social distance between blacks and whites. As young girls, white women learn they must fear black men and boys and need to be protected from them.

There were other things to fear about blacks. "I do remember as soon as we would drive though a bad area (a black neighborhood), we would all sit there and put the locks down on the car. You always tried to look down and not to look. I was always thinking, 'please don't do anything,'" admitted Maxine Schneider. "Yes, I do remember a fear of getting caught in the wrong section of town," she continued. Maxine went on to talk about being very scared of blacks because of the riots that happened in the city. "I mean I lived through the curfew. You had to be in by 11 o'clock. You just didn't know what to expect. On TV you would see the city burning and then you were really scared, really frightened." Maxine's family did not live anywhere near the black community yet she still was afraid that blacks would invade and destroy her neighborhood. Even indirect contact left negative impressions. The lesson was clear: blacks were deviant, destructive, and violent.

Another reason for not associating with blacks was the implication that blacks not only had different values but also had undesirable ones. "I always thought they were poor, and I felt sorry for them," says Maxine, who also remembers driving throught what her mother called "jigaboo city" on the way into town from the suburbs. "I just couldn't understand why they would let their homes get so ramshackle. It was always so terrible and yet there was always a big Cadillac in the front yard. I always thought their values were so strange. Why would you buy a car when your house was so bad?"

Still another lesson white women learned as young girls was to act in a benevolent way toward blacks. Alice Booth, a senior executive in the financial industry, told us, "From the early days, there was a black nurse who used to take care of me. There was a racial difference at that time between blacks and whites. They were always people who worked for you. We always had a maid and a washwoman because we didn't have a washing machine. We took our wash to someone who did it. You were taught kindness. Well, I would have to call it 'servitude respect' if I had to put a name on it. These people worked for you and you were to be good to them. You remembered them on special occasions like Christmas." These whitely scripts taught young white girls about being paternalistic toward blacks, and it taught them about racial hierarchy. Whites in positions of authority and superiority were to be good to black people. Even though Alice's family could not afford a washing machine, they were able to assume a superior position to blacks because the blacks served them.

Embedded in the notion of "servitude respect" was the inherent inferiority of black people—an idea consistent with racial attitudes and policies of a pre–civil rights society. Cecilia Monroe learned about paternalism by observing her father's interactions with the black men he employed. "My father, when he owned this small lumber mill, had ten to fifteen black men working for him. He took very good care of those men. He bailed them out of jail. Some of them would go off and spend their money on gambling and drinking. Their wives wouldn't have any money for food for their children. He would give their wives money. He was very protective of them. And yet he was also prejudiced. It was like we were always superior. We looked after them, and it was sad that they weren't as intelligent as we were. That was kind of a paradox for me."

A different lesson was learned during childhood by some of the girls— that whites should be color blind. In this context, whitely scripts teach white girls to believe there are no differences between black and whites. Ann Gilbert remembers being told by her mother that blacks "are no different than you and me." Her mother also taught Ann the proper way of referring to black people. In Ann's words, "I can remember her saying to me, 'They're not niggers.' You don't call them that! It's not nice. You call them colored people. That was a southern way of referring to black people." Other women, too, remember their parents as color blind. Gloria Goldberg describes her father as "a diehard FDR liberal" who insisted on standing up for his black employees. She shared one particular incident in which her father would not tolerate discrimination against one of his employees. "It angered him that someone would judge someone based on color and race."

Being color blind meant more than just not seeing differences between blacks and whites. Being color blind was exemplary behavior for a white person—the proper behavior to display. But for all its laudatory attributes it hides a more pernicious assumption: if blacks and whites are the same under the skin, there is no racism in the United States, for blacks have the same chances as whites to make it in society. There is something naïvely unaware about the conclusion Gloria Goldberg reaches about the blacks who worked for her father. "The only black people I knew worked for Dad. But they were superior people because they were confident and good."

Parents, too, sometimes transmitted contradictory messages about color blindness to their daughters. It was striking to hear women describe parents as "truly color blind" in one moment only to later recite a childhood story where racial difference took center stage. In other cases, one parent was not prejudiced, while the other one was. Marilyn Paul told us, "I used to secretly suspect that my mother would like to be a member of the John Birch Society, but she was too ashamed to voice it out loud because my father would have divorced her on the spot. Because she was the one who had to wash our mouths out with soap, it took me years to realize my mother's tendencies. I remember every once in a while hearing some pretty derogatory comments about blacks from her. The one thing I heard from her was 'You must never say this outside the family.' She said you can have your own private beliefs in America but you must never express them in public."

Lessons of whiteliness can be summed up in the words of writer Margo Jefferson: "To become successfully male or white means that you should accept as right and natural a system that subtly, or blatantly declares you the most intelligent, handsome, and gifted of all people."[13] To Jefferson's observation we would add that young white girls learn that white people are the most responsible, the most generous, the most hard working, the most good willed, and the most ethical of people, which brings us to the question of their racial privilege.[14]

On Being Privileged

The concept of white privilege arose in the '90s to describe the hidden benefits of being a member of the dominant race: such benefits include power, status and entitlement.[15] Peggy McIntosh, associate director of the Wellesley College Center for Research on Women, suggests being a member of the dominant culture, "allows whites to be confident, comfortable, and oblivious," something blacks do not share. Author Maurice Berger thinks of white privilege as the "ability of whites to live their lives without having to think about the color of their skin. While other factors might endanger us, our race does not generally threaten our survival or well-being; nor does it provide us with a daily barrage of suspicious glances, physical and emotional evasion, closed doors and thoughtless comments and insults."[16]

When asked if they felt privileged, a majority of the white women we interviewed discounted the idea. "Being white is probably easier than being black," they would answer, but "it does not necessarily mean privilege." Jean Hendrick explained: "You never get a situation where all things are equal." For Jean, class moderated the issue of privilege between whites and blacks. "I think some educated black women can clearly be more privileged and sought after than some white women. I think we're getting past the point, to a large degree, in our country where just being white is an advantage." Jean's thoughts of black women being more in demand in companies is in reference to their "twofer" status—being black and female. While this phenomenon may get black women in the front door of many companies, it is not an indication of their future career success.

Many white women agreed with Jean's position. To these women, professional black women had the same degree of opportunity and received the same level of rewards in the workplace as white women, making racial discrimination a moot cause. Maurice Berger believes that middle-class blacks make whites comfortable because they "often think that middle-class blacks no longer suffer the indignities of prejudice, unlike their less fortunate ghetto brothers and sisters. Middle-class blacks have economic and social standing to insulate them."[17]

Marilyn Paul told us, "Having grown up in an upper-middle-class family, I started out ahead of the game; I was so conversant with the rules that success was easier for me. Being a white woman is a privilege and an advantage." Being from an upper-class family helps Marilyn to recognize

some of the ways she is privileged. However, she so firmly believes in meritocracy that in another moment she is willing to deny her own sense of
privilege in order to subscribe to the notion that organizations are based
in meritocracy; that all employees start out on an even playing field: "Privilege is bullshit. Nobody gets all the benefits in the world; you have to
work real hard to make it work." From Marilyn's perspective, talent, hard
work, and solid performance at work are the primary factors in determining who advances in the work place. Personal privilege does not translate into organizational privilege.

If whiteness has its advantages, then the system of meritocracy gives all
players an equal opportunity to prove themselves, regardless of their race.
The meritocratic ideal in the United States promises that people who contribute effort and ability will be rewarded with advancement and income.
References to "the land of opportunity" abound, brought to life by images
of employees who rise from the factory floor to the upper echelons of a
company. To the extent that people believe there is plenty of opportunity,
they approach the workplace as the site of individualistic competition to
move ahead.[18] The corollary to the belief in meritocracy is the idea that
people who do not get ahead have only themselves to blame for displaying
inadequate effort and ability.

If a black woman works as hard, if she is as responsible, if she is as ethical, if she is as loyal a team player, and if given the chance, she demonstrates an ability to advance the business, she will be aptly rewarded. Or,
will she? A belief in meritocracy negates how important certain dynamic
forces are in propelling someone up the corporate structure. A belief in
meritocracy ignores the power of informal networks and influential relationships with people high in the company ranks, those endorsed with
authority and decision-making power. Black women are often excluded
from such networks and have fewer opportunities to develop critical connections with important people. A belief in meritocracy also inhibits a
white woman's understanding of the systemic obstacles in the organizational structure (i.e., the reward and promotion systems) and culture (i.e.,
rituals, beliefs, and accepted behaviors) that work against black women.
Rather than seeing systemic indiscretions, white women who ascribe to
meritocracy tend to blame the victim.[19] A persistent vocalization of
racism involves white people attributing black people's slower economic
advancement to individual traits rather than to structural factors.[20]

As we pointed out previously, upper-middle-class women in particular
received the message from their parents that they could be anything they

wanted to be. Their upper-middle-class upbringing provided them with the resources and cultural capital to bolster success. In telling their stories, these women focus on the importance of talent and hard work as the key traits for success. The structural sources of priviledge were not central to their stories.

As long as the workplace is perceived as a fair game, there is less of a need to make changes. The quest becomes how to play the game artfully and credibly, rather than how to contest the game. From this position, the self rather than the system becomes the target of change.[21] It is tempting for white women to believe in meritocracy and to follow the individualistic course that this ideal prescribes. The mentality of "I'll show them" is based on the belief, and hope, that talent will triumph in the end, and that hard work will ultimately be recognized and rewarded.

But not all the white women interviewees bought into the ideology of meritocracy; not all refuted the idea of being privileged. There were a few, like Linda Butler, who candidly acknowledged her privilege as a white woman. Linda believes that having a sense of privilege is culturally instilled in whites, even as she is bothered by whites who believe they are "chosen people." "It is something that, for the most part, white people grow up with; even if nobody tells you, you grow up feeling that we are just a little better than anybody else in the whole world. I don't think it's white versus black necessarily. I think it's white versus anybody that is not white. And white males are the most extreme."

The black women we interviewed also described an upbringing that exhorted success through meritocracy, but with a subtly different slant. Women like Julia Smith, Patricia Triggs, Karen Brown, and Dawn Stanley, for example, were also taught that they could accomplish whatever they wanted in the world. But they knew that their achievement would challenge society's racist restrictions. To them meritocracy means they can enter the company and perform to the best of their ability *while critiquing the injustices of the system.*

What About Learning Blackness?

Just as there are racial scripts white girls are taught about the appropriate roles, behaviors, and attitudes in their interactions with blacks, black women, too, are socialized to adhere to defined roles and performances in their associations with white people. All of the black women we interviewed consciously lived the reality of being black and female every day throughout their lives. And they continue to experience race at the offices where they work and in the communities where they live. Their stories of learning blackness are explicitly captured in the Flashbacks section.

Julia Smith, for instance, had a powerful lesson when she accompanied her grandparents to the voting polls in Mississippi. Her account (given in chapter 4) of hearing a young white boy call her grandfather a nigger was a crucial lesson; in that moment she became aware of the lack of respect white people had for black people. But watching her grandfather's response to this denigration was just as critical. When he ignored the white boy's epithet, it taught her not to let white people's racism interfere with her goal and mission in life; she learned that some battles just are not worth fighting.

By standing on a stool to clean a poor white woman's kitchen, Ruthie Mae White learned very early in her life that black people were in a subordinate position to white people. But she also learned that not all white people were alike when a white lawyer intervened in her life by showing her respect and dignity, thereby raising her self-worth and allowing her to set higher expectations for herself. Dawn Stanley received a very different lesson. She learned the complexities of race within her own race, because of her light complexion and silky hair. She learned that dark-skinned black people often hold light-skinned blacks in contempt because of their greater acceptance by whites, and she learned that "passing"— when fair-skinned blacks pass for white and turn their backs on the black community—was not an option for brown-skinned blacks. Dawn learned she had to prove her blackness and loyalty toward the black race.

Finally, Patricia Triggs learned there were two racial scripts for her to learn: one black, the other white. Walking the fine line between two worlds in an integrated school setting, Patricia learned the importance of hanging out with the brothers and sisters to avoid being labeled a "Sally," a black woman who is trying to be white. She learned the value of interacting with the white kids, and most important, learned the value of being able to compete on their level. From this she learned to stand tall; she learned the power of navigating in two separate but connected worlds.

Living in Two Worlds

The need to develop a way of navigating in two separate worlds marks one of the sharpest differences between the professionals we studied, in that it was unique to the black women. The white women grew up in a mono-cultural world and strove to work in a monocultural corporate world. Growing up, they were insulated in the whiteness of their communities of origin and didn't develop skills to operate in other environments.

Black women, though, were raised with a bicultural sensibility. Always acutely aware of their blackness, they developed a rich sense of racial iden-tity—a richness that they carry into the white world. But, by necessity, they also developed separate roles that allow them to move comfortably in the white world—a set of behaviors that white people accept and that serves to reduce tension with white people. This amalgamation of roles works for them in the white world.

"Biculturalism" is a way they structure their lives to have rich and sat-isfying experiences in both the personal and professional spheres.[22] Young black girls like Julia Smith and Patricia Triggs first learned armoring at home as a way to protect themselves against racism. As women, they extended this shield as they developed bicultural life structures: on the one hand, they built their careers in the white world; on the other, they cultivated significant personal relationships, leisure-time activities, and spirituality within the black community.[23] Such bicultural life structures allow black women to move back and forth between the black and white cultural contexts in their lives. Each cultural context was developed within vastly different socio-historical conditions that contribute to each one having its own set of social requirements, values, and behavior patterns that make demands on the women. As young girls, black women learn to manage these often-contradictory cultural settings, unlike white women, who tend to grow up in monocultural environments. A bicultural life structure enables a black woman to hold on to her African-American rootedness without being totally assimilated into white society.

Dawn Stanley, for example, characterized the black and white com-munities in her life as "two separate drawers, two separate faces, and two separate uniforms. I get up Monday through Friday and I think about act-ing, behaving, and interacting with one group of people where I am more formal and maintain an emotional distance. Then on Friday evenings, I close the door to my office. The weekend is back to me, back to family, back to being in safe territory. It's not that I don't do things with white folks from time to time, but my worlds are not very integrated, they are separate and distinct . . . It's just two closets: they both work and I know what to expect in both of them."

Having a bicultural life structure can be a source of empowerment for black women. It enables a woman to draw on resources, traditions, and belief systems from multiple cultural contexts, thereby giving her a sense of spiritual, emotional, and intellectual wholeness. One director of marketing at a Southern regional branch location of a major Fortune 100 financial services corporation gave an example from her life: To celebrate the holiday season, she plans and hosts two separate Christmas parties in her home. The first is a small gathering organized for her white colleagues and professional associates, and scheduled early on Friday evening. She hires a black professional caterer, and together they plan a menu of hors d'oeuvres. A case of California wine is ordered for the event. An elaborate table is set by the Christmas tree in the living room. On the night of the affair, guests arrive promptly at five o'clock wearing the appropriate attire and are greeted by the elegantly dressed hostess and her husband. Hired waiters serve an array of delicacies as classical versions of Christmas music play softly in the background. Guests mingle and talk throughout the evening, chatting about work, families, and social events. By eight o'clock the last guest has left, and the caterer is busy cleaning up.

The second party she organizes for friends, sorority sisters, and fraternity brothers, family members and professional associates—all of whom are black. It takes place on the Saturday after the white Christmas gathering. The same caterer is hired. However, this time a full feast is planned: honey-baked ham, turkey, chitterlings, potato salad, marinated black-eyed peas, and collard greens. The food is placed on the kitchen table, and all eat from paper plates. The dessert table by the Christmas tree is laden with pound and coconut cakes, sweet potato pies, banana pudding, and a huge crystal punch bowl filled to its rim with eggnog spiked with rum, brandy, and bourbon. Guests, casually dressed, begin to arrive at nine o'clock, and continue showing up after eleven. Pulsating sounds of rhythm, soul, and jazzy Christmas music emanate from the stereo in the family room. Some people talk, but most are dancing. The party does not wind down until three-thirty in the morning.

Creating a bicultural life structure also enables black women to cope more effectively with the tensions of working in hostile work environments. "The white world, as best I can describe it, is me being a guest in someone else's home," said Brenda Boyd. "When I am around white people," Karen Brown told us, "I am much more aware and alert about everything that is going on around me. My antennas are coming out the back of my head, out of my ears, out of my feet. But when I am around my people, in my community, my antennas are relaxed. It takes a lot of energy to be around white folks all day."

Not all of the black women we talked with described living bicultural lives. Rather, they speak of themselves as centered in one universe, one they describe as richly diverse. They are not interested in being "incog-Negro," a black person who attempts to disguise, hide, or deny their racial identity. Their willingness to reveal their sense of identity keeps them strongly connected to black womanhood. These women see African-Americans as an important part of the national fabric, and because of that, carry inside them a sense of self-worth that many black women in a white world have to fight to discover.

"I don't know if you would call it being in a limbo world or if you would call it having access to things that have been traditionally opened only to whites," Julia Smith told us. She continued, "I guess the notion of functioning in a white world becomes uncomfortable when you view yourself as having sort of given up and you have cut away a piece of yourself in order to deal with white people. Now I am not saying that I open my life like a book to white folks, but I am clear on who I am. I think I'm accepted on my own terms to a certain extent as a black woman. I position myself not as a threat, but as person of strength. That's important to do."

What about the fact that many black women still see themselves as being marginal players in their companies? Does Julia Smith ever feel this tension? "Without a doubt," she responded. Then she reframed the issue. "I think that black folks are more prone to view work as a job that we leave at the end of the day. It's largely because we have not been given the opportunity to feel vested in the welfare of a company. So, we go into work with the attitude of, 'This is a job we perform and after we complete the job we split.' I think white folks, because they feel like it's theirs—they have a vested interest—do have a sense of ownership. I mean, it's theirs. And there is a higher probability that they actually have something vested in the outcome. They are more prone to really fuse work and their social life together as one value system with little separation."

12

❖

IMAGES OF OTHER

AS MORE AND MORE women enter managerial positions, the relationships they establish with each other will be critical not only to the advancement of their careers, but to their company's competitive edge. Strategic planning, financial maneuvering, and savvy marketing may be do-or-die features of a company's survival, but these are not enough to sustain growth. The very heart and soul of a company's productivity rests upon the relationships among its employees. Especially as women in managerial positions increase in number, they need to develop dynamic, collaborative relationships with each other. If this is no easy task among women in general, it is even harder across racial lines. Racial stereotypes and distorted images hamper black and white women from building authentic bonds both at work and in their personal lives. This chapter examines the perceptions with which black and white women regard each other in the workplace—as colleagues, supervisors, and subordinates.

Relationships begin first by perception. Perceptions influence how a black woman feels about a white woman, how she will approach her, what she will expect from her, and the ways she is willing to interact with her—and vice versa. Accompanying perceptions are the attributes we give them. Negative attributes can cause us to stereotype others. Unfortunately, black and white women's perceptions of each other often jeopardize their chances to work effectively with one another and to connect as women.

The fragile relationship between black and white women is rarely discussed openly. This chapter breaks that silence by exploring the often-taboo issues that undermine supportive bonds between black and white women.

Historical Context

Most of the present-day tensions in the professional relationships between black and white women can be traced not only to the environments and conditions that shaped their lives, but also to a past historical context, a history of pain, betrayal, frustration, disappointment, anger, envy, and mistrust. This history begins with the institution of slavery and the dichotomized constructions of black and white women. Black women were no more than chattel, forced to labor in the fields and to procreate to maintain a slave labor pool.[1] In stark contrast, white women were seen as pure and chaste and were to be protected.[2] The legacy of slavery deeply affected both the perceptions of and the kind of relationship possible between black and white women. As a result, historian Patricia Morton notes, "Women of each race were thereby rendered a fractured self, denied a full and diverse identity by the culture of patriarchy and slavery and encouraged always to reject that racially designated female other."[3]

In more contemporary times, tensions among black and white women persisted. While the women's movement of the late '60s was a watershed event for women's rights, it also signaled serious disconnections between women, particularly along the lines of race. According to feminist critic bell hooks, white women's "rhetoric of sisterhood and solidarity suggested that women in America were able to bond across both class and race boundaries," but no such coming together actually occurred.[4] White women activists omitted the experiences of black women in their writings on feminism. In consciousness-raising groups, white women silenced black women's voices when they attempted to tell their stories of what it meant to be a woman of color in a society that oppressed them.[5] Also, bell hooks adds, "feminists tended to evoke an image of woman as a collective group."[6] Thus issues such as poverty, unemployment, health care, and child care—issues pertinent to black women—were pushed to the back burner of the feminist agenda or fell between the cracks all together.

Many black women came away from the women's movement feeling angry and rejected, and sensing that white women were abetting racism. Many withdrew from the feminist movement. Ruth Frankenberg, a sociologist who was also active in the women's movement, confesses, "It seems as though we white feminists responded with confusion over accusations of racism; guilt over racism; anger over repeated criticism; dismissal over stasis."[7]

Our national survey data provided ample evidence of disconnections between black and white women. Overall, white women appear to perceive the relationship between white and black women to be better than black women believe it to be. For example, 44 percent of the white women said that it is easy to relate to black women. Only 36 percent of the black women, however, described the relationship as easy. Black women were less trusting of their white counterparts. Ninety percent of the black women reported conflicts at work with white women, but only 4 percent of the white women said they had conflicts with black women.

A significant percentage of the black women, 90 percent, believed they competed with white women for jobs in their companies. Only 10 percent of the white women believed they were competing with black women. Why is this? The black women managers were more likely to work for white women or have one as a colleague. Of the white women interviewed, few had a black female boss and fewer still had black women as peers. Because white women constituted the majority of women in upper-management positions, black women managers were more likely to be subordinate to white women managers than the other way around. When a white woman came in contact with a black woman on the same management level, she was often in another area of the company, thus diminishing opportunities for them to work together. However, both groups of women reported the tendency to stay away from each other in social interactions. And neither group reported a willingness to discuss their cultural differences with the other.

Perceptions of Other

Brenda Boyd: "She can never hear anything intelligent from me, and so it's that kind of racism where she just refuses to acknowledge the validity of my role. So she'll deal with anyone else around me, but she will never deal with me directly."

Maxine Schneider: "When she greets you, it's a whole thing about being black first. She wears her blackness. I think she has a chip on her shoulder. Too often she expects extraordinary measures. She wants exceptions. But this is a business environment and you either cut it or you don't."

As the two responses above reveal, the black and white women in our study had strong—and different—impressions of each other in their professional lives. The most obvious and consistent impression black women conveyed about white women was their colleagues' lack of racial identity. In their eyes, white women were attentive to women's issues—willing to rally around sexual discrimination—but unlikely to recognize racial discrimination, let alone act upon it.

In her role as vice president of human resources, Karen Brown regularly holds informal meetings with senior women in the company to talk about workplace change. Not surprisingly, it is a white female group. In one of these meetings, Karen brought up the topic of diversity. "When you talk about diversity, of course, it means race to them." Karen recalled. "The conversation becomes a low-energy, intellectual conversation: What are we going to do about the Hispanics and Blacks?" After the conversation changed to women's issues, Karen noticed an immediate change in the demeanor of the white group. "The room lights up, and it's stars and spangles. Everyone starts talking at once and they get all animated. Two days later, one of the white women who was at the meeting said to me, 'Did you notice that the room changed when we started talking about women's issues, how it got all exciting and the discussion was emotional?' I thought to myself, we could have an intellectual conversation about race," Karen then added in a dry tone, "but when it comes right down to it, that's my problem."

Karen's story demonstrates how, to white women, the category of "women" really means white women. By separating "diversity" issues (read race) from "women's" issues, the plight of black women and other women of color often remain invisible. The story also underscores how white women sometimes miss the racial perspective. For instance, the white woman questioner who approached Karen appears to be conscious that something caused the room to become more animated yet she doesn't seem to know exactly why it occurred. A great many of the black women we interviewed offered similar anecdotes and echoed Karen's observations. Black women interpret white women's self-interest on gender issues both as a lack of empathy and a lack of concern for their nonwhite colleagues. They see white women taking care of themselves, supporting those policies that benefit mostly white women. Thus, black women feel they are left standing alone on matters that positively impact the work conditions of minorities. When white women miss the racial perspective, black women feel abandoned by their white female colleagues, making it difficult for black women to build authentic relationships with them.

A majority of the white women had no impressions of black women because they had so little interaction with black women in the companies where they worked. A number of white women frankly admitted that they had no contact with black women in organizational settings: "There are no black women in similar leadership roles at my bank." "I don't know any black women in the company." "I have only minimal contact with black women." Without a reference point, some of the white women were unable to offer perceptions of black women. These responses are sad testimonies to how few black women are in management positions in American companies.

When we probed white women further for descriptions of black women peers we noted that some white women struggled to identify any black woman as a reference point. More typically a white woman identified a black woman in a subordinate position, such as a secretary. If they could not identify someone in a subordinate position at work, then they talked about a black woman who existed in another dimension of their lives. Usually this black woman turned out to be the family maid during childhood or someone they were currently employing as a domestic.

At other times, there was a tendency for white women to respond to our questions by referring to black men, often not realizing they had switched gender. This occurred even through we explicitly asked for their perceptions of black women. In this context, black women were lumped together with black men, losing their gender identity: there was no distinction made between black women and men. Linda Butler's comment serves as a good illustration: "I will have to honestly say that I do not know a black person well enough to really answer that question. The one person I can think of that I do have a pretty good relationship with is in human resources. He heads up what we call our EEO area."

Because of a lack of contact with black women as colleagues and peers, some white women did not have the kinds of interactions that enabled them to develop relationships with black women. Within their work environments, white women were surrounded with whiteness; their associates were all white. Whiteness was the taken-for-granted racial lens through which they perceived their associates and companies. Living racially separated personal lives only served to heighten the inescapability of whiteness.[8]

Invoking Fractured Images

Despite initial responses that were sometimes vague, especially in the case of the white women when they were pushed to be more specific, both black and white women revealed images of each other that arose out of deeply embedded gender stereotypes. Although they may not have used these particular labels, a number of the women we interviewed invoked the characteristics of the following stereotypes to describe women of the other race. These stereotypes reinforced images of other women as nurturers, as compromisers, and as sexual manipulators. The images that contemporary corporate women have of each other continue to reflect traditional ways women have been forced to seek power in a masculine world. Yet their images of other also indicate a fractured and distorted view of womanhood.

BLACK WOMEN'S IMAGES OF WHITE WOMEN

Let us start with the images black women had of white women, first by introducing a description of a stereotype, then by using the women's real words to bring the image to life.

The "Miss Anne" stereotype refers to an elegant but callous white woman, originally the mistress of a plantation house and its slaves. Put on a pedestal by white men for her virtue, she derived her power from her position as wife, daughter, mother, and sister to the white slave owner; to maintain this power, she willingly deferred to her husband in all things.[9] This Miss Anne originated in African-American literature.[10] In the words of literary critic Mary Ann Doane, "the white woman profited from her place in the protected shadow of the white male's assertion of racial power and mastery."[11] Consequently, her power derived from her position as wife, daughter, mother and sister to the white slave owner. As Hazel Carby points out, "white women who felt that caste was their protection aligned their interests with patriarchal power."[12]

Black women use the Miss Anne image to describe a white woman who garners status and power in the organization by catering to the needs of her white male bosses. She not only aligns herself with white male power brokers, but places herself in a subservient position when inter-acting with them, refusing to stand up for her own beliefs and ideas. As Brenda Boyd put it, "You know, they perpetuate this line about this being a woman-friendly company and it doesn't seem to dawn on them that we are not in charge, that the people laughing all the way to the bank aren't us. I just find it awesome that they get smacked down, sat down, and treated like little girls."

Such women are quick to come to the defense of their white male sup-porters, often acting as their talking heads, echoing and supporting their views and values to fellow workers. Black women feel such women are unsure about their authority in the company, and deep down are afraid of being seen as incompetent. However, the foundation on which a Miss Anne builds her power base can easily collapse. Miss Anne retains her sta-tus for only as long as the white men who support her remain in power. She is perceived as having access to white men, who teach her the rules of the corporate game, rules necessary for moving ahead in the workplace. She learns how to fit into the work environment.

"White women are very familiar to white men," Patricia Triggs explained, "This is someone they know. This could be their sister, their daughter, the mother, or the girl next door. They are comfortable with these women." Julia Smith described Miss Anne somewhat differently: "White women have godfathers, which is how they have gotten where they are in this company." Because of white women's perceived access to white men, many black women believe a white woman who acts like a Miss Anne has the upper hand in advancing her own career. She learns from the master players—white men. But she gets caught in a bind when it comes to speaking out against company practices. Speaking out jeopard-izes her fragile status.

The "Snow Queen" refers to a cold, unfriendly white woman who focuses on her own ambition at the expense of her relationships with coworkers and friends. Originally found in the Scandinavian fairy tale written by Hans Christian Anderson,[13] the Snow Queen is a woman who is alienated from her own emotions and incapable of genuine friendship or love.

The Snow Queen imagery cropped up in many of the black women's descriptions of white women they had observed or had known in their work life, especially those who were very senior in the company. They described these women as being cold, insensitive to others, controlling, over-ambitious, isolated, and unable to connect with their colleagues. Dawn Stanley observed, "If I look at the white women who are above me,

I have a hard time looking at them as role models because they are all the prototypical female executive bitches: tough, nasty women; high strung, with big egos. They are the women who fought their way up. Now, they're going to make everyone below them suffer a little pain, too. Take for example one of our divisional heads. She can be very cunning when she wants, but she always has her own agenda and will do whatever she has to do to get her agenda on the table."

The Snow Queen's source of power in a company derives from her canny ability to "use the patriarchal system for her own ends," without questioning the implications or effects on others, especially other women.[14] Indeed, she refuses to identify with other women at work because she is detached from her femininity. She is a solo player. The Snow Queen is reminiscent of the Iron Maiden discussed in the breakthrough book *Men and Women of the Corporation* by Rosabeth Moss Kanter.[15] Like the Snow Queen, the Iron Maiden was seen as a tough and hostile woman. The Snow Queen has derived her authority in the company by being the first female to successfully scale her way up the company's hierarchy. But being the first women has a high cost. A woman must learn to endure a hostile work environment and to accept demeaning feedback from her male supervisors. Consequently, she may suffer from stomach anxiety attacks or experience some other physical aliment from trying to prove she is just as talented, if not more so, than her male counterparts. All this frustration and pain comes with the territory of being the first white woman entering a male-dominated profession.

In the Snow Queen's struggle to succeed, she adopts masculine behavioral traits: self-centeredness, a confrontational attitude, and an authoritarian style. But the same aggressive behaviors that get a white man promoted can get a white woman derailed. If she is able to succeed, she carries with her the reputation for being a "she-devil."[16] In time, however, her reputation can work against her, especially as she continues to alienate co-workers and those above her. When this happens, she is vulnerable and her career eventually topples.

The image that appeared most frequently in the women's narratives was the "Femme Fatale." The Femme Fatale refers to an inappropriately flirtatious white woman who manipulates men's desire for her own purposes. She plays a dangerous game, using her sexuality for professional gain. This female representation emerged as a central figure in the nineteenth-century texts of such writers as Gautier and Baudelaire.[17] She later appeared as the "vamp in Scandinavian and American silent cinema, the diva of Italian film, and the Femme Fatale of film noir of the forties."[18] Possessed with uncontrollable ambition, she uses her sexuality to manipulate men to get what she wants. In an organizational setting, a Femme Fatale obtains her power and status through her sexuality.

Black women were cautious when sharing their observations of a Femme Fatale. Patricia Triggs, for example, couched it this way, "I would not say that white women's use of sexuality is excessive or extraordinarily widespread, but in every company I've worked in there is at least one officer who everybody knows slept with men to get to the top. So, it's still here. I'm not trying to say that all white women do this to get ahead. That's not fair. Some white women do good work and work hard to get where they are."

Patricia's comment underscores the notion that one way a Femme Fatale is thought to use her sexuality is by having sexual liaisons with white men in exchange for career advancement. Other black women echoed this perception. In each case, a Femme Fatale was described in a subordinate position to a senior white male. These were not described as romantic interludes; rather, these liaisons were perceived as purely instrumental affairs to advance a woman's career.

Such blatant use of sexuality was not limited to sexual relationships with senior white males. Black women also mentioned a Femme Fatale's flirtatious behavior and use of sexual innuendo in the presence of white male colleagues; she used her body, her tone of voice, or her style of dress to seductively attract the attention of men. "Whether it is the softer voice or just the tilt of the head," said Dawn Stanley, "there's always some little sexual thing going on." Julia Smith put it another way, "I've seen white women use their femininity much more than black women to get promotions. I've seen some white women wear something tight and a little suggestive. They really turn it on in the presence of senior management."

In a company a Femme Fatale often gets trapped in the sexual object role, which is hard to play down. Forming sexual liaisons with white men in exchange for career mobility can in the long run compromise a woman's career. The white woman who sleeps her way to the top is such a common stereotype that such an image is often projected onto a woman without any evidence. It may stem from the age-old attitude that a white woman could never achieve executive status based on her own intelligence, merit, and talent. What is striking in the comments of black women is that they perceive a Femme Fatale's use of sexuality as a source of power unavailable to them.

The perceptions of the black women may be less a reflection of the actions of white women than it is about the taboos preventing the black women from displaying sexuality in the workplace—especially in their interactions with white men. While white women struggle to overcome a legacy of restrictive Victorian values about sexuality, black women struggle to defy the denigrating images of black women as oversexed and hot-blooded. So they do not dare display any sexual behaviors, especially in the workplace. When Anita Hill accused Clarence Thomas, now a Supreme Court Justice, of sexually harassing her at the Equal Employment Opportunity Commission, she was mercilessly portrayed as a wanton, sexually promiscuous, insatiable black woman both in the popular press and in the black community.[19] The strength of the stereotype is proved by the success of the media campaign against the prudent—even proper—Professor Hill. A black woman linked sexually to a white man stirs even more dangerous stereotypes. Such a liaison plays upon the historical racial-sexual legacy of black women who were forced to be the concubines of white men. So professional black women struggle mightily to be perceived as respectable and shrink from using their sexuality to gain status from white men.

WHITE WOMEN'S IMAGES OF BLACK WOMEN

White women were perplexed when asked of their perceptions of black women, because so few of them had any significant interaction with them professionally. A small number of white women in our sample, however, did have collegial relationships with black women at work. The white women's perceptions of black women were different in that, unlike the black women, white women had no perceptions of black women in a sexualized role with white or black men. There was no mention of sexual innuendos, sexual liaisons, or flirtations by blacks. If anything, white women's social construction of black women was asexual.

Historian Darlene Clark Hine's concept of a "culture of dissemblance" is useful in this discussion. Hine's concept provides insight on how black women were taught as girls to conceal public displays of sexuality, sexual abuse, and exploitation as a means to survive in an oppressive society.[20] To the extent that black professional women can successfully hide their sexuality, it may be difficult for white women to pick up any sexual overtones in the behavior of black women. Mary Ann Doane adds another provocative point: "In the historical scheme of rape, lynching, and castration, which reveals a complex articulation of power and sexuality in relation to both white women and black men, the black woman disappears as an actor because she can only be an embarrassment to any lingering ideals of white male morality or white female compassion."[21] The two primary stereotypical images white women had of black women were the "Mammy" and "Sapphire."

The "Mammy" refers to a motherly, self-sacrificing black woman who takes care of those around her. The mythological image of the Mammy was born out of the literature of the antebellum South: she was the loyal, hard-working, caring, and trustworthy slave who was the chief caretaker of the plantation's master and his family. Much of the mythology surrounding the Mammy stresses her strong maternal devotion toward those she cares for. In the white women's narratives, the Mammy becomes the emotionally competent earth mother, still in the caretaker role. This contemporary Mammy is nurturing, supportive, all giving, and self-sacrificing. She "comforts the weary and the oppressed while championing the causes of others," according to Tavistock consultant Rhetaugh Graves Dumas.[22] White women view the Mammy as an advocate of other blacks in the company.

Joyce Canton's observation typified other white women's characterizations of the Mammy. "Black female managers," she said, "have a tendency to be a little more demonstrative in style. I've watched how the senior women look out for the younger black women and men in the company. There is always one who will organize a group, make sure they meet, and be responsible for their welfare. She is always available for consultation and willing to lend a hand if help is needed. Management looks to her when there are minority problems. And they better listen to her, because she doesn't take excuses from anybody." Joyce added an interesting assumption in support of her observation: "I think their behavior is partially based on the fact that they come from a matriarchal society where women run things."

This is not the first time the Mammy image has been used in describing black professional women. In her pioneering study of black women executives, Rhetaugh Graves Dumas offered a brilliant analysis of the Mammy among black women who have leadership roles in white companies. In our study, white women perceived the Mammy as a senior ranking woman or an older black woman. She is described as being competent in her work, but her emotional and nurturing style casts a shadow over her other professional strengths. Dumas notes that a Mammy's power "is derived from her relationships in the informal [organizational] system . . . and her willingness to put her person at the disposal of those around her. And it can be maintained only as long as she is willing or able to provide what is demanded of her."[23]

"Sapphire" refers to a dramatic, bossy black woman who is full of complaints and mistrust. The opposite of the nurturing Mammy, Sapphire first appeared on the American pop culture scene on the radio program *Amos and Andy*, soon followed by the 1950s television sitcom of the same name. The prototypical "black bitch," she is portrayed as the wisecracking, angry black female. Her bossing of black men forms a cornerstone in the black matriarch mythology. Another characteristic of the Sapphire is her ability to sass back in a stinging and impudent tone. Joanne Braxton, a professor of American Studies and English at the College of William and Mary, traces the origin of the word "sass" to West Africa where the "poisonous sassy tree grows." According to Braxton, "a decoction of the bark of this tree was used as a poisoning . . . for punishing accused witches . . . women spoken of being wives of Exu, the trickster God."[24]

In the white women's narratives, a modern-day Sapphire is a black woman with an attitude. But here her hostility and impatience surface in the office rather than at home. A Sapphire is described as being aloof, rude, self-centered, and lazy. Sandra Martin remembered a black woman she encountered during the early years in her career, when they had the same job title. "She was terrible to me," Sandra recalled, and "rude to everyone." In the white women's descriptions, such a woman does not bother to extend herself to the aid of others, black or white. She is not trusting of anyone, particularly, but especially keeps her distance from white colleagues.

Linda Butler's comments elaborate on this point. "I think black women tend to be a lot more reserved and a lot more cautious, which works against them a little bit. I have a black female who works for me and is really good. But what is really hanging her up is that she doesn't trust anyone. She won't open up to anyone You come here everyday. You spend all kinds of time here and you have to develop relationships with people. She sets herself up. She's an island. She doesn't confide in me."

One of the most frequent observations made by several of our white interviewees was that "black women wear their blackness on their sleeve." By this they perceive a black women's hypersensitiveness to racism and a militant attitude toward whites. When a Sapphire acts out her hostility, white women do not know how to respond. A Sapphire is someone who uses race as a means of getting sympathy from whites in the workplace. When this happens, she is rarely viewed as a good worker. Instead, white women see her as trying to move ahead in a company based on the color of her skin rather than the skills she possesses. As Sandra Martin observed, "You have to produce. A lot of times a black woman will duck responsibility; she thinks she is better than she actually is." Sandra was not the only white woman to voice this opinion.

Often, when a black woman is too outspoken and aggressively pursues privileges that are customarily given to whites, she can find herself seen as a Sapphire, and can quickly find herself marginalized in the company. Her bosses and colleagues may respond more to her behavior rather than her performance. That is, her outspokenness gets in the way of people being able to see her talent. Gradually, she is cut off from support from other blacks and sympathetic whites in the company. Unable to respond to constructive feedback or to soften her aggressive nature, her career in a company may be short-lived.

PUTTING THE IMAGES INTO PERSPECTIVE

Stereotypical images of professional women are not new phenomena in managerial literature. As we mentioned earlier, Rosabeth Moss Kanter's classic, *Men and Women of the Corporation,* discussed the stereotypical informal roles professional women are molded into by men in order to maintain the familiar and everyday patterns of social interactions. Kanter's Mother, Seductress, Pet, and Iron Maiden figures are reminiscent of the images black and white women held of each other. However, there are several distinctions. First, Kanter's images depict the views white men have of white women, and convey men's covert responses to women's sexuality and their traditional sex roles. The stereotypes are not racialized so as to have meaning for black women. (During the time of Kanter's study, black women were an anomaly in most U.S. corporations.) Second, Kanter based her observations and analysis on numerical demographics, so at the time the low number of women working in a male-dominated company made them tokens and encapsulated them into limited gender specific roles.

Still, the caricatures of Miss Anne, the Snow Queen, the Femme Fatale, the Mammy, and Sapphire are as painful for us to read just as they are grotesque for us to accept. Yet, vestiges of these images surround us, in one form or another, every day. "What caricatures of bloodless fragility and broiling sensuality still imprint our psyches, and where did we receive these imprints?" Adrienne Rich poignantly asks.[25] Miss Anne, the Snow

Queen, the Femme Fatale, the Mammy, and Sapphire are still alive and well. In fact, new negative images of women are emerging. Take, for example, the "killer woman" as described by cultural critic Benjamin DeMott in his book *Killer Woman Blues*.[26] This is a woman who has traded in her femininity for the very worst of masculine traits. Writer Emily Eakin describes her as being "everywhere money and power congregate, hiring, firing, and barking orders with one steely eye trained on her prospects for advancement, the other glued to the bottom line."[27] Lawyer Marcia Clark, Internet guru Esther Dyson, *New York Times* columnist Maureen Dowd, and physician and editor of the *New England Journal of Medicine* Marcia Angell are among the successful professional women whom DeMott characterizes as treacherous killer women.[28] We consciously apply such destructive images to ourselves, to women of our own race, and to women of other races. Some of today's most successful and powerful women—whether in the business world, the political world, the entertainment world, or the larger culture—have been boxed in by mutations of Miss Anne, the Snow Queen, the Femme Fatale, the Mammy, and Sapphire.

Miss Anne. A Yale-trained lawyer, a best-selling author, and a corporate board member, Hillary Clinton fell into the contemporary Miss Anne trap. While still First Lady, she decided to run for a seat in the U.S. Senate representing New York. Newspapers across the country were abuzz about the "chilly reception" she received from the very women she was expected to attract as supporters. Women, especially white women, have seen Hillary Clinton as someone who uses her husband's power and status to leverage her own political ambitions and is willing to overlook his transgressions.[29] "We finally had the opportunity to have a strong First Lady, but she used her marriage for personal gain," said one woman quoted in the *New York Times*. "I can't get over that."[30]

The Snow Queen. One of the first women to head a Fortune 500 company as CEO of Mattel Incorporated, the world's largest toy manufacturer, Jill Barad's biggest success was revitalizing a forty-three-year-old doll, Barbie. Her downfall came as a result of a sharp two-year decline in stock for Mattel and a string of resignations from the senior executive team. During her rise at Mattel and early in her top executive role, Barad was a media darling, characterized by her femininity, good looks, style, and charisma, as well as her outstanding skills in the marketing arena. But when it was clear Mattel was in trouble, all the good press quickly soured, and the characterizations of Barad echoed the stereotype of the Snow

Queen. Barad turned from being a warm, charming marketing guru and team player to a demanding, uncooperative, self-absorbed, obsessed, nasty, and financially unsavvy Snow Queen.[31]

The Femme Fatale. In 1979, a twenty-nine-year-old woman armed with an M.B.A. from Harvard went to work at the Bendix Corporation. There she reported to the highly regarded and dashing CEO, Bill Agee. After her alleged affair with Agee made headlines in newspapers across the country, Mary Cunningham went from being a brilliant and competent upstart to the Femme Fatale of the decade. And she paid an extraordinarily high price, losing her job and seeing her professional credibility tarnished. In her memoir, *Power Play*, Cunningham tries to make sense of what happened to her. She writes, "The fact that I had achieved some credibility and was physically attractive played into people's worst insecurities and awakened their most suspicious instincts. Sometimes the easiest outlet for jealousy is the old stereotype, 'Oh, she must be where she is because she's sleeping with the boss.'"[32]

The Mammy. Born into poverty in rural Mississippi, abandoned by her mother as a small child and then reclaimed by her, Oprah Winfrey was traumatized by childhood sexual abuse at the hands of relatives. She became pregnant at the age of fourteen, only to lose the baby. Oprah has survived some of the most horrific experiences known to womanhood. She made what was kept secret in the lives of many women public by sharing her story and, in the process, built a production empire estimated at $725 million.[33] Oprah's compassionate, down-to-earth, and caring style has made her one of talk television's most beloved personalities. She has been labeled the "High Priestess of Positivity," the "Empress of Empathy," and "the older big sister."[34] Yet critics in the black community focus on Oprah's over-the-top caretaking—her solicitation of her public's woes and hardships—ignoring her accomplishments and characterizing her as a modern-day Mammy.[35]

Sapphire. When Whoopi Goldberg burst audaciously onto the silver screen, she had already established herself as a Sapphire—not just in the wisecracking, street-smart characters she had been showcasing in her one-woman Broadway shows, but also in her political life. Whoopi jokingly has crowned herself the "Mighty Afro-Deity."[36] Adversaries rarely miss an opportunity to criticize her potent style, but does she care? Not one bit. Goldberg has never shied from sassing others, regardless of their status or power. Whether she is on or off stage, she is in your face, profane and protean. This philanthropist and author is unafraid to use her piercing wit and willful voice to make the world a more human place.

Harsh stereotypes continue to surround powerful women who use their talent, do not conceal their ambition, and honor their ability for having unprecedented influence. The Bureau of Labor Statistics reported that the number of women in managerial and professional positions has grown 14.6 percent to five million in the last five years.[37] However, the percentage of these women in executive positions or in high positions with commanding authority is still relatively low. "Today, only about 5 percent of those who run major corporations and other major organizations are women—mostly white women—or men of color," writes sociologist Joe Feagin. "While white women are more common than people of color at the top of such organizations, they have not yet penetrated these decision-making heights in anything akin to proportionate numbers. Sex discrimination remains a central aspect of this society, and changes are coming slowly."[38]

Companies are dealing not just with issues of sex discrimination, but also with the problem of how to let high-powered women—black or white—assume influence and command. Women who wield power and influence tap into primitive images held by both men and women regarding femininity and power. Psychiatrist Theodore Rubin reminds us "we think, talk, relate, invent, calculate, create, and even feel through the use of representational symbols."[39] The representational symbols for women remain symbols of good, evil, motherhood, relationship, morality, sexuality, status, and wealth.[40]

The images of Miss Anne, the Snow Queen, the Femme Fatale, the Mammy, and Sapphire are steeped in the interlocking legacy of racial, gender, and class oppression in our society. The descriptions of female colleagues elicited in our interviews revealed not just the persistence of the stereotypes, but the very real office tensions between black and white women. The findings illustrate not only how one woman perceives the other across the racial line, but also how women are perceived to exact influence with white men, the power brokers in companies.

White women may be attached economically and socially to the privileges society makes available to white men, but the price of access to these privileges is dependence and submission (Miss Anne), or isolation (the Snow Queen). On the other hand, black women are subjected to racism and kept in a subordinate position through exclusion—they have no attachment to white men. Ultimately, both groups of women are denied power by the status quo position of white men in corporate America. Their sphere of power may be severely limited to the customary and historical ways women have been allowed to influence male-dominated institutions—through care-taking (The Mammy) and sexuality (The Femme Fatale). Or the women may box themselves in by attempting to dismantle male dominance through rage and anger (Sapphire). Until companies fully recognize and legitimatize the power of both black and white women, each group will continue to lobby for influence in ways that eventually undermine all women while maintaining white male dominance.

EPILOGUE

We plead to each other
We all come from the same rock
We all come from the same rock
Ignoring the fact that we bend
at different temperatures
that each of us is malleable
up to a point.

Yes, fusion is possible
But only if things get hot enough—
All else is temporary adhesion,
patching up.

—CHERRÍE MORAGA, THE WELDER

OUR SEPARATE WAYS began as a vision of three African-American women: Stella Nkomo, Ella L. J. Edmondson Bell, and Toni Denton. We dreamed of telling the stories of the women who walked, talked, and fought their way up the corporate ladder of some of the most prestigious companies in America. These women were the first generation of their race to hold managerial or executive positions. Yet their stories remained untold.

At the time, Stella was an associate professor of management at the University of North Carolina at Charlotte, a large, urban state-operated campus; Ella was an assistant professor at Yale's School of Organization and Management, an elite, Ivy League setting; and Toni was an assistant professor at Norfolk State University, a historically black Southern college. We all held advanced degrees in managerial sciences. We met at an Academy of Management Meeting in 1987 and quickly discovered our common interest in doing research on the intersection of race, class, and gender.

In the managerial sciences, unlike the social sciences, such a research topic was not considered mainstream even in the late '80s. We decided to jointly conduct a research project exploring the black and white women's journeys into and their experiences in corporate America. Our first task was to find resources to do the study. Ours was one of 15 (out of 600) applications accepted by the Rockefeller Foundation's Changing Gender Roles in Post-Industrial Societies competition. Additional funding from the Ford Foundation enabled us to continue our research. We assembled a research team that included two white women: Lisa Horvath, a graduate student at Yale; and Susan Corriher, a psychologist who had returned to school to obtain an M.B.A. at the University of North Carolina at Charlotte. Jennifer Ire, a Caribbean woman working on a doctorate degree in family psychology at the University of Massachusetts at Amherst, also joined the project.

Much time went into recruiting women to participate in the project. It took us a year to identify, make initial contact with, and then schedule interviews with the 120 women we eventually settled on. It took another three years to actually conduct the life history interviews. During this stage of the project, the research team worked hard to design life history interview guides and survey instruments and to organize a system for transcribing and filing interviews.

But the real odyssey of passion, pain, determination, and courage came from unintended outcomes of this intellectual inquiry. Our research team was buffeted by the very phenomena we were studying. Exploring the complexities of women's lives and the impact of race on relationships between black and white women meant that issues of trust, authority, and how to give voice surfaced among members of the research team. The three principal investigators were black women inquiring into the lives of not only black women, but also white women. Being black women in the position of authority and inquiring into the lives of whites was atypical in the social sciences. We had long and difficult conversations with our white associates on how to frame questions to white women, particularly on those related to race. We had frank and tense discussions on whether our questions on racial identity and on experiences with black women were setting white women up to appear insensitive to race and to the plight of their black women colleagues.

One story stands out. Lisa Horvath met Ella several hours after completing an interview with a white female participant, obviously flustered and upset. Suddenly, Lisa broke down in tears, confessing a fear that when Ella read the finished interview she would interpret the woman's responses as being racist. Though the white graduate student had already reached that conclusion, she struggled to accept and acknowledge it. Lisa always believed in calling people on racist behavior. This time she did not, causing her to be disappointed by her own lack of response. Still, she felt an allegiance to the white woman she had interviewed. Our colleague was caught in the horrible position of trying to protect the woman she had interviewed from the woman who, at the end of the process, would be responsible for interpreting and telling her story.

The two women—teacher and student—sat in silence for a long time. It was the kind of silence that makes people anxious and uncomfortable. It took courage for the student to reveal what she was feeling and to trust. And it took control and compassion for Ella to support her junior colleague.

What was the right response in this situation?

This is the kind of transformative experience that is at once most difficult and most important for black and white female colleagues. If women have any hope of building authentic and deep relationships with each other they must be honest, confronting feelings of discomfort and pain, and learning to move forward. Moving forward requires talking about assumptions of one another and letting judgments surface. It means admitting the ways denial of racism or anger over racism work against the strong desire to become true allies. The conversations can be tearful, they can be animated, and they can be sharp. This is the kind of struggle it takes to build a lasting collegial bond.

The energy generated by Ella and Lisa was infectious, quickly spreading throughout the entire research team. Four black women, including one Caribbean woman, and two white women participated in a dialogue that allowed all to cross new borders and build new bridges. We became aware of how much our language kept getting in our way, how having empathy was easier said than done, and how there were few models of alliances between black and white women we could rely on. We discovered that in our lives there were few safe spaces where we could come together to really learn of the other. But we also began to forge the fusion Cherríe Moraga underscores in her poem *The Welder*: we began to see how bringing women together across racial lines was possible when we had courage enough to engage in the struggle.

> *The life history may be thought of as a process that blends together the consciousness of the investigator and the subject, perhaps to the point where it is not possible to disentangle them.*

—GELYA FRANK

The behind-the-scenes account of this study would be incomplete without Stella and Ella sharing the impact of this study on their lives. (In 1991 our project suffered a loss when Toni Denton withdrew to be able to concentrate more fully on her personal life.) As black women academics, we discovered that the lives of the black women managers who had graciously allowed us in mirrored our own. We too were in the vanguard, being in the first wave of black academics to serve on primarily white faculties at business schools. We have learned about our own identities as we sought to ask other women about theirs. We have felt ambiguity, confusion, joy, and loss over the course of the project.

During the course of our academic careers, each of us was told at various points we had placed ourselves in a research ghetto or that we were doing "heart" work by making race, gender, and class the central foci of our research. Yet the reason we sought doctorates was to be able to use our intellects and skills to contribute to positive social change. We were inspired by and wanted to emulate the scholarly tradition of W. E. B. DuBois, the preeminent black sociologist.[1]

Our Separate Ways certainly afforded us the opportunity to pursue scholarly work that addresses barriers facing women in the workplace and in the larger society. But we quickly learned that there were personal costs associated with doing the research. One of the greatest challenges was to decide to reveal secrets, especially the carefully guarded thoughts and feelings about black life that African-Americans rarely reveal to their white counterparts. We did not want to be perceived as race traitors, especially to the women who entrusted to us their precious stories. Many of our interviewees did not want it to be known that they had mothers who mistreated or abandoned their daughters, were raised by black fathers who were too controlling and even abusive, or that in some part of their lives they had cleaned white people's kitchens in order for their families to have food to eat. They did not want their stories to make them appear weak or helpless. Such are the taboo subjects that do not get discussed around the water fountain at work.

We also struggled over reporting that one of the major stresses in the lives of black women was not having a significant personal relationship with men. Again, this comes across as politically incorrect; this is not the kind of sentiment a professional career woman ought to express. But in the case of some of these highly accomplished women, going home at night meant facing a nonexistent personal life and recognizing that the prospects of finding a mate similar in background and stature were quite slim.

We are breaking a long silence. We fear that one consequence of our decision is that people, even including black women, will not be comfortable reading this book. But we believe that if true change is to come for all women then we must make our differences explicit so they can be fully understood. As noted anthropologist and educator Johnnetta Cole so eloquently stated, "To address our commonalities without dealing with our differences is to misunderstand and distort that which separates as well as that which binds us as women."[2]

For those who persist and do read our book regardless of the anxieties it may stir, we would like to offer a concrete set of positive steps that will help not just the professional lives of black and white women, but also the companies they serve.

We stressed in our Prologue that this book is intended to help black and white women, their colleagues, and their organizations. In the Introduction we posed a number of questions that reflected what we heard from the women in this study. While we cannot answer each of those questions, we can help readers think through the broader implications of our research, by offering the following guidance.

- *Black women do not neatly fit into either of the two groups in which they are usually placed: women professionals or black professionals.* Nor should companies try to make them fit into one group or the other. Black women face both racism and sexism in their corporate life. Companies should not assume that programs and initiatives addressing gender issues will solve all of the problems black women face. Conversely, policies and practices aimed at enhancing racial diversity may also miss issues unique to black women. We have a simple suggestion for CEOs and others who ask: "Who are they? Where do they fit?" Ask the black women in your company about their lives, their goals, and their particular concerns. Few will have qualms about telling you of their experiences in the face of earnest interest.

• *White colleagues should sponsor and support black women.* They must learn to both understand black women and be advocates for their development and advancement. If anything, the narratives of the black women in this study have been a cry to be accepted for who they are, not for who people think they are or who they want them to be. The narratives indicated that many worked for white supervisors who did not fully understand their talents or who were not willing to give them meaningful assignments. This happened despite their outstanding educational backgrounds and proven competence. The black women in our study experienced more demotions and lateral moves than their white women counterparts. Many felt it was difficult for them to get credit for excellent work or for colleagues to get past the stereotypes of black women being incompetent.

• *Black women want deeply to be themselves and be able to express their cultural identity.* This identity has been a source of strength in their lives—allowing them to withstand and prevail in spite of the obstacles encountered in their careers. Companies need to sensitize and train majority group managers, both male and female, about the unique challenges facing black women—a complex web of pressures emanating from both racism and sexism in the workplace and from the extra burden they carry in their communities. When black women end up as the conscience of their company, championing the cause of others who feel oppressed or excluded, their own needs can suffer.

• *Companies must support black and white women's networks.* This will help to alleviate the isolation all women feel—especially black women, or other women of color who are few in number in the managerial ranks in their companies. It will also enable the women to build constructive collegial bonds with one another. While a company may take pride in placing a lone black woman in a prominent position, it must also be keenly aware of the ways in which it is making her vulnerable to the extreme pressures brought by performance anxiety, tokenism, and demanding communities. We are not suggesting that black women not be promoted to showcase a company's commitment to affirmative action, but white colleagues must understand the pressures this places on them. Companies must find ways to offer concrete support and enable the women's success. Indeed, since black women have been taught from early life to "armor" themselves, many are reluctant to reveal their pain. So they put on extra armor. Overarmoring can end up immobilizing them to the point they feel they have no way out.[3]

• *Companies must build upon black women's talents and institute policies and practices that incorporate their concerns and special challenges.* We have discussed the extent to which black women withhold fully committing to their organizations. Company leaders must not use this as justification for not making an effort to recruit and retain black women. When black women feel fully accepted and embraced, they will fully vest themselves in their companies.

• *One way to attract and retain black women managers is to show them that you are prepared to assist their communities and the causes important to them.* This can only be a win-win situation. The ethics of giving back is a significant part of how black women make sense of their work and lives. Giving to their communities in various ways such as through recruitment, training, or philanthropy will strengthen black women's connections to the company. It will reap benefits for the company in both retention and good community relations.

Black and White Women Together

For trusting, authentic relationships between black and white women to develop, black women must know that if they are not represented, their white sisters will speak for them and will be advocates for ending both racism and sexism in the companies where they work. Black and white women managers in corporate America are often trapped in a mutual perceptual illiteracy about one another. The fragile bond of gender is not enough to overcome the divisiveness of race. Black women often lament that while white women may speak out against sexism they do not bring the same energy to confronting racism.

For many white women, confronting the possibility of their racism is not only agonizing but also often incomprehensible. Before coming together with black women, white women should seek out other white women to talk about their apprehensions and confusion about race, including their own racial membership. Many white women spoke of their disappointment over not connecting to other white women at work. They felt unsupported by their female colleagues. White women can get caught up in assimilating white male models of behavior at work, becoming competitive, instrumental, and individualistic. Added to this is their belief that gender does not matter at work. Such behavior sabotages any chance of connecting with or supporting other women.

Black women need safe spaces in their lives to take off the armor that they have been wearing since childhood. Armor left on for too long can make a spirit heavy and burdened. It can cause a black woman to become emotionally brittle. When this happens, she is not open to constructive feedback or support from others and she maintains a defensive stance toward her colleagues and her loved ones. This is the beginning of a downward spiral that can affect black women's performance at work, as well as their personal relationships. As sociologist Kesho Scott suggests, "The habits of surviving that we mistakenly thought made us whole make no sense to us now."[4] We suggest that black women, when feeling out of control or overwhelmed, seek out a qualified therapist, spiritual counselor, mentor, or coach who can help them learn how to effectively cope and to create fulfilling lives.

One truth raised in this book is the dark side of women's relationships with each other, especially across racial lines. Women are expected to be nurturing, supportive, caring, and loving in their relationships with other women. Women bond. Women make good friends. We are thought of as naturally building and attending to relationships. Men and women alike reinforce the good behaviors associated with females being the ideal caretakers within our society. Women who break this conventional wisdom of femininity, those who act within the dark side of negative emotions, are often called any number of nasty names. So it is extremely difficult for women to publicly acknowledge the the dark side of their relationships. Competition, envy, jealousy, pettiness, rage, and scorn remain hidden and repressed for the sake of maintaining the ideal feminine self. Infusing race into the situation only serves to make matters worse.

Coming face to face with the racial undercurrents that exist in black and white women's relationships hurts deeply, forcing each to own the disfigured image she has constructed of the other. By not attending to this racial shadow, all the hurt, frustration, guilt, and ambivalence continues to fester. The seed of hope for changing this situation is for us as women to struggle through the darkness. We cannot change our tarnished history, but we can begin to build sturdy bridges today. We can establish positive, healthy relationships between one another. Yes, it takes courage, it takes reaching out, it takes forgiving, it takes listening, and it takes accepting, but it is possible. Our reward for doing so is creating a new energy that allows us to be our true selves, to become more authentic in our relationships, and to grow into women who will make a difference in the companies where we work, in our families, and in the communities we live in.

Appendix A
The Women

Main Participants

These are the key women whose narratives we intensively focused on in *Our Separate Ways*.

Black Women

Name	Title
Brenda Boyd	Vice President of Corporate Giving
Karen Brown	Vice President of Human Resources
Colleen Powell	Corporate Treasurer
Julia Smith	Vice President, Financial Industry
Dawn Stanley	Vice President, Marketing
Patricia Triggs	Strategist, Product Marketing
Ruthie Mae White	Vice-President, Mortgage Originations

White Women

Name	Title
Linda Butler	Vice President of Corporate Affairs
Joyce Canton	Vice President, Director of Marketing
Gloria Goldberg	Vice President, Investment Banker

Jean Hendrick	Senior Vice President
Sandra Martin	Senior Vice President of Human Resources
Marilyn Paul	Marketing Executive
Maxine Schneider	Director of Corporate Affairs

Supplemental Participants

We have also used information from other women's narratives to illuminate various points.

Black Women

Name	Title
Dannette Brown	Sales Manager
Deidre Gainey	Regional Manager, Banking
Whitney Hamilton	Director of Public Relations, Consumer Products Company
Mamie Jefferson	Vice President
Deborah Jones	Production Executive
Anna Smalls	Vice President
Eliza Washington	Regional Branch Manager
Deidre White	Senior Executive, Consumer Products
Shawn White	President

White Women

Name	Title
Alice Booth	Vice President
Gina Davidson	General Executive Manager
Ann Gilbert	Investment Banker
Cecilia Monroe	Senior-Level Manager
Sylvia Whitaker	Senior Executive

❖

Appendix B
Life History Interviews

Recruitment

The women we interviewed were drawn from two sites: the New York Tri-state area and the Charlotte/Atlanta region. The main reason for these sites was the location of the researchers at the time the research was undertaken. We used a two-tier recruitment process.

First, because our focus was on understanding the women's life journeys, we used sources that would lead us directly to women managers. Thus, we contacted a number of women's professional organizations for their assistance in locating women to participate in our study. Among these contacts were the National Coalition of Female Executives, the National Association of Bank Women, the National Coalition of 100 Black Women, the National Black M.B.A. Association, and the Delta Sigma Theta Sorority (a black women's national sorority). While this is not an exhaustive list of all the groups contacted, it does indicate the types of organizations used in our recruitment efforts. We sent a description of the research project to the president of each organization. A follow-up phone contact was made with the president of the organization. When requested, formal presentations at organizational meetings were made to explain the scope and purpose of the research. These efforts had a snowball effect. Our conversations with presidents of the organizations and our presentations at meetings resulted in recommendations to contact other women and other organizations. Meetings with individual women resulted in referrals of other women in their firms for participation in the study.

Second, once a pool of women was identified, a master list was compiled of potential research participants at each site. The final list consisted of 200 white and 297 black women managers. This list formed the basis of a computerized database. We reviewed this list to assure a wide representation of companies, industries, and positions. A letter introducing the project and inviting their participation was sent to a smaller random sample of women on the list.

The letter described the purpose of the project, the interview process, and the time commitment required. The letter was followed by a phone call to discuss the project further and to ascertain whether the women met the criteria for inclusion.

TABLE B-1 *Profile of Interviewees*

Characteristic	Black Women	White Women
Education		
High school	1.6 percent	0.0 percent
Some college	9.7	5.9
B.A./B.S. degree	19.4	23.5
Some graduate school	12.9	14.7
Graduate degree	56.5	55.9
Undergraduate Degree		
Liberal arts	58.9	75.0
Business	25.0	25.0
Education	7.1	0.0
Engineering	0.0	0.0
Other	8.9	0.0
Graduate Degree		
Liberal arts	10.8	30.0
Business	67.6	55.0
Education	8.1	5.0
Engineering	0.0	0.0
Other	13.5	10.0
Job Type*		
Line	68.9	48.1
Staff	31.1	51.9
Management Level*		
Top	19.4	45.2
Middle	51.6	51.6
Lower	29.0	3.2

The major criteria were: (1) the women must be currently holding a management position in a private sector company. Management positions were defined as those in which the job holder is directly supervising a group of individuals or has authority and responsibility for a particular unit or area of business; and (2) they must exhibit a willingness to commit time and energy and to share life experiences. If a woman did not fit the criteria or she declined participation, another potential interviewee was selected from the master list. Generally, once the women understood the nature of the project, they were open to participation. A majority of the women who declined had prior commitments that precluded their participation. Participants were assured confidentiality and told that all interviews would be recorded. A profile of the women interviewed is in Table B-1.

Characteristic	Black Women	White Women
Years of Work Experience	14.3 years	15.3 years
Median Age	40.8	41.5
Marital Status*		
Never married	35.0 percent	29.4 percent
Married	44.4	61.8
Divorced or separated	20.6	8.8
Widowed	0.0	0.0
Children		
No	60.3	64.7
Yes	39.7	35.3
Industry		
Manufacturing (durable)	11.3	8.8
Manufacturing (nondurable)	22.6	11.8
Finance/Banking	29.0	32.4
Insurance	0.0	11.8
Communications	16.1	17.6
Retail	3.2	5.9
Personal business services	3.2	5.9
Entertainment	6.5	0.0
Real estate	1.6	0.0
Other	6.5	5.9

*Chi-Square tests indicate significant differences at the .05 level.

Interviews

The interviews were semistructured and conducted in two parts. We used a combination of structured and open-ended questions that guided the participants through key themes while allowing for elaboration. The questions were essentially the same for the black and white women except for certain questions. We indicate the wording adjustment for white women in brackets. Below are a description of the major sections and a sampling of questions in each section. Even though our interviews were semistructured, they were conducted so as to allow each woman to pursue particular issues in her life and career that were personally meaningful and significant. A complete copy of the interview protocol is available upon request. Most interviews took place at the participant's office or home, with a smaller number held at some other mutually agreed-upon site.

INTERVIEW PROTOCOL

Part I: Early Life Experiences

In the first part of our interview, I'm going to ask you several questions about your childhood and early life, so I want you to take a few minutes to think about your childhood experiences—things such as your parents, the old neighborhood, and school experiences.

1. Where did you grow up?

2. Tell me about your mother. Did she work when you were a child? What kind of work did she do? (Probing questions: Was your mother very involved in her work? That is, did she talk about her work at home? Did she bring work home? Did she like her job(s)?)

3. How are you like your mother? How are you unlike your mother?

4. What was your relationship like with your mother?

5. What messages or advice did your mother give you about being a black woman [a woman]?

6. Now, tell me about your father. What kind of work did he do? (Probing questions: Did he work at more than one job while you were growing up? Was your father very involved in his work? That is, did he talk about his work at home? Did he bring work home? Did he like his work?)

7. How are you like your father? How are you unlike your father?

8. What was your relationship like with your father?

9. What messages or advice did your father give you about being a black woman [a woman].

10. How many children were in your family? Where were you in the birth order? How would you characterize your parents' expectations of you and your siblings? (Probe: Did you receive different messages from the ones given to your brother(s)?)

11. Who were the significant people in your life as a child? (This can include immediate and extended family, friends, individuals in the community, and anyone else you particularly remember.)

12. Were you taught special values about being a girl? What were the values? Did your parents have different expectations of you because you were a girl?

13. What was your neighborhood like? What was its racial, ethnic, and class mix?

14. As a child, how did you first become aware that you were black or that there was something different about being black? [As a child, how did you first become aware that you were a member of an ethnic group?]

15. Were you taught special values about being black? What were the values? How were you taught them? [Were you taught special values about being a member of your ethnic group? What were the values? How were you taught them?]

16. How did your parents talk about race? About issues of being black? Did they ever talk about your role as a black person as you grew older? [How did your parents talk about race? Were you aware of being part of the dominant group? Was this talked about? How was it talked about? Did they ever talk about your role as a white person as you grew older?]

Now let's focus on your school experiences.

1. What type of elementary school did you attend? What was the racial composition of the school? How were you treated in school?

2. Were you treated in any special ways because of your race [ethnicity] while in elementary school?

3. Were you treated in any special ways because of your gender while in elementary school?

4. In high school what was the racial composition?

5. What activities did you participate in while in high school?

6. What supports were there for you in high school? What obstacles? Were any of the obstacles due to your race [ethnicity]? How did they affect you? Were any of the supports due to race [ethnicity]? How did they affect you?

7. While you were in high school did you think about going to college? Did you think a lot about your future? Do you remember having any career plans? Describe them.

8. Did your teachers or counselors encourage you to plan for a career?

9. What was your ideal vision of being an adult? What were you taught to aspire to? Who taught you? How were you taught?

10. While you were growing up, what historical events stand out in your mind?

College and Graduate School

1. What factors were important in your choosing a college? What major did you choose? Why?

2. Where did you attend college? Who were the important people and influences in your decision to attend college?

3. Was it predominantly a black or white setting? How did this impact your experiences in college?

4. Who were your friends in college?

5. Did you go to graduate school? What led you to choose graduate school?

Closing the Interview

How have you been feeling about the many things we talked about today? What's been easiest to talk about? What's been hardest? Has anything you've said felt like a real surprise to you? Anything you feel you'd like to restate or rediscuss? Any final thoughts before we wrap things up? I'd like to arrange/confirm your second interview. Any final questions before we say good-bye?

Thank you for the opportunity you've given us to learn from your life experience. We do appreciate your honesty and will respect your privacy about your experiences accordingly.

Part II: Early Adult Experiences

The next set of questions focus on your career and other aspects of your early adult life.

Transition from First Interview

1. How did your career and life plans evolve from your early life influences, such as your family and school experiences?

2. At what point in your life did you decide on your career goals? How have your career goals changed? Why?

3. What expectations did you have for your life when you were twenty—personally, socially, and for your career?

4. What other factors contributed to your career selection?

5. When did you become involved in a significant relationship? Can you talk a little about your first adult love? What made this person special?

In this second interview, I'd like to get some idea of your public world: those life dimensions that reflect your career, professional activities, and career aspirations.

1. Can you tell me about your current job? What's the nature of your work?

2. What is a typical workweek like for you? How many hours do you work? How often do you work on weekends? How often do you travel out of town for your job?

3. What has been your exposure to high-level executives? What did you learn from this exposure?

4. What was your first "quantum leap"—movement to a job with significantly more responsibility, challenge, and pressure than prior jobs?

5. What do you see as critical turning points in your career? Why?

6. What's the biggest job challenge you have ever faced?

7. What kinds of personal sacrifices have you had to make to get to where you are today?

8. How has your company helped in your achieving success? What other support would you have liked?

9. We sometimes invest in developmental activities that we hope will pay off. Have you done this? Which of these activities have proven to be particularly valuable? (Probe: Education? Courses? Workshops?) Which of these were a waste of time?

10. How have you changed significantly as a person over the course of your career? What changes do you like? Which changes don't you like?

11. How would you assess your career at this point? Are you behind, ahead, or about where you expected to be in your career?

12. Where do you see your career moving? What's next for you?

General Company Questions

1. Do you think the road to the top is different for black women in comparison to black men, white women, or white men?

2. Do you believe some parts of the company are more likely to produce top
black female executives (managers) than others? Which ones, and why?

3. Are there certain specific jobs or types of jobs you see as critically important in seasoning black female managers on the way up?

4. Do you see any differences between black and white women's styles in
your company? What are they? (Can you give me an example of that?)
When are you most likely to be aware of those differences? Can you tell
me a story that illustrates those differences?

5. Some companies have recently developed programs and policies to help their
employees with their family lives. What one change would improve both the
quality of your home life and your productivity at work? In what specific ways
would this change improve your personal life? Your productivity at work?

Relationships with Others

1. As a black woman, have you experienced discrimination in your company? Tell me a little bit about those experiences. How did you respond
when you became aware of the discrimination? What about sex discrimination? [As a woman, have you experienced sex discrimination in your
company? Tell me a little bit about those experiences. How did you
respond when you became aware of the discrimination?] What about
sexual harassment?

2. How important to you is it that you develop close relationships with other
women at work?

3. Are there white women [black women] in your firm that you turn to for
support—either emotional or task related? In what situations would you
turn to a white woman [black woman] in your firm for support? Can you
tell me about one of those times?

4. Would you say that you are particularly close to any of the white women
[black women] colleagues in your company? Tell me about this relationship.
In what ways are you close? How did the relationship develop? Do you ever
discuss your cultural differences? Has race ever been an issue in the relationship? How has the relationship changed over the course of time?

5. Are there white female [black female] colleagues that you find you have
conflicts with? Can you tell me about a time when you were particularly

troubled by a conflict with a white female [black female] colleague? (Probe: How did you handle the situation? Do you think race was an issue?)

Private World

(Note: Questions used varied according to participant's marital and parental status.) Now I'd like you to respond to some questions concerning your private world: those life dimensions that reflect significant relationships, family, leisure activities, and support groups.

1. Let's talk about how you spend your time away from your job. What life dimensions other than work are important to you? Are there specific things you do away from your job that really make you happy?

2. What are the demands, constraints, and choices for you in your personal life? Of the ones you've identified, which ones have a direct impact on your career? Are there things that make you crazy?

3. Are you currently involved in an intimate (committed relationship or marriage) relationship?

4. How many years have you and your partner been together? How did you meet? What attracted you to your partner? How has the relationship evolved?

5. What kind of work does your significant other do? Do the two of you spend time talking about your jobs? What kind of things do you talk about? Have you ever shared your career dreams with each other?

6. How do you and your significant other spend your leisure time together?

7. What does it take to manage a two-career family? How do you organize your schedule to balance your personal life with your professional life?

8. In what ways do family responsibilities affect your work life, such as your ability to accept promotions, spend informal time with your colleagues, or simply being able to concentrate on your job?

9. If forced to choose between your family and your career, which would gain precedence for you? I am really interested in how women make these choices. Can you tell me a story about a situation in which you chose your career over family? Could you tell me a story about a situation in which you chose family over career?

10. Tell me about the community where you live: What are its distinctive characteristics? Is the community racially integrated? How long have you lived in the community?

11. What are the ages and sex of your children, starting with the oldest child?

12. What arrangements do you have with your husband/partner concerning household chores, household decisions, and child care? Do you feel your partner is supportive? Are there special concerns related to child care? Please give me some examples.

13. What does it mean to be a professional woman raising a child/children? How does your race influence the way you raise your children?

14. I am particularly interested in learning how your family and women friends provide you support. In what kinds of situations do they support you? How do they communicate their support? What kinds of support do they provide?

15. Do you have a fantasy of how your personal life will be five years from now? Create a verbal photograph of this fantasy in terms of significant relationships, things you believe in, and dimensions that will be important in your life.

Bicultural Life Dimensions
This last set of questions concentrates on what it means to be a black woman [white woman] in the broader society.

1. Some people describe blacks as being in a limbo-like position in this society, that is, being neither in or out—or often feeling on the outside looking in. [Some people describe whites as being privileged, in a dominant position in society. That is, often feeling as if their group is the 'in group.'] Considering this statement, what does it mean to be a black [white] woman? What are the most important parts of your identity? How do you take care of yourself emotionally? What do you cherish about being a black woman [white woman]? Are there any things about being black [white] that bother you?

2. Are there parts of yourself you feel cut off from in regard to your culture, race, or gender?

3. Are there experiences of subtle as well as blatant racial discrimination (racism/sexism) that have affected your life? Have you seen this happen to white [black] women? How do you feel about such experiences?

4. Do you perceive any constraints in your life success that are grounded in issues of race and/or gender? How are you confronting such constraints?

5. How would you characterize your relationship with whites [blacks] in your personal life? Do you have a close relationship with a white [black] person, for example, a friend? How has the relationship developed? What kinds of social activities do you share together? Are there tensions in your relationship? Can you give me an example?

Closing

How have you been feeling about the many things we talked about today? What's been easiest to talk about? What's been hardest? Has anything you've said felt like a real surprise to you? Anything you feel you'd like to restate or rediscuss? Any final thoughts before we wrap up? Any final questions before we say good-bye?

Thank you for the opportunity you've given us to learn from your life experience. We do appreciate your honesty and will respect your privacy about your experiences accordingly.

Analysis of the Interviews

Analysis of the life history interviews was a long, complicated process. The theory and concepts in this book were developed inductively, working qualitatively from the narratives generated by the life history interviews. We used what is known as a grounded theory approach in our analysis. A grounded theory is one that is inductively derived from the study of the phenomenon it represents.[1] This approach is particularly suitable to understudied phenomena. Thus, as we explained in the Introduction, we did not begin with hypotheses to be empirically tested and proven. Rather, we started with the six broad questions listed in the Introduction to this book, which were based on our theoretical framework, and incorporated a number of factors we believed important to understanding the life and career experiences of women executives.

First, all the interviews were taped and transcribed. There were thousands of pages of transcribed interview data. In essence we had a biography for each woman interviewed. The interviews were read several times to note core ideas and concepts, to recognize emotive stories, and to locate themes. According to life history methodology, emotive stories often communicate significant points and explanations for events and/or behavior.[2] We focused on the following domains: family and early childhood experiences, education, career choice, race and gender identity, organizational experiences, and personal life. Second, a preliminary coding scheme was developed based on the general patterns and themes reflected in the narratives. A second reading was done to refine the codes. Each interview was then coded. To check reliability, the interviews were coded a second time by a different set of coders. The inter-rater reliability from this process met acceptable standards. To handle the volume of data, we used the qualitative data analysis software Ethnograph for the coding process. This program enabled us to group the data by codes, to compare themes, and to check frequency of themes across the interviews.

Hence, the findings and themes reported throughout the book represent dominant and significant patterns in the data. Throughout the analysis process, we sought to integrate across themes to identify how themes related to each other and to the broader questions guiding our study. For example, we wanted to know how early life experiences affected the women's careers and their responses to corporate life. Our interpretation of the data allowed us to subsequently develop theoretical constructs and conclusions about the significant factors explaining the differences and similarities in their life stories and the effects on their careers and organizational experiences. We then sought out the broader significance of what we heard by asking if our themes and conclusions supported, modified, or contradicted any existing theories or concepts.

In presenting our findings we have attempted to stay true to life history methodology. Life history methodology focuses on the ways in which individuals account for and theorize about their lives over time. The method allows researchers to access the sense of reality about the world held by those interviewed. In other words, the story an individual tells about his or her life is subjectively constructed—it is how that person makes sense of and attaches meaning to his or her experiences. We wanted to be certain that the women's voices speak for themselves. But life history scholars also recognize that life histories cannot be told without constant reference to changes in the larger historical, cultural, and social environment. Hence our interpretation attempts to blend the women's perspectives while providing an analytical lens to their constructions.[3]

Appendix C
National Survey

In addition to the in-depth interviews, we conducted a random survey of 1,461 African-American and white women managers. The sample included women graduates of five M.B.A. programs and two professional women's associations. In addition, each woman we interviewed also completed a survey. A total of 825 surveys were returned for a response rate of 56 percent. The final number of usable surveys we received totaled 290 African-American women and 535 white women managers. The survey focused on the women's current job and organizational experiences in addition to their careers and personal lives: It was divided into eight major sections: Career Dynamics, Current Job, Race and Gender Dynamics at Work, Family and Social Life, Personal Dimensions of Racial and Ethnic Identity, Stress Factors in Professional and Personal Life, Demographic Background, and Career History. Some of the items for the survey were specifically developed for the research while others were taken from previously validated scales. Table C-1 provides a profile of the women surveyed.

Since the survey focused on the women's current job and organizational experiences, its significant findings are integrated into the later chapters of the book. Several analyses were done to examine differences in the career and organizational experiences of black and white women although we relied primarily on t-tests and Chi-Square statistics. We only report significant differences at the .05 level or higher in the book.

Sample of Survey Items

I. Career Dynamics

Respondents indicated the extent of agreement with each item using a scale ranging from 1 = strongly disagree to 5 = strongly agree. Some items were reverse coded.

1. I enjoy my career.

2. My profession fits me and reflects my personality.

3. My career is an integral part of my life.

4. I am satisfied with my career progress to date.

TABLE C-1 *National Survey Profile*

Characteristic	Black Women	White Women
Education		
High school	0.4 percent	0.8 percent
Some college	2.8	3.9
B.A./B.S. degree	9.2	7.7
Some graduate school	11.3	7.7
Graduate degree	76.3	80.0
Undergraduate Degree		
Liberal arts	58.7	71.0
Business	24.2	18.2
Education	2.6	3.0
Engineering	6.4	2.5
Other	7.9	5.3
Graduate Degree		
Liberal arts	3.2	5.4
Business	87.0	86.4
Education	1.8	2.4
Engineering	0.5	0.5
Other	7.7	5.2
Job Type*		
Line	61.3	70.0
Staff	38.7	30.0
Management Level*		
Top	13.5	32.1
Middle	46.6	48.1
Lower	39.9	19.8

5. In my company, there is a person who will sponsor me by creating opportunities for career advancement.

II. Current Job

Respondents indicated the extent of agreement with each item using a scale ranging from 1 = strongly disagree to 5 = strongly agree. Some items were reverse coded.

1. Generally speaking, I am very satisfied with my current position.

2. I fit the image of a manager.

3. My assignments are challenging.

4. I have a good relationship with my boss.

Characteristic	Black Women	White Women
Years of Work Experience	12.6 years	14.0 years
Median Age	39.8	40.4
Marital Status*		
Never married	42.5 percent	25.1 percent
Married	43.5	59.9
Divorced or separated	12.6	13.5
Widowed	1.4	1.5
Children		
No	70.5	61.8
Yes	29.5	38.2
Industry		
Manufacturing (durable)	15.9	12.4
Manufacturing (nondurable)	13.8	9.6
Medical/Health care	3.9	6.2
Finance/Banking	21.6	26.4
Insurance	2.8	4.5
Transportation	2.8	1.3
Communications and utilities	16.3	12.1
Retail	1.8	2.5
Personal business services	6.4	7.2
Entertainment	2.1	1.1
Real estate	1.1	1.3
Other	11.4	15.4

Note: Some totals do not equal 100 percent due to rounding.

*Chi-Square tests indicate significant differences at the .05 level.

5. I have considerable decision-making power in my position.

6. I have the opportunity to use my knowledge and skills.

III. Race and Gender Dynamics at Work

Respondents rated each item using a scale ranging from 1 = never to 5 = always. Some items were reverse coded.

1. I am conscious of my racial [ethnic] identity at work.

2. I become self-conscious when I am the only black woman [woman] among my colleagues.

3. I have to perform better than my male colleagues.

4. I feel accepted and a member of my company's team.

5. I have experienced sex discrimination.

6. Race relations in my company are good.

IV. Family and Social Life

Respondents rated each item using a scale ranging from 1 = never to 5 = always. Some items were reverse coded.

1. I have a full social life.

2. I have limited time for friends and social activities.

3. I can manage my personal life with my career.

4. My spouse/significant other is supportive of my career goals.

5. I have little time to pursue personal interests.

V. Personal Dimensions of Race and Ethnicity

Respondents rated each item using a scale ranging from 1 = never to 5 = always. Some items were reverse coded.

1. I identify with the black community [my ethnic community].

2. I have white [black] women friends.

3. I socialize with my white [black] women friends.

4. I feel comfortable in an integrated social setting if people discuss race.

5. I am open to discussion of race relations with a black [white] person.

VI. Stress Factors in Professional and Personal Life

Respondents rated each item using a scale ranging from 1 = never to 5 = always. Some items were reverse coded.

1. Child care

2. Getting household help

3. Managing illness

4. Care of older family members

5. Career pressures

6. Conflicts with spouse or significant other

VII. Demographic Background

1. Date of birth

2. Educational level

3. Marital status

4. Information about spouse if married

5. Children

6. Current job title

7. Industry

8. Salary level

9. Size of company

VIII. Career History

Respondents were asked to reconstruct their career history, indicating positions and tenure in each position.

❖

NOTES

Prologue

1. Louis Harris and Associates, *A Survey of Leaders on Leadership Development and Empowerment for Black Women*, conducted for National Coalition of 100 Black Women, study no. 864010 (New York: Louis Harris and Associates, August 1986), table 26.
2. The percentages total more than 100 percent because the CEOs could choose more than one black female.
3. In February 1988, *Black Enterprise Magazine* issued its first report on black managers in corporate America. Its list of black managers did not include any black women.
4. U.S. Department of Labor, Bureau of Labor Statistics unpublished data, 1988, 1995, and 1996. This information is updated periodically on the Department of Labor's Web site at <http://www.dol.gov/dol/wb>.
5. The most recent list published appears in the February 2000 issue of *Black Enterprise Magazine*, "The Top 50 Blacks in Corporate America," 107–142. There are eight black women and forty-two black men on the list. Six of the black men on the list have made it to the CEO seat in companies that include Dun & Bradstreet, Alliant Energy Corporation, Symantec Corporation, Avis Rent A Car, and Maytag Corporation. None of the eight women holds such a position.
6. U.S. Department of Labor, Bureau of Labor Statistics, unpublished data, 1988,

1995, and 1996. See also U.S. Department of Labor, current employment figures, unpublished data, 1988, 1995, and 1999.

7. The 25 October 1999 edition of *Fortune* (96–126) featured an article on the fifty most powerful women in American business. This was the magazine's second annual ranking of the fifty most powerful women in business. Power was defined by revenues and profits controlled, influence within a company, the importance of the business in the global economy, and its effect on culture and society. On the list were two black women, Oprah Winfrey and Ann Fudge, executive vice president of Kraft Foods, both of whom had slipped to lower rankings compared to their previous rankings. See also the work of Natalie Sokoloff, *Black Women and White Women in the Professions* (New York: Routledge, 1992). Her research demonstrates a racial hierarchy among women in access to professional jobs: only when white women gain access to higher level positions traditionally held by men are black women then able to fill the jobs previously occupied by white women.

Introduction

1. Marilyn Hennig and Anne Jardim are also the founders of the M.B.A. program at Simmons College. This was the first graduate program exclusively for women interested in management. Their book was one of the first about women managers. See Marilyn Hennig and Anne Jardim, *The Managerial Woman: The Survival Manual for Women in Business* (New York: Pocket Books, 1978).

2. Ann M. Morrison et al., *Breaking the Glass Ceiling: Can Women Reach the Top of America's Largest Corporation* (Reading, MA: Addison-Wesley, 1987).

3. Dawn-Marie Driscoll and Carol R. Goldberg, *Members of the Club: The Coming of Age of Executive Women* (New York: Free Press, 1993).

4. Rosabeth Moss Kanter, *Men and Women of the Corporation* (New York: Basic Books, 1977).

5. Two of these studies are Anne Tsui, Thomas Egan, and Charles O'Reilly, "Being Different: Relational Demography and Organizational Attachment," *Administrative Science Quarterly* 37 (1992): 549–579; and Eric Hoffman, "The Effects of Race-Ratio Composition on the Frequency of Organizational Communication," *Social Psychology Quarterly* 48, no. 1 (1985): 17–26. Tsui, Egan, and O'Reilly examined the effects of increasing demographic diversity in organizations on psychological and behavioral attachment to the organization, individual commitment, attendance, and tenure intentions. The whites in their study had a larger negative response to increased work group heterogeneity than nonwhites. As a work group included more African-Americans, whites began to show psychological discomfort. In a study of the influence of varying relative proportions of black supervisors on the frequency of different types of group and organizational level

communication, Hoffman found decreased interpersonal communication frequency among the supervisory cadre as the minority composition of the work group increased.

6. For a good discussion of continuing challenge of increasing diversity in the workplace, see Robert J. Grossman, "Race in the Workplace," *HR Magazine* 45, no. 3 (2000): 41–45. See also Pushkala Prasad, Albert J. Mills, Michael Elmes, and Anshuman Prasad, eds., *Managing the Organizational Melting Pot: Dilemmas of Workplace Diversity* (Thousand Oaks, CA: Sage Publications, 1997); and Fred Lynch, *The Diversity Machine: The Drive to Change the "White Male Workplace"* (New York: Free Press, 1997).

7. Although we focus in this book on black women's experiences, we realize that current managerial research and theory do not address experiences of other women of color. It was beyond the scope of our methodology and resources to attempt to include a comprehensive study of the different groups of women who fall under the umbrella of "women of color." For discussions of the broad effects of race and ethnicity on women of color, see Bernard M. Ferdman, "The Color and Culture of Gender in Organizations," in *Handbook of Gender and Work*, ed. Gary N. Powell (Thousand Oaks, CA: Sage Publications, 1999). There are also a few studies of the workplace experiences of other women of color. See Denise A. Segura, "Inside the Work Worlds of Chicana and Mexican Immigrant Women," in *Women of Color in U.S. Society*, ed. Maxine Baca Zinn and Bonnie Thornton Dill (Philadelphia: Temple University Press, 1994), 95–111; and Esther Ngan-Ling Chow, "Asian American Women at Work," in *Women of Color in U.S. Society*, ed. Maxine Baca Zinn and Bonnie Thornton Dill (Philadelphia: Temple University Press, 1994), 203–227.

8. We should point out that the early research on women in management and their careers tended to use the same theories used to study the careers of male managers. It is only in recent years that alternative models of women's career experiences have appeared. See, for example, Judi Marshall, *Women Managers: Travellers in a Male World* (Chichester, England: Wiley, 1984); and Joan Gallos, "Exploring Women's Development: Implications for Theory, Practice, and Research," in *Handbook of Career Theory*, ed. Michael Arthur, David T. Hall, and Barbara Lawrence (Cambridge: Cambridge University Press, 1989).

9. David A. Thomas and John J. Gabarro, *Breaking Through: The Making of Minority Executives in Corporate America* (Boston: Harvard Business School Press, 1999).

10. Ella L. Bell, "The Bicultural Life Experience of Career-Oriented Black Women," *Journal of Organizational Behavior* 11 (1990): 461–464.

11. David A. Thomas, "Mentoring and Irrationality: The Role of Racial Taboos," *Human Resource Management* 28, no. 2 (1989): 279–290. Thomas's research is the only study we know of that specifically addresses the sexual tensions underlying cross-race and cross-gender protégé/mentor relationships.

12. Catalyst, *Women of Color in Corporate Management Executive Summary* (New York: Catalyst, 1999), 8.

13. Patricia Hill Collins, *Black Feminist Thought: Knowledge, Consciousness, and the Politics of Empowerment* (New York: Routledge, 1990). The work of Patricia Hill Collins is part of a growing body of work by black feminist scholars. A central theme in this scholarship is the emphasis upon intersectionality—the intersection of race, gender, and class in women's lives. See also Angela Davis, *Women, Race, and Class* (New York: Random House, 1981); bell hooks, *Feminist Theory: From Center to Margin* (Boston: South End Press, 1984); Gloria Hull, Patricia Bell Scott, and Barbara Smith, eds., *All the Women Are White, All the Blacks Are Men, But Some of Us Are Brave: Black Women's Studies* (Old Westbury, NY: Feminist Press, 1982); Deborah King, "Multiple Jeopardy, Multiple Consciousness: The Context of a Black Feminist Ideology," *Signs: Journal of Women in Culture and Society* 14, no. 1 (1988): 42–72; Audre Lorde, *Sister Outsider* (Trumansburg, NY: Crossing Press, 1984); and Toni Morrison, ed., *Race-ing Justice, En-gendering Power: Essays on Anita Hill, Clarence Thomas, and the Construction of Social Reality* (New York: Pantheon, 1992).

14. Aida Hurtado, "Relating to Privilege: Seduction and Rejection in the Subordination of White Women and Women of Color," *Signs: Journal of Women in Culture and Society* 14 (1989): 844.

15. Philomena Essed, *Understanding Everyday Racism* (Newbury Park, CA: Sage Publications, 1991), 47–53. There were fifty-five women in Essed's study ranging in age from twenty to forty-five. About one third of the women were students and the rest were professionals.

16. Ibid., 50.

17. Yanick St. Jean and Joe Feagin, *Double Burden: Black Women and Everyday Racism* (Armonk, NY: M. E. Sharpe, 1998), 16–17.

18. *Gender* is a very slippery term. Most scholars would agree that it has something to do with social behaviors and characteristics of men and women. But there is no single well-accepted definition. What is clear is that scholars are careful to distinguish between sex and gender, and to define gender as a social construction. For a nuanced discussion of the difference between sex and gender, see Myra Marx Ferree, Judith Lorber, and Beth B. Hess, *Revisioning Gender* (Thousand Oaks, CA: Sage Publications, 1999), xv–xxvi.

19. Elizabeth Fox-Genovese, *Feminism Without Illusions: A Critique of Individualism* (Chapel Hill: University of North Carolina Press), 120.

20. J. B. Miller, *Toward a New Psychology of Women* (Boston: Beacon Press, 1976); Carol Gilligan, *In a Different Voice* (Cambridge: Harvard University Press, 1982).

21. Judith Rosener, "Ways Women Lead," *Harvard Business Review* 68, no. 6 (1990): 119–120. In the book *Women's Ways of Knowing*, Belenky and her colleagues offer a cogent explanation for why women might place more importance than

men on building relationships at work. The findings from their in-depth study of 135 women were compared to findings from studies of men. They concluded women are motivated more by a "morality of responsibility" than a "morality of rights" (male orientation), and that women tend to define themselves more in terms of relationships and connections to others. See M. F. Belenky et al., *Women's Ways of Knowing* (New York: Basic Books, 1986). However, results from comprehensive reviews of gender difference studies indicate inconsistent results. Some studies find no differences; sometime there are "stereotypical" differences; and sometimes there are non-stereotypical differences. Two of these reviews are Gary N. Powell, "One More Time: Do Female and Male Managers Differ?" *Academy of Management Executive* 4 (1990): 68–74; and A. H. Eagly and B. T. Johnson, "Gender and Leadership Style: A Meta Analysis," *Psychological Bulletin* 108, no. 2 (1990): 233–256.

22. In recent years there have been a number of analyses of the significance of gender in organizations and in management. For example, see the work of Lotte Bailyn, *Breaking the Mold: Women, Men and Time in the New Corporate World* (New York: Free Press, 1993); Marta Calas and Linda Smircich, "Rewriting Gender in Organization Theory," in *Rethinking Organizations*, ed. M. Reed and M. Hughes (London: Sage Publications, 1992), 227–253.; David L. Collinson, David Knights, and Margaret Collinson, *Managing to Discriminate* (London: Routledge, 1990); Joyce Fletcher, *Disappearing Acts: Gender, Power and Relational Practice at Work* (Cambridge, MA: MIT Press, 1999); Silvia Gherardi, *Gender Symbolism and Organizational Culture* (London: Sage Publications, 1995); and Joanne Martin, "Deconstructing Organizational Taboos: The Suppression of Gender Conflict in Organizations," *Organization Science* 1 (1990): 339–359. See Gary N. Powell, ed., *Handbook of Gender and Work* (Thousand Oaks, CA: Sage Publications, 1999), for a comprehensive overview of the literature on gender and work.

23. Janet Z. Giele, "Crossovers: New Themes in Adult Roles and the Life Cycle," in D. McGuigan, ed., *Women's Lives: New Theory, Research, and Policy* (Ann Arbor: University of Michigan Center for Continuing Education of Women, 1980); and Ruth Josselson, *Finding Herself: Pathways to Identity Development in Women* (San Francisco: Jossey-Bass, 1987). See Gallos, "Exploring Women's Development." Gallos argues that career theories have been largely built on male models of success and work. She lays out the elements critical to studying women's development.

24. Katherine Gerson, *Hard Choices: How Women Decide About Work, Career, and Motherhood* (Berkeley: University of California Press, 1985); and Sue J. Freeman, *Managing Lives: Corporate Women and Social Change* (Amherst: University of Massachusetts Press, 1990). Gerson examines the individual preferences and structural conditions that shape women's choices among employment, marriage, and childbearing. However, her sample consisted only of white women.

25. Gordon W. Allport, *The Nature of Prejudice* (Reading, MA: Addison-Wesley, 1954), 110.

26. Ella L. Bell and Stella M. Nkomo, *Barriers to Workplace Advancement Experienced by African-Americans*; a special report prepared for the U.S. Department of Labor Glass Ceiling Commission, 1994; and Taylor Cox, Jr., *Cultural Diversity In Organizations: Theory, Research, and Practice* (San Francisco: Berett-Koehler Publishers, 1993); Thomas and Gabarro, *Breaking Through.*

27. For an excellent analysis of the formation of racial identity for white women see Ruth Frankenberg, *White Women, Race Matters: The Social Construction of Whiteness* (Minneapolis: University of Minnesota Press, 1993).

28. Gerda Lerner, *Why History Matters: Life and Thought* (New York: Oxford University Press, 1997), 181.

29. Karen Sacks, "Toward a Unified Theory of Class, Race, and Gender," *American Ethnologist* 16, no. 3 (1989).

30. Lerner, *Why History Matters*, 181.

31. Stuart A. Hall, "Cultural Identity and Cinematic Representation," *Framework* 36 (1989): 68.

32. Stuart A. Hall, *Representation: Cultural Representation and Signifying Practices* (London: Sage Publications, 1997), 2.

33. Taylor Cox, *Cultural Diversity in Organizations.*

34. Erik H. Erikson, *Life History and the Historical Moment* (New York: W. W. Norton, 1975), 20.

35. C. Wright Mills, *The Sociological Imagination* (New York: Oxford University Press, 1959), 3–4.

36. Norman Denzin, *Interpretive Biography: Qualitative Research Methods* No. 17 (Newbury Park, CA: Sage Publications, 1989).

37. Janet Z. Giele and Glen H. Elder, Jr., *Methods of Life Course Research: Qualitative and Quantitative Approaches* (Thousand Oaks, CA: Sage Publications, 1998), 17–20.

38. Helen S. Farmer & Associates, *Diversity and Women's Career Development: From Adolescence to Adulthood* (Thousand Oaks, CA: Sage Publications, 1997); and Josselson, *Finding Herself.*

39. Research studies indicate significant race-of-interviewer effects in cross-race interview situations (see Nora Cate Schaeffer, "Evaluating Race-of-Interviewer Effects in a National Survey," *Sociological Methods and Research* 8 (1980): 400–419; and Kenneth D. Bailey, *Methods of Social Research*, 3d ed. (New York: Free Press, 1987). For example, Schaeffer concluded that "race of interviewer effects on items with racial content were large and fairly consistent for black and white respondents" (p. 417). Bailey concluded that responses to questions dealing with such sensitive matters as sex, religion, or race relations may be affected by the characteristics of the interviewer. For us, the key driver was choosing a method that would allow our participants to be forthright and authentic in

sharing their life stories with us. Therefore, our approach was to match interviewee race with interviewer race.

40. Gail Sheehy, *New Passages: Mapping Your Life Across Time* (New York: Random House, 1995), 33–43.

Chapter 1: Lost Childhoods

1. Dolores E. Janiewski, *Sisterhood Denied: Race, Gender, and Class in a New
South Community* (Philadelphia: Temple University Press, 1985).

2. Mimi Conway, *Rise Gonna Rise: A Portrait of Southern Textile Workers* (New
York: Anchor Books, 1979).

3. Andrew Billingsley, *Climbing Jacob's Ladder: The Enduring Legacy of African-
American Families* (New York: Simon & Schuster, 1992), 49.

4. U.S. Census Bureau, *Census of the Population: Characteristics of the Population* (Washington, DC: 1961), table 218.

5. Carol Stack, *Call to Home: African-Americans Reclaim the Rural South* (New
York: Basic Books, 1999), xvii.

6. Stephanie J. Shaw, *What a Woman Ought to Be and to Do: Black Professional
Women Workers During the Jim Crow Era* (Chicago: University of Chicago
Press, 1996), 38.

7. Collins, *Black Feminist Thought*, 22.

8. Historians point out that early white feminists embraced individualism as an
important value that was not available to women. According to historian Linda
Kerber, individualism was the ultimate experience of educated, middle-class
white men, who had the luxury to discover themselves and self-actualize. Hence
in their argument for the right to vote, white feminists stressed the significance
of the individual self. For a more detailed discussion of this point, see Linda Kerber, "Women and Individualism in America," *Massachusetts Review* 1, no. 1
(1997): 598; and Elizabeth Cady Stanton, "The Solitude of Self," in *The History
of Woman Suffrage*, volume IV, ed. Elizabeth Cady Stanton, Susan B. Anthony,
and Matilda Joslyn Gage (Rochester, NY: Source Book Press, 1970).

9. Robert N. Bellah et al., *Habits of the Heart: Individualism and Commitment in
American Life* (Berkeley: University of California Press, 1985), 153.

10. Hope Edelman, *Motherless Daughters: The Legacy of Loss* (New York: Ban-
tam/Doubleday, 1994), 41.

11. Carol Stack, *All Our Kin: Strategic Survival in a Black Community* (New York:
Harper & Row, 1974), 60.

Chapter 2: Their Fathers' Daughters

1. Several studies have documented this relationship. See, for example, Hennig and
Jardim, *The Managerial Woman*; and Carol Pearson, *Awakening the Heroes*

Within: Twelve Archetypes to Help Us Find Ourselves and Transform Our World (San Francisco: Harper San Francisco, 1991).

2. Betty Carter, "Fathers and Daughters," in *The Invisible Web: Gender Patterns in Family Relationships*, ed. Marianne Walters et al. (The Women's Project in Family Therapy) (New York: Guilford Press, 1988), 11.

3. Billingsley, *Climbing Jacob's Ladder*, 243.

Chapter 3: Comfortable Families, Uncomfortable Times

1. Albert Gross, *The Scarsdale Controversy, 1948–1954* (New York: Columbia University, 1958).

2. Ibid., 34.

3. Linda McDowell, *Gender, Identity, and Place: Understanding Feminist Geographies* (Minneapolis: University of Minnesota Press, 1999), 92.

4. Ibid., 4.

5. For more information regarding racial identity development among blacks, see William E. Cross, *Shades of Black: Diversity in African-American Identity* (Philadelphia: Temple University Press, 1991), 203.

6. Beverly Daniel Tatum, *Why Are All the Black Kids Sitting Together in the Cafeteria? And Other Conversations About Race* (New York: Basic Books, 1997), 43.

7. Ibid., 44.

Chapter 4: Executives in Training

1. McDowell, *Gender, Identity, and Place*, 106.

2. The term *armor* has been used in the psychotherapy literature to describe an adaptive mechanism for coping with racial oppression. See Beverly Greene, "African American Women," in *Women of Color: Integrating Ethnic and Gender Identities in Psychotherapy*, ed. L. Comas-Diaz and B. Greene (New York: The Guilford Press, 1994), 23. Elsewhere in the social science literature, armor is strongly related to several other concepts, including *dual socialization* [Janice Hale-Benson, *Black Children: Their Roots, Culture and Learning Styles*, rev. ed. (Baltimore, MD: Johns Hopkins University Press, 1986), 62; and Beverly Greene, "What Has Gone Before: The Legacy of Racism and Sexism in the Lives of Black Mothers and Daughters," *Women and Therapy* 9 (1990): 210] and *racial-socialization* [Beverly Greene, "Racial Socialization: A Tool in Psychotherapy with African American Children," in *Working with Culture: Psychotherapeutic Interventions with Ethnic Minority Youth*, ed. L. Vargas and J. Koss-Chioino (San Francisco: Jossey-Bass, 1992) 64; and M. F. Peters, "Racial Socialization of Young Black Children," in *Black Children: Social, Educational and Parental Environments*, ed. H. P. McAdoo and J. L. McAdoo (Newbury Park, CA: Sage Publications, 1985), 168].

3. Annie G. Rogers, "The Development of Courage in Girls, and Women" (unpublished manuscript, Harvard School of Education, 1991), 38.

4. Kesho Y. Scott, *The Habit of Surviving: Black Women's Strategies for Life* (New Brunswick, NJ: Rutgers University Press, 1991).

5. Ibid., 200.

Chapter 5: Breaking In

1. Pamela J. Schreiber, "Women's Career Development Patterns," in *Women's Career Development Across the Lifespan: Insights and Strategies for Women, Organizations, and Adult Educators*, ed. Laura J. Bierema (San Francisco: Jossey-Bass, 1998), 5.

2. For a review of gender-specific theories, see Samuel H. Osipow and Louise F. Fitzgerald, *Theories of Career Development*, 4th ed. (Needham Heights, MA: Allyn & Bacon, 1996), 248–266.

3. In recent years a number of scholars have offered alternative career development theories for women. See, for example, Barbara A. Gutek and Laurie Larwood, *Women's Career Development* (Thousand Oaks, CA: Sage Publications, 1987); Helen S. Farmer & Associates, *Diversity and Women's Career Development*; Judi Marshall, "Re-visioning Career Concepts: A Feminist Invitation," in *Handbook of Career Theory*, eds. Michael B. Arthur, Douglas T. Hall, and Barbara S. Lawrence (Cambridge: Cambridge University Press, 1989); and N. E. Betz and L. F. Fitzgerald, *The Career Psychology of Women* (New York: Academic Press, 1987).

4. Teresa Amott and Julie Matthaei, *Race, Gender, and Work: A Multicultural Economic History of Women in the United States* (Boston: South End Press, 1996), 95. In chapter 5, Amott and Matthaei trace the history and influence of the "cult of domesticity"—the ideal of husband/breadwinner and wife/full-time homemaker marriage that emerged among U.S.–born whites in the 1820s. This ideal portrayed the model white woman as a mother who stayed a home to care for the family. She was wholesome, passive, delicate, pure, submissive, calm, and dependent.

5. We should point out that we did not ask the women directly about the feminist movement or the civil rights movement. Our question was: "What historical events stand out in your mind when you were growing up?"

6. Amott and Matthaei, *Race, Gender, and Work*, 412.

7. The cult of domesticity ideology did not have the same relevancy for black women as white women.

8. Amott and Matthaei, *Race, Gender, and Work*, 412.

9. See Phyllis A. Wallace, *Black Women in the Labor Force* (Cambridge: MIT Press, 1980), 21.

10. Mary C. King, "Occupational Segregation by Race and Sex, 1940–1988," *Monthly Labor Review* (April 1992). This article offers a detailed discussed of occupational segregation and its trends for the period.

11. Amott and Matthaei, *Race, Gender, and Work*, 125, 158. There were so few women in managerial positions in the late 1960s that Harvard Business School had to abandon a planned study of women in management. See Cynthia Fuchs Epstein, "Institutional Barriers: What Keeps Women out of the Executive Suite," in *Bringing Women into Management*, eds. F. E. Gordon and M. H. Strober (New York: McGraw-Hill, 1975).

12. Amott and Matthaei, *Race, Gender, and Work*, 158.

13. Nelle Swartz et al., *A New Day for the Colored Women Workers: A Study of Colored Women in Industry in New York City* (1 March 1919), 5. This monograph describes a study undertaken to understand the experience of black women in factory jobs and also to assess their potential as factory workers. At the time there was strong prejudice against allowing black women into the more skilled and better-paid work. The study was conducted in 242 factories in the New York City area. Black women, white women, and their employers were interviewed. Interestingly, the research team for the study included a black investigator and a white investigator. It appears to be one of the first cross-race studies of women in factory work. The report also highlighted the tensions between black and white women in the factory. White women often refused to work side by side with black women. See also Dolores E. Janiewski's study of women workers in the tobacco and textile industries in Durham, North Carolina, *Sisterhood Denied*.

14. Amott and Matthaei, *Race, Gender, and Work*, 338. The feminization of clerical jobs occurred in earnest between 1920 and 1930. In 1900, 6.9 percent of employed white women worked in clerical occupations. By 1960 that number was 34.5 percent.

15. Amott and Matthaei, *Race, Gender, and Work*, 338. In 1930, 25.3 percent of white women were employed in clerical positions compared with 0.6 percent for African American women. In 1960, the figures were 34.5 percent and 8.0 percent respectively.

16. Natalie J. Sokoloff, *Black Women and White Women in the Professions* (New York: Routledge, 1992).

17. Department of Labor, Bureau of Labor Statistics, *Handbook of Labor Statistics* (Washington, DC: GPO, 1983), table 16, 44–48.

18. Department of Education, *Digest of Education Statistics* (Washington, DC: GPO, 1972), 99.

19. It is nearly impossible to find data on degrees conferred that simultaneously incorporate sex and ethnic/racial category. Data were located for 1980–1981 showing that 805 black women earned master's degrees in business and management compared with 1,554 black men, 35,380 white men, and 12,094 white women. See Department of Education, *Digest of Education Statistics* (1982).

20. See Sokoloff, *Black Women and White Women in the Professions*, for an excellent analysis of the changes in women's occupations over the years.

21. Department of Labor, Bureau of Labor Statistics, *Handbook of Labor Statistics* (Washington, DC: GPO, 1983), 44–48.

22. Influential studies done by management scholar Virginia Schein in 1973 and 1975 found that both male and female managers believed that successful managers possessed an abundance of characteristics that were more associated with men in general than with women in general. Her research is powerful because it demonstrates the extent to which women themselves were socialized into the male stereotyping of managerial jobs. See Virginia Schein, "The Relationship Between Sex Role Stereotypes and Requisite Management Characteristics," *Journal of Applied Psychology* 57 (1973): 95–100; and Virginia Schein, "Relationships Between Sex Role Stereotypes and Requisite Management Characteristics Among Female Managers," *Journal of Applied Psychology* 60 (1975): 340–344.

23. Helen Farmer & Associates, *Diversity and Women's Career Development*, 109–111.

24. L. R. Gaskill, "Women's Career Success: A Factor Analytic Study of Contributing Factors," *Journal of Career Development* 3, no. 17 (1991): 167–178.

25. Richard Harker, Cheleen Mahar, and Chris Wilkes, eds., *An Introduction to the Work of Pierre Bourdieu* (New York: St. Martin's Press, 1990). See especially chapter 5 on education.

26. Jeffrey H. Greenhaus and Gerald A. Callanan, *Career Management* (Fort Worth, TX: Harcourt Brace College Publishers, 1994): 121.

27. Gallos, "Exploring Women's Development," 114–121.

28. Mary Catherine Bateson, *Composing a Life* (New York: Atlantic Monthly Press, 1989), 1–18.

29. Edgar Schein, *Career Dynamics: Matching Individual and Organizational Needs* (Reading, MA: Addison-Wesley Publishing Company, 1978), 127.

30. Shaw, *What a Woman Ought to Be and to Do*, 2. This book is based on records of the lives of approximately eighty African-American women who worked throughout the country in feminized professions—as social workers, librarians, nurses, and teachers—from the 1880s to the 1950s. Other scholars have also written about the tradition of giving back to the community among professional African-American women. For example, see Lynda F. Dickson, "The Third Shift: Black Women's Club Activities in Denver, 1900–1925," in *Women and Work: Exploring Race, Ethnicity, and Class*, ed. Elizabeth Higginbotham and Mary Romero (Thousand Oaks, CA: Sage Publications, 1997), 216–234. According to Dickson, members of federated clubs organized by black women were for the most part middle-class and employed outside the home in helping professions (e.g., social work, nursing, teaching, and counseling). Their club work created a third work shift, contributing to racial uplift efforts within their communities. See also the work of Paula Giddings, *When and Where I Enter: The Impact of Black Women on Race and Sex in America* (New York: William Morrow, 1984). Both educated, middle-class black and white women responded

to the negative, patriarchal conditions in which they lived by forming women's clubs. Of course, these clubs were racially segregated. For white women, the club movement was a response to exclusion from male occupations and professional groups. For black women, it was more of doing race work to improve the often oppressive social conditions for both black women and men. Bridges between the women were not built because their social and economic interests were different, complicated by the fact of white women's emphasis on gender issues only. This fault line between black and white women has never been fully eradicated and even surfaced in the women's narratives about their perceptions of one another.

31. Shaw, *What a Woman Ought to Be and to Do*, 4–6.
32. The origin of this phrase was the motto of the National Association of Colored Women founded in 1896 under the leadership of Mary Church Terrell, daughter of a millionaire former slave. See Amott and Matthaei, *Gender, Race, and Work*, 163.
33. See the work of Joseph E. Rosenbaum, *Career Mobility in a Corporate Hierarchy* (Orlando, FL: Academic Press, 1984); and Taylor Cox, Jr. and Celia V. Harquail, "Career Paths and Career Success in the Early Career Stages of Male and Female M.B.A.'s," *Journal of Vocational Behavior* 39 (1991): 54–75.
34. Cynthia Cockburn, *In the Way of Women: Men's Resistance to Sex Equality in Organizations* (Ithaca, NY: ILR Press, 1991), 17.

Chapter 6: Fitting In

1. For a full description of how organizational cultures are gendered, see Silvia Gherardi, *Gender, Symbolism and Organizational Culture.* Beverly Alimo-Metcalfe, in "Women in Management: Organizational Socialization and Assessment Practices that Prevent Career Advancement," *International Journal of Selection and Assessment* 1, no 2 (1993): 68–83, makes the point that management and management effectiveness are often assumed to be consistent with characteristics valued in men.
2. John P. Wanous, *Organizational Entry: Recruitment, Selection, Orientation, and Socialization of Newcomers*, 2d ed. (Reading, MA: Addison-Wesley Publishing Company, 1992), 193–235.
3. J. A. Chatman, "Matching People and Organizations: Selection and Socialization in Public Accounting Firms," *Administrative Science Quarterly* 36 (1991): 459–484.
4. There are several models of the socialization process. Most notable are models developed by Edgar E. Schein, John Van Maanen, and Daniel C. Feldman. See Schein, *Career Dynamics*; John Van Maanen, "People Processing: Strategies of Organizational Socialization," *Organization Dynamics* 7 (1978): 18–36; Daniel C. Feldman, "A Contingency Theory of Socialization," *Administrative Science*

Quarterly 21 (1976): 433–452; and John Van Maanen and Edgar E. Schein, "Toward a Theory of Organizational Socialization," in *Research in Organizational Behavior*, vol. 1, ed. Barry Staw (Greenwich, CT: JAI Press, 1979), 209–266.

5. Wanous, *Organizational Entry*, 200.

6. We could locate only one study that examined differences in person-organization fit among diverse groups of managers. See Kay Lovelace and Benson Rosen, "Differences in Achieving Person-Organization Fit Among Diverse Groups of Managers," *Journal of Management* 22, no. 5 (1996): 703–723. Lovelace and Rosen found that African-American managers reported achieving significantly poorer organization fit compared with other subgroups. White female and Hispanic managers did not report less organization fit than did white male managers.

7. Kanter, *Men and Women of the Corporation*, 207.

8. Ibid.

9. M. E. Heilman, C. J. Block, and J. A. Lucas, "Presumed Incompetent? Stigmatization and Affirmative Action Efforts," *Journal of Applied Psychology* 77 (1992): 536–544. The authors found that dominant group members often perceive minorities and women employed in nontraditional positions in organizations as beneficiaries of affirmative action. They are more likely to be perceived as incompetent by their coworkers because of their perceived status.

10. Thomas F. Pettigrew and Joanne Martin, "Shaping the Organizational Context for Black American Inclusion," *Journal of Social Issues* 43, no. 1 (1987): 41–78.

11. Pamela Braboy Jackson, Peggy A. Thoits, and Howard F. Taylor, "Composition of the Workplace and Psychological Well-Being: The Effects of Tokenism on America's Black Elite," *Social Forces* 74, no. 2 (1995): 530–557.

12. This concept reflects one of the defensive functions of a well-developed black identity described by William E. Cross in his work on black identity development. See William E. Cross, *Shades of Black: Diversity in African-American Identity* (Philadelphia: Temple University Press, 1991).

13. Kecia M. Thomas, Layli D. Phillips, and Stephanie Brown, "Redefining Race in the Workplace: Insights from Ethnic Identity Theory," *Journal of Black Psychology* 24, no. 1 (1998): 76–92. Research in psychology suggests that issues related to race and racism are more likely to exert their influence on the self-efficacy of blacks. Additionally, Thomas and her colleagues suggest that one benefit of a strong racial identity is immunization from racism that may affect self-efficacy and motivation to succeed.

14. Patricia Hill Collins, "Learning from the Outsider Within: The Sociological Significance of Black Feminist Thought," *Social Problems* 33, no. 6 (1986): 14–32.

15. N. J. Allen and J. P. Mevery, "The Measurement and Antecedents of Affective, Continuance, and Normative Commitment to the Organization," *Journal of Occupational Psychology* 63 (1990): 13.

16. Interestingly, this is a pretty consistent finding in studies of high achieving

women. Many point to the importance of receiving a message from fathers about being anything they want to be. Jill Barad, the former CEO of Mattel Toys and at one time one of the highest and most prominent female executives in corporate America, credits her success to growing up in a household with a father who always told her, "You can be anything you want to be—just be good at it. Put your mind to it, learn what you need to, and go for it" (as cited in Pearson, *Awakening the Heroes Within*, 37).

17. See Lynn Weber and Elizabeth Higginbotham, "Black and White Professional-Managerial Women's Perceptions of Racism and Sexism in the Workplace," in *Women and Work: Exploring Race, Ethnicity, and Class*, ed. Elizabeth Higginbotham and Mary Romero (Thousand Oaks, CA: Sage Publications, 1997), 153–175.

18. Aida Hurtado, *The Color of Privilege: Three Blasphemies on Race and Feminism* (Ann Arbor: University of Michigan Press, 1996), 14. Others have also written about the contradictory position of white women to privilege and gender subordination. For example, Catherine MacKinnon argues, "Women who comply or succeed are elevated to models, tokenized by success on male terms or portrayed as consenting to their natural place and dismissed as having participated if they complain." Catherine A. MacKinnon, "Feminism, Marxism, Method, and the State: An Agenda for Theory," *Signs: Journal of Women in Culture and Society* 7, no. 31 (1982): 530.

19. Lovelace and Rosen, "Differences in Achieving Person-Organization Fit," 718.

Chapter 7: Barriers to Advancement

1. There are a number of studies of the glass ceiling. In fact the term first appeared in an article by Carol Hymowitz and Timothy Schellhardt, "The Glass Ceiling," in "The Corporate Woman: A Special Report," *Wall Street Journal*, 24 March 1986. Also see Ann Morrison et al., *Breaking the Glass Ceiling: Can Women Make It to the Top of America's Largest Corporations?* (Reading, MA: Addison-Wesley, 1988, 1992); Lisa Mainero et al., "Gender Gap in the Executive Suite: CEOs and Female Executives Report on Breaking the Glass Ceiling," *Academy of Management Executive* 12 (1998): 28–42; Gary N. Powell, "The Glass Ceiling: Explaining the Good and Bad News," in *Women in Management: Current Research Issues*, vol. 2, ed. Marilyn J. Davidson and Ronald J. Burke (London: Sage Publications, 2000), 236–249; and Catalyst, *Census of Women Corporate Officers and Top Earners* (New York: Catalyst, 1997). There are also several studies completed by the U.S. Department of Labor through its Glass Ceiling Commission. See *Good for Business: Making Full Use of the Nation's Human Capital: A Fact-Finding Report of the Federal Glass Ceiling Commission* (Washington, DC: GPO, 1995).

2. Again we want to point out that much of the glass ceiling research has been done on white populations.

3. Other studies point out that minority women feel they are at greater disadvantage than white women, white men, or male members of minority groups. See, for example, Mor Barak, David A. Cherin, and Sherry Berkman, "Organizational and Personal Dimensions in Diversity Climate: Ethnic and Gender Differences in Employee Perceptions," *Journal of Applied Behavioral Science* 34, no. 1 (1998): 82–104; and Ellen E. Kossek and S. C. Zonia, "Assessing Diversity Climate: A Field Study of Reactions to Employer Efforts to Promote Diversity," *Journal of Organizational Behavior* 14 (1993): 61–81.

4. A budding body of research demonstrates that different combinations of gender and race can produce distinctive work experiences. See, for example, Darlyne Bailey, Donald Wolfe, and C. R. Wolfe, "The Contextual Impact of Social Support Across Race and Gender: Implications for African-American Women in the Workplace," *Journal of Black Studies* 26, no. 3 (1996): 297–307; Stella Nkomo and Taylor Cox, Jr., "Gender Differences in the Upward Mobility of Black Managers: Double Whammy or Double Advantage?" *Sex Roles* 21 (1989): 825–839; Roy L. Austin and Hiroko H. Dodge, "Despair, Distrust, and Dissatisfaction Among Blacks and Women, 1973–1987," *Sociological Quarterly* 33, no. 4 (1992): 579–598; S. M. Crow, L. Y. Fok, and S. J. Hartman, "Who Is at Greater Risk of Work-Related Discrimination—Blacks or Homosexuals?" *Employee Responsibilities and Rights Journal* 11, no. 1 (1998): 15–26; Susan J. Lambert and Karen Hopkins, "Occupational Conditions and Workers Sense of Community: Variations by Gender and Race," *American Journal of Community Psychology* 23, no. 2 (1995): 151–179; Weber and Higginbotham, "Black and White Professional-Managerial Women's Perceptions," 153–175; and Janice D. Yoder and Patricia Aniakudo, "Outsider Within the Firehouse: Subordination and Difference in the Social Interactions of African-American Firefighters," *Gender and Society* 11, no. 8 (1997): 324–341.

5. Other researchers have referred to the everydayness of racism experienced by African-Americans. For example, Philomena Essed, in her book *Understanding Everyday Racism: An Interdisciplinary Theory* (Newbury Park, CA: Sage Publications, 1991), 50, uses the term *everyday racism* to refer to the integration of racism into everyday situations through practices that activate underlying power relations. See also reference to bouts of racism and sexism described by the African-American women studied by Angela Farrar in her unpublished doctoral dissertation, "It's All About Relationships: African-American and European American Women's Hotel Management Careers" (Ph.D. diss., Virginia Polytechnic Institute and State University, 1995).

6. Jane Mills, *Woman Words: A Dictionary of Words About Women* (New York: Free Press, 1989). Mills draws her example from the scholarly work of Casey Miller and Kate Swift, *Words and Women: New Language in New Times* (London: Victor Gollancz, 1977).

7. According to black feminist thinker bell hooks: "White women and men justified the sexual exploitation of black women by arguing that they were the initiators of

sexual relationships with men. From such thinking emerged the stereotype of black women as sexual savages, and in sexist terms as sexual savages, a nonhuman, an animal cannot be raped." See bell hooks, *Ain't I a Woman: Black Women and Feminism* (Boston: South End Press, 1981), 52.

8. Karen M. Ruggiero and Donald M. Taylor, "Why Minority Group Members Perceive or Do Not Perceive the Discrimination That Confronts Them: The Role of Self-Esteem and Perceived Control," *Journal of Personality and Social Psychology* 72, no. 2 (1997): 373–389. In their study, women, Asians, and blacks reacted to negative feedback after information about the probability of discrimination. Results of their study suggested that minority group members minimize discrimination because the consequences of doing so are psychologically beneficial.

9. Other researchers have documented this effect. Because of low expectations for blacks and other minority groups, successful performance creates contradictory effects. In one study, researchers found that dominant group participants set lower-minimum-competency standards, but higher ability standards, for female than for male and for black than for white applicants. They concluded that although it may be easier for low-status group members to meet (low) standards, these same people must work harder to prove that their performance is ability based. See Monica Biernat and Diane Kobrynowicz, "Gender- and Race-Based Standards of Competence: Lower Minimum Standards but Higher Ability Standards for Devalued Groups," *Journal of Personal and Social Psychology* 72, no. 3 (1997): 544–557.

10. See a discussion of these cultural images in K. Sue Jewell, *From Mammy to Miss America and Beyond: Cultural Images and the Shaping of U.S. Policy* (London: Routledge, 1993), 35–75. Also read Barbara Christian, *Black Feminist Criticism: Perspectives on Black Women Writers* (Elmsford, NY: Pergamon Press, 1985).

11. In her study of black women managers in Great Britain, Linda Martin also found it was difficult for the women to be seen beyond their race and gender. Linda Martin, "Power, Continuity, and Change: Decoding Black and White Women Managers' Experience in Local Government," in *Women in Management: A Developing Presence,* ed. Morgan Tanton (London: Routledge, 1994).

12. Sharon Collins, "Black Mobility in White Corporations: Up the Ladder but out on a Limb," *Social Problems* 44 (1997): 59.

13. Thomas and Gabarro, *Breaking Through,* 73–75.

14. When Catalyst surveyed 461 women executives (predominantly white), the women cited stereotyping as the number one obstacle to their advancement followed by exclusion from informal networks. Catalyst, *Women in Corporate Leadership Progress and Prospects* (New York: Catalyst, 1996).

15. There are a number of studies on gender stereotyping. For example, see N. Nicholson and M. A. West, *Managerial Job Change: Men and Women in Transition.* (Cambridge: Cambridge University Press, 1988); and Susan T. Fiske,

"Controlling Other People: The Impact of Power on Stereotyping," *American Psychologist* 48 (1993): 612–628.

16. See the work of Deborah Tannen, *You Just Don't Understand: Women and Men in Conversation* (New York: Ballantine, 1990); and L. Smith-Lovin and C. Brody, "Interruptions in Group Discussion: The Effects of Gender and Group Composition," *American Sociological Review* 54 (1989): 434–453.

17. Cockburn, *In the Way of Women*, 142.

18. As bell hooks notes: "While assimilation is seen as an approach that ensures successful entry of black people into the mainstream, at its very core it is dehumanizing. Embedded in the logic of assimilation is the white supremacist assumption that blackness must be eradicated so that a new self, in this case a 'white' self, can come into being." See bell hooks, *Talking Back: Thinking Feminist, Thinking Black* (Boston: South End Press, 1989), 67.

19. Judy B. Rosener, *America's Competitive Secret: Utilizing Women As a Management Strategy* (New York: Oxford University Press, 1995).

20. Jeff Hearn and P. Wendy Parkin, "Gender and Organizations: A Selective Review and Critique of a Neglected Area," in *Gendering Organizational Analysis*, ed. Albert J. Mills and Peta Tancred (London: Sage Publications, 1992).

21. Harvard Business School Professor Herminia Ibarra studied informal networks of middle managers in several industries. She reported that minority managers had fewer intimate informal relationships than did white managers of both genders. See Herminia Ibarra, "Race, Opportunity, and Diversity of Social Circles in Managerial Networks," *Academy of Management Journal* 38 (1995): 673–703. Other research reported that black women are the race and gender group least likely to receive mentoring from the highest status managers in the company, white men. See the research reported in David A. Thomas, "The Impact of Race on Managers' Experiences of Developmental Relationships," *Journal of Organizational Behavior* 2, no. 4 (1990): 479–492.

22. In a study of authority hierarchies at work, Gail McGuire and Barbara F. Reskin found that black women faced higher authority and earnings penalties than either black men or white women. Compared with black men and white women, black women lost more authority and earnings because employers failed to reward their credentials in the same way as they did white men's. Gail McGuire and Barbara F. Reskin, "Authority Hierarchies at Work: The Impacts of Race and Sex," *Gender and Society* 7, no. 4 (1993): 487–507.

Chapter 8: Climbing over the Barriers

1. See N. Nicholson and M. West, *Managerial Job Change: Men and Women in Transition* (Cambridge: Cambridge University Press, 1988). Nicholson and West use this term in their study of managerial job changes. See also B. White, C. L.

Cox, and Cary L. Cooper, *Women's Career Development: A Study of High Flyers* (Oxford: Blackwell Press, 1992).

2. See, for example, White, Cox, and Cooper, *Women's Career Development.* White, Cox, and Cooper studied the careers of forty-eight British women executives to examine success factors. Out-spiraling moves were one of the main factors in the women's success.

3. Thomas and Gabarro refer to this phenomenon as "The tax of prejudice is time." Thomas and Gabarro, *Breaking Through,* 74.

4. Weber and Higginbotham, "Black and White Professional-Managerial Women's Perceptions," 53–75.

5. Clayton P. Alderfer, "An Intergroup Perspective on Group Dynamics," in *Handbook of Organizational Behavior,* ed. Jay W. Lorsch (Englewood Cliffs, NJ: Prentice Hall, 1987), 190–222.

6. See Sharon Hurley, "Speaking Up: The Politics of Black Women's Labor History," in *Women and Work: Exploring Race, Ethnicity, and Class,* vol. 6, ed. Elizabeth Higginbotham and Mary Romero (Thousand Oaks, CA: Sage Publications, 1997): 28–51. Focusing on the work/family nexus, work identity and consciousness, and black female resistance, Hurley illuminates the issues and spaces contested by African-American women as they seek to survive and even empower themselves and members of their families and communities in the face of exploitation.

7. Patricia Hill Collins, *Fighting Words: Black Women and the Search for Justice* (Minneapolis: University of Minnesota Press, 1998), 119–120.

8. Janis Sanchez Hucles, "Jeopardy Not Bonus Status for African-American Women in the Workforce: Why Does the Myth of Advantage Persist?" *American Journal of Community Psychology* 25, no. 5 (1997): 565–580.

9. David A. Thomas, "The Impact of Race on Managers' Experiences of Developmental Relationships (Mentoring and Sponsorship): An Intra-Organizational Study," *Journal of Organizational Behavior* 11, no. 6 (1990):479–492; and Belle R. Ragins, "Diversified Mentoring Relationships in Organizations: A Power Perspective," *Academy of Management Review* 22 (1997): 482–521.

10. Kathy Kram, *Mentoring at Work* (Glenville, IL: Scott, Foresman & Co., 1985).

11. Meg A. Bond, "The Multitextured Lives of Women of Color," *American Journal of Community Psychology* 25, no. 5 (1997): 737–738.

12. The research of Raymond Friedman points to the value of these networks for African-Americans. He found that minority network groups provide positive benefits that outweigh the negative effects of symbolic separation. Raymond Friedman, "Defining the Scope and Logic of Minority and Female Network Groups: Can Separation Enhance Integration?" in *Research in Personnel and Human Resource Management,* vol. 14, ed. Gerald R. Ferris (Greenwich, CT: JAI Press), 307–349. On the implications of these networks for social change, see

Maureen Scully and Amy Segal, "Passion with an Umbrella: Grassroots Activists in the Workplace," *Research in the Sociology of Organizations* (forthcoming).

13. See the research of Sally Ann Davies-Netzley, "Women Above the Glass Ceiling: Perceptions on Corporate Mobility and Strategies for Success," *Gender and Society* 12, no. 3 (1998): 339–355; and Robin Ely, "The Power in Demography: Women's Social Construction of Gender Identity at Work," *Academy of Management Journal* 38 (1995): 589–634.

14. See Lisa A. Mainero's study of fifty-five high-profile executive women for a similar emphasis on a "proven track record" as a key for success. Mainero also found that the women believed working within corporate norms was important to career advancement. Lisa A. Mainero, "On Breaking the Glass Ceiling: The Political Seasoning of Powerful Women Executives," *Organizational Dynamics* 22 (Spring 1994): 4–20. We are assuming all of the women in her sample were white since she does not mention the racial breakdown of the fifty-five she interviewed.

15. It is very important to emphasize that while this study is a comparative study of the career experiences of black and white women managers, we are not attempting to dismiss the reality of the dominance of white males in managerial and executive positions. It must be remembered women managers of all races and ethnicities cluster near the bottom of corporate hierarchies relative to white men. Our goal was to challenge the assumption that all women experience managerial careers in the same way, pointing to the importance of the intersection of race, gender, and class in shaping their professional identities.

16. See Susan E. Martin, "Outsider Within the Station House: The Impact of Race and Gender on Black Women Police," *Social Problems* 41 (1994): 383–400; and Winifred R. Poster, "The Challenges and Promises of Class and Racial Diversity in the Women's Movement: A Study of Two Women's Organizations," *Gender and Society* 9 (1995): 659–79. These studies suggest that white women may be co-opted into solidarity with high-status white men, which ends up distancing them from building relationships with women of color.

Chapter 9: Making Change

1. Parts of this chapter are taken from the unpublished manuscript "Tempered Radicalism Revisited: Black and White Women Making Sense of Black Women's Enactments and White Women's Silence" by Ella L. J. Edmondson Bell, Debra E. Meyerson, Stella M. Nkomo, and Maureen Scully. We deeply appreciate the insights of Debra and Maureen and the valuable contributions they continue to make to our work.

2. In another interesting finding, an overwhelming percentage of black women believed their careers had benefited from affirmative action. This implies two things for black women: that without government policies and intervention, the

number of minorities entering corporate America would be lower; and that meritocracy alone has a limited impact on advancing their careers. Only 27 percent of white women believed their careers had benefited from affirmative action, despite the fact that white women's careers have advanced the most due to affirmative action.

3. Debra E. Meyerson and Maureen Scully, "Tempered Radicalism and the Politics of Ambivalence and Change," *Organizational Science* 6, no.5 (1995): 585–600.

4. Ibid., 584.

5. Fran Ostrower, *Why the Wealthy Give: The Culture of Elite Philanthropy* (Princeton, NJ: Princeton University Press, 1995).

6. St. Clair Drake and Horace R. Cayton, *Black Metropolis: A Study of Negro Life in a Northern City* (Chicago: University of Chicago Press, 1993), 394.

7. Shaw, *What a Woman Ought to Be and to Do*, 38.

8. Collins, *Black Feminist Thought*, 95, 147, 144.

9. Shaw, *What a Woman Ought to Be and to Do*, 35.

10. For us the term *homeland* is borrowed from the South African system apartheid. "Homelands were government-designated areas of land where people from varying black ethnic groups were restricted to live." We give the meaning of homeland a different twist. "Urban homelands denote not only a geographic place, but, because communities undergo transitions, erode, and sometimes even vanish, homelands represent a given period of time. In the time between the 1960s and the 1970s, homelands were where a majority of African-Americans lived, where they shared a common way of life that was separate from white America." See Ella Edmondson or Ella E. Bell, "Infusing Race into the U.S. Discourse on Action Research," in *Handbook on Action Research*, ed. Peter Reason and Hilary Bradbury (London: Sage Publications, forthcoming), 49.

11. Maureen Scully, "Meritocracy," in *Dictionary of Business Ethics*, ed. R. Edward Freeman and Patricia Wehane (London: Blackwell Publishers, 1977).

12. For a fuller explanation of this point, see L. R. Della Fave, "The Meek Shall Not Inherit the Earth: Self-Evaluation and the Legitimacy of Stratification," *American Sociological Review* 45 (1980): 955–971; and Maureen Scully, "The Irony of Meritocracy: How a Legitimating Ideology Generates and Redirects Disbelief" (working paper, MIT Sloan School of Management, 1995).

13. Kanter, *Men and Women of the Corporation*.

14. Hurtado, "Relating to Privilege," 833–855.

Chapter 10: Work Isn't Everything

1. The sociologist Patricia Hill Collins makes the point that as a collectivity, women experience distinctive gendered mechanisms of control that remain

specific to women's patterns of inclusion within race-class groups. Specifically, regardless of actual family composition, all women encounter the significance of American society's preoccupation with family. See Collins, *Fighting Words*, 119–120.

2. Daniel J. Levinson, *The Seasons of a Woman's Life* (New York: Alfred A. Knopf, 1996).

3. We should point out that more recently men, too, are increasingly required to juggle their work and family lives because of the greater number of women who have joined the labor force. But at the time these women entered their careers, it was not a central issue faced by their male colleagues. See the work of Lotte Bailyn, *Breaking the Mold: Women, Men and Time in the New Corporate World* (New York: Basic Books, 1995).

4. Comas-Diaz and Greene, "Women of Color with Professional Status," in *Women of Color*, 362.

5. For an excellent summary of the work-family literature, see Jeffrey H. Greenhaus and Saroj Parasuraman, "Research on Work, Family, and Gender," in *Handbook of Gender and Work*, ed. Gary Powell (Thousand Oaks, CA: Sage Publications, 2000), 391–412.

6. A number of writers have documented the scarcity of black professional men and its consequences for black professional women. An 8 March 1994 *Wall Street Journal* article by Dorothy J. Gaiter, "The Gender Divide: Black Women's Gains in Corporate America Outstrip Black Men's," reported that between 1982 and 1992, the number of black women in corporate American grew at a heady 125 percent. At the same time the number of black professional females for every black professional man increased from 1.2 to 1.8. For white women the numbers were 0.62 and 0.94 for the same period. See also David A. Price's column, "A Good Man Is Hard to Find" *Wall Street Journal*, 21 February 1995, A26. The reasons black professional women are outstripping black men are complex, but most research cites crime, drugs, inadequate education, and corporate attitudes that hinder their employment.

7. Ibid.

8. U.S. Department of Labor, Bureau of Labor Statistics, unpublished data for the years 1988, 1995, and 1999.

9. F. N. Schwartz, "Management Women and the Facts of Life," *Harvard Business Review* 67, no. 1 (1989): 65–76.

10. See the research of Arlie Hochschild, *The Second Shift* (New York: Viking, 1989).

11. See Billingsley, *Climbing Jacob's Ladder*, 243.

12. Uma Sekaran, "Quality of Life in Dual-Career Families," in *Dual-Career Families* (San Francisco: Jossey-Bass, 1986). See especially chapter 3.

13. Christian, *Black Feminist Criticism*.

14. Comas-Diaz and Greene, *Women of Color*, 350.

Chapter 11: The Racialized Self

1. Ruth Frankenberg, *Displacing Whiteness: Essays in Social and Cultural Criticism* (Durham, NC: Duke University Press, 1997), 6.

2. Maurice Berger, *White Lies: Race and the Myths of Whiteness* (New York: Farrar, Straus, and Giroux, 1999), 203. Joe Feagin, in *Racist America: Roots, Current Realities, and Future Reparations* (New York: Routledge, 2000), strongly echoes this point.

3. Berger, *White Lies*, 166.

4. Frankenberg, *Displacing Whiteness*, 6.

5. Tatum, *Why Are All the Black Kids Sitting Together in the Cafeteria?* 16.

6. Ibid.

7. Berger, *White Lies*, 166.

8. Ruth Frankenberg, *White Women, Race Matters: The Social Construction of Whiteness* (Minneapolis, University of Minnesota Press, 1993), 148.

9. Marilyn Frye, *Willful Virgin: Essays in Feminism, 1976–1992* (Freedom, CA: Crossing Press, 1992), 151.

10. Alison Bailey, "Despising an Identity They Taught Me to Claim," in *Whiteness: Feminist Philosophical Reflections*, ed. C. J. Cuomo and K. Q. Hall (Lanham, MD: Rowman & Littlefield Publishers, Inc., 1999), 96–97.

11. Judith Butler, *Gender Trouble: Feminism and the Subversion of Identity* (New York: Routledge Press, 1990), 33.

12. Adrienne Rich, "Disloyal to Civilization: Feminism, Racism and Gynephobia," in *On Lies, Secret and Silence: Selected Prose, 1966–1978* (New York: W. W. Norton & Company, 1978).

13. Margo Jefferson, "Revisions: On Defining Race, When Only Thinking Makes It So," *New York Times*, 22 March 1999, The Arts/Cultural Desk.

14. Bailey, *Despising an Identity*, 97.

15. While most scholars of race relations have embraced the use of white privilege, some have not. Philosopher Naomi Zack points out a problem with the term's use, "Even in the most racist of cultures, there is no legal tradition that grants special rights to whites so much as there is a present social practice and a past legal history of excluding nonwhites from the privileges assumed to belong to all citizens, in the second sense of the dictionary meaning of privilege. The idea of white privilege, then, must be an elliptical reference to the result of discrimination and exclusion of nonwhites. To call the result a privilege, which means a positive, specifically granted absolute advantage, rather than a relative one clouds the issue of disparities between whites and nonwhites." See Naomi Zack, "White Ideas," in *Whiteness: Feminist Philosophical Reflections* (Boulder, CO: Rowman & Littlefield Publishers, Inc., 1999), 78.

16. Berger, *White Lies*, 168.

17. Ibid., 55.

18. Scully, *The Irony of Meritocracy.*
19. William Ryan, *Blaming the Victim* (New York: Vintage Books, 1971).
20. Claude M. Steele, "Race and the Schooling of Black Americans," *Atlantic Monthly*, April 1992; and Claude M. Steele and Joshua Aronson, "Stereotype Threat and the Intellectual Test Performance of African Americans," *Journal of Personality and Social Psychology* 69 (1995): 797–811.
21. For articles reflecting this point of view, see Della Fave, "The Meek Shall Not Inherit the Earth," 955–971; and Joanne Martin and Deborah Meyerson, "Women in Power: Conformity, Resistance, and Disorganized Coaction," in *Power and Influence in Organizations*, ed. R. M. Kramer and M. A. Neale (Thousand Oaks, CA: Sage Publications: 1998), 311–348.
22. Bell, "The Bicultural Life Experience of Career-Oriented Black Women."
23. For a broader understanding of biculturalism and how black professional women organize bicultural life structures, see Bell, "The Bicultural Life Experience of Career-Oriented Black Women," 459–477.

Chapter 12: Images of Other

1. A number of excellent books on the experiences of black women during slavery have helped correct the distortions in the historiography of that era. Historian Deborah Gray White argues in *Aren't I a Woman: Female Slaves in the Plantation South* (New York: Norton, 1985) that black women were unprotected from hard labor, brutality, and rape. In other words, female slaves were placed symbolically outside the boundaries of womanhood and femininity. Other texts of this genre include Angela Davis's *Women, Race, and Class* (New York: Vintage Books, 1981), and Jacqueline Jones's eloquent study of the work and family life of black women from slavery to contemporary times in *Labor of Love, Labor of Sorrow: Black Women, Work and the Family from Slavery to Present* (New York: Basic Books, 1985). Poignant testimonies of the actual conditions of slave women can be found in slave narratives. See especially Harriet A. Jacobs, *Incidents in the Life of a Slave Girl*, ed. Jean Fagan Yellin (Cambridge: Harvard University Press, 1987); and Melton A. McLaurin, *Celia: A Slave* (Athens, GA: University of Georgia Press, 1991).
2. See historian Darlene Clark Hine, "For Pleasure, Profit, and Power: The Sexual Exploitation of Black Women: Historical Perspectives," in *African-American Women Speak Out on Anita Hill–Clarence Thomas*, ed. G. Smitherman (Detroit, MI: Wayne State University Press, 1995), 178. Hine's analysis is critical to understanding the contradictory position of white women relative to their gender and race. While white women were privileged and advantaged because of their race, they have been victims of sexism because of their gender. Yet, the very same gender constructions that sexually exploited them also propped up their worth at the expense of black women.

3. Patricia Morton, *Disfigured Images: The Historical Assault on Afro-American Women* (New York: Greenwood Press, 1991), 9. Morton stresses how the devalued imagery of black womanhood stood in antithetical relationship to an ideal white womanhood; one could not exist without the other.

4. bell hooks, *Ain't I a Woman*, 136. In fact, strains and differences between black and white women trace back historically to the suffrage movment. As white female suffragists fought for the vote, Sojourner Truth had to defiantly ask, "Ain't I a woman?" Truth and other black women of their time clearly understood that their lives were not solely affected by gender and that their experiences of womanhood were not included in how white women were framing the movement. Additionally, black women who attempted alignment with white reformers were often expected to prioritize sex over race.

5. In addition to bell hooks, from a social science perspective, see Amott and Matthaei, *Race, Gender, and Work*; Aida Hurtado, *Color of Privilege*; and Kimberly Springer, ed., *Still Lifting, Still Climbing: African American Women's Contemporary Activism* (New York: New York University Press, 1999). For a philosophical perspective, see Elizabeth V. Spelman, *Inessential Woman: Problems of Exclusion in Feminist Thought* (Boston: Beacon Press, 1988). Finally, for literary approaches, review Barbara Smith, ed., *Home Girls: A Black Feminist Anthology* (New York: Kitchen Table Press, 1983); and Audre Lorde, *Sister Outsider.*

6. hooks, *Ain't I a Woman*, 141.

7. Ruth Frankenberg, *White Women, Race Matters*, 2.

8. Ibid., 9.

9. Hazel Carby, *Reconstructing Womanhood* (Cambridge: Harvard University Press, 1987), 115.

10. There are other sources for Miss Anne. According to Jane Mills, Miss Anne is "used to denote the female head of a household or family in C15th in late middle English." See Mills, *Womanwords*, 164.

11. Mary Ann Doane, *Femmes Fatales: Feminism, Film Theory, and Psychoanalysis* (New York: Routledge, 1991), 244.

12. Hazel Carby, *Reconstructing Womanhood* , 115.

13. Fairy tales, according to Marie Louise Von Franz, a Jungian scholar, "represent the archetype in their simplest and most concise form . . . and afford us the best clues to the understanding of the processes going on in the collective psyche." Marie Louise Von Franz, *Interpretation of Fairytales* (San Francisco: Shambala Publications, 1996), 2.

14. Linda Schierse Leonard, *Meeting the Madwoman: An Inner Challenge for Feminine Spirit* (New York: Bantam Books, 1993), 35.

15. Kanter, *Men and Women of the Corporation*, 236.

16. An excellent case in point is that of Ann Hopkins, who worked as a CPA at Price Waterhouse. Hopkins sued Price Waterhouse charging sex discrimination. Hopkins,

the only woman in her firm, was denied promotion to partner despite having outstanding work performance because her male colleagues characterized her as
overly aggressive, unduly harsh, difficult to work with, and impatient with staff.
One partner described her as "macho." In a meeting with a senior partner about
her candidacy, she was told that to improve her chances for partnership she
should "walk more femininely, talk more femininely, dress more femininely,
wear make-up, style her hair, and wear jewelry." Hopkins took her case all the
way to the U.S. Supreme Court. Price Waterhouse was found guilty of sex discrimination. The court ruled that her gender played a role in the negative decision not to promote her. She was punished for displaying behavior valued in
males. See *Price Waterhouse v Hopkins*, 490 US 228, 247 (1989).

17. Doane, *Femmes Fatales*, 1.
18. Ibid., 2. Doane uses the femme fatale image as a signpost to address questions of
    the implications of knowledge and sexuality and their impact on feminism in a
    variety of discourses: philosophy, psychoanalysis, and cinema. Her discussion of
    the relationship between Victorian notions of racial difference and the femme
    fatale myth is fascinating and quite illuminating for understanding the deep
    roots of negative sexual images of black women.
19. Ella L. Bell, "Myths, Stereotypes, and Realities of Black Women: A Personal
    Reflection," *Journal of Applied Behavioral Science* 28 (1992): 363–372.
20. Darlene Clark Hine, "Rape and Inner Lives of Black Women in the Middle West:
    Preliminary Thoughts on the Culture of Dissemblance," *Signs* 14, no. 4 (1989):
    912–929.
21. Doane, *Femme Fatales*, 222.
22. Rhetaugh Graves Dumas, "Dilemmas of Black Females in Leadership," in *The
    Black Woman*, ed. La Frances Rodgers-Rose (Beverly Hills, CA: Sage Publica-
    tions, 1980), 207.
23. Ibid., 208.
24. Joanne Braxton, *Black Women Writing Autobiography: A Tradition Within a
    Tradition* (Philadelphia: Temple University Press, 1989), 31. Braxton traces the
    definition of *sass* in the *Oxford English Dictionary* and Amanda Smith's *An
    Autobiography: The Story of the Lord's Dealings with Mrs. Amanda Smith*
    (Chicago: Meyer and Brothers, 1893), 386–389. Quoting Smith, Braxton wrote,
    "I don't know if anyone has ever found what the composition of this sassy wood
    really is; but I am told it is a mixture of certain barks. They say that it is one of
    their medicines that they used for punishing witches so you cannot find out
    what it is. The accused had two gallons to drink. If she throws up, she has gained
    her case."
25. Adrienne Rich, "Disloyal to Civilization: Feminism, Racism, and Gynophobia," 298.
26. Benjamin DeMott, *Killer Woman Blues: Why Americans Can't Think Straight
    About Gender and Power* (Boston: Houghton Mifflin, 2001).

27. Emily Eakin, "Women Behaving Badly," *New York Times Book Review*, 28 January 2001, 12.
28. DeMott, *Killer Woman Blues*, 45–50.
29. "Fame a Two-Edged Sword for the Candidate Clinton," *New York Times*, 27 September 2000.
30. "The Trouble with Hillary," *Harper's Bazaar*, August 2000, 124.
31. See "Mattel's Lack-of-Action Figures," *Business Week*, 21 February 2000, 50; "Trouble in Toyland," *Business Week*, 15 March 1999, 40; and "The Rise of Jill Barad," *Business Week* 25 May 1988, 112.
32. Mary Cunningham, *Power Play: What Really Happened at Bendix* (New York: Simon & Schuster, 1984), 277.
33. "The Cult of Oprah Inc.," *Irish Times*, 5 August 2000, city edition, magazine launch, 61.
34. See Ibid.; and "Why We Love Oprah," *Detroit News*, 19 June 2000, 1.
35. "Here's Red Clay in Your Eye: Magazine Talks Tough," *Atlanta Journal and Constitution*, 4 August 1994, entertainment city life section; and "Weighing the Odds Against Oprah," Gannett News Service, 8 November 1990, Richard Prince section.
36. Carrie Rickey, "The Continuing Evolution of the 'Mighty Afro-Deity,'" *Baltimore Sun*, 5 January 1997.
37. "Deportment Gap: In Today's Workplace, Women Feel Freer to Be, Well, Women," *Wall Street Journal*, 7 February 2000, A1.
38. Joe R. Feagin, *Racist America*, 185.
39. Theodore Rubin, *Anti-Semitism: A Disease of the Mind* (New York: Continuum Publishing Company, 1990), 25.
40. Ibid. We believe it is important to take into consideration the unconscious ways in which these stereotypical images linger. Theodore Rubin employs the concept of symbol sickness to refer to bigotry-oriented illnesses including anti-Semitism. He argues that because we organize our world through the use of representational symbols, symbols come to have value associations and take on meaning relative to the culture or society as well as the individual's personal experience. The symbols and their meanings are deeply embedded in our psyches and become pictures in our minds that affect our behavior and perceptions.

Epilogue

1. Ella Edmondson Bell and Stella M. Nkomo, "Postcards from the Borderlands: Building a Career from the Outside/Within," *Journal of Career Development* 26, no. 1 (1999): 69–84.
2. Johnnetta Cole, ed., *All American Women: Lines That Divide, Ties That Bind* (New York: Free Press, 1986).
3. There are cases in the popular press of black women professionals who toppled

because of these extraordinary burdens. Suicide was their way of coping. One tragic case is Dianna Green, who overcame growing up fatherless in Miami and racial barriers to become a senior vice president at Duquesne Light, leading the corporation through nine tumultuous years of downsizing. But she was unable to overcome having her performance heavily scrutinized and fulfilling the multiple demands on her time. Single and childless, she was believed to be the pillar of strength both within her company and in the African-American community where she selflessly gave her time. Very few of those in the corporation or in the community knew the burdens she was carrying including discrimination charges from a terminated white staffer. As one of her friends observed, "She rarely had anyone to fall back on." Taken from Carol Hymowitz and Faju Narisott, "Lonely at the Top: A Promising Career Comes to a Tragic End and a City Asks Why," *New York Times*, 9 May 1997, 1, A8.

4. Scott, *Habit of Surviving*, 187.

Appendix B: Life History Interviews

1. For a full discussion of grounded theory see Anselm Strauss and Juliet Corbin, *Basics of Qualitative Research: Grounded Theory Procedures and Techniques* (Newbury Park, CA: Sage Publications, 1990).
2. Herbert J. Rubin and Irene S. Rubin, *Qualitative Interviewing: The Art of Hearing Data* (Thousand Oaks, CA: Sage Publications, 1995), 231.
3. For a full discussion of this point see Gill Musson, "Life Histories," in *Qualitative Methods and Analysis in Organizational Research*, ed. Gillian Syjmon and Catherine Cassell (London: Sage Publications, 1998), 10–27.

Bibliography

Acker, J. "Gendering Organization Theory." In *Gendering Organizational Analysis*, edited by A. Mills and P. Tancred, 248–260. Newbury Park, CA: Sage Publications, 1992.

Alderfer, C. P. "An Intergroup Perspective on Group Dynamics." In *Handbook of Organizational Behavior*, edited by J. W. Lorsch, 190–222. Englewood Cliffs, NJ: Prentice Hall, 1987.

Alderfer, C. P., et al. "Diagnosing Race Relations in Organizations." *Journal of Applied Behavioral Science* 16 (1980): 135–166.

Alimo-Metcalfe, B. "Women in Management Organizational Socialization and Assessment Practices that Prevent Career Advancement." *International Journal of Selection and Assessment* 1, no. 2 (1993): 68–83.

Allen, N. J., and J. P. Mevery. "The Measurement and Antecedents of Affective Continuance and Normative Commitment to the Organization." *Journal of Occupational Psychology* 63 (1990): 13.

Allport, G. *The Nature of Prejudice*. Reading, MA: Addison-Wesley, 1954.

Amott, T. L., and J. A. Matthaei. *Race, Gender, and Work: A Multicultural Economic History of Women in the United States*. Boston: South End Press, 1991.

Andersen, H. C. *The Snow Queen*. Woodbury, NY: Barron's Educational Series, 1985.

Andersen, M. L., and P. Hill Collins. *Race, Class, and Gender.* Belmont, MA: Wadsworth, 1991.

Angelou, M. *And Still I Rise: A Book of Poems by Maya Angelou.* New York: Random House, 1978.

Anthias, F. "Race and Class Revisited—Conceptualizing Race and Racisms." *Social Review* 38 (1990): 19–42.

Aptheker, N. *Tapestries of Life: Women's Work, Women's Consciousness, and the Meaning of Daily Experience.* Amherst: University of Massachusetts Press, 1989.

The Archetype of the Collective Unconscious: Collected Works of C. G. Jung. Princeton, NJ: Princeton University Press, 1971.

Austin, R. "Sapphire Bound!" *Wisconsin Law Review* 3 (1989): 539–578.

Austin, R. L., and H. H. Dodge. "Despair, Distrust, and Dissatisfaction Among Blacks and Women, 1973–1987." *Sociological Quarterly* 33 (1992): 579–598.

Bailey, A. "Despising an Identity They Taught Me to Claim." In *Whiteness: Feminist Philosophical Reflections,* edited by C. J. Cuomo and K. Q. Hall. Lanham, MD: Rowman & Littlefield Publishers, Inc., 1999.

Bailey, K. D. *Methods of Social Research,* 3d ed. New York: Free Press, 1987.

Bailyn, L. *Breaking the Mold: Women, Men and Time in the New Corporate World.* New York: Free Press, 1993.

Baldwin, J. A. "The Psychology of Oppression." In *Contemporary Black Thought,* edited by M. K. Asante and A. S. Vandi. Beverly Hills, CA: Sage, 1980.

Barkley, E. "African American Women's Quilting: A Framework for Conceptualizing and Teaching African American Women's History." *Signs: Journal of Women in Culture and Society* 14 (1989): 921–929.

Baron, J. N., et al. "The Structure of Opportunity: How Promotion Ladders Vary Within and Among Organizations." *Administrative Science Quarterly* 31 (1986): 248–273.

Barrett, M. "The Concept of Difference." *Feminist Review* 26 (1987): 29–41.

Baskerville, D. M., S. H. Tucker, and D. Whittingham-Barnes. "Women of Power and Influence in Corporate America." *Black Enterprise Magazine* 22 (1991): 39–90.

Bateson, M. C. *Composing a Life.* New York: Atlantic Monthly Press, 1989.

Belenky, M. F., et al. *Women's Way of Knowing.* New York: Basic Books, 1986.

Bell, D. *Faces at the Bottom of the Well.* New York: Basic Books, 1992.

Bell, E. L. "Myths, Stereotypes, and Realities of Black Women: A Personal Reflection." *Journal of Applied Behavioral Science* 28 (1992): 363–376.

Bell, E. L., et al. "Women of Color in Management: Toward an Inclusive Analysis." In *Women in Management: Trends, Issues, and Challenges in Managerial Diversity,* edited by E. Fagenson. Newbury Park, CA: Sage Publications, 1993.

Bell, E. L., and S. M. Nkomo. "Postcards from the Borderlands: Building a Career from the Outside/Within." *Journal of Career Development* 26, no. 1 (1999): 69–84.

_____. "Theorizing Race and Gender in Organizations: Expanding the Women in Management Paradigm." Unpublished manuscript, MIT, The Sloan School, 1995.

Bellah, R., R. Madsen, W. Sullivan, A. Swidler, and S. M. Tipton. *Habits of the Heart: Individualism and Commitment in American Life.* Berkeley: University of California Press, 1985.

Berger, M. *White Lies: Race and the Myths of Whiteness.* New York: Farrar, Straus, and Giroux, 1999.

Bernikow, L. *Among Women.* New York: Harmony Books, 1980.

Betz, N. E., and L. F. Fitzgerald. *The Career Psychology of Women.* New York: Academic Press, 1987.

Biernat, M., and D. Kobrynowicz. "Gender- and Race-Based Standards of Competence: Lower Minimum Standards but Higher Ability Standards for Devalued Groups." *Journal of Personal and Social Psychology* 72 (1997): 544–557.

Billingsley, A. *Climbing Jacob's Ladder: The Enduring Legacy of African-American Families.* New York: Simon & Schuster, 1992.

Blanton, M. *Racial Theories.* Cambridge: Cambridge University Press, 1987.

Bolton, R. *Gal: A True Life.* New York: Harcourt Brace & Company, 1994.

Bond, M. A. "The Multitextured Lives of Women of Color." *American Journal of Community Psychology* 25 (1997): 737–738.

Borak, Mor, D. A. Cherin, and S. Berkman. "Organizational and Personal Dimensions in Diversity Climate: Ethnic and Gender Differences in Employee Perceptions." *Journal of Applied Behavioral Science* 34 (1998): 82–104.

Bouma D., and J. Hoffman. *The Dynamics of School Integration: Problems and Approaches in a Northern City.* Grand Rapids, MI: William B. Eardman's Publishing Co., 1968.

Boyd, J. *In the Company of My Sisters: Black Women and Self-Esteem.* New York: Dutton Books, 1993.

Bracey, J. H., A. Meier, and E. Rudivic. *Black Nationalism in America.* Indianapolis, IN: The Boss-Merrill Company, Inc., 1970.

Braxton, J. *Black Women Writing Autobiography: A Tradition Within a Tradition.* Philadelphia: Temple University Press, 1989.

Breines, W. *Young, White, and Miserable: Growing Up in the Fifties.* Boston: Beacon Press, 1992.

Brenner, O. C., et al. "The Relationship Between Sex Role Stereotypes and Requisite Management Characteristics Revisited." *Academy of Management Journal* 32 (1989): 662–669.

Brewer, R. M. "Theorizing Race, Class and Gender: The New Scholarship of Black Feminist Intellectuals and Black Women's Labor." In *Theorizing Black Feminisms: The Visionary Pragmatism of Black Women,* edited by S. M. James and A. P. A. Busia. New York: Routledge, 1993.

Brockner, J., and L. Adsit. "The Moderating Impact of Sex on the Equity-Satisfaction Relationship: A Field Study." *Journal of Applied Psychology* 71 (1986): 585–590.

Brown, E. B. "Imagining Lynching: African-American Women, Communities of

Struggle, and Collective Memory." In *African American Women Speak Out on Anita Hill–Clarence Thomas*, edited by Geneva Smitherman. Detroit, MI: Wayne State University Press, 1995.

Butler, J. *Gender Trouble: Feminism and the Subversion of Identity.* New York: Routledge Press, 1990.

Calas, M., and L. Smircich. "Rewriting Gender in Organization Theory." In *Rethinking Organizations*, edited by M. Reed and M. Hughes. London: Sage Publications, 1992.

———. "Using the 'F' Word: Feminist Theories and the Social Consequences of Organizational Research." *Academy of Management Best Paper Proceedings* (1989): 355–359.

Caraway, N. *Segregated Sisterhood: Racism and Politics of American Feminism.* Knoxville: University of Tennessee Press, 1991.

Carby, H. *Reconstructing Womanhood.* Cambridge: Harvard University Press, 1987.

Carter, B. "Fathers and Daughters." In *The Invisible Web: Gender Patterns in Family Relationships*, edited by M. Waters, et al. (The Women's Project in Family Therapy). New York: Guilford Press, 1988.

Catalyst. *Census of Women Corporate Officers and Top Earners.* New York: Catalyst, 1997.

———. *Women of Color in Corporate Management Executive Summary.* New York: Catalyst, 13 July 1999.

Chatman, J. A. "Matching People and Organizations: Selection and Socialization in Public Accounting Firms." *Administrative Science Quarterly* 36 (1991): 459–484.

Chodorow, N. *The Reproduction of Mothering.* Berkeley: University of California Press, 1978.

Chodorow, N., and S. Contratio. *Rethinking the Family: Some Feminist Questions.* Boston: Northeastern University Press, 1992.

Chow, E. N. "Asian American Women at Work." In *Women of Color in U.S. Society*, edited by M. B. Zinn and B. T. Dill. Philadelphia: Temple University Press, 1994.

Christian, B. *Black Feminist Criticism: Perspectives on Black Women Writers.* Elmsford, NY: Pergamon Press, 1985.

———. "A Race for Theory." *Feminist Studies* 14 (Spring 1988): 67–79.

Chusmir, L. H., et al. "Self-Confidence of Managers in Work and Social Situations: A Look at Gender Difference." *Sex Roles* 26 (1992): 497–512.

Chusmir, L. H., and J. Mills. "Gender Differences in Conflict Resolution Styles of Managers: At Work and At Home." *Sex Roles* 20 (1989): 149–163.

Clark, K. *Dark Ghetto.* New York: Harper's Press, 1965.

Clinton, C. *The Plantation Mistress: Woman's World in the Old South.* New York: Pantheon Books/Random House, 1982.

Cockburn, C. *In the Way of Women: Men's Resistance to Sex Equality in Organizations.* Ithaca, NY: ILR Press, 1991.

Collins, P. H. *Black Feminist Thought: Knowledge, Consciousness, and the Politics of Empowerment.* New York: Routledge, 1990.

_____. *Fighting Words: Black Women and the Search for Justice.* Minneapolis: University of Minnesota Press, 1998.

Collins, S. "The Marginalization of Black Executives." *Social Problems* 36 (1989): 317–331.

Collinson, D. L., D. Knights, and M. Collinson. *Managing to Discriminate.* London, Routledge, 1990.

Comas-Diaz, L., and B. Greene. "African American Women." In *Women of Color: Integrating Ethnic and Gender Identities in Psychotherapy.* New York: Guilford Press, 1994.

_____. "Women of Color with Professional Status." In *Women of Color: Integrating Ethnic and Gender Identities in Psychotherapy.* New York: Guilford Press, 1994.

Conway, M. Rise *Gonna Rise: A Portrait of Southern Textile Workers.* New York: Anchor Books, 1979.

Cose, E. *Rage of a Privileged Class.* New York: Harper Collins, 1993.

Courlander, H. *A Treasury of Afro-American Folklore.* New York: Crown Publishers, 1976.

Cox, T. J. *Cultural Diversity In Organizations: Theory, Research, and Practice.* San Francisco: Berett-Koehler Publishers, 1993.

Cox, T. J., and S. M. Nkomo. "Invisible Men and Women: A Status Report on Race as a Variable in Organizational Behavior Research." *Journal of Organizational Behavior* 11 (1990): 459–477.

Cox, T., Jr., and C. V. Harquail. "Career Paths and Career Success in the Early Career Stages of Male and Female M.B.A.'s." *Journal of Vocational Behavior* 39 (1991): 54–75.

Crapanzano, V. "Life Histories." *American Anthropologist* 86 (1984): 953–959.

Crenshaw, K. "Demarginalizing the Intersection of Race and Sex: A Black Feminist Critique of Antidiscrimination Doctrine, Feminist Theory, and Antiracist Politics." In *Feminist Legal Theory: Foundations,* edited by D. K. Weisberg, 383–395. Philadelphia: Temple University Press, 1989.

_____. "Whose Story Is It Anyway? Feminist and Antiracist Appropriations of Anita Hill." In *Race-ing Justice, En-gendering Power: Essays on Anita Hill, Clarence Thomas, and the Construction of Social Reality,* edited by T. Morrison. New York: Pantheon Books, 1994.

Cross, W. E. J. *Shades of Black: Diversity in African-American Identity.* Philadelphia: Temple University Press, 1991.

Crow, S. M., L. Y. Fok, and S. J. Hartman. "Who is at Greater Risk of Work-Related Discrimination—Blacks or Homosexuals?" *Employee Responsibilities & Rights Journal* 11 (1998): 15–26.

Cunningham, M. *Power Play: What Really Happened at Bendix.* New York: Simon & Schuster, 1984.

Davies-Netzley, S. A. "Women Above the Glass Ceiling: Perceptions on Corporate Mobility and Strategies for Success." *Gender and Society* 12 (1998): 339–355.

Davis, A. *Women, Race and Class*. New York: Random House, 1981.

Davis, M., et al. "Emotion and Work in Supervisor-Subordinate Relations: Gender Differences in the Perception of Angry Displays." *Sex Roles* 26 (November/December 1992): 513–531.

DeMott, B. *Killer Woman Blues: Why Americans Can't Think Straight About Gender and Power*. Boston: Houghton Mifflin, 2001.

Denzin, N. *Interpretive Biography: Qualitative Research Methods No. 17*. Newbury Park, CA: Sage Publications, 1989.

Dickson, L. F. "The Third Shift: Black Women's Club Activities in Denver, 1900–1925." In *Women and Work: Exploring Race, Ethnicity, and Class*, edited by E. Higginbotham and M. Romero, 216–234. Thousand Oaks, CA: Sage Publications, 1997.

Dill, B. T. "The Dialectics of Black Womanhood." *Signs: Journal of Women in Culture and Society* 4 (1979): 543–55.

Dion, K. L., and R. A. Schuller. "Ms. and the Manager: A Tale of Two Stereotypes." *Sex Roles* 22 (1990): 569–577.

Doane, M. A. *Femmes Fatales: Feminism, Film Theory, Psychoanalysis*. New York: Routledge, 1991.

Dobbins, G. H. "Equity vs. Equality: Sex Differences in Leadership." *Sex Roles* 15 (1986): 513–525.

Drake, S. C., and H. R. Cayton. *Black Metropolis: A Study of Negro Life in a Northern City*. Chicago: University of Chicago Press, 1993.

Dreher, G. F., and R. A. Ash. "A Comparative Study of Mentoring Among Men and Women in Managerial, Professional, and Technical Positions." *Journal of Applied Psychology* 75 (1990): 539–546.

Driscoll, D. M., and C. R. Goldberg. *Members of the Club: The Coming of Age of Executive Women*. New York: Free Press, 1993.

DuCille, A. "Occult of True Black Womanhood." In *Skin Trade*. Cambridge, MA: Harvard University Press, 1996.

Dumas, R. G. "Dilemmas of Black Females in Leadership." In *The Black Woman*, edited by L. F. Rogers-Rose, 203–215. Beverly Hills, CA: Sage Publications, 1980.

Duveen, G., and B. Lloyd. "The Significance of Social Identities." *British Journal of Social Psychology* 25 (1986): 219–230.

Eagly, A. H., and B. T. Johnson. "Gender and Leadership Style: A Meta-Analysis." *Psychological Bulletin* 108 (1990): 233–256.

Eagly, A. H., et al. "Gender and the Evaluation of Leaders. A Meta-Analysis." *Psychological Bulletin* 111 (1992): 3–22.

Eakin, E. "Women Behaving Badly," *New York Times Book Review*, 28 January 2001, 12.

Edelman, H. *Motherless Daughters: The Legacy of Loss*. New York: Bantam/Doubleday, 1994.

Eichenbaum, L., and S. Orbach. *Between Women: Love, Envy, and Competition in Women's Friendships.* New York: Viking Press, 1987.

Eisenstein, Z. R. *The Color of Gender: Reimagining Democracy.* Berkeley: University of California Press, 1994.

Ely, R. "The Power in Demography: Women's Social Construction of Gender Identity at Work." *Academy of Management Journal* 38 (1995): 589–634.

Epstein, C. F. "Institutional Barriers: What Keeps Women Out of the Executive Suite." In *Bringing Women into Management,* edited by F. E. Gordon and M. H. Strober. New York: McGraw-Hill, 1975.

Erikson, E. *Life History and the Historical Moment.* New York: W. W. Norton and Co., 1975.

Essed, P. *Understanding Everyday Racism: An Interdisciplinary Theory.* Newbury Park, CA: Sage Publications, 1991.

Estes, C. T. *Women Who Run With Wolves.* New York: Valentine Books, 1993.

Fagenson, E. "At the Heart of Women in Management Research: Theoretical and Methodological Approaches and Their Biases." *Journal of Business Ethics* 9 (1990): 267–274.

Farmer, H. S., & Associates. *Diversity and Women's Career Development: From Adolescence to Adulthood.* Thousand Oaks, CA: Sage Publications, 1997.

Farrar, A. "It's All About Relationships: African-American and European American Women's Hotel Management Careers." Ph.D. diss., Virginia Polytechnic Institute and State University, 1995.

Faulkner, J. "Women in Interracial Relationships." *Women and Therapy* 2 (1983): 193–203.

Fave, D., et al. "The Meek Shall Not Inherit the Earth: Self-Evaluation and the Legitimacy of Stratification." *American Sociological Review* 45 (1980): 955–971.

Feagin, J. *Racist America: Roots, Current Realities, and Future Reparations.* New York: Routledge, 2000.

Federal Glass Ceiling Commission. *Good for Business: Making Full Use of the Nation's Human Capital: A Fact-Finding Report of the Federal Glass Ceiling Commission.* Washington, DC, 1995.

Feldman, D. C. "A Contingency Theory of Socialization." *Administrative Science Quarterly* 21 (1976): 433–452.

Ferdman, B. M. "The Color and Culture of Gender in Organizations." In *Handbook of Gender and Work,* edited by G. N. Powell. Thousand Oaks, CA: Sage Publications, 1999.

Fernandez, J. P. *Racism and Sexism in Corporate Life: Changing Values in American Business.* Lexington, MA: Lexington Books, 1981.

Ferree, M. M., J. Lorber, and B. B. Hess, eds. *Revisioning Gender.* Thousand Oaks, CA: Sage Publications, 1999.

Fiske, S. T. "Controlling Other People: The Impact of Power on Stereotyping." *American Psychologist* 48 (1993): 612–628.

Fletcher, J. *Disappearing Acts: Gender, Power and Relational Practice at Work.* Cambridge, MA: MIT Press, 1999.

Fowlkes, D. *White Political Women: Paths from Privilege to Empowerment.* Knoxville: University of Tennessee Press, 1992.

Fox-Genovese, E. *Feminism Without Illusions: A Critique of Individualism.* Chapel Hill: University of North Carolina Press, 1991.

_____. *Within the Plantation Household.* Chapel Hill: University of North Carolina Press, 1988.

Frankenberg, R. *Displacing Whiteness: Essays in Social and Cultural Criticism.* Durham, NC: Duke University Press, 1997.

_____. *White Women, Race Matters: The Social Construction of Whiteness.* Minneapolis: University of Minnesota Press, 1993.

Freeman, S. J. *Managing Lives: Corporate Women and Social Change.* Amherst: University of Massachusetts Press, 1990.

Friedman, R. "Defining the Scope and Logic of Minority and Female Network Groups: Can Separation Enhance Integration?" In *Research in Personnel and Human Resource Management,* vol. 14, edited by G. R. Ferris, 307–349. Greenwich, CT: JAI Press, 1996.

Frye, M. *Willful Virgin: Essays in Feminism, 1976–1992.* Freedom, CA: Crossing Press, 1992.

Gallos, J. "Exploring Women's Development: Implications for Career Theory, Practice, and Research." In *Handbook of Career Theory,* edited by A. Hall, D. Hall, and B. Lawrence, 110–132. Cambridge: Cambridge University Press, 1989.

Gaskill, L. R. "Women's Career Success: A Factor Analytic Study of Contributing Factors." *Journal of Career Development* 17 (1991): 167–178.

Gerson, K. *Hard Choices: How Women Decide About Work, Career, and Motherhood.* Berkley: University of California Press, 1985.

Gherardi, Silvia. *Gender Symbolism and Organizational Culture.* London: Sage Publications, 1995.

Gibson, A. L. *Growing Up Black and Female in America.* New York: Harlem River Press, 1995.

Giddings, P. *When and Where I Enter: The Impact of Black Women on Race and Sex in America.* New York: William Morrow and Company, Inc., 1984.

Giele, J. Z. "Crossovers: New Themes in Adult Roles and the Life Cycle." In *Women's Lives: New Theory, Research, and Policy,* edited by D. McGuigan. Ann Arbor: University of Michigan Center for Continuing Education of Women, 1980.

Giele, J. Z., and G. H. Elder, Jr. *Methods of Life Course Research: Qualitative and Quantitative Approaches.* Thousand Oaks, CA: Sage Publications, 1998.

Gilligan, C. *In a Different Voice.* Cambridge, MA: Harvard University Press, 1982.

Gleason, J. *Oya: In Praise of the Goddess.* Boston: Shambhala, 1977.

Glenn, E. N. "From Servitude to Service Work: Historical Continuities in the Racial

Division of Paid Reproductive Labor." *Signs: Journal of Women in Culture and Society* 18, no.1 (1992): 1–43.

Gray, D. *Ain't I a Woman: Female Slaves in the Plantations South*. New York: Norton, 1985.

Greene, E. B. "African-American Women." In *Women of Color: Integrating Ethnic and Gender Identities in Psychotherapy*, edited by L. Comas-Diaz and E. B. Greene, 10–29. New York: Guilford Press, 1994.

_____. "Racial Socialization: A Tool in Psychotherapy with African-American Children." In *Working with Culture: Psychotherapeutic Interventions with Ethnic Minority Youth*, edited by L. Vargas and J. Koss-Chioino. San Francisco: Jossey-Bass, 1992.

_____. "Sturdy Bridges: The Role of African-American Mothers in the Socialization of African-American Children." *Women and Therapy* 10 (1990): 205–225.

_____. "What Has Gone Before: The Legacy of Racism and Sexism in the Lives of Black Mothers and Daughters." *Women and Therapy* 10 (1990): 207–230.

Greenhaus, J. H., and G. A. Callanan. *Career Management*. Fort Worth, TX: Harcourt Brace College Publishers, 1994.

Greenhaus, J. H., et al. "Job Performance Attributes and Career Advancement Prospects: An Examination of Gender and Race Effects." *Organizational Behavior and Human Decision Processes* 55 (1993): 276–297.

_____. "Research on Work, Family and Gender." In *Handbook of Gender and Work*, edited by G. Powell. Thousand Oaks, CA: Sage Publications, 2000.

Gregory, A. "Are Women Different and Why Are Women Thought to Be Different? Theoretical and Methodological Perspectives." *Journal of Business Ethics* 9 (1990): 257–266.

Gross, A. *The Scarsdale Controversy, 1948–1954*. New York: Columbia University, 1958.

Grossman, R. J. "Race in the Workplace." *HR Magazine* 45 (March 2000): 41–45.

Gutek, B. A., and L. Larwood. *Women's Career Development*. Thousand Oaks, CA: Sage, 1987.

Guy-Sheftal, B. *Daughters of Sorrow: Attitudes Towards Black Women, 1880–1920*. Brooklyn, NY: Carlson Publishing, 1990.

Gwin, M. *Black and White Women of the Old South: The Peculiar Sisterhood in American Literature*. Knoxville: University of Tennessee Press, 1985.

Hacker, A. *Two Nations: Black and White, Separate, Hostile, and Unequal*. New York: Charles Scribner and Sons, 1992.

Hale-Benson, J. *Black Children: Their Roots, Cultures and Learning Styles*. Baltimore: John Hopkins Press, 1986.

Hall, N. *The Moon and the Virgin: Reflections on the Archetypal Feminine*. San Francisco: Harper & Row, 1980.

Hall, S. A. "Cultural Identity and Cinematic Representation." *Framework* 36 (1989): 68–81.

_____. *Representation: Cultural Representation and Signifying Practices.* London: Sage Publications, 1997.

Hansen, D. G. *Strained Sisterhood: Gender, Class in the Boston Female Anti-Slavery Society.* Amherst: University of Massachusetts Press, 1993.

Harker, R., C. Mahar, and C. Wilkes., eds. *An Introduction to the Work of Pierre Bourdieu.* New York: St. Martin's Press, 1990.

Harris, A. "Race and Essentialism in Feminist Legal Theory." In *Feminist Legal Theory: Foundations,* edited by D. K. Weisberg, 348–353. Philadelphia: Temple University Press, 1989.

Hearn, J., and P. W. Parkin. "Gender and Organizations: A Selective Review and Critique of a Neglected Area." In *Gendering Organizational Analysis,* edited by A. J. Mills and P. Tancred. London: Sage Publications, 1992.

Heilman, M. E., C. J. Block, and J. A. Lucas. "Presumed Incompetent? Stigmatization and Affirmative Action Efforts." *Journal of Applied Psychology* 77 (1992): 536–544.

Heimannsberg, B., and C. J. Schmidt, eds. *The Collective Silence: German Identity and the Legacy of Shame.* San Francisco: Jossey-Bass Publishers, 1993.

Hennig, M., and A. Jardim. *The Managerial Women.* New York: Pocket Books, 1978.

Higginbotham, R. B. "African-American Women's History and the Meta Language of Race." *Signs: Journal of Women in Culture and Society* 17 (1992): 251–274.

Hine, D. C. "For Pleasure, Profit, and Power: The Sexual Exploitation of Black Women: Historical Perspectives." In *African-American Women Speak Out on Anita Hill–Clarence Thomas,* edited by G. Smitherman. Detroit: Wayne State University Press, 1995.

_____. "Rape and Inner Lives of Black Women in the Middle West: Preliminary Thoughts on the Culture of Dissemblance." *Signs: Journal of Women in Culture and Society* 14 (1989): 912–929.

Hochschild, A. *The Second Shift.* New York: Viking, 1989.

Hoffman, E. "The Effects of Race-Ratio Composition on the Frequency of Organizational Communication." *Social Psychology Quarterly* 48 (1985): 17–26.

hooks, b. *Ain't I a Woman: Black Women and Feminism.* Boston: South End Press, 1981.

_____. *Feminist Theory: From Center to Margin.* Boston: South End Press, 1984.

Hucles, J. S. "Jeopardy Not Bonus Status for African-American Women in the Workforce: Why Does the Myth of Advantage Persist?" *American Journal of Community Psychology* 25 (1997): 565–580.

Hull, G., P. B. Scott, and B. Smith, eds. *All the Women Are White, All the Blacks Are Men, But Some of Us Are Brave: Black Women's Studies.* Old Westbury, NY: Feminist Press, 1982.

Hurley, S. "Speaking Up: The Politics of Black Women's Labor History." In *Women and Work: Exploring Race, Ethnicity and Class,* vol. 6, edited by E. Higginbotham and M. Romero, 28–51. Thousand Oaks, CA: Sage Publications, 1997.

Hurtado, A. *The Color of Privilege: Three Blasphemies on Race and Feminism.* Ann Arbor: University of Michigan Press, 1996.

———. "Relating to Privilege: Seduction and Rejections in the Subordination of White Women and Women of Color." *Signs: Journal of Women in Culture and Society* 14 (1989): 833–855.

Hymowitz, C., and T. Schellhardt. "The Corporate Woman: A Special Report/The Glass Ceiling." *Wall Street Journal,* 24 March 1986.

Ibarra, H. "Homophily and Differential Returns: Sex Differences in Network Structure and Access in an Advertising Firm." *Administrative Quarterly* 37 (1992): 422–447.

———. "Race, Opportunity, and Diversity of Social Circles in Managerial Networks." *Academy of Management Journal* 38 (1995): 673–703.

Imber-Black, Roberts, et al. *Rituals in Families and Family Therapy.* New York: Norton & Company, 1988.

Imel, M. A., and D. M. Imel. *Goddesses in World Mythology: A Biographical Dictionary.* New York: Oxford University Press, 1993.

Irons, E. D., and G. W. Moore. *Black Managers: The Case of the Banking Industry.* New York: Praeger, 1985.

Jackson, P. B., P. A. Thoits, and H. F. Taylor. "Composition of the Workplace and Psychological Well-Being: The Effects of Tokenism on America's Black Elite." *Social Forces* 74 (1995): 530–557.

Jacobi, J. *Complex Archetype Symbol in the Psychology of C. G. Jung.* New York: Princeton University Press, 1969.

Jacobs, H. A. "Women's Entry into Management: Trends in Earnings, Authority, and Values Among Salaried Managers." *Administrative Science Quarterly* 37 (1992): 282–301.

James, J. *Resisting State Violence: Radicalism, Gender and Race in U.S. Culture.* Minneapolis: University of Minnesota Press, 1996.

James, S. M., and A. P. A. Busia. *Theorizing Black Feminisms: The Visionary Pragmatism of Black Women.* New York: Routledge, 1993.

Janiewski, D. E. *Sisterhood Denied: Race Genera and Class in a New South Community.* Philadelphia: Temple University Press, 1985.

Jeanquart-Barone, S. "Trust Differences Between Supervisors and Subordinates: Examining the Role of Race and Gender." *Sex Roles* 29 (1993): 1–11.

Jewell, K. S. *From Mammy to Miss America and Beyond: Cultural Images and the Shaping of U.S. Policy.* London: Routledge, 1993.

Jhally, S., and J. Lewis. *Enlightened Racism.* Boulder: Westview Press, 1992.

Jones, J. *Labor of Love, Labor of Sorrow: Black Women, Work, and the Family from Slavery to the Present.* New York: Basic Books, 1985.

Jones, L. *Bulletproof Diva: Tales of Race, Sex, and Hair.* New York: Bantam Doubleday Dell Publishing Group, 1994.

Josselson, R. *Finding Herself: Pathways to Identity Development in Women*. San Francisco: Jossey-Bass, 1987.

Josselson, R., and A. Lieblich, eds. *The Narrative Study of Lives*. Newbury Park, CA: Sage Publications, 1993.

Jung, C. G. *Collected Works: Archetypes and Collective Unconscious*, translated by R. F. C. Hull. New Jersey: Princeton University Press, 1959.

Lambert, S. J., and K. Hopkins. "Occupational Conditions and Workers Sense of Community: Variations by Gender and Race." *American Journal of Community Psychology* 23 (1995):151–179.

Kanter, R. M. *Men and Women of the Corporation*. New York: Basic Books, 1977.

Kerber, L. "Women and Individualism in America." *Massachusetts Review* 1, no. 1 (1997).

Kessler-Harris, A., and K. Brodkin-Sacks. *Women, Households, and the Economy*. New Brunswick: Rutgers University Press, 1987.

King, D. K. "Multiple Jeopardy, Multiple Consciousness: The Context of a Black Feminist Ideology." *Signs: Women in Culture and Society* 14 (1988): 42–72.

King, M. C. "Occupational Segregation by Race and Sex, 1940–1998." *Monthly Labor Review* (April 1992).

Kirchmeyer, C. "Nonwork–Work Spillover: A More Balanced View of the Experiences and Coping of Professional Women and Men." *Sex Roles* 28 (1993): 531–552.

Kossek, E. E., and S. C. Zonia. "Assessing Diversity Climate: A Field Study of Reactions to Employer Efforts to Promote Diversity." *Journal of Organizational Behavior* 14 (1993): 61–81.

Kram, K. *Mentoring at Work*. Glenville, IL: Scott, Foresman & Co., 1985.

Langness, L. L., and F. Gelga. *Lives: An Anthropological Approach to Biography*. Novato, CA: Chandler & Sharp Publishers, Inc, 1981.

Larwood, L., and M. M. Wood. *Women in Management*. Lexington, MA: Lexington Books, 1977.

Leonard, L. S. *Meeting the Madwoman: An Inner Challenge for Feminine Spirit*. New York: Bantam Books, 1993.

Lerner, G. *Why History Matters: Life and Thought*. New York: Oxford University Press, 1997.

Levinson, D. J. *The Seasons of a Woman's Life*. New York: Alfred A. Knopf, 1996.

Levinson, D. J., et al. *The Seasons of a Man's Life*. New York: Alfred A. Knopf, 1978.

Lionnet, I. *Autobiographical Voices: Race, Gender, Self-Portraiture*. Ithaca, NY: Cornell University Press, 1989.

Lorber, J. *Paradoxes of Gender*. New Haven, CT: Yale University Press, 1994.

Lorber, J., and S. A. Farrell, eds. *The Social Construction of Gender*. Newbury Park, CA: Sage Publications, 1991.

Lorde, A. *Sister Outsider: Essays and Speeches*. Trumansburg, NY: Crossing Press, 1984.

Lovelace, K., and B. Rosen. "Differences in Achieving Person-Organization Fit Among Diverse Groups of Managers." *Journal of Management* 22 (1996): 703–723.

Lynch, F. *The Diversity Machine: The Drive to Change the "White Male Workplace."* New York: Free Press, 1997.

Mack, R. W. *Our Children's Burden: Studies of Desegregation in Nine American Communities.* New York: Random House, 1968.

MacKinnon, C. A. "Feminism, Marxism, Method, and the State: An Agenda for Theory." *Signs: Journal of Women in Culture and Society* 7 (1982): 530.

_____. *Feminism Unmodified: Discourses on Life and Law.* Cambridge, MA: Harvard University Press, 1987.

_____. *Only Words.* Cambridge, MA: Harvard University Press, 1993.

_____. *Toward a Feminist Theory of the State.* Cambridge, MA: Harvard University Press, 1989.

Mainero, L. "On Breaking the Glass Ceiling: The Political Seasoning of Powerful Women Executives." *Organizational Dynamics* 22, no. 4 (1994): 5–20.

Mainero, L., et al. "Gender Gap in the Executive Suite: CEOs and Female Executives Report on Breaking the Glass Ceiling." *Academy of Management Executive* 12 (1998): 28–42.

Major, C. *Juba to Jive: A Dictionary of African-American Slang.* New York: Penguin Books, 1994.

Marshall, J. "Revisiting Career Concepts: A Feminist Invitation." In *Handbook of Career Theory*, edited by M. B. Arthur, et al. Cambridge: Cambridge University Press, 1989.

Marshall, J. *Women Managers: Travellers in a Male World.* Chicester, England: Wiley, 1984.

Martin, J. "Deconstructing Organizational Taboos: The Suppression of Gender Conflict in Organizations." *Organization Science* 1 (1990): 339–359.

Martin, L. "Power, Continuity and Change: Decoding Black and White Women Managers' Experience in Local Government." In *Women in Management: A Developing Presence*, edited by Morgan Tanton. London: Routledge, 1994.

Martin, S. E. "Outsider Within the Station House: The Impact of Race and Gender on Black Women Police." *Social Problems* 41 (1994): 383–400.

Maslow, E. "Storybook Lives: Growing Up Middle Class." In *Liberation Now.* New York: Dell Publishing Company, 1991.

"Mattel's Lack of Action Figures." *Business Week*, 21 February 2000, 50.

Mayer, J., and J. Abramson. *Strange Justice: The Selling of Clarence Thomas.* Boston: Houghton-Mifflin Company, 1994.

Mbiti, J. S. *African Religions and Philosophy.* New York: Doubleday & Co., 1970.

McDowell, L. *Gender, Identity, and Place: Understanding Feminist Geographies.* Minneapolis: University of Minnesota Press, 1999.

McGuire, G., and B. F. Reskin. "Authority Hierarchies at Work: The Impacts of Race and Sex." *Gender & Society* 7 (1993): 487–507.

McLaurin, M. A. *Celia: A Slave.* Athens, GA: University of Georgia Press, 1991.

Meier, A., and E. Rudivick. *Black Nationalism in America.* Indianapolis: The Bobbs-Merrill Company, Inc, 1970.

Meyerson, D. E., and M. Scully. "Tempered Radicalism and the Politics of Ambivalence and Change." *Organizational Science* 6 (1995): 585–600

Miller, C., and K. Swift. *Words and Women: New Language in New Times.* London: Victor Gollancz, 1977.

Miller, J. B. *Toward a New Psychology of Women.* Boston: Beacon Press, 1976.

Mills, A. J., and P. Tancred. *Gendering Organizational Analysis.* London: Sage Publications, 1992.

Mills, C. W. *Sociological Imagination.* New York: Oxford University Press, 1959.

Mills, J. *Womanwords: A Dictionary of Words About Women.* New York: Free Press, 1992.

Mindel, C. H., et al. *Family Lifestyles of America's Ethnic Minorities: An Introduction.* New York: Elsevier, 1988.

Minuchin, S., and H. C. Fishman. *Family Therapy Techniques.* Cambridge, MA: Harvard University Press, 1981.

Moraga, C., and G. Anzaldua, eds. *This Bridge Called My Back: Writings by Radical Women of Color.* Watertown, MA: Persephone Press, 1981.

Morrison, A., et al. *Breaking the Glass Ceiling: Can Women Reach the Top of America's Largest Corporations?* Reading, MA: Addison-Wesley, 1987.

Morrison, T., ed. *Race-ing Justice, En-gendering Power: Essays on Anita Hill, Clarence Thomas, and the Construction of Social Reality.* New York: Pantheon Books, 1992.

Morton, P. *Disfigured Images: The Historical Assault on Afro-American Women.* New York: Greenwood Press, 1991.

Murray, P. *Song in a Weary Throat: An American Pilgrimage.* New York: Harper & Row, 1987.

Nicholson, N., and M. West. *Managerial Jobs Change: Men and Women in Transition.* Cambridge: Cambridge University Press, 1988.

Nieva, V. F., and B. A. Gutek. *Women and Work: A Psychological Perspective.* New York: Praeger, 1981.

Nkomo, S. M. "The Emperor Has No Clothes: Rewriting 'Race in Organizations.'" *Academy of Management Review* 17 (1992): 487–513.

Nkomo, S. M., and T. Cox, Jr. "Gender Differences in the Upward Mobility of Black Managers: Double Whammy or Double Advantage?" *Sex Roles* 21 (1989): 825–839.

Olson, J. E., et al. "Having It All? Combining Work and Family in a Male and a Female Profession." *Sex Roles* 23 (1990):515–533.

Omni, M., and H. Winant. *Racial Formation in the United States: From the 1960s to the 1980s.* New York: Routledge, 1986.

Osipow, S., and L. F. Fitzgerald. *Theories of Career Development,* 4th ed. Needham Heights, MA: Allyn & Bacon, 1996.

Ostrower, F. *Why the Wealthy Give: The Culture of Elite Philanthropy.* Princeton, NJ: Princeton University Press, 1995.

Pearson, C. *Awakening the Heroes Within: Twelve Archetypes to Help Us Find Ourselves and Transform Our World.* New York: Harper, 1991.

Peters, M. F. "Racial Socialization of Young Black Children." In *Black Children: Social, Educational, and Parental Environments,* edited by H. P. McAdoo and J. L. McAdoo. Newbury Park, CA: Sage Publications, 1985.

Pettigrew, T. F., and J. Martin. "Shaping the Organizational Context for Black American Inclusion." *Journal of Social Issues* 43 (1987): 41–78.

Pinckney, A. *Black Americans.* Englewood Cliffs, NJ: Prentice Hall, 1987.

Pinderhughes, E. *Understanding Race, Ethnicity, and Power: The Key to Efficacy in Clinical Practice.* New York: Free Press, 1989.

Poster, W. R. "The Challenges and Promises of Class and Racial Diversity in the Women's Movement: A Study of Two Women's Organizations." *Gender & Society* 9 (1995): 656–679.

Powell, G. N. "The Glass Ceiling: Explaining the Good and Bad News." In *Women in Management: Current Research Issues,* vol. 2, edited by M. J. Davidson and R. J. Burke, 236–249. London: Sage Publications, 2000.

_____. *Handbook of Gender and Work.* Thousand Oaks, CA: Sage Publications, 1999.

_____. "One More Time: Do Female and Male Managers Differ?" *Academy of Management Executive* 4 (1988): 68–75.

_____. *Women and Men in Management.* Newbury Park, CA: Sage Publications, 1993.

Prasad, P., et. al, eds. *Managing the Organizational Melting Pot: Dilemmas of Workplace Diversity.* Thousand Oaks, CA: Sage Publications, 1997.

Price, D. A. "A Good Man Is Hard to Find." *Wall Street Journal,* 21 February 1995.

Ragins, B. R. "Diversified Mentoring Relationships in Organizations: A Power Perspective." *Academy of Management Review* 22 (1997): 482–421.

Rhodes, D. L. *Justice and Gender.* Cambridge: Harvard University Press, 1989.

Rich, A. "Disloyal to Civilization: Feminism, Racism, Gynophobia." In *On Lies, Secrets and Silence: Selected Prose 1966–1978.* New York: W. W. Norton & Company, 1978.

_____. *Of Woman Born: Motherhood as Experience and Institution.* New York: W.W. Norton & Co., 1976.

"The Rise of Jill Barad." *Business Week,* 25 May 1988, 112.

Riger, S., and P. Galligan. "Women in Management: An Exploration of Competing Paradigms." *American Psychologist* 35 (1980): 902–910.

Rivkin, E. T. "The Black Woman in South Africa: An Azanian Profile" In *The Black Woman Cross-Culturally,* edited by F. C. Steady. Cambridge, MA: Schenkman Publishing Company, 1981.

Roberts, J. "Setting the Frame: Definitions, Functions, and Typology of Rituals." In *Rituals in Families and Family Therapy*, edited by E. Imber-Black, J. Roberts, and R. Whiting. New York: Norton, 1988.

Roethlisberger, F., and W. Dickson. *Management and the Worker*. New York: Wiley, 1939.

Rogers, A. "The Development of Courage in Girls and Women." Unpublished manuscript, Harvard School of Education, 1991.

Rollins, J. *Between Women: Domestics and Their Employers*. Philadelphia: Temple University Press, 1985.

Rosenbaum, J. E. *Career Mobility in a Corporate Hierarchy*. Orlando, FL: Academic Press, 1984.

Rosener, J. "Ways Woman Lead." *Harvard Business Review* 68, no. 6 (1990): 119–120.

Rosener, J. B. *America's Competitive Secret: Utilizing Women as a Management Strategy*. New York: Oxford University Press, 1995.

Rothman, B. K. *Recreating Motherhood: Ideology and Technology in a Patriarchal Society*. New York: W. W. Norton, 1989.

Rubin, H. J., and I. S. Rubin. *Qualitative Interviewing: The Art of Hearing Data*. Thousand Oaks, CA: Sage Publications, 1995.

Rubin, T. *Anti-Semitism: A Disease of the Mind*. New York: Continuum Publishing Company, 1990.

Ruggiero, K. M., and D. M. Taylor. "Why Minority Group Members Perceive or Do Not Perceive the Discrimination that Confronts Them: The Role of Self-Esteem and Perceived Control." *Journal of Personality and Social Psychology* 72 (1997): 373–389.

Ryan, W. *Blaming the Victim*. New York: Vintage Books, 1971.

Sacks, K. *Caring By the Hour: Work, Women and Organizing at Duke Medical Center*. Urbana: University of Illinois Press, 1988.

———. "Toward a Unified Theory of Class, Race, and Gender." *American Ethnologist* 16 (1989).

St. Jean, Y., and J. Geagin. *Double Burden: Black Women and Everyday Racism*. Armonk, NY: M. E. Sharpe, 1998.

Schaeffer, N. C. "Evaluating Race-of-Interviewer Effects in a National Survey." *Sociological Methods and Research* 8 (1980): 400–419.

Schein, E. *Career Dynamics: Matching Individual and Organizational Needs*. Reading, MA: Addison-Wesley, 1978.

Schein, V. "The Relationship Between Sex Role Stereotypes and Requisite Management Characteristics." *Journal of Applied Psychology* 57, 1973): 95–100.

———. "Relationships Between Sex Role Stereotypes and Requisite Management Characteristics Among Female Managers." *Journal of Applied Psychology* 60 (1975): 340–344.

Schneer, J. A., and F. A. Reitman. "Effects of Alternate Family Structures on Managerial Career Paths." *Academy of Management Journal* 36 (1993): 830–843.

Schneider, D. M., and R. T. Smith. *Class Differences and Sex Roles in American Kinship and Family Structure.* Englewood Cliffs, NJ: Prentice-Hall, 1973.

Schreiber, P. J. "Women's Career Development Patterns." In *Women's Career Development Across the Lifespan: Insights and Strategies for Women, Organizations and Adult Educators,* edited by L. J. Bierema. San Francisco: Jossey-Bass, 1998.

Schwartz, F. N. "Management Women and the New Facts of Life." *Harvard Business Review* 67, no. 1 (1989): 65–76.

Scott, K. Y. *The Habit of Surviving: Black Women's Strategies for Life.* New Brunswick, NJ: Rutgers University Press, 1991.

Scott, P. *Double Stitch: Black Women Writing About Mothers and Daughters.* Boston: Beacon Press, 1991.

Scully, M. "The Irony of Meritocracy: How a Legitimating Ideology Generates and Redirects Disbelief." Working paper, MIT, The Sloan School.

———. "Meritocracy." In *Dictionary of Business Ethics,* edited by R. Edward Freeman and P. Werhane. London: Blackwell, 1997.

Segura, D. A. "Inside the Work Worlds of Chicana and Mexican Immigrant Women." In *Women of Color in U.S. Society,* edited by M. B. Zinn and B. T. Dill. Philadelphia: Temple University Press, 1994.

Sekaran, U. *Dual-Career Families.* San Francisco: Jossey-Bass, 1986.

Shaw, S. J. *What a Woman Ought to Be and Do: Black Professional Women's Workers During the Jim Crow Era.* Chicago: University of Chicago Press, 1996.

Sheehy, G. *New Passages: Mapping Your Life Across Time.* New York: Random House, 1995.

Simmel, G. "The Sociological Significance of the 'Stranger.'" In *Introduction to the Science of Sociology,* edited by R. E. Park and E. W. Burgess, 322–327. Chicago: University of Chicago Press: 1921.

Smith, B., ed. *Home Girls: A Black Feminist Anthology.* New York: Kitchen Table—Women of Color Press, 1983.

Smith-Loving, L., and C. Brody. "Interruptions in Group Discussion: The Effects of Gender and Group Composition." *American Sociological Review* 54 (1989): 434–453.

Sokoloff, N. *Black Women and White Women in the Professions.* New York: Routledge, 1992.

Spelman, E. V. *Inessential Woman: Problems of Exclusion in Feminist Thought.* Boston: Beacon Press, 1988.

Spence, D. F. *Narrative Truth and Historical Truth.* New York: Norton, 1982.

Springer, K., ed. *Still Lifting, Still Climbing: African American Women's Contemporary Activism.* New York: New York University Press, 1999.

Stacey, J. *Brave New Families: Stories of the Domestic Upheaval in Late Twentieth Century America.* New York: Basic Books, 1990.

Stack, C. *All Our Kin: Strategic Survival in a Black Community.* New York: Harper & Row, 1974.

_____. *Call to Home: African Americans Reclaim the Rural South.* New York: Basic Books, 1996.

Stanton, E. C. "The Solitude of Self." In *The History of Woman Suffrage,* volume IV, edited by E. C. Stanton, S. B. Anthony, and M. J. Gage. Rochester, NY: Source Book Press, 1970.

Steady, F. C., ed. *The Black Woman Cross-Culturally.* Cambridge: Schenkman Publishing Company, 1981.

Steele, C. M. "Race and the Schooling of Black Americans." *Atlantic Monthly,* April 1992.

Steele, C. M., and J. Aronson. "Stereotype Threat and the Intellectual Test Performance of African Americans." *Journal of Personality and Social Psychology* 69 (1995): 797–811.

Stone, M. *Ancient Mirrors of Womanhood: A Treasury of Goddess and Heroine Lore from Around the World.* Boston: Beacon Press, 1979.

Swartz, N., et al. *A New Day for the Colored Woman Worker: A Study of Colored Women in Industry in New York City.* New York, 1919.

Tannen, D. *You Just Don't Understand: Women and Men in Conversation.* New York: Ballantine, 1990.

Tatum, B. *Assimilation Blues: Black Families in a White Community.* New York: Greenwood Press, 1987.

Tatum, B. D. *Why Are All the Black Kids Sitting Together in the Cafeteria? And Other Conversations About Race.* New York: Basic Books, 1997.

Teish, L. Jambalaya: *The Natural Woman's Book of Personal Charms and Practical Rituals.* San Francisco: Harper & Row, 1985.

Thomas, D. A. "The Impact of Race on Managers' Experiences of Developmental Relationships." *Journal of Organizational Behavior* 2 (1990): 479–492.

————. "Mentoring and Irrationality: The Role of Racial Taboos." *Human Resource Management* 28 (1989): 279–290.

Thomas, D. A., and J. J. Gabarro. *Breaking Through: The Making of Minority Executives in Corporate America.* Boston: Harvard Business School Press, 1999.

Thomas, K. M., L. D. Phillips, and S. Brown. "Redefining Race in the Workplace: Insights from Ethnic Identity Theory." *Journal of Black Psychology* 24 (1998): 76–92.

Thompson, R. F. *Flash of the Spirit.* New York: Vintage Books, 1984.

————. *Faces of the Gods: Art and Altars of Africa and African-Americans.* New York: Museum for African Art, 1993.

Thorne, B., ed. *Rethinking the Family: Some Feminist Questions.* Boston: Northeastern University Press, 1992.

"Trouble in Toyland." *Business Week,* 15 March 1999, 40.

"The Trouble with Hillary," *Harper's Bazaar,* August 2000.

Trudier, R. *From Mammies to Militants: Domestics in Black American Literature.* Philadelphia: Temple University Press, 1982.

Tsui, A., T. Egan, and C. O'Reilly. "Being Different: Relational Demography and Organizational Attachment." *Administrative Science Quarterly* 37 (1992): 549–479.

Van Maanen, J. "People Processing: Strategies of Organizational Socialization." *Organization Dynamics* 7 (1978): 18–36.

Van Maanen, J., and E. E. Schein. "Toward a Theory of Organizational Socialization." In *Research in Organizational Behavior*, vol. 1, edited by B. Staw. Greenwich, CT: JAI Press, 1979

Von Franz, M. L. *Interpretation of Fairytales.* San Francisco: Shambala Publications, 1996.

Wanous, J. P. *Organizational Entry: Recruitment, Selection, Orientation and Socialization of Newcomers.* Reading, MA: Addison-Wesley Publishing Company, 1992.

Wallace, P. *Black Women in the Labor Force.* Cambridge, MA: MIT Press, 1980.

Ware, V. *Beyond the Pale: White Women, Racism, and History.* London: Verso, 1992.

Waters, M., et al. *The Invisible Web: Gender Patterns in Family Relationships.* New York: Guilford Press, 1988.

Watson, L. C., and M. B. Watson Franke. *Interpreting Life Histories: An Anthropological Inquiry.* New Brunswick, NJ: Rutgers University Press, 1985.

Weber, L., and E. Higginbotham. "Black and White Professional Managerial Women's Perceptions of Racism and Sexism in the Workplace" In *Women and Work: Exploring Race, Ethnicity, and Class*, edited by E. Higginbotham and M. Romero, 153–175. Thousand Oaks, CA: Sage Publications, 1997.

Webster, S. "Ethnography as Storytelling." *Dialectical Anthropology* 8 (1983): 185–206.

"Weighing the Odds Against Oprah." Gannett News Service, Richard Prince Section, 8 November 1990.

Weinberg, M., et al. *Three Myths: An Exposure of Popular Misconceptions About School Desegregation.* Atlanta: Southern Regional Council, 1976.

Wellman, D. *Portraits of White Racism.* Cambridge: Cambridge University Press, 1993.

West, C., and D. H. Zimmerman. "Doing Gender." In *The Social Construction of Gender*, edited by J. Lorber and S. A. Farrell, 13–37. Newbury Park, CA: Sage Publications, 1991.

White, B., C. L. Cox, and C. L. Cooper. *Women's Career Development: A Study of High Flyers.* Oxford: Blackwell Press, 1992.

White, D. G. *Aren't I a Woman? Female Slaves in the Plantation South.* New York: W. W. Norton, 1985.

Wiley, M. G., and A. Eskilson. "Gender and Family/Career Conflict: Reactions of Bosses." *Sex Roles* 19 (1988): 445–466.

Wolfe, D. and C. R. Wolfe. "The Contextual Impact of Social Support Across Race and Gender: Implications for African-American Women in the Workplace." *Journal of Black Studies* 26 (1996): 297–307.

Yellin, J. F., ed. *Incidents in the Life of a Slave Girl.* Cambridge: Harvard University Press, 1987.

Yoder, J. D., and P. Aniakudo. "Outsider Within the Firehouse: Subordination and Difference in the Social Interactions of African-American Firefighters." *Gender and Society* 11 (1997): 324–341.

Zack, N. "White Ideas." In *Whiteness: Feminist Philosophical Reflections*, edited by C. J. Cuomo and K. Q. Hall. Lanham, MD: Rowman & Littlefield Publishers, Inc., 1999.

Zinn, M. B. *Race and the Reconstruction of Gender.* Memphis: Center for Research on Women, 1992.

Zinn, M. B., and B. Dill-Thornton. *Women of Color in U.S. Society.* Philadelphia: Temple University Press, 1993.

INDEX

About the Authors

Dr. Ella L. J. Edmondson Bell is the Leon E. Williams Visiting Professor of Business Administration at the Tuck School of Business at Dartmouth. She will be joining the faculty at Tuck in the fall of 2001. She has served on the faculties of the Sloan School of Management at MIT and the School of Organization and Management at Yale. A former Scholar-in-Residence at the Mary Ingraham Bunting Institute of Radcliffe College, Bell is a nationally and internationally recognized scholar on the management of race, gender, and change in organizational life. She is a consultant to Fortune 500 companies, nonprofit organizations, and public policy institutions.

Dr. Stella M. Nkomo is a Professor of business leadership at the University of South Africa Graduate School of Business Leadership. A former Scholar-in-Residence at the Mary Ingraham Bunting Institute of Radcliffe College, Nkomo has contributed internationally recognized work on race and gender in organizations and managing diversity to numerous journals, edited volumes, and magazines. She served as Chair of the Women in Management Division of the Academy of Management and is a member of the Board of Governors of the Academy of Management and the Center for Creative Leadership.